50 YEARS
lonely planet
OF TRAVEL

ANDALUCÍA

Mark Julian Edwards, Anna Kaminski,
Paul Stafford, Rachel Webb

CONTENTS

Plan Your Trip

The Guide

Tapas

Benalmádena (p158)

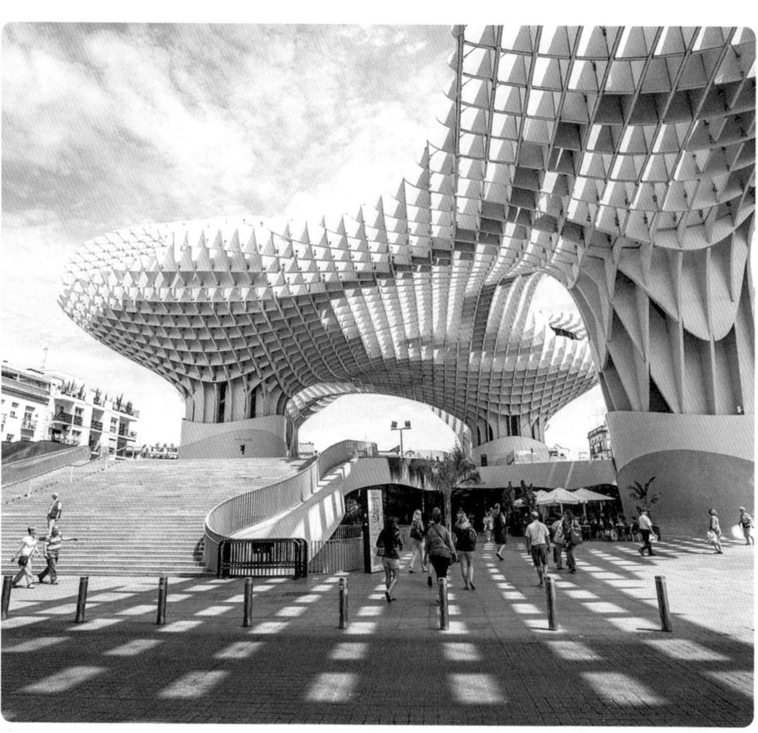

Las Setas, Sevilla (p64)

ANTONIO CIERO REINA/SHUTTERSTOCK ©

Axarquía (p183)

ANDALUCÍA

THE JOURNEY BEGINS HERE

Living in a small *pueblo blanco* (white town) in Axarquía, I've come to appreciate the morning and sunset views down the valley all the way to the Mediterranean, the mountains looming right behind my house. I explore them on foot whenever I have free time, and the scenic, winding mountain roads to other remote villages. As a gastronavigator, I have deep respect for the Andalucians' fierce devotion to their local produce and I love impromptu road trips to the remoter reaches of Huelva, Almería, Córdoba and other provinces because I always make some exciting edible discovery: the world's first organic caviar producer in a village in Granada, a tiny bar in Córdoba specialising in live and biodynamic wines, a small-scale olive-oil producer in Baeza experimenting with olive beer while tackling the challenges climate change poses to his olive harvest.

Anna Kaminski

@ackaminski

My favourite experience is trekking along the coast in Parque Natural Cabo de Gata-Nijar, stopping at remote white-sand coves, then finishing the day with creative seasonal dishes at Asador la Chumbera.

WHO GOES WHERE

Our writers and experts choose the places which, for them, define Andalucía

ALEX TIHONOVS/SHUTTERSTOCK ©

Málaga for me is about contrasts – talking about life with fishermen over *espetos*, then enjoying a luxurious *hammam* experience. The beaches provide perfect conditions for swimming, the vibe looking down at the city from the rooftop bars is exquisite and the food has a uniquely local flavour.

Mark Julian Edwards

@markjulianedwards

Mark is a travel and culture journalist and co-author of Faces of Mallorca.

JOSE ARCOS AGUILAR/SHUTTERSTOCK ©

An old-world mystique still clings to the **Sierra de Aracena**'s hilly countryside, where castle-topped towns are connected by networks of sylvan footpaths. But when the earth is scraped away at Minas de Riotinto's open pits, it's like the hues of the earth belong to some fairy-tale land, rather than this oft-overlooked corner of Andalucía.

Paul Stafford

@paulrstafford

Paul is a journalist and photographer.

M-MARTINEZ/GETTY IMAGES ©

Cazorla Natural Park is dramatic scenery, rugged wilderness, charming, sleepy towns and never-ending views. Burbling rivers for cooling down in summer and snow-covered mountain plains in winter – a year-round nature binge that provides new experiences on every visit.

Rachel Webb

@rachelspaniola

Rachel is an estate agent, travel journalist and long-term resident of northern Andalucía.

Sevilla
Explore Sevilla's Giralda and awe-inspiring Gothic cathedral (p56)
Parque Nacional de Doñana
Spot the shy Iberian lynx (p103)
Aracena
Taste the finest *jamón ibérico* (p97)
Belalcázar
Santa Eufemia
Peñarroya-Pueblonuevo
Pozoblanco
EXTREMADURA
Llerena
CÓRDOB
PORTUGAL
Parque Natural Sierra de Aracena y Picos de Aroche
Rosal de la Frontera
Jabugo
Aracena
Alájar
Santa Olalla del Cala
Constantina
Córdoba
Minas de Riotinto
Nerva
Río Guadalquivir
Almodóvar del Río
Palma del Río
Valverde del Camino
SEVILLA
Villanueva de los Castillejos
Montilla
HUELVA
Carmona
Écija
Río Genil
Río Tinto
Sevilla
Marchena
Lepe
Huelva
Almonte
Osuna
Ayamonte
Los Palacios y Villafranca
Utrera
Morón de la Frontera
Punta Umbría
Parque Nacional de Doñana
Campillo
Golfo de Cádiz
Matalascañas
Anteque
Lebrija
Olvera
El Chorro
Sanlúcar de Barrameda
Arcos de la Frontera
Zahara de la Sierra
MÁLAGA
Jerez de la Frontera
Ronda
Jerez de la Frontera
Sip extra-aged sherries at Bodegas Tradicíon (p125)
Ubrique
Fuengiro
Cádiz
CÁDIZ
Jimena de la Frontera
Medina Sidonia
Marbel
Chiclana de la Frontera
Estepona
San Pedro de Alcántara
Vejer de la Frontera
La Línea de la Concepción
Costa de la Luz
Barbate
Algeciras
Atlantic Ocean
Gibraltar (UK)
Bolonia
Strait of Gibraltar
Tarifa
Zahara de la Sierra
Descend into Sierra de Grazalema's Garganta Verde (p133)
Cádiz
Feel flamenco rhythms at La Perla (p114)
Bolonia
Wander through Roman seafront settlement Baelo Claudia (p142)

Córdoba
Purchase Moorish-style Guadamecí leather art (p190)
Jaén
Look down from Castillo de Santa Catalina (p216)
Parque Natural Sierras de Cazorla, Segura y las Villas
Follow a turquoise river to its source (p209)
Pulpí
Climb inside the Geoda de Pulpí crystal (p273)
La Carolina
Villanueva del Arzobispo
Segura de la Sierra
JAÉN
Linares
Andújar
Bailén
Úbeda
Río Guadalquivir
Baeza
Cazorla
Parque Natural Sierras de Cazorla, Segura y las Villas
Caravaca de la Cruz
MURCIA
Empanadas (2107m)
Porcuna
Albánchez de Mágina
Quesada
Huéscar
Jaén
Martos
Parque Natural Sierra Mágina
Pozo Alcón
Vélez Rubio
Baena
Parque Natural Sierras Subbéticas
Alcalá la Real
Baza
Huércal-Overa
Albox
Priego de Córdoba
Lucena
Iznalloz
Río Almanzora
Geoda de Pulpí
GRANADA
Guadix
Iznájar
Vera
Loja
Granada
ALMERÍA
Garrucha
Mulhacén (3482m)
Parque Natural Sierra Nevada
Sorbas
Tabernas
Ohanes
Carboneras
Trevélez
Níjar
La Maroma (2065m)
Capileira
Ugíjar
Parque Natural de Cabo de Gata-Níjar
Órgiva
Almería
Cómpeta
Motril
Adra
San José
Málaga
Torre del Mar
Nerja
Almuñécar
Almerimar
Golfo de Almería
Costa de Sol
Parque Natural Cabo de Gata-Níjar
Take a clifftop path to Playa San Pedro (p264)
Granada
Admire the unparalleled beauty of the Alhambra (p230)
Málaga
Deep dive into Picasso's career at Museo Picasso (p152)
Parque Nacional Sierra Nevada
Jump into gin-clear river pools while canyoning (p244)
Mediterranean Sea
0 50 km
0 25 miles

BEAUTIFUL BEACHES

Whether you're looking for a deserted stretch of white sand, a family-friendly beach, lapped at by gentle waves and packed with sun loungers, a secluded pebbled cove to bare all, or a wind-battered stretch of coast for kitesurfing, Andalucía's Costa de la Luz and Costa del Sol have a beach to suit your needs. While some are accessible via steep paths along precipitous cliffs, others have car parks, beachside restaurants and plentiful other facilities.

Beach season

The official season is June to September, with lifeguards and beach equipment for rent on busier beaches. However, many are open year-round.

Parking problems

Parking spots can be hard to find at the most popular beaches during peak season, and some beaches are shuttle access only, so plan accordingly.

Water gear

Bring your own snorkelling mask and reef booties for visits to remote beaches bookended by cliffs, since there's often good underwater visibility and no equipment rental.

Playa San Pedro (p264)

BEST BEACH EXPERIENCES

Revel in the remote white-sand **Playa San Pedro** in Parque Natural Cabo de Gata-Níjar, reachable via a precarious clifftop path. ❶ (p264)

Crest turquoise waves on your boogie board or simply lie back and take in the glorious sweep of golden sand at **Bolonia**'s main beach. ❷ (p142)

Sun your buns, toast your feet on hot pebbles or snorkel in the clear waters at the clothing-optional **Playa Cantarriján**, near Nerja. ❸ (p256)

Take to the water in a kayak or on a paddleboard in **La Herradura**'s horseshoe-shaped bay on the Costa Tropical. ❹ (p255)

Munch on grilled catch-of-the-day at a *chiringuito* and visit the beautiful Sea Life aquarium in **Benalmádena Costa**. ❺ (p158)

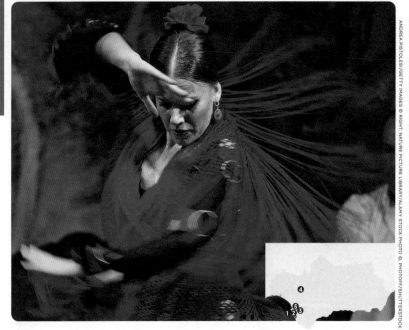

FAB FLAMENCO

Plaintive, *duende*-inducing laments, fast-paced, urgent *bulerías*, the staccato rhythm of heels on a wooden stage, the *jaleo* of handclaps, the acapella *martinetes* and *carceleras* – no other music sums up the Andalucian experience better than flamenco, born of hardship in the Roma barrios of Jerez, Sevilla and Cádiz.

Tablao or peña?

Choose between seeing flamenco at a *tablao* (polished, tourist-oriented flamenco show) or a more spontaneous live performance at a *peña* (club for flamenco aficionados).

Flamenco museums

Immerse yourself in the history of flamenco at the interactive Museo del Baile Flamenco in Sevilla (p62) and at the Centro Andaluz de Flamenco in Jerez (p126).

BEST FLAMENCO EXPERIENCES

Lose yourself at Cádiz's **La Cava** – a rustic taverna hosting thrice-weekly *tablaos*. ❶ (p125)

Ride the vibes with aficionados at the romantically run-down **La Perla** in Cádiz. ❷ (p125)

Sip sherry from the barrel and see a performance at **El Guitarrón** in Jerez. ❸ (p126)

Witness a superb performance at Sevilla's **Museo del Baile Flamenco**, in the intimate basement space or the courtyard. ❹ (p62)

Attend a top-notch, semi-spontaneous experience at Jerez **Centro Cultural Flamenco**. ❺ (p126)

MOUNTAIN THRILLS

If mere hiking doesn't give you enough of a rush, and scaling Andalucía's highest peaks is insufficiently exciting, get up close and personal with the plunging cliffs, deep gorges bisected by rivers and snow-covered mountains by soaring above them, straining every muscle and sinew by clawing your way up craggy rock faces, and skiing the winter slopes.

Canyoning gear

If you've never canyoned before, never fear: canyoning operators provide drysuits, helmets, harnesses and other gear. A reasonable level of fitness is a must, though.

Skiing into spring

Europe's southernmost ski resort in the Sierra Nevada is also one of the continent's highest, and snow often lingers from November well into May.

Seasonal adventure

Canyoning season is May to September, ideal for escaping the summer heat. Vie ferrate are best tackled from September to May; summers are too hot.

BEST MOUNTAIN ADVENTURE EXPERIENCES

Take to the skies in a flight above **Sierra de Grazalema** with Zero Gravity. ❶ (p131)

Whizz down zip lines and scramble along mountain obstacle courses with Nevadensis in the **Sierra Nevada.** ❷ (p253)

Abseil down waterfalls and jump into river pools with Sierra Nevada's Nevadensis or with Horizon in **Sierra de Grazalema.** ❸ (p131)

Get breathless at the height of 3300m as you fly down the **Sierra Nevada**'s lofty slopes in a spray of powder. ❹ (p252)

Bring your own climbing gear and tackle dozens of climbing routes near **Caminito del Rey** or brave El Torcal de Antequera. ❺ (p175)

MOORISH MASTERPIECES

Eight centuries of Moorish rule left an indelible imprint on Andalucía. It's in the whitewashed houses and palaces clad in colourful tile work, church towers that were once minarets, the tangle of narrow lanes, the fountains that dot city streets, the hillsides terraced for irrigated agriculture, the Arabic-style bathhouses and, of course, in the grand architecture, such as Granada's Alhambra and Córdoba's Mezquita that's testimony to the sophisticated bygone civilisation.

ALBA PEREZ ENRIQUEZ/SHUTTERSTOCK © LEFT: TAKASHI IMAGES/SHUTTERSTOCK ©, HANS GEEL/SHUTTERSTOCK ©

Alhambra tickets

The Alhambra's incredible popularity means that you need to book your entry weeks in advance; don't forget timed slot tickets to Palacios Nazaríes.

Virtual legacy

Before visiting Medina Azahara, tour the site virtually, with headsets that allow you to wander through the (currently off-limits) Salón de Abd ar-Rahman III.

Sunset views

It's well worth visiting Almería's Alcazaba just as the sun dips towards the horizon for particularly atmospheric views of Barrio Almedina and the port beyond.

Medina Azahara (p193)

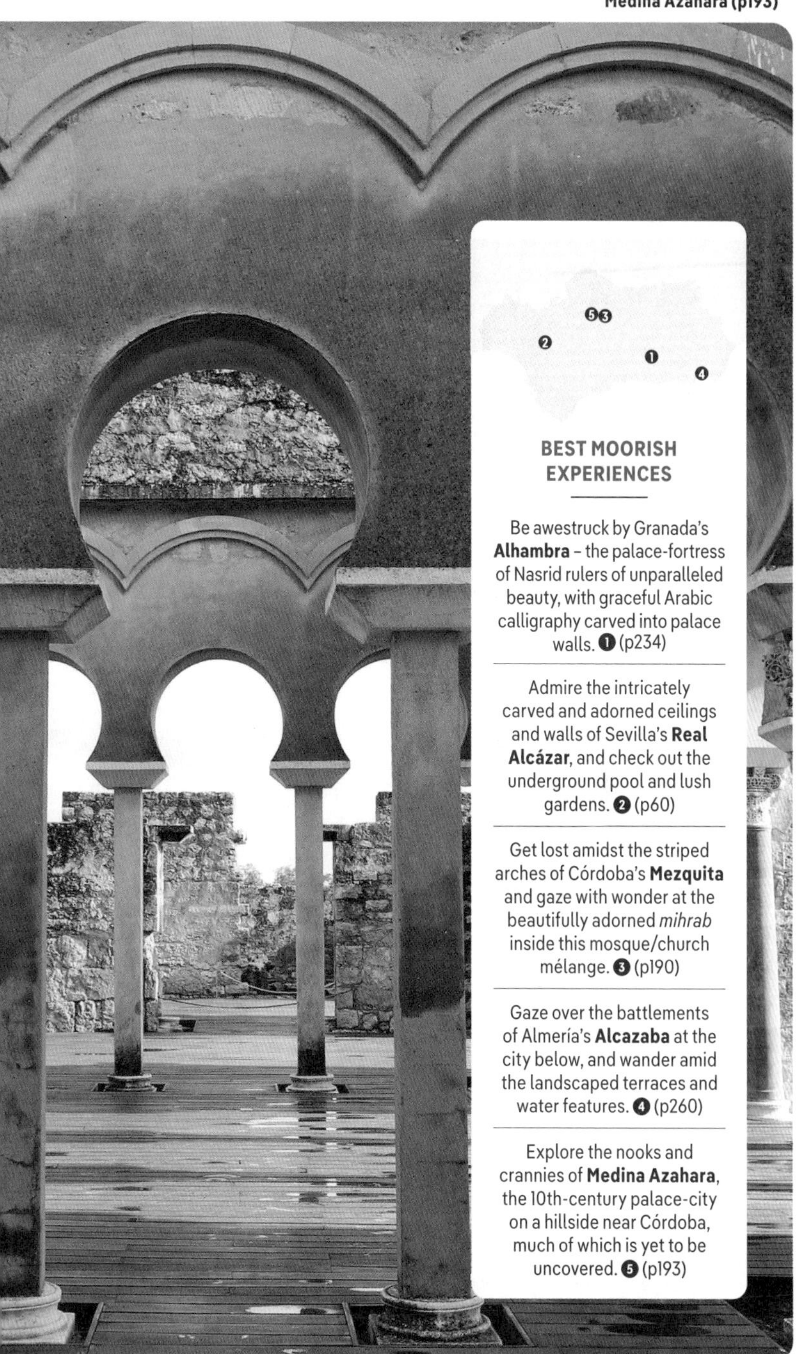

BEST MOORISH EXPERIENCES

Be awestruck by Granada's **Alhambra** – the palace-fortress of Nasrid rulers of unparalleled beauty, with graceful Arabic calligraphy carved into palace walls. ❶ (p234)

Admire the intricately carved and adorned ceilings and walls of Sevilla's **Real Alcázar**, and check out the underground pool and lush gardens. ❷ (p60)

Get lost amidst the striped arches of Córdoba's **Mezquita** and gaze with wonder at the beautifully adorned *mihrab* inside this mosque/church mélange. ❸ (p190)

Gaze over the battlements of Almería's **Alcazaba** at the city below, and wander amid the landscaped terraces and water features. ❹ (p260)

Explore the nooks and crannies of **Medina Azahara**, the 10th-century palace-city on a hillside near Córdoba, much of which is yet to be uncovered. ❺ (p193)

PABKOV/SHUTTERSTOCK © MURALS BY D*FACE AND OBEY; RIGHT: CATALIN EREMIA/SHUTTERSTOCK ©; UNAI HUIZI PHOTOGRAPHY/SHUTTERSTOCK ©

Soho, Málaga (p155)

CONTEMPORARY ART

Andalucía's largest cities are filled with art. The birthplace of Picasso, Málaga dazzles with museums and gritty street art; Sevilla regularly features superb local talent; Almería showcases cutting-edge photography; while Granada's streets are daubed with murals by Andalucía's answer to Banksy.

QR codes

In art museums, zoom in on QR codes with your smartphone for more detailed information on exhibits in English.

Explore further

Widen your artistic horizons at Málaga's (p152) Centre Pompidou, Centro de Arte Contemporáneo, and Sevilla's Museo de Bellas Artes (p69).

BEST CONTEMPORARY ART EXPERIENCES

Get an overview of Picasso's creative periods at Málaga's superb **Museo Picasso.** ❶ (p152)

Go on a self-guided urban art hunt in Málaga's **Lagunillas district**, as well as Soho. ❷ (p155)

Immerse yourself in exhibitions at Almería's **Centro Andaluz de la Fotografía.** ❸ (p260)

Admire installations at Sevilla's **Centro Andaluz de Arte Contemporáneo.** ❹ (p71)

Seek out El Niño's most famous murals at Lorca's childhood home in **Fuente Vaqueros.** ❺ (p230)

GO BELOW

There's a rich, labyrinthine underworld in Andalucía: shimmering caverns filled with stalactites and stalagmites, dark tunnels leading to enormous glittering crystals that you can climb inside, underground rivers flowing steadily in the dark, and spelunking adventures await the intrepid. Above ground, ancient caves showcase millennia-old paintings and other signs of early human habitation.

Advance bookings

Underground caves are accessible via guided tour; book well ahead for the Geoda de Pulpí. Minimum group numbers required for some spelunking adventures.

Spelunking tips

Dress in clothes you're prepared never to wear again, as well as comfortable closed-toed shoes. Reasonable levels of fitness a boon; claustrophobia a bane.

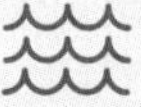

Watery adventures

Exploring the Sorbas's Cueva del Agua involves rappelling down sheer walls, hanging in a harness above the abyss and wading through chest-deep cold water.

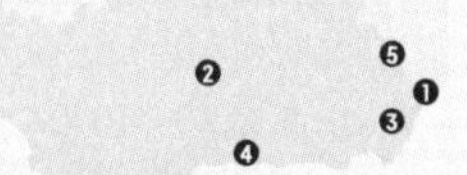

BEST CAVE EXPERIENCES

Tour tunnels glistening with mineral deposits, and climb inside the sparkling cave of **Geoda de Pulpí**. 1 (p273)

Look for Neolithic rock paintings inside the **Cueva de los Murciélagos** near Zuheros and gasp over the fantastic rock formations. 2 (p200)

Admire the stalactite and stalagmite formations inside the **Cuevas de Sorbas**, and wriggle through to reach remoter galleries. 3 (p273)

See extraordinary rock formations at the **Cueva de Nerja**, with a cathedral-like interior shaped by water five million years ago. 4 (p180)

Be greeted by millennia-old figures and other anthropomorphic shapes at **Cueva de los Letreros**. 5 (p263)

FROM GRAPE TO GLASS

Though Andalucía is the oldest wine-producing region in Spain, most of its wines are not as well known as those from Spain's north. More's the pity; the varied, rugged terrain is responsible for a huge variety of tipples, many by small producers. Whether you're a sherry aficionado, a lover of dessert wines, someone who enjoys trying interesting blends from varietals grown at high altitude, or an oenophile with a passion for live wines, you'll find them here.

Wine tasting

Many wine and sherry bodegas offer tastings of multiple wines; some offer food pairings. Book ahead, particularly for non-Spanish-language visits.

Bodega tours

While it's possible to arrange tours of the wine-making facilities at many bodegas, it's easiest in the Sherry Triangle, Montilla-Moriles and vineyards around Ronda.

Buying wine

You needn't drift into insolvency in your quest for the perfect bottle: decades-old sherries, rare live rosés and robust Granada reds cater to all budgets.

Bodegas Alvear (p198)

BEST VITICULTURAL EXPERIENCES

Investigate the sustainable **Bodega Anchurón** on the Altiplano near Guadix, powered by renewable energy and producing high-altitude, single-origin reds. ❶ (p243)

Pair extra-aged sherries at **Bodegas Tradicíon** in Jerez with a visit to its private 14th- to 19th-century Spanish art collection with paintings by Great Masters. ❷ (p127)

Tour the characterful 1792 **Bodegas Hidalgo–La Gitana** in Sanlúcar and taste its superlative *manzanilla* and VORS sherries on the vine-draped patio. ❸ (p129)

Marvel at Montilla's **Bodegas Alvear** (one of Spain's oldest), tour the premises and sample the treacle-sweet PX dessert wine, alongside other fortified vintages. ❹ (p198)

Sip Cartojal and aged dessert wines at the 19th-century **Bodegas Málaga Virgen**. ❺ (p174)

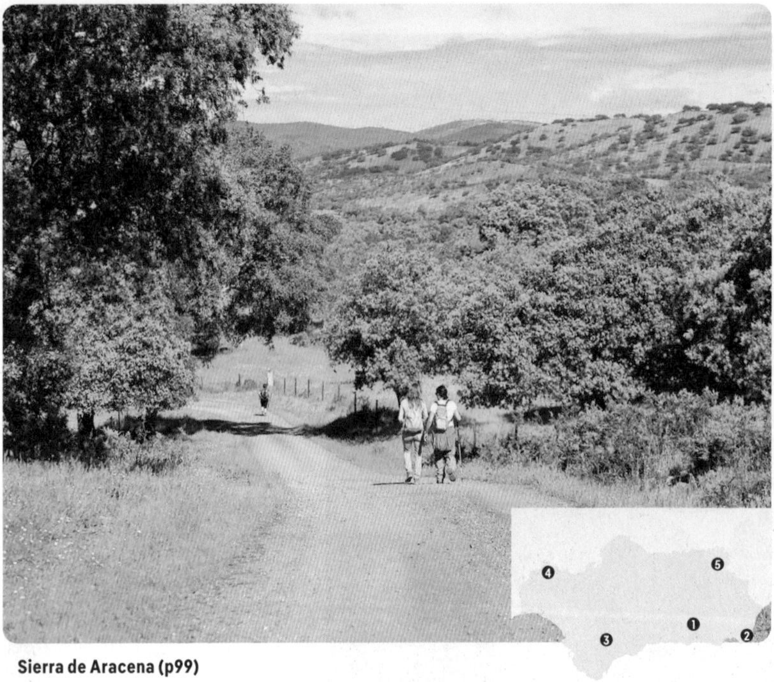

Sierra de Aracena (p99)

HAPPY TRAILS

Long-distance trails through craggy mountains throw down a gauntlet to experienced trekkers, while less demanding day hikes connect villages along centuries-old paths and clifftop trails lead you to remote beaches. Whether you're looking to summit mainland Spain's tallest peak or simply wander down to a secluded stretch of sand, Andalucía delivers.

Maps and apps

If embarking on a hike, equip yourself with a decent map of the area by Editorial Alpina. Gaia GPS is a hugely useful mapping app.

Hiking season

May, June, September and October are best, weather-wise. July and August are ideal for the high Sierra Nevada but unbearably hot elsewhere; fire risk abounds.

BEST HIKING EXPERIENCES

Scale **Mulhacén** – Spain's highest peak – in the rugged Parque Nacional Sierra Nevada. ❶ (p248)

Find your own slice of beach paradise during clifftop jaunts in the **Parque Natural Cabo de Gata-Níjar.** ❷ (p264)

Summit El Torreón for Morocco views in **Parque Natural Sierra de Grazalema.** ❸ (p130)

Wander through valleys between timeless villages in the **Sierra de Aracena.** ❹ (p99)

Follow a river to its source and scramble to mountain passes in **Parque Natural Cazorla.** ❺ (p209)

LEATHER, MARBLE & WOOL

Moorish-style vases produced using age-old clay-working and glazing techniques, marble chiselled into elaborate sculpture, woollen ponchos woven on looms... Andalucía's artisan tradition stretches back for centuries. Some villages are known for one craft, while others have workshops used by multiple generations of the same family. Purchasing from the artisans helps keep Andalucía's artistic heritage alive.

Artisans at work

Many village artisans are happy to be observed while they work with their material of choice. Items are usually available for purchase in the workshop/shop.

Esparto grass

The tradition of weaving footwear, containers and decorative items from esparto grass has remainsed virtually unchanged since Neolithic times and is currently enjoying a revival.

Moorish ceramics

Hispano-Moresque ware is Islamic-style pottery dating back to Andalucía's Al-Andalus era, with blue and gold dominating, as well as white tin-glaze and metallic lusterware techniques.

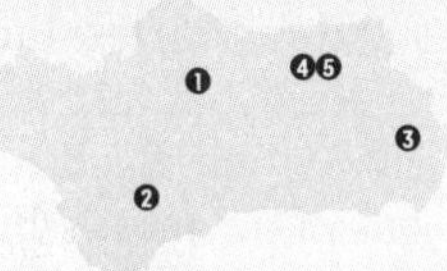

BEST CRAFT EXPERIENCES

Marvel over unique Moorish-era Guadamecí leather art by José Carlos Villarejo García in Córdoba's **Casa-Museo del Guadamecí Omeya**. ❶ (p194)

Grab a woven woollen scarf at **Artesanía Textil** in Grazalema, or pick up a durable blanket or two. ❷ (p132)

Shop for abstract marble sculpture or find some utilitarian kitchenware at **Artesanía Muro** in Macael. ❸ (p262)

Admire blue-glazed ceramics produced using surviving Moorish-era kilns at Úbeda's **Museo de Alfarería Paco Tito**. ❹ (p219)

Decorate your home with a woven bull's head or shop with your sustainably produced esparto hold-all from **Ubedies Artesanía**. ❺ (p219)

REMARKABLE ROMAN RELICS

Italy aside, few European countries can lay claim to such a vast wealth of remains of the Roman civilisation. Baetica to its conquerors, Andalucía was one of the most affluent parts of the Roman Empire, and the well-preserved Roman amphitheatres, baths, temples, mosaics, villas and towns are testimony to that. Many are found in spectacular locations, set against the backdrop of the ocean or mountains, which only adds to their millennia-old appeal.

Theatre performances

Summer performances at the reconstructed Baelo Claudia Roman amphitheatre are incredibly popular, so make sure you get your tickets well ahead of time.

Footwear

The remoter Roman sights are accessed via uneven paths, and some require extensive walking, so make sure you wear comfortable footwear.

Shadeless sights

Consider the time of year when visiting; in July and August, remnants of Roman towns provide no shade and are mercilessly hot; bring ample drinking water and a hat.

Teatro Romano (p118)

BEST ROMAN EXPERIENCES

Marvel at Cádiz's sensitively reconstructed **Teatro Romano** – the largest in Spain at the time, with room for 10,000 spectators. ❶ (p118)

Duck inland from the Costa de la Luz to the whitewashed **Medina Sidonia** to appreciate the town's well-preserved Roman road and underground sewers. ❷ (p121)

Follow an ancient Roman stone path from Benaocaz to the remains of the Roman town of **Ocuri**, in the Sierra de Crazalema. ❸ (p121)

Wander through the forum, and past the aqueduct, temples, basilica and garum tanks of **Baelo Claudia**, the prosperous city by the sea in Bolonia. ❹ (p121)

Peruse the quirky mosaics in the villa remnants in Sevilla's Roman settlement of **Itálica**, as well as its vast amphitheatre. ❺ (p75)

Málaga (p152)

RENAISSANCE AND GOTHIC MONUMENTS

Often built atop Nasrid mosques and monuments to comprehensively seal the victory of the Catholic kings against the Moors, Andalucía's grandest cathedrals and palaces are symphonies in stone. Renaissance columns intermingle with Gothic flying buttresses, with exceptionally fine Spanish plateresque elements appearing on many a facade.

Take your time

The pleasure's in the detail: these remarkable buildings will yield their many secrets if you take your time to explore (and peruse the QR codes).

Prominent architect

Diego de Siloé was one of the most important Renaissance architects, responsible for the Granada Cathedral and Granada school of sculpture.

BEST RENAISSANCE & GOTHIC EXPERIENCES

Head to the *cubiertas* (roof) of **Málaga**'s cathedral for panoramic city views. ❶ (p152)

Contemplate the vast Renaissance edifice of **Granada**'s cathedral. ❷ (p230)

Scale the mighty bell tower of **Sevilla**'s awe-inspiring Gothic cathedral. ❸ (p56)

Marvel over the facade of the Palacio Juan Vázquez de Molina in **Úbeda**. ❹ (p218)

Be mesmerised by **Baeza**'s Palacio del Jabalquinto with its spectacular patio arcade. ❺ (p219)

WHERE THE WILD THINGS ARE

Andalucía's varied terrain – mountains, deep gorges, rolling hills, dense woodland and swamplands – makes up a variety of habitats, essential to the survival of all manner of furred and feathered creatures, from the Iberian lynx and the ibex to raptors. You may also spot large pelagics in the Strait of Gibraltar, teeming with marine life.

Bring binoculars

Whether you're a keen birder or a casual appreciator of wildlife, pack some binoculars to get a closer look at hooved, feathered and finned life.

Whale-watching season

Some of Tarifa's pelagics are seasonal: come in July and August for a chance to spot killer whales, and in spring to glimpse sperm whales.

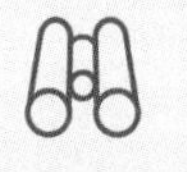

Iberian lynx

Formerly critically endangered, Andalucía's iconic Iberian lynx is bounding back, with 400 or so big cats split between Sierra Morena and Parque Nacional de Doñana.

BEST WILD EXPERIENCES

Hop on a boat in **Tarifa**, with marine conservationists pointing out various species as you cruise the Strait of Gibraltar. ❶ (p138)

Test your luck to spot lynx in the wild; the alternative is compelling webcam footage at **Parque Nacional de Doñana**'s visitor centre. ❷ (p103)

Hike in the upper reaches of **Parque Nacional Sierra Nevada**, and look out for graceful ibex scrambling effortlessly up bare rock. ❸ (p244)

Visit **Parque Natural Cazorla** and catch sight of bearded vultures, brought back from near extinction. ❹ (p213)

Go birdwatching in **Parque Natural Cabo de Gata-Níjar**, where you'll find flamingos on the salt marsh, plus dozens of other species. ❺ (p264)

WHITE TOWNS

Cascades of brilliant white houses spilling down steep hillsides are a typical Andalucian spectacle. *Pueblos blancos* typically have a dramatically sited location and a volatile frontier history. Choosing your favourite while road-tripping along winding mountain roads is a near-impossible task. While *pueblos blancos* are dotted all over Andalucía, the best examples are concentrated in the northeastern Cádiz province and in the mountainous Granada Alpujarras.

PHILIP REEVE/SHUTTERSTOCK © LEFT: CARON BADKIN/SHUTTERSTOCK ©, EUSEBIO TORRES/SHUTTERSTOCK ©

Almond blossoms

Road-trip through Granada's Alpujarras villages in February in order to catch the almond trees in bloom and the hillsides wreathed in almost ethereal white.

Moros y Cristianos

If you pass through Válor in October, you can be forgiven for thinking that a war's broken out when the Moors vs Christians struggle is re-enacted with enthusiasm.

Via verde

Whizz between some of the *pueblos blancos* in the Sierra de Grazalema on two wheels along a *via verde* (defunct railway repurposed as cycling track).

Capileira (p244)

❺ ❹❶ ❷ ❸

BEST WHITE TOWN EXPERIENCES

Gaze in awe at the cave houses in **Setenil de las Bodegas** – a remarkable village dug deep into the cliff face. ❶ (p134)

Base yourself in lofty **Capileira** – the highest village in the Alpujarras – to tackle Spain's highest peak and numerous other mountain trails. ❷ (p244)

Stay in a charming boutique hotel and follow your taste buds around hilltop **Vejer de la Frontera**'s many excellent restaurants and tapas bars. ❸ (p136)

Look down on the turquoise Zahara Reservoir from the rugged, Moorish-flavoured **Zahara de la Sierra** and hike into the Sierra de Grazalema's Garganta Verde. ❹ (p133)

Follow a carpet of olive groves to **Zuheros** – the ideal hiking base for exploring the canyons of the Sierras Subbéticas that overlook the village. ❺ (p200)

REGIONS & CITIES

Find the places that tick all your boxes.

Sevilla & Huelva
p51
Sevilla
p56
Cádiz & Gibraltar
p109
Málaga
p147

Sevilla & Huelva

MUDÉJAR MARVELS & RURAL IDYLLS

Seductive flamenco rhythms, striking architecture, lively tapas bars – Andalucía's 'Golden Age' capital is the place to be moved by *duende* and explore the cultural heritage funded by wealth from the 'New World'. By contrast, quiet beaches and vast national parks await in the bucolic, tree-filled hinterland of Huelva.

p51

Cádiz & Gibraltar

ANDALUCIAN CULTURAL HEARTLAND WITH BEACHES

Andalucía's southwestern corner has everything: culture, buzzy cities, sand and mountains. Water-sports fiends flock to white-sand beaches, gourmands await bluefin-tuna season and sherry aficionados further their education in the bodegas of the 'Sherry Triangle'. Inland, enticing *pueblos blancos* (white towns) are launchpads for mountain escapades, while sultry Cádiz and Jerez rock to flamenco rhythms.

p109

Córdoba & Jaén

HISTORY, CULTURE & PROTECTED NATIONAL PARKS

Mesmerising Moorish architecture meets a thriving dining scene in Córdoba, while bucolic Jaén bristles with ancient castles and welcomes you with the Renaissance wealth of historic Úbeda and Baeza. A carpet of olive groves covers the hills, leading you to the mountains, forests and waterfalls of Parque Nacional Cazorla.

p185

Córdoba & Jaén
p185

Granada & Almería
p225

Málaga

BEYOND THE COSTA DEL SOL

Contemporary art, Roman ruins and white-sand beaches: Andalucía's south coast has them all, from the 'museum capital' and Picasso's birthplace of Málaga to the beach-adorned Costa del Sol. North and east of the capital, rock climbers and hikers head for the mountains of Axarquía and around Antequera and El Chorro.

p147

Granada & Almería

MASTERPIECE ARCHITECTURE & OUTDOOR ADVENTURE

Europe's finest Moorish palace awaits in Granada, home of Andalucía's best tapas scene. Beyond, the snowy peaks and age-old villages of the Sierra Nevada beckon mountain adventurers. On the coast, the ancient city-port of Almería is a gateway to superb beaches, Wild West desert and giant glittering gems underground.

p225

Albaicín district, Granada (p233)

ITINERARIES

Cultural Heartlands

Allow: 10 days **Distance:** 818km

This loop takes you from Sevilla's grand cathedral and medieval streets to the magnificent Moorish monuments of Granada and Córdoba to the Renaissance architecture of Úbeda, the old-school tapas bars of seaside Cádiz and the flamenco clubs of Jerez, with superb dining en route.

1

SEVILLA 2 DAYS

Begin in **Sevilla** (p56), where you can explore its monumental cathedral, the Alcázar (royal palace), and the tile-clad Hospital de la Caridad. Wander the lanes of Santa Cruz, sampling tapas and going to one of the flamenco *peñas* (clubs). Venture across the river for modern art at Centro Andaluz de Arte Contemporáneo and Triana's old-school eateries.

1-hour train trip

2

CÓRDOBA 2 DAYS

Split your time in **Córdoba** (p190) between the historical centre and the remains of the Moorish palace-city Medina Azahara, on the outskirts. In the city, allow plenty of time to absorb the Mezquita, taking in the Alcázar, the synagogue, the tapas bars and the flowering patios of Palacio de Viana. Take the pedestrian Roman Bridge across the river at night.

2½-hour bus ride

3

ÚBEDA 1 DAY

Head across fields of olive groves to historic **Úbeda** (p218). Wander the streets of the Unesco-listed old town, admiring Renaissance palaces and a centuries-old synagogue. Delve into Jewish history by touring historic mansions with Vandelvira (vandelviraturismo.com).

2-hour bus ride

***Detour:** Head to the sister city of **Baeza** (p219) to explore its remarkable Renaissance buildings. 3 hours*

CASTILLA-LA MANCHA
EXTREMADURA
Pozoblanco
Llerena
CÓRDOBA
JAÉN
Bailén
Linares
Andújar
Úbeda
Baeza
Cazorla
Córdoba
2hr30min
Aracena
Río Guadalquivir
Parque Natural Sierra Mágina
Pozo Alcón
Jaén
2hr
Palma del Río
SEVILLA
Montilla
Parque Natural Sierras Subbéticas
Alcalá la Real
1hr
START
Écija
Río Genil
Lucena
Carmona
Iznalloz
Guadix
Almonte
Sevilla
Osuna
Loja
Mulhacén (3482m)
Utrera
2hr15min
Granada
Parque Nacional de Doñana
Campillos
Antequera
GRANADA
Parque Natural Sierra Nevada
4hr30min
Jerez de la Frontera
MÁLAGA
Málaga
Arcos de la Frontera
Ronda
Nerja
Motril
END
Cádiz
Fuengirola
Marbella
Chiclana de la Frontera
CÁDIZ
Estepona
Costa de Sol
Costa de la Luz
Gibraltar (UK)
Strait of Gibraltar
Tarifa
0 50 km
0 25 miles

4 GRANADA ⏱ 3 DAYS

Continue south to **Granada** (p230) and allow a day for the remarkable Alhambra alone. The hilly, Unesco-listed *barrio* (district) of Albaicín, the cathedral and royal tombs, and Realejo's street art and sensational tapas bars will easily gobble up another day or two.

2¼-hour train trip

***Detour:** Head to **Guadix** (p240) to visit the centuries-old, unique cave houses of the Altiplano. ⏱ 4 hours*

5 RONDA ⏱ 1 DAY

In historic **Ronda** (p160), wander down into the gorge for the best views of the iconic bridge, returning to peruse the quirky museums, tour the Plaza de Toros and descend into the water cistern of the Casa del Rey Moro.

4½-hour train trip

***Detour:** Leaving Ronda, stop in **Arcos de la Frontera** (p134) to admire the pueblo blanco's castle and valley views from its lofty perch. ⏱ 3 hours*

6 JEREZ DE LA FRONTERA ⏱ 1 DAY

Heading back to Sevilla, slow down and spend a day in **Jerez** (p125), the cradle of Andalucian horse culture, the home of sherry and one of the three cornerstones of flamenco. Tour a bodega or two, relax in a Moorish-style *hammam*, sample cuisine and attend a passionate flamenco performance before a nightcap at one of the city's *tabancos* (sherry taverns).

ITINERARIES

Costa del Sol & Luz Beaches

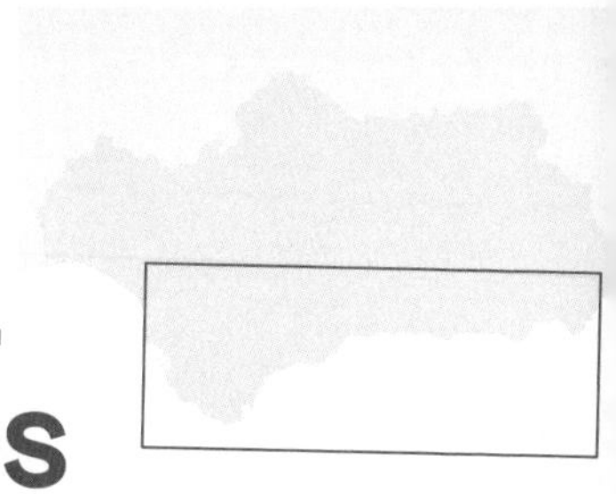

Allow: 7 days
Distance: 453km

Andalucía's Costa del Sol and Costa de la Luz feature many of Spain's most beautiful beaches, with vast crescents of white sand, secluded coves and pebble beaches attracting sun-worshipers and water-sports enthusiasts alike. This coastal jaunt takes in the best of both coasts, from secluded strands to glitzy resort towns.

❶

SAN JOSÉ ⏱1 DAY

Base yourself in **San José** (p267), the main seaside town at the heart of Parque Natural Cabo de Gata-Níjar. From here, hike or drive to the spectacular Playa de los Genoveses – the park's most popular beaches – or the even more striking Playa de Mónsul.

3-hour drive

***Detour:** Stop in **Almería** (p257) on your way west to experience the Moorish charm of this ancient port city.* ⏱*4 hours*

❷

NERJA ⏱1 DAY

Defined by the promontory of Balcón de Europa and silhouetted against Sierra de Almijara, the town of **Nerja** (p180) lets you choose between the *chiringuitos* (snack bars) of buzzy Playa de Burriana, sheltered Playa Calahonda cove and its main beach, Playa el Salón.

1-hour drive

***Detour:** For a more tranquil scene, pebbly **Playa el Cañuelo** (p181) and clothing-optional **Playa Cantarriján** (p256) are a 10-minute drive east.*

❸

MÁLAGA ⏱2 DAYS

With its appealing historic centre, palm-lined seafront promenade and a heavyweight clutch of museums, **Málaga** (p152) – the birthplace of Picasso and hometown of Antonio Banderas – has much more to offer besides a handful of decent city beaches. While away a few hours in a *chiringuito* by the sea, immerse yourself in art at the Picasso Museum, or get sucked into Málaga's nightlife in Soho.

20-minute drive

4 BENALMÁDENA & MIJAS 1 DAY

At the town of **Benalmádena** (p158), check out coastal views from a Buddhist stupa and enjoy fresh seafood by the marina. A short drive away is the attractive old heart of **Mijas** (p158), where you can admire works by Dalí, Miró and Picasso at its Centre for Contemporary Art.

2½-hour drive

***Detour:** Heading west, stop in glitterati haunt **Marbella** (p159) for a coffee and a stroll around the appealing casco antiguo (old town). 2 hours*

5 TARIFA 1 DAY

At **Tarifa** (p138), a compact, walled old town with North African flavour, Andalucía's windiest settlement draws kitesurfers and windsurfers to its wide, white-sand beaches. Sign up at a kiting school or go whale-watching in the Strait of Gibraltar.

45-minute drive

***Detour:** On your way north, admire the Roman town of **Baelo Claudia** (p121), or simply relax on the stupendous, dune-backed beach at **Playa de Bolonia** (p142). 2 hours*

6 ZAHARA DE LOS ATUNES 1 DAY

Boogie-boarding on the foam-crested turquoise waves is a must at **Playa de Zahara** (p142), a powder-white, 8km-long beach on the Costa de la Luz. When you finally emerge from the sea, salty-skinned and sun-drunk, peruse the boutiques of this formerly sleepy fishing village.

***Detour:** Hike the scenic coastal **Sendero de Acantilado** (p124) between Los Caños and Barbate. 3 hours*

OSZO/SHUTTERSTOCK ©

Pradollano, Sierra Nevada (p252)

ITINERARIES

Mountains & Hills

Allow: 8 days **Distance:** 720km

From the snow-tipped Sierra Nevada and the rugged Grazalema and Almijara ranges to the hills of Sierras Subbéticas, the forested Parque Nacional Cazorla and the vast limestone Rock of Gibraltar – fresh-air fiends will find challenges here, but there are gentler pursuits aplenty.

1

PARQUE NATURAL SIERRAS DE CAZORLA 2 DAYS

Use picturesque Cazorla as your launchpad for exploring the **Parque Natural Sierras de Cazorla, Segura y las Villas** (p209). The strenuous 20km-loop from the town up to the Pico Gilillo peak is a superb day hike.

3¼-hour drive

Detour: *Drive to the stupendously scenic* ***Sendero de Río Borosa*** *(p210) hiking trail. 8 hours*

2

CAPILEIRA 2 DAYS

The loftiest village in the Sierra Nevada's Barranco de Poqueira, **Capileira** (p244) is the most popular starting point for climbing Mulhacén (3482m) – mainland Spain's highest mountain. There are gentler rambles nearby, too.

2½-hour drive

Detour: *The demanding* ***Siete Lagunas loop hike*** *(p246) from nearby Trevélez is arguably even more scenic, with waterfalls and views. 1 day*

3

ZUHEROS 1 DAY

Approaching **Zuheros** (p200), a *pueblo blanco* in the Sierras Subbéticas, feels highly dramatic: it looms ahead, overlooked by a crag-top castle. Challenge yourself by hiking the rocky gorge of Cañón de Bailón, returning via the road past the Cueva de los Murciélagos, or take a tour to that cave and simply marvel at the traces of Neolithic rock paintings inside.

1-hour drive

ZDENEK MATYAS PHOTOGRAPHY/SHUTTERSTOCK ©, ECUADORPOSTALES/SHUTTERSTOCK ©, DAVAIPHOTOGRAPHY/SHUTTERSTOCK ©

CÓRDOBA
JAÉN
Villaviciosa de Córdoba
Linares
Sendero de Río Borosa
Montoro
Andújar
Parque Natural Sierras de Cazorla
1 START
Constantina
Córdoba
Porcuna
Quesada
Río Guadalquivir
Jaén
Parque Natural Sierra Mágina
3hr15min
Palma del Río
Baena
Montilla
Alcalá la Real
Carmona
Écija
Río Genil
3 Zuheros
Baza
SEVILLA
Lucena
Parque Natural Sierras Subbéticas
GRANADA
Iznalloz
Guadix
Osuna
1hr
2hr30min
Loja
Granada
Parque Natural Sierra Nevada
Mulhacén (3482m)
Campillos
Capileira
Trevélez
Setenil de las Bodegas
4 Antequera
2hr
2
Ugíjar
El Chorro
La Maroma (2065m)
Grazalema
5
Parque Natural Sierra de Grazalema
Ronda
MÁLAGA
Nerja
Motril
Adra
Málaga
Almerimar
Marbella
Fuengirola
Costa de Sol
2hr15min
San Pedro de Alcántara
CÁDIZ
Estepona
Mediterranean Sea
Algeciras
6 Gibraltar (UK)
END
0 50 km
0 25 miles
Tarifa

4

ANTEQUERA 1 DAY

Basing yourself in **Antequera** (p168), a castle-topped white town, explore the limestone formations of El Torcal de Antequera along several trails. A gentle, 1km-long ramble from Antequera brings you to the striking Bronze Age dolmen site.

2-hour drive

Detour: *Drive to El Chorro for* ***El Caminito del Rey*** *(p175; sign up in advance), to hike the boardwalk through the canyon. 4 hours*

5

SIERRA DE GRAZALEMA 1 DAY

In the **Sierra de Grazalema** (p130), the namesake village is your gateway to the demanding El Torreón (1648m) summit, with views as far as Morocco. An alternative is the descent into the precipitous Garganta Verde.

2¼-hour drive

Detour: *Drive to* ***Setenil de las Bodegas*** *(p134) and wander around the unique cave houses of this village, built deep into the cliffs. 3 hours*

6

GIBRALTAR 1 DAY

Rest your legs (a little) by taking the cable car to the top of the Rock in **Gibraltar** (p144) and meeting the simian residents at the Apes' Den (just make sure not to carry any food with you!). Easy strolls to O'Hara's Battery and the plexiglass-floored Skywalk give you tremendous, 360-degree views of the town below, the Mediterranean and both sides of the Rock.

ITINERARIES

Gourmet Trail

Allow: 4 days
Distance: 139km

Multiple delectable courses of bluefin tuna; sea-salt-tinged *manzanilla* sherry straight from the barrel; old-school tapas flying across a bar surrounded by bullfighting memorabilia; and fusion dishes served on the terrace of a hilltop *pueblo blanco* are just some of the foodie experiences on offer in this gourmand-friendly corner of Andalucía.

1 JEREZ DE LA FRONTERA

1 DAY

Elegant **Jerez** (p125) beckons with its old-world charm, sunny plazas, graceful architecture and, of course, its centuries-old tradition of making sherry. Tour famed sherry manufacturers Bodegas Tradición or González-Byass, see flamenco at a *tabanco* and treat yourself to a Michelin-starred dinner at LÚ, Cocina y Alma.

30-minute drive

2 SANLÚCAR DE BARRAMEDA

1 DAY

Sanlúcar's (p129) coastal location and microclimate has infused its unique *manzanilla* sherry with a distinctive tang. Sample *amontillado* at Bodegas Hidalgo–La Gitana, or the exceptional 15-year-old *manzanilla pasada* at Bodegas Barbadillo. Feast on seafood, including fried anemone, while people-watching at Casa Balbino, or indulge in food-and-wine pairings at El Espejo.

1-hour drive

Parque Natural de Doñana
Lucio de los Ánsares
HUELVA
Río Guadalquivir
SEVILLA
Lebrija
Trebujena
El Cuervo
Golfo de Cádiz
Bonanza
2 Sanlúcar de Barrameda
30min
Jedula
START
1 Jerez de la Frontera
El Puerto de Santa María
1hr
Río Guadalete
Rota
Bahía de Cádiz
Cádiz 3
Puerto Real
CÁDIZ
San Fernando
Medina Sidonia
Isla de León
Bahía de Cádiz
Chiclana de la Frontera
Isla de Sancti Petri
Sancti Petri
1hr
Novo Sancti Petri
Costa de la Luz
Conil de la Frontera
Santa Lucía
Vejer de la Frontera 5
END
15min
El Palmar
Zahora
Los Caños de Meca
4 Barbate
Parque Natural de la Breña y Marismas de Barbate
Costa de la Luz
ATLANTIC OCEAN
Strait of Gibraltar
0 20 km
0 10 miles

3

CÁDIZ 1 DAY

Eat your way around **Cádiz** (p114), breakfasting on churros at the Mercado Central de Abastos and haunting old-school tapas bars Casa Manteca and El Faro de Cádiz come evening. Fusion dining at La Candela or Sonámbulo is a must.

1-hour drive

***Detour:** Take a catamaran to **Puerto de Santa María** (p121) for more sherry. Book ahead for sensational set menus at Michelin-starred Aponiente.*

4

BARBATE HALF-DAY

Scruffy around the edges, the busy fishing port of **Barbate** (p123) is one of the centres of the seasonal *almadraba* tuna catch. Don't miss a blowout meal at 'tuna temple' El Campero; then buy jars of tuna in Iberian pork fat at the Herpac factory shop.

15-minute drive

***Detour:** Whizz up the coast to **Conil** (p143) for other restaurants specialising in* atún rojo *(bluefin tuna).*
3 hours

5

VEJER DE LA FRONTERA HALF-DAY

Finish up at hilltop Moorish-town **Vejer** (p136). Choose between Moroccan-accented meals at El Jardín de Califa, La Judería's fusion bites or mind-blowing *arróz con ibéricos* at Elmuro, or learn to cook Andalucian specialities with Annie B.

***Detour:** Gorge yourself on beautiful wood-fired local meats at **Restaurante la Castillería** (p137) in nearby Santa Lucía. 3 hours*

CKTRAVELS.COM/SHUTTERSTOCK ©

WHEN TO GO

Answer: whenever you want. Andalucía is a year-round destination, though the beaches are at their best outside July and August.

Long daylight hours, plenty of sun and sand, and year-round sunshine are just some of the reasons to come to Andalucía. Water sports dominate all year, with kayakers, snorkellers, swimmers and kitesurfers flocking to the beaches of Costa de la Luz and Costa del Sol. City vacations are ideal anytime, apart from scorching July and August. Andalucía is also a superb trekking destination, with mountain ranges to explore and long-distance trails to hike; for this, shoulder seasons are best. You might consider olive- and grape-harvest season (autumn) if you wish to visit bodegas and olive-oil producers at the liveliest time of year. Factor in the altitude when packing, since there's a world of difference between the Sierra Nevada and coastal resorts.

Want a bargain?

Resorts aside, prices don't vary much between seasons. Along the Costa del Sol and Costa de la Luz, however, accommodation is priciest from early July till late August.

I LIVE HERE

Ute Mergner, owner of Bodega Etu-Vinos, Europe's smallest, most southerly bodega, specialising in limited-production, handcrafted organic wines.

"Every month is exciting when you're tending vines. To watch them burst into leaf in spring with the promise of grapes, right through to the autumnal colour splash ahead of pruning at the end of the year. May–June is also very exciting, as that's when the grapes start to form and I can tell what level of production the harvest holds, as long as the grapes remain healthy."

Feria de Agosto, Málaga

CALIMA

The Calima is a phenomenon that occurs in spring, when the hot southeasterly wind brings sand and dust from the Sahara. Visibility becomes very low, the sky acquires a red, Martian tinge and air quality is extremely poor for three to five days.

Weather through the year

JANUARY	FEBRUARY	MARCH	APRIL	MAY	JUNE
Ave. daytime max: **15°C**	Ave. daytime max: **17°C**	Ave. daytime max: **20°C**	Ave. daytime max: **24°C**	Ave. daytime max: **27°C**	Ave. daytime max: **32°C**
Days of rainfall: 5.8	Days of rainfall: 5.2	Days of rainfall: 4.8	Days of rainfall: 4.7	Days of rainfall: 3.3	Days of rainfall: 1.2

ATLANTIC VERSUS MEDITERRANEAN

Beach holidays in Andalucía revolve around either the Atlantic Ocean or the Mediterranean Sea. The average water temperature in both is around 22 degrees Celsius during the summer months, while in winter it hovers around 16 degrees Celsius.

Carnivals & parties

Every February, Cádiz throws mainland Spain's largest **Carnaval** (p114). This 10-day spectacle, famous for its wit and best embodied by scathingly humorous *chirigotas* (satirical folk songs), comprises parades, fancy dress and local band competitions. **Feb**

In late February or early March, Jerez – the self-styled *cuna* (cradle) of flamenco – gets taken over by fiery flamenco performances, held all over town for two weeks during the **Festival de Jerez** (p125). **Feb or Mar**

Sevilla's legendary week-long **Feria de Abril** (p54) – Andalucía's biggest fair – kicks off in April. *Sevillanos* dress up in traditional gear, drink sherry, parade on horseback and dance *sevillanas* (flamenco-influenced folk dances). **Apr**

Andalucía's second-biggest party – the **Feria de Agosto** (p151) – takes place in Málaga in mid-August, with dancing, parades, dressing up to the nines, fairground rides and a massive fireworks show over the harbour. **Aug**

Quirky festivals

During Córdoba's **Fiesta de los Patios** (p196) in May, homeowners deck out private courtyards with flowers to compete for prizes awarded for the 'best patio'. **May**

You can fly high above the mountain of El Yelmo in Jaén province during the three-day **Festival international del Aire** that celebrates paragliding, held on the first weekend in June. **Jun**

Taking place in Guadix (p240) in August, the **Festival de Cascamorras** centres on an age-old dispute revolving around the sacred image of the Virgen de la Piedad. During the three-day fest, participants smear themselves in oil and fight over the virgin. **Aug**

Tiny Válor in Granada's Alpujarras hosts **Moros y Cristianos** (p251) in October – a noisy, colourful, four-day re-enactment of the 1568 Moorish rebellion against Christian rule, played out with gusto on the main square. **Oct**

I LIVE HERE

Annie Manson (Annie B) is an Andalucian food expert based in Vejer de la Frontera. @anniebspain

"Each May I get excited about the arrival of the bluefin tuna. It's an excitement that must have been felt in this area for centuries as it heralded the restocking of tuna supplies such as air-dried *mojama*. These massive fish have an inbuilt radar to find the gap of the Strait of Gibraltar, beyond which are the warm Mediterranean waters they need for spawning. Along the coast are ancient lookout towers to watch for the first tuna arriving."

Mojama

FEELING HOT, HOT, HOT!

Andalucía's Almería province is Spain's (and Europe's!) sunniest, with over 300 days of sunshine per year. However, the hottest cities are Sevilla and Córdoba, with temperatures soaring into the 40s in July and August.

JULY
Ave. daytime max: **36°C**
Days of rainfall: 0.3

AUGUST
Ave. daytime max: **36°C**
Days of rainfall: 0.4

SEPTEMBER
Ave. daytime max: **32°C**
Days of rainfall: 2.2

OCTOBER
Ave. daytime max: **26°C**
Days of rainfall: 5.5

NOVEMBER
Ave. daytime max: **20°C**
Days of rainfall: 6.0

DECEMBER
Ave. daytime max: **16°C**
Days of rainfall: 6.3

LEFT: SOPHIE PICARD/SHUTTERSTOCK © RIGHT: MURRAY CLOSE/GETTY IMAGES ©

Casa de Pilatos, Sevilla (p65)

GET PREPARED FOR ANDALUCÍA

Useful things to load in your bag, your ears and your brain

Clothes

Dress nicely: Spain is a fashion-forward, well-dressed nation, and in Andalucian cities people make an effort and go for a smart-casual look. Dress up for high-end restaurants, though elsewhere it's more flexible. Beachwear is appropriate on the beach but generally not on a city street.
Layers: Bring a fleece, windbreaker, waterproof, sweater and even a coat if visiting in the winter months or planning to scale mountains.
Footwear: Flip-flops and sandals are ideal for beach holidays, but you'll want sturdy footwear – walking shoes with decent grip at the least – both for hiking trails and for hilltop villages and towns where streets can be steep and the cobbles slippery.
Hats: In summer, hats are an absolute must. Warm hats are a good idea for mountains in winter.

Manners

Be like the locals and linger over a coffee on a terrace, or a sit-down meal at a restaurant.

Greet friends and strangers alike with a kiss on each cheek (unless you're both men).

If invited to an Andalucian home, dress nicely and bring a bottle of wine.

Don't visit churches for tourism purposes during Mass and other worship services.

READ

South from Granada (Gerald Brenan; 1957) A Bloomsbury intellectual tries village life in Las Alpujarras in the 1920s.

Three Plays (Federico García Lorca; 1930s) Andalucía's greatest playwright's three classic tragedies, about passion and trapped lives.

The Ornament of the World (María Rosa Menocal; 2002) Examines the tolerance and sophistication of Moorish Andalucía.

Driving Over Lemons (Chris Stewart; 1999) An anecdotal bestseller about life on a small Alpujarras farm.

Words

'hola' (oh-lah) is how you say 'hello'.

'buenos días' (bweh-nohs dee-ahs), 'good day', is a more formal way of greeting someone, while **'buenas tardes'** (bweh-nahs tahr-des), 'good afternoon', is used from noon onwards, and **'buenas noches'** (bweh-nahs noh-ches), 'good evening/good night', is used from 8pm in both greeting and farewell.

Use **'usted'** ('you') in polite company and **'tu'** with friends and children.

'como está?' (koh-moh es-tah) is how you greet friends and ask 'how are you?'

You should respond **'bien, y usted/tu?'** (b'yen, eee oos-ted/too), meaning 'I'm fine, and you?'

'por favor' (por fa-vohr) is the standard way to say 'please'. It is also what you use in restaurants to summon the waiter.

'gracias' (gra-si-ahs) is 'thank you'.

Say **'disculpe'** (deh-skool-peh), meaning 'excuse me', to get someone's attention.

Say **'permiso'** (per-mee-soh) when you want to get past someone in a crowd.

'no entiendo' (no en-tien-doh) is how you say 'I don't understand'.

'salud!' (sa-lood) literally means 'health'. You say it both as a 'cheers!' toast and instead of 'bless you' after someone sneezes.

When ordering food an excellent way to try local specialities is to ask **'qué es la especialidád de la casa?'** (ke ehs la es-pes-yal-i-dad deh la cah-sah).

'socorro!' (soo-koh-roo) means 'help!'

WATCH

Marshland (Alberto Rodríguez; 2014) A suspenseful story of detectives investigating murders in the Guadalquivir delta.

The Disappearance of García Lorca (Marcos Zurinaga; 1997) A journalist investigates the death of the great Spanish playwright.

Living Is Easy with Eyes Closed (David Trueba; 2013) It's 1966 and three Spanish music fans search for John Lennon, who's shooting a film in Almería.

Indiana Jones and the Last Crusade (Steven Spielberg; 1989) Spielberg classic shot at Playa de Mónsul, Desierto de Tabernas and Guadix.

LISTEN

Antología (Paco de Lucía; 1995) Two dozen tracks by the incomparable flamenco guitar maestro.

La leyenda del tiempo (Camarón de la Isla; 1979) The great flamenco voice of modern times.

Bulería (David Bisbal; 2004) Classic *andaluz* pop of the kind that reverberates around every summer fiesta.

La voz de mi silencio (El Barrio; 2007) Top album of flamenco's urban poet from Cádiz.

NITO/SHUTTERSTOCK ©

Salmorejo

THE FOOD SCENE

You haven't fully experienced Andalucía until your taste buds have taken a tour of the region's rich edible repertoire.

Talk to any Andalucian and they'll express strong, passionate opinions about the dishes and wines of their region, profoundly shaped by the rugged terrain and proximity to the sea. Traditionally poor and underdeveloped economically compared to other Spanish regions, Andalucía is Spain's agricultural heartland, producing the lion's share of Europe's fruit and vegetables, as well as a quarter of the world's olive oil.

The Mediterranean's marine wealth has drawn successive civilisations and invaders to Andalucía's shores, with many stamping their influence on the region's cuisine, from fishing techniques employed by the Phoenicians to spices from North Africa.

Andalucian cuisine stands out for its simplicity and quality of ingredients, celebrated in distinctive regional dishes and village specialities. But there is room for innovation as well, with gourmet food stalls alongside traditional *charcuterías*; new wine-producing techniques resulting in live, organic and biodynamic wines; and Michelin-starred restaurants mingling with old-school *tabernas* and tapas bars in the bigger cities.

Ancient roots

Andalucía's multifaceted cuisine is rooted in its proximity to the Atlantic and the Mediterranean; the annual bluefin tuna migration led Phoenicians to pioneer the *almadraba* net-fishing technique 3000 years ago. The cultivation of olives here goes back to Roman times, and it's thought that gazpacho – Andalucía's signature cold soup – may well have originated from the Roman *caspa*, an olive-oil and bread gruel.

Best Andalucian dishes

SALMOREJO
A savoury gazpacho topped with hard-boiled egg and *jamón*

BERENJENAS CON MIEL
Crispy aubergine slices drizzled with honey or sugarcane syrup

AJOBLANCO
Cold almond-and-garlic soup, often topped with fresh grapes or melon

JAMÓN IBERICO DE BELLOTA
The most highly prized of Andalucía's cured hams

But it's the Moors who truly shaped Andalucian cuisine, bringing with them apricots, artichokes, carob, sugar, aubergines, grapefruits, carrots and numerous spices completely unknown in Spain before Nazrid rule. They also introduced rice and saffron, key ingredients in paella, Spain's quintessential dish.

Bounty from the land

Coastal Andalucía is not alone in its devotion to local produce. Andalucians justifiably claim that the olive oil and *jamón* (cured ham) produced here are Spain's finest.

Spanish *jamón* is deep red, marbled with buttery fat. At its best, it smells like the forest and the field. It's divided into salted and semidried *jamón serrano* (from the meat of white-coated pigs); *jamón ibérico* (from black-coated pigs indigenous to the Iberian peninsula); and *jamón ibérico de bellota* (acorn-fed Iberian pigs) – the most sought-after designation.

The ritual of mopping up olive oil with some bread has almost sacred status here. Andalucía's Jaén province alone produces almost a quarter of the world's olive oil. Extra-virgin olive oil is made from the somewhat spicy *picual* olive, which dominates Jaén, and the *hojiblanca* variety (fruity, grassy and nutty), grown predominantly around Málaga and Sevilla provinces.

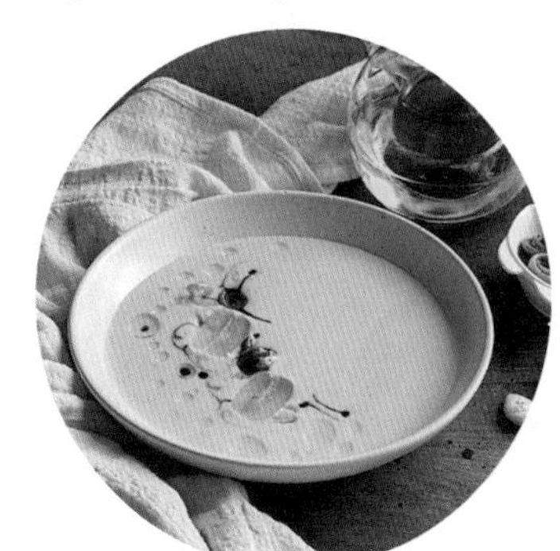

Ajoblanco

Bounty from the sea

That old saying about the Costa del Sol megaresorts once being nothing more than a string of fishing villages is largely true. The seasonal delicacy of *almadraba* tuna aside, most seafood here is wonderfully affordable. For those living near the coast, heading for their favourite *chiringuito* (beachside seafood restaurant) for a long lunch of fried or grilled fish is a much-loved weekend pastime.

BEST GOURMAND FESTIVALS

Fiestas de Vendimia (p125) This two-week September grape-harvest extravaganza in Jerez sees flamenco, horse events and the treading of the first grapes.

Ruta del Atún (p122) In May and June, the fishing towns of Zahara de los Atunes, Barbate, Conil and Tarifa host gastronomic events revolving around bluefin tuna.

Feria de la Manzanilla (p128) A big *manzanilla*-sherry-fuelled fair kicks off Sanlúcar's summer in early June.

Gastrojazz (p113) Jazz accompanies all manner of gastronomic events in foodie haven Vejer de la Frontera in July.

Noche del Vino, Cómpeta (p183) Cómpeta celebrates its sweet local muscatel wine on 15 August, with a traditional treading of the grapes followed by fiery flamenco performances – and endless free cups of the tipple.

Fiestas de Vendimia (p125)

TARTAR DE ATÚN ROJO Seasonal bluefin tuna served raw and lightly seasoned

ESPETOS DE SARDINAS Sardine skewers, grilled to perfection at beachside charcoal grills

TORTILLA DE CAMARONES Fritters made with tiny shrimp, chickpea and wheat flour, onion and parsley

FRITURA DE PESCADO Fried seafood platters including *boquerones* (anchovies) and *puntillitas* (tiny squid)

Local specialities

When travelling around Andalucía, keep your eyes peeled for these regional treats.

Seafood favourites

Pescaíto frito Literally 'fried fish'; extra-virgin olive oil and flash-fried, lightly battered fish
Cazón en adobo Dogfish (small shark) marinated in vinegar, battered with spices and fried
Ortiguillas Fried sea anemones, with their own unique flavour (a little like oysters)
Boquerones Anchovies, either fried or marinated in garlic, olive oil and vinegar
Chanquetes Similar to whitebait and served deep-fried
Chipirones or chopitos Battered and fried baby squid
Camarones rojas/blancas Local shrimp (red from Almería and white from Huelva), served chilled with mayo, sprinkled with salt
Tortillitas de camarones Shrimp fritters

Tortillitas de camarones

Meaty dishes

Rabo de toro Oxtail, braised for hours
Puchero Traditional vegetable and chickpea stew, with *pringá* (mixed meats) served separately
Migas Fried breadcrumbs, cooked with garlic, meat, olive oil and sometimes offal
Morcilla Black pudding, made from pig's blood, spices and sometimes rice
Callos a la Andaluza Slow-cooked tripe stew with chickpeas – a winter favourite

Sweet treats

Pan de Cádiz Nutty-flavoured Cádiz sweet with marzipan filling
Buñelos Fried sweets made with flour, yeast, milk and sugar, around since medieval times
Roscos Fried sugar-covered dough rings of Moorish origin
Borrachuelos Malagueños Filled sweet pastries, bathed in wine and fried during Semana Santa in Málaga
Castañas asadas Chestnuts roasted over hot coals at street stalls; an autumn treat

MEALS OF A LIFETIME

Bagá, Jaén (p218) Playful tasting menu by Pedro Sánchez features local, seasonal ingredients with unusual pairings.

La Brunilda, Sevilla (p69) Brilliantly executed fusion creations at one of Sevilla's best tapas haunts, with a superb wine list.

Damasqueros, Granada (p237) In the Realejo *barrio*, renowned chef Lola Marín presides over weekly market-fresh menus embodying Granada's culinary heritage.

Casa Manteca, Cádiz (p115) Elbow your way to the bar to order *payoyo* cheese with asparagus marmalade at this old-school institution filled with bullfighting paraphernalia.

El Campero, Barbate (p143) The 10-course tasting menu utilises every edible morsel of bluefin tuna.

THE YEAR IN FOOD

SPRING

Strawberries, asparagus, artichokes, peas and broad beans appear at greengrocers, with yet more fruit and vegetables ripening in the greenhouses of the 'breadbasket of Europe'. Bluefin tuna season begins on the coast.

SUMMER

Market stalls groan under the weight of aubergines, peaches, cherries, apricots and heat-beating melons and watermelons. Head to the coast for *espetos*, bountiful between May and October.

AUTUMN

Time for food festivals, since it's harvest season for olives and grapes. Foraged mushrooms and wild game on mountain menus; it's also pig-slaughter season, with *jamón* and other prized products cured during the colder months.

WINTER

It's orange harvest season, and goat's and sheep's milk cheeses mature during winter. Meaty stews appear on menus and it's the best time of year to sample *rabo de toro* (slow-cooked oxtail).

JOSE ALCAIDE FOTOGRAFO/SHUTTERSTOCK ©

HOW TO... Visit a winery

Andalucía is Spain's oldest wine-producing region, and the industry has enjoyed a renaissance in recent years. The region's vineyards vary dramatically, from the rolling countryside of Jaén and Córdoba and steep mountainsides of Málaga and Granada to Almería's arid, desert-like terrain. These terroirs, plus new wine-making techniques from ambitious vintners and experimentation with biodynamic wines, make for a very exciting scene. Focus on sherries alone, or travel across the whole region in search of that elusive bodega that makes your taste buds sing. Many wineries and bodegas offer tastings and guided tours; some come with superb restaurants offering pairings. Below is a step-by-step list for planning your wine-tasting trip to Andalucía.

1. Pick a season

Vineyards and sherry bodegas can be visited year-round – but if your heart is set on participating in the grape harvest, or you'd like to visit a wine festival, aim for late September or early October. Traditional foot-stomping is confined to small, traditional producers, but this is an excellent time to observe the entire process.

2. Choose the region

Andalucía has six Denominaciónes de Origens (DO) appellations for wines of exceptional quality: Cádiz's Sherry Triangle (sherry production); Sanlúcar de Barrameda (unique, delicate *manzanilla* sherry); Córdoba's Montilla-Moriles (fortified wines); Málaga province (sweet dessert wines and dry whites made from moscatel and Pedro Ximénez grapes); and Sierras de Málaga and Condado de Huelva (excellent, refreshing whites). There are also 16 Vinos de la Tierra regions, which cover Almería's dessert wines (p257), Granada's complex Altiplano blends (p243) and more.

3. Select a winery

After settling on a region, search online for wineries offering tours (andalucia.org/en/eno-gastronomy/andalusian-wine). Those in popular locations are usually multilingual, though booking ahead for non-Spanish tours is essential. While there's a good chance of same-day bodega tour bookings in Jerez, remote wineries on Granada's Altiplano require more notice.

4. Savour the wine

You've done the tour, you know how wine is made, and you can tell your *oloroso* from your *amontillado*. It's time to kick back and sip your selection of post-tour tipples.

LIVE WINES

There is no official definition of what a 'live' (or 'natural') wine is. All wine contains bacteria, but to protect wines from bad bacteria, sulphites are typically added to stabilise them – by killing all bacteria. Some vintners believe that artificial stabilisation of wine goes against its essence and prevents it from 'evolving' – so live wines are essentially organic wines that contain no sulphites. Córdoba's wonderful Jugo Vinos Vivos (facebook.com/quierojugovivo) specialises in experimental live wines from small producers all over Andalucía (some of which welcome visitors). Otherwise, look out for Duende 2018, Purulio 2017 and La Traviesa Blanco 2019.

OWAIN LACEY/SHUTTERSTOCK ©

El Torcal de Antequera (p174)

THE OUTDOORS

With its year-round sunny climate, miles of coastline, national parks and mountain ranges, Andalucía is a veritable playground.

Andalucía has a coastline hundreds of miles long that throws down a gauntlet to water-sports enthusiasts. Inland, the region bristles with mountain ranges, where hikers can challenge themselves with precipitous ascents and long-distance hiking trails. Europe's southernmost ski resort beckons, while daredevils can scale rock faces and vie ferrate. Whatever your passion, Andalucía delivers.

Hiking

Whether you're a seasoned trekker looking to scale the highest mountain on the Spanish mainland, or gentle coastal rambles are more your bag, Andalucía has trails to suit all abilities, and walking gets you to where most visitors never go. All of Andalucía's *parques naturales* (natural parks) and *parques nacionales* (national parks) are criss-crossed by well-marked trails, ranging from half-hour strolls to full-day mountain ascents and long-distance adventures. Scenery ranges from plunging cliffs and terraced olive groves to snow-sprinkled mountains. Andalucía is bisected by three *senderos de gran recorrido* (GRs; long-distance footpaths). You can also string together day walks into multiday treks, sleeping along the way in hotels, *hostales* (budget hotels) and campgrounds, or the occasional mountain refuge.

To beat the heat and avoid the months when some mountain trails are closed by

Adrenaline thrills

CANYONING
Abseil rock faces and slide down waterfalls with Nevadensis (p253) in Las Alpujarras.

ROCK CLIMBING
Tackle hundreds of routes in the gorge near El Chorro (p171) or shimmy up the crag of El Torcal de Antequera (p174).

CYCLING
See the countryside along *vías verdes* fashioned out of old railway lines (p207) or go mountain biking in Parque Nacional Sierra Nevada (p244).

FAMILY ADVENTURES

Go **whale- and dolphin-watching** in the Strait of Gibraltar from Tarifa (p138).

Ride horses between villages amid spectacular mountains in the Alpujarras (p253).

Cycle in parts of the Sierra de Grazalema along a *vía verde* (p207).

Take part in an **olive harvest** and learn how olive oil is made near Baeza (p222).

Go **boogie-boarding** off the main beach in Zahara de los Atunes (p142).

Spend the day on one of the many **white-sand beaches** on the Costa del Sol (p180).

Take a **boat/4WD tour** of Parque Nacional Doñana near Sanlúcar (p104).

Go **snorkelling** and observe fish life off Playa Maro near Nerja (p180).

Explore **underground caverns** in Almería's Cuevas de Sorbas (p273).

snowfall, it's best to hike during spring and autumn. Signage is steadily improving but can still be iffy. The best markers are in the *parques naturales* and *nacionales*, and on major routes such as the long-distance GR7, identified by red-and-white paint splashes. It's well worth investing in good hiking maps of the area where you plan to hike; Editorial Alpina produces some of the best.

Kitesurfing, windsurfing & surfing

Thanks to the strong *levante* and *poniente* winds that blow across the Strait of Gibraltar, Cádiz's Costa de la Luz plays host to Europe's liveliest windsurfing and kitesurfing scene. Windsurfing, popular since the early 1980s, has since been overtaken in popularity by kitesurfing. The choppy seas off the Costa de la Luz aren't always beginner territory. May, June and September are usually the best months (calmer water, fewer people). Tarifa is Europe's windsurfing and kitesurfing capital, while Los Caños de Meca, northwest of Tarifa, is another surfing/kitesurfing hot spot. Tarifa in particular has no shortage of kitesurfing and windsurfing schools, run by professional multilingual instructors. Surfers head to El Palmar for Andalucía's best board-riding waves.

Skiing, Sierra Nevada

Diving & snorkelling

Andalucía has some decent spots for underwater exploration, mostly along its eastern coastline in Granada and Almería provinces, though there are some interesting wreck dives around Gibraltar, while the western part of Andalucía's Mediterranean tends to be subject to strong currents and waves, and is not for novices. Cabo de Gata in Almería has clear protected waters and varied underwater terrain comprising seagrass, caves, crevices, canyons and a wreck. Reef fish, octopuses, corals and relatively warm waters off the Costa Tropical in Granada make for good year-round diving and snorkelling, with the gentle, shallow sea off La Herradura ideal for beginners.

SKIING & SNOWBOARDING

Visit Europe's most southerly ski resort, the Sierra Nevada (p252), with 110km of runs.

PARAGLIDING

Soar above Parque Natural Sierra de Grazalema (p131) or El Yelmo (p213) in Parque Natural Sierras de Cazorla, Segura y las Villas.

HORSE RIDING

Trek mountain trails in the Sierra Nevada (p253).

VIE FERRATE

Tackle ladders, cables, bridges and zip lines with RSG Aventura (p131) in the Sierra de Grazalema and Nevadensis (p253) in the Sierra Nevada.

ACTION AREAS

Where to find Andalucía's best outdoor activities.

Kitesurfing/Windsurfing

1. Tarifa Town Beach (p139)
2. Playa de los Lances (p139)
3. Playa de Valdevaqueros (p139)
4. Los Caños de Meca (p139)
5. Palmones (p139)

Extreme Adventures

1. Cuevas de Sorbas (p273)
2. Sierra de Grazalema (p131) Zero Gravity
3. Sierra Nevada (p253) Nevadensis
4. Pradollano (p252)
5. El Torcal de Antequera (p174)
6. Gruta de las Maravillas (p98)

Wildlife Watching

1. Parque Nacional de Doñana (p103)
2. Tarifa (p138)
3. Parque Nacional Sierra Nevada (p244)
4. Parque Natural Sierras de Cazorla, Segura y las Villas (p209)
5. Parque Natural Cabo de Gata-Níjar (p264)
6. Parque Natural Sierra de Grazalema (p130)

CASTILLA-LA MANCHA
Parque Natural Sierra de Andújar
La Carolina
Parque Natural Sierras de Cazorla, Segura y las Villas
Segura de la Sierra
JAÉN
Linares
Andújar
Bailén
Caravaca de la Cruz
Río Guadalquivir
Baeza
Úbeda
Cazorla
Empanadas (2107m)
Porcuna
Albánchez de Mágina
Quesada
Huéscar
Jaén
Martos
Parque Natural Sierra Mágina
Pozo Alcón
Vélez Rubio
Baena
Parque Natural Sierras Subbéticas
Alcalá la Real
Baza
Priego de Córdoba
Iznalloz
Río Almanzora
Albox
Huércal-Overa
GRANADA
Guadix
Iznájar
Vera
Garrucha
Loja
Granada
Mulhacén (3482m)
Parque Nacional Sierra Nevada
ALMERÍA
Sorbas
Ohanes
Tabernas
Trevélez
Níjar
Carboneras
La Maroma (2065m)
Capileira
Ugíjar
Parque Natural Cabo de Gata-Níjar
Órgiva
Almería
Cómpeta
San José
Málaga
Torre del Mar
Nerja
Almuñécar
Motril
Adra
Almerimar
Golfo de Almería
Costa de Sol
Mediterranean Sea

Hiking

1. Parque Nacional Sierra Nevada (p244)
2. Parque Natural Sierras de Cazorla, Segura y las Villas (p209)
3. Parque Natural Cabo de Gata-Níjar (p264)
4. Parque Natural Sierra de Grazalema (p130)
5. Sierra Norte (p87)
6. Bosques del Sur (p210)
7. Caminito del Rey (p175)

Snorkelling/Diving

1. Playa de Maro (p180)
2. La Herradura (p255)
3. 'La Chocolita' (p264)
4. Cueva del Francés (p264)
5. Playa La Isleta (p264)
6. Piedra de los Meros (p264)
7. Cala los Amarillos (p264)

N
0 50 km
0 25 miles

ANDALUCÍA

THE GUIDE

Chapters in this section are organised by hubs and their surrounding areas. We see the hub as your base in the destination, where you'll find unique experiences, local insights, insider tips and expert recommendations. It's also your gateway to the surrounding area, where you'll see what and how much you can do from there.

Alcázar de los Reyes Cristianos (p192)

VICPHOTORIA/SHUTTERSTOCK ©

Plaza de España (p66)

THE MAIN AREAS

SEVILLA
Spain's essence condensed. p56

CARMONA
Forts and Mudéjar architecture. p77

CONSTANTINA & CAZALLA
Rugged wilderness hikes. p86

SEVILLA & HUELVA

MUDÉJAR MARVELS AND RURAL IDYLLS

Secluded natural spaces, overlooked beaches and religious spectacles, with the passions of Sevilla, the beguiling Andalucian capital, at its heart.

The term 'Golden Age' is bandied about quite liberally when it comes to Sevilla. Itálica was Ancient Rome's first Spanish city, but Sevilla's first truly prosperous period was in the 11th century under the Moorish Abbadid dynasty. Under it, the city rose to prominence as capital of the most powerful, wealthy and learned kingdom in the southern Iberian Peninsula.

Sevilla remained one of Europe's largest cities well into its official Golden Age during the 16th and 17th centuries, an era that was Catholic by nurture, bloody by nature. The vast amounts of wealth pouring in from the New World often found their way to Sevilla up the Guadalquivir River, while Christopher Columbus's first trans-Atlantic voyage set sail from near Huelva.

Even flamenco, the art form largely associated with Andalucía, had a Golden Age here in the 19th century. The numerous *tablao* flamenco theatres, where spectators can enjoy a drink and a show, are a legacy of the *café cantante*, the first of which was opened in Sevilla by legendary flamenco singer Silverio Franconetti.

Those iconic, seductive rhythms, suffused with impassioned vocals, intense hand claps, and decisive stamping on wooden floorboards, still float through the sultry air of Sevilla and Huelva today.

These two provinces are also home to some of the remotest tree-filled hinterlands of Andalucía, where nature reserves, Spain's largest *parque nacional* (national park) and some of the country's best quiet beaches are found.

HUELVA
Quieter beaches and Columbus's ships. p91

ARACENA
Charming hill town. p97

PARQUE NACIONAL DE DOÑANA
Flamingo and lynx haven. p103

Find Your Way

The Sierra Morena cuts a diagonal swath through western Andalucía, with verdant, hilly hinterlands on one side, and dry, sweltering plains commandeered by farmland and cities on the other. Choose a landscape to match your desired pace.

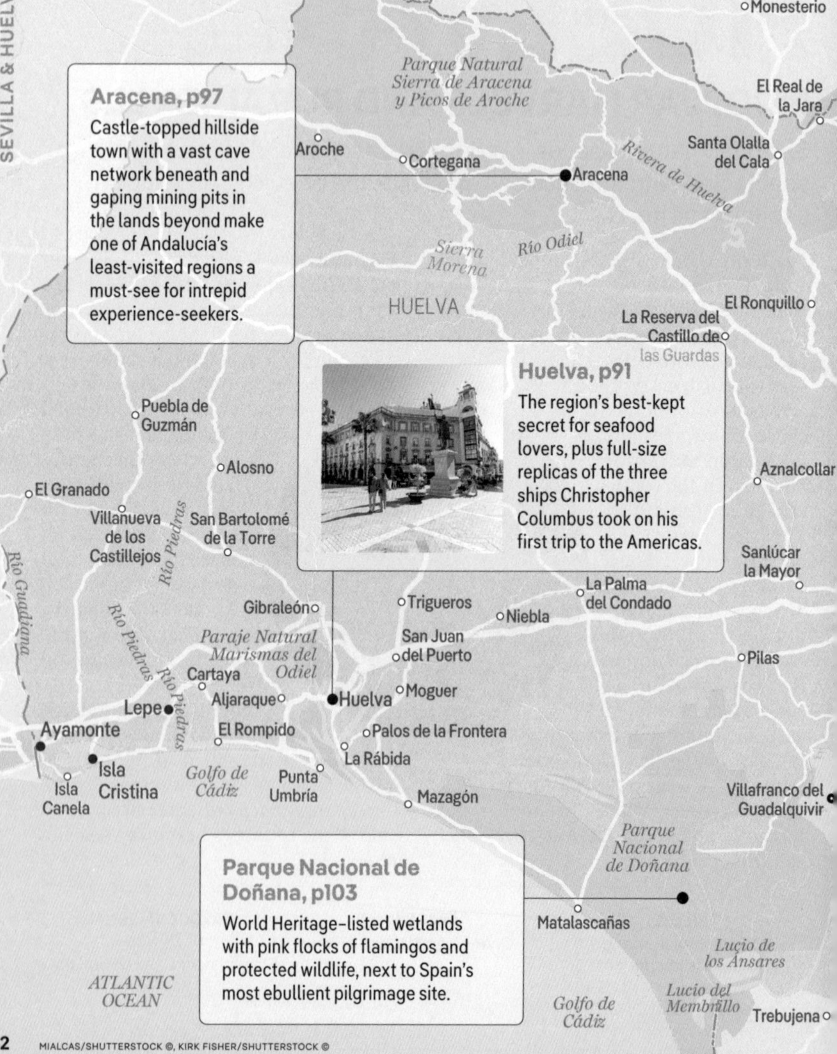

Aracena, p97

Castle-topped hillside town with a vast cave network beneath and gaping mining pits in the lands beyond make one of Andalucía's least-visited regions a must-see for intrepid experience-seekers.

Huelva, p91

The region's best-kept secret for seafood lovers, plus full-size replicas of the three ships Christopher Columbus took on his first trip to the Americas.

Parque Nacional de Doñana, p103

World Heritage–listed wetlands with pink flocks of flamingos and protected wildlife, next to Spain's most ebullient pilgrimage site.

CAR

Consider hiring a car if you want to veer away from the main hubs in this region, especially further north into the Sierra Morena. Discover the truly Andalucian rural charm in serene villages and remote beaches this way.

BUS

The region's best transport links emanate from a Sevillan nucleus. Roads towards Osuna, Carmona, Huelva and Aracena are regularly plied by buses. Two companies, Alsa and Damas, connect Sevilla and Huelva to the rest of Andalucía, as well as other major Spanish and Portuguese cities.

TRAIN

Sevilla is well served by efficient Renfe trains from Madrid, and sees multiple daily services to and from Cádiz, Córdoba, Huelva and Málaga. Additionally, regional Media Distancia trains connect many smaller towns and the Sierra Norte.

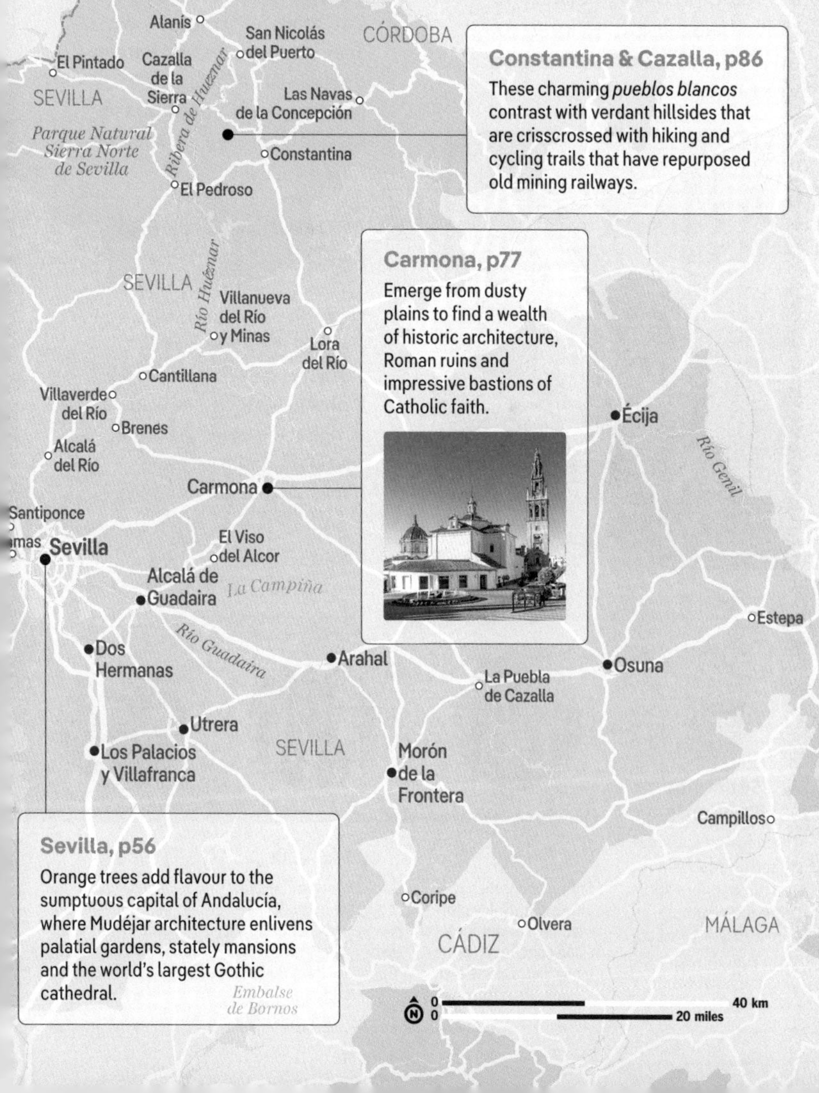

Constantina & Cazalla, p86

These charming *pueblos blancos* contrast with verdant hillsides that are crisscrossed with hiking and cycling trails that have repurposed old mining railways.

Carmona, p77

Emerge from dusty plains to find a wealth of historic architecture, Roman ruins and impressive bastions of Catholic faith.

Sevilla, p56

Orange trees add flavour to the sumptuous capital of Andalucía, where Mudéjar architecture enlivens palatial gardens, stately mansions and the world's largest Gothic cathedral.

Plan Your Time

Explore some of Spain's finest landmarks over a few days in Sevilla or find your perfect Andalucian ambling pace to delve deeper into Roman ruins, an overlooked coastline and bucolic hilly interiors.

KIRK FISHER/SHUTTERSTOCK ©

Barrio Santa Cruz (p62)

A flying visit to Sevilla

- **Sevilla** (p56) embodies many facets of the Andalucian psyche. Start with a wander around the narrow cobblestone streets of Barrio Santa Cruz. Then look out over the rooftops from the **Catedral's** (p56) Giralda tower. Seek afternoon shade in **Parque de Maria Luisa** (p66), where landmarks such as the **Plaza de España** (p66) are ensconced amid sculpted gardens.

- The next day, visit the **Real Alcázar** (p60) early, before spending the afternoon exploring the north side of the Centro district, taking in Spanish masterpieces at the **Museo de Bellas Artes** (p69) and modern design at the **Setas** (p64). Cap your stay off with a moving **flamenco** (p62) performance.

Seasonal highlights

Spring and autumn offer the ideal balance of atmosphere and agreeable climate. In summer, build a siesta into your itinerary to skip the hottest hours of day.

MARCH

Spring brings meadow flowers, and pleasant weather creates ideal hiking conditions on the many Sierra Norte and Aracena trails.

MARCH–APRIL

Sevilla hosts Andalucía's biggest festival. The Semana Santa is among the most fervent Christian Holy Weeks in all of Spain.

APRIL

Sevillanos take to the streets again for the Feria de Abril, with horse parades, sherry drinking and traditional attire.

JOSERPIZARRO/SHUTTERSTOCK ©, JULIA MLOZANO/SHUTTERSTOCK ©, SHOOTDIEM/SHUTTERSTOCK ©

One week to roam

- After two days in Sevilla, hire a car and make the short drive to **Carmona** (p77) for its rich historical heritage. Continue eastwards to the bell-tower-filled skyline of **Écija** (p84). The next day, experience **Sierra Norte's** (p89) pretty *pueblo blanco* of **Constantina** (p86), then road-trip through the cork oak forests for panoramic views from atop **Castillo de Alanís** (p90).

- Switch directions towards Sevilla to see the Roman ruins at **Itálica** (p75) on the way to the Wild West–style pilgrimage town **El Rocío** (p106). From here, take a 4WD guided tour of **Parque Nacional de Doñana** (p103) in search of Iberian lynx and flamingos.

More time to explore

- Following further Sevilla explorations, delve into the hinterlands of **Huelva province** (p93), stopping at **Almonaster la Real's** (p102) impressive *mezquita* (mosque), and descending deep beneath the hilltop castle at **Aracena** (p97) into the mesmerising caves at **Gruta de las Maravillas** (p98). Next, take a walk around **Cortegana** and enjoy the views from the **Castillo** (p100). Then hop on the train from **Minas de Riotinto** (p101) to trundle alongside a blood-red river.

- Near **Huelva** (p91), board replicas of Columbus's ships in **La Rábida** (p94). Visit the home of Nobel laureate Juan Ramón Jiménez in **Moguer** (p94), or dig your toes into the sand on Huelva's **beaches** (p95).

MAY

The Romería del Rocío sees over a million people venerate the Virgin in colourful style on Pentecost (Whitsunday) weekend.

JUNE

As the mercury climbs ever higher, it's time to hit the beaches along Huelva's coastline.

SEPTEMBER

Thousands attend events at the Bienal de Flamenco, the world's premier flamenco festival, every even-numbered year.

NOVEMBER

Waterfowl and flamingos flock to the wetlands of Huelva, particularly at Parque Nacional de Doñana.

SEVILLA

Sevilla, the Andalucian capital and jewel in the region's cultural crown, is a luminous introduction to this region of Spain. A rich blend of cultures and historical phases goes into every detail of the magnificent Mudéjar architecture, into every sultry note of the flamenco guitar, and infuses the animated nightlife that spills from bars and bodegas, invigorating the plazas and narrow cobbled streets of the city.

Great civilisations, including the Moors, the Romans and the Reyes Católicos (Catholic Monarchs) of the Spanish Empire have left an indelible mark on Sevilla. So too have the Jewish and Roma cultures, along with countless generations of homebred *sevillanos*, through the centuries. You'll see this diversity everywhere, in the architecture, the culture and the varied cuisine. The city's well-heeled past endures into the present, through aristocratic palaces, romantic streets scented with orange blossom, and Unesco-listed landmarks, such as the imposing Gothic cathedral.

TOP TIP

You can cover much of Sevilla on foot, with trams, city bikes and scooter rentals offering neat alternatives to getting around. Local buses depart from within the Plaza de Armas bus station to the ruins at Itálica roughly every 30 minutes.

Giralda Tower & Catedral de Sevilla

SEVILLA'S ARCHITECTURAL CENTREPIECE

When Castilian king Fernando III captured Sevilla from the Almohad dynasty in 1248, he ordered that the 12th-century great mosque be converted into a church. At the turn of the 15th century, Sevilla's Catholic leaders were so confident in their rule that they began to get ambitious: 'Let's construct a church so large future generations will think we were mad', they are rumoured to have said.

To see the Catedral is to think they may just have been brilliant. Still the world's largest Gothic building, officially known as the Catedral de Santa María de la Sede, it is a veritable feast of artworks and skilled craftwork, both inside and out. Flying buttresses, cheeky gargoyles and lavish Gothic ornamentation decorate the exterior of this remarkable feat of creation, which bears testament to the inspirational power of religious fervour.

The visitor entrance is through the Puerta de Lagarto. Look up and you'll see a stuffed crocodile hanging from the ceiling. Immediately on your left, a gentle ramp swirls up through **La Giralda**, a former minaret repurposed as the cathedral's noteworthy bell tower. Expansive views over Sevilla from the belfry are the reward for your exertion.

Back at the bottom of the Giralda, heading clockwise, the often-closed Capilla Real contains some important royal tombs, including the remains of the city's Christian conqueror, Fernando III, in a silver urn.

GIVE YOUR FEET A BREAK

There are plenty of great places near the cathedral to take a load off.

Amorino is an ice-cream shop with creative presentation and alfresco seating. **Bodega Santa Cruz** is open from breakfast until late at night, serving coffees, beers and a variety of tapas, including smaller on-the-go bites. Keep it historic at **Casa Morales**, a cheery tapas bar that's been going since 1850. It's notable for its sherry, *albondigas* (meatballs) and *croquetas*.

La Giralda

Next, enter the series of rooms to your left and you'll uncover some major art treasures, including a Goya in the Sacristía de los Cálices, a Zurbarán in the Sacristía Mayor, and Murillo's shining *La inmaculada* in the Sala Capitular.

Still hugging the exterior wall, the four sturdy figures carrying an ornately carved catafalque mark the Tomb of Columbus, which contains the purported remains of the revered voyager; something that DNA testing in 2006 upheld as fact.

Perhaps the finest design is saved for the *retablo* (altarpiece), which lies at the very heart of the cathedral in the Capilla Mayor. Intricately carved from wood and covered in gold leaf, it was started in 1482 by Flemish sculptor Pieter Dancart, who dedicated the rest of his life to it, with others completing it long after his death. Over 1000 intricately carved figures depict biblical scenes and characters.

Only a few sections of the Catedral – such as the Puerta del Perdón (the cathedral's exit) on Calle Alemanes, and the Patio de los Naranjos to which it leads – retain facets of the original mosque. You'll pass through the patio, which contains 66 orange trees and a Visigothic fountain, on your way out.

MORE HOLY STROLLERS?

The cavernous **Iglesia Colegial del Divino Salvador** (p63) is a delightful baroque church to wander around, where practically every inch is carved and crafted. You can get a combined entry ticket.

WHERE TO STAY IN BARRIO SANTA CRUZ

Hotel Alfonso XIII
A local landmark. Classic neo-Mudéjar facade, complete with glazed tiles and terracotta bricks. **€€€**

Pensión San Pancracio
Book ahead for these simple private rooms with shared bathrooms in Sevilla's historic heart. **€**

Legado Alcázar
Upscale rooms with wood-beamed ceilings. Adjoining Real Alcázar; its peacocks may visit your balcony. **€€€**

SEVILLA

SIGHTS

1 Acuario de Sevilla
2 Alameda de Hércules
3 Antigua Fábrica de Tabacos
4 Archivo General de Indias
5 Barrio de Santa Cruz
6 Basílica de La Macarena
7 Capilla de San José
8 Casa de Pilatos
9 Casa de Salinas
10 Catedral & Giralda
11 Centro Andaluz de Arte Contemporáneo
12 Centro Cerámica Triana
13 Hospital de la Caridad
14 Hospital de los Venerables Sacerdotes
15 Iglesia Colegial del Divino Salvador
16 Iglesia de San Luis de los Franceses
17 Metropol Parasol
18 Museo Antiquarium
19 Museo Arqueológico
20 Museo Casa de la Ciencia
21 Museo de Artes y Costumbres Populares
22 Museo de Bellas Artes
23 Museo del Baile Flamenco
24 Pabellón de la Navegación
25 Palacio de la Condesa de Lebrija
26 Palacio de las Dueñas
27 Parque de María Luisa
28 Parroquia de Santa María Magdalena

29 Plaza de América
30 Plaza de España
31 Plaza de Toros de la Real Maestranza
32 Real Alcázar
33 Torre del Oro
34 Torre Schindler

ACTIVITIES, COURSES & TOURS
35 Kayak Sevilla
36 Taller Flamenco

Acuario de Sevilla (p66)

ANIBAL TREJO/SHUTTERSTOCK ©

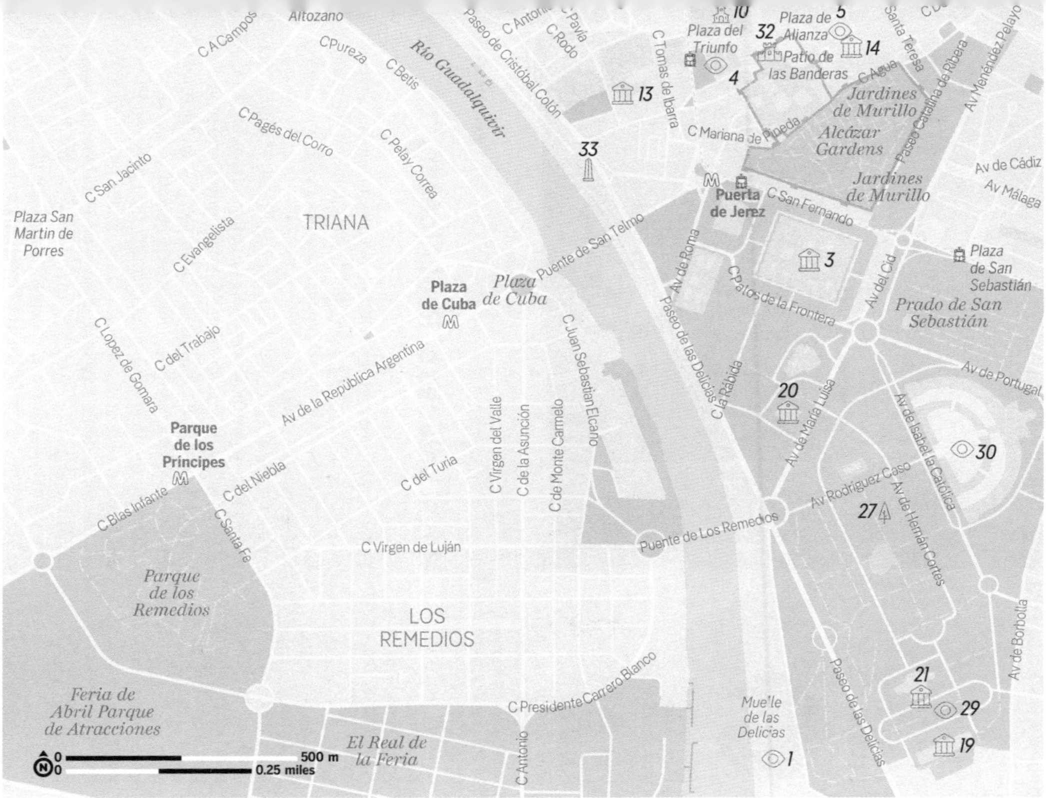

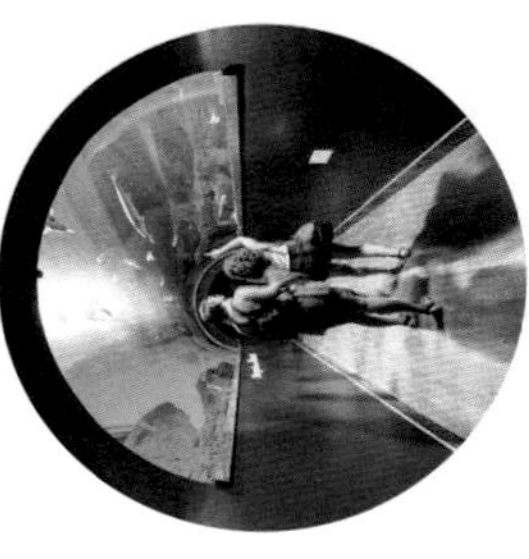

WHY I LOVE SEVILLA

Paul Stafford, Lonely Planet writer. *@paulrstafford*

Once, after a rather late night out around the Alameda, I was walking home through the Plaza del Triunfo, outside the cathedral, when I saw two people in full flamenco dress dancing in the light of the moon for nobody but themselves, tinny music jangling from a phone. That sums Sevilla up so neatly for me, as a place where, despite so many major sights, the traveller's reward is in the little snatched moments of private beauty. There is so much detail, so much artistic ingenuity and brilliance. It's as though everybody is keen to leave only the best of themselves in Sevilla. As such, the moments that move you most are often the least expected.

Real Alcázar

Regal palaces at Real Alcázar

MUDÉJAR MEETS CHRISTIAN STYLE

Exquisitely decorated and with a labyrinthine quality that will keep you exploring for many hours, the palaces, rooms and gardens of Sevilla's royal palace complex make for a memorable must-see spectacle.

Since the 10th century, Moorish rulers and Spanish monarchs chose to preside over their kingdoms from the Real Alcázar, tearing down, augmenting, redesigning and rebuilding various sections of the sprawling complex to suit their tastes and whims. The result is delightfully eclectic.

Entry to the Real Alcázar is through the dusty red **Puerta del León** on Plaza del Triunfo. As you pass into a small plaza, the **Sala de la Justicia** is on your left. Note its beautiful Mudéjar plasterwork and *artesonado* (a wooden ceiling of interlaced beams with decorative insertions). On the other side is the pretty **Patio del Yeso**, part of the 12th-century Almohad palace, complete with a pond stuffed with goldfish (good for keeping the mosquitoes at bay). Taken together, these three sections give a good flavour, albeit on a smaller scale, of what's to come.

WHERE TO STAY IN BARRIO SANTA CRUZ

Hotel Puerta de Sevilla
Cosy rooms with crisp white and floral designs in a modernist building from 1929. **€€**

Hotel Casa 1800
Stately old mansion mere minutes from the cathedral and Real Alcázar. Complimentary afternoon tea. **€€€**

Hotel Amadeus
Period furniture and a swanky rooftop hot tub in the heart of the old *judería* (Jewish quarter). **€€€**

Next is the open space of the **Patio de la Montería**. You can imagine the king's entourage, gathered here on horseback, ready to head out on a hunt. The **Casa de la Contratación**, on the western side of the square, was where trade with Spain's American colonies was once controlled.

But it is Pedro I's (1350–69) additions that garner the greatest admiration. You'll struggle to find a more perfect exhibition of the Mudéjar ethos than in the **Palacio de Don Pedro**, where rooms feel both decadent and homely.

At the heart of this palace is the sublime central courtyard, the **Patio de las Doncellas**. The sunken garden at its core, surrounded by beautiful arches, plasterwork and tiling, was uncovered by archaeologists in 2004 from beneath a 16th-century marble covering. Other highlights include the golden-tiled dome ceiling of the **Cuarto del Principe**, and the spectacular **Salón de Embajadores**, originally Pedro I's throne room, with a wooden, star-patterned dome, symbolising the universe, that was added in 1427.

Above this level is the **Cuarto Real Alto**, guided tours of which are ticketed separately and only run when the royal family is not in residence. Meanwhile, the style changes drastically on entering **Palacio Gótico**, which was remodelled for Carlos I in the 16th century and is now known as the **Salones de Carlos V** (after his additional title as Holy Roman Emperor Charles V).

Once you've explored the rooms and palaces, the **Jardines de los Reales Alcázares** offer a refreshing assemblage of shaded paths between mazes of myrtle, fish-filled ponds and lofty palm trees. The highlight is the **Galeria de Grutesco**, a 17th-century porticoed gallery offering views over the gardens and a former Almohad well.

SEVILLA'S QUIRKIER DRINKING SPOTS

El Garlochi
Try the *sangre de Christo* (Christ's blood), a sacrilegious cocktail in a bar impeccably designed to look like a baroque church.

La Carbonería
Tintos (red wines), beers and light bites in a former coal warehouse, where you might catch an impromptu flamenco performance if lucky.

Pecata Mundi
It initially looks like your traditional wooden bar, tiled-walls establishment. Closer inspection reveals papier-mâché masks and goat skulls amid the spirits.

Archivo de Indias architecture

RECORDS OF AN EMPIRE

The building that held the Spanish Empire's official document and map archive since 1785 is inscribed on Unesco's World Heritage list, along with the Catedral and Alcázar. Most documents at the Archivo General de Indias have since been relocated, but the building, with its exquisite black, white and rose marble interiors, now hosts free exhibitions of photography and archive highlights, such as excerpts from Christopher Columbus's logbooks.

MORE MUDÉJAR?

For a mini-Alcázar without the hordes, see the privately owned, 16th-century **Casa de Pilatos** (p65). Explore at your leisure, allowing time to appreciate the sculpted gardens and delicate tile work.

WHERE TO STAY IN CENTRO & ARENAL

Hotel Casa de Colón
Stylish neo-Mudéjar comfort; stained-glass windows, bare brick walls and clawfoot bathtubs by the cathedral. **€€€**

Santiago 15 Hotel Casa Palacio
Rooms are spacious with elegantly inventive furnishings. Plus a columned lobby. **€€**

La Banda
Perennial favourite, due to its stunning rooftop terrace, the staff's sociable ethos and evening events. **€**

WHERE TO SEE FLAMENCO

La Casa del Flamenco
Deeply moving shows often showcasing three styles of flamenco, woven together by a virtuoso guitar performance.

Pura Esencia
As the spiritual home of Roma flamenco practitioners, *tablaos* like Pura Esencia are big in Triana.

Casa de la Guitarra
Shows in this space balance singing, guitar and dance perfectly, surrounded by antique flamenco guitars.

Teatro Flamenco Sevilla
These larger shows bring more performers onto the stage for a grander spectacle.

Tablao Flamenco Andalusí
Beautiful dresses and passionate dancing backed by wistful vocals, guitar and *cajón* (box drum) in these skilled performances.

Casa de la Memoria
In Palacio Lebrija's former stables. The most intimate of shows, if you can bag a stage-side seat.

Narrow streets of Barrio Santa Cruz

TAPAS BARS AND LIVELY SQUARES

To the east of the cathedral lies Sevilla's pre-Inquisition Jewish quarter, Santa Cruz. It might just be that in these rambling, narrow cobbled alleyways, overhung with colourful window boxes, you fall in love with Sevilla. Lose your way to find yourself in plazas packed with diners at the many restaurants and tapas bars, such as **Bodega Santa Cruz**, around here.

Hospital de los Venerables Sacerdotes frescoes

ART AND HEALING

Towards the end of their lives, Sevilla's Catholic priests moved to this 17th-century former hospice. Pass first through the chapel, straight ahead of the entrance, with its lavish ceiling frescoes by Valdés Leal. Another highlight of this impressive museum is **Centro Velázquez**. Its collection of 17th-century paintings includes *Santa Rufina* by Diego Velázquez and *San Pedro penitente de los Venerables* by Bartolomé Murillo. There's also an excellent anonymous painting of Sevilla as it may have looked in 1660.

Flamenco

AN IMPASSIONED ANDALUCIAN ART FORM

In Sevilla, you'll frequently hear the emotive arpeggios of a flamenco guitar, unusual rhythmic cadences of the *palmas* clapping style, and impassioned vocals that signify a flamenco performance. Chance encounters in the street are common, but nothing beats a live show.

Start by getting your head around flamenco's history at the **Museo del Baile Flamenco**, which uses interactive displays, some beautiful traditional dresses and imagery from flamenco's 19th-century Sevilla heyday. The museum morphs into a venue at night, with multiple shows in its courtyard and smaller basement space. There are dozens of *tablaos* (rehearsed flamenco shows with drinks and dinner), and *peñas* (private clubs) putting on nightly performances in Sevilla.

Better yet, get involved yourself. **Taller Flamenco**, near La Macarena (p70), offers fantastic classes on various aspects of flamenco. A good place to start is with *compás y palmas*, which explores the unique clapping and accented

WHERE TO STAY IN CENTRO & ARENAL

Hotel Abanico
Distinctive tile work and arabesque touches evoke Sevilla's baroque and Mudéjar sensibilities. €€

EME Catedral Mercer
Rooms with innovative interior designs. Also home to La Terraza, the city's most coveted rooftop bar. €€€

Oasis Palace Hostel
Buzzing hostel in a 19th-century mansion with luxury features, including a rooftop pool and deck. €

Iglesia Colegial del Divino Salvador

GO TO A MATCH

Football is big in Sevilla, and two local teams, **Sevilla FC** and **Real Betis Balompié**, are regular features in Spain's top division: La Liga. Derby day, aka El Gran Derbi, is a particularly raucous affair that has divided the city since 1915. Match tickets are available directly from either club's website (available in English).

rhythmical style that lies at the heart of flamenco. There are also guitar, singing and dance classes in a group or one-to-one format.

Lavish Iglesia Colegial del Divino Salvador

BRASHLY BAROQUE

A minute's walk from Sevilla's striking **Ayuntamiento** (city hall) lies one of Sevilla's most extravagant baroque churches. A pretty, mannerist red brick exterior conceals the profusion of decoration within, culminating in a series of mighty gold altarpieces stretching up towards a luminous domed ceiling above the nave. The ornamentation depicts Catholicism at its most graphic, including carvings of Christ already dead on the cross, and a pelican nourishing its young with its own blood. This 17th-century building replaced the largest mosque from the Caliphate era, which in turn had replaced a Roman forum.

FLAMENCO'S ORIGINS

Discover flamenco's diverse influences, from Roma to Almohad, that made the art form what it is today in the Andalucía Storybook (p304).

WHERE TO STAY NEAR ALAMEDA DE HÉRCULES

Corner House
Right on the Alameda, with minimalist modern decor, hanging lamps and a rooftop terrace. **€€**

H10 Corregidor Boutique
Some 19th-century features, blended into a modern space (2021 renovation). Rooftop plunge pool terrace. **€€**

Hotel Sacristía de Santa Ana
Gorgeous rooms in an 18th-century townhouse with courtyard. Perfect for history and architecture fans. **€€**

THE POET KING

In the 11th century, when Sevilla was Andalucía's most powerful *taifa* (sect/kingdom), the city enjoyed a relative period of calm, intellectual rule under the Abbadid dynasty. The dynasty's third and final ruler, al-Mu'tamid ibn Abbad (c 1040–95), was even known as 'the Poet King'. Love and war are recurrent themes in his work, such as this stanza from *To Salma, from battle*:

'When the battle-alarms
Threaten, Salma, thy arms
Are around me.'

With Christian armies pushing ever southward, al-Mu'tamid rallied assistance from the Berber Muslim Almoravids, whose ferocity brought success, but whose zealotry also brought greed. The Almoravids soon usurped Sevilla and al-Mu'tamid died in their captivity a few years later.

HENRIQUEWESTIN/SHUTTERSTOCK ©, ARCHITECT: JÜRGEN MAYER

Las Setas

Las Setas & Antiquarium

A TALE OF TWO SEVILLAS

Some of the best views of the cathedral come from atop one of Sevilla's more modern constructs. Officially called the **Metropol Parasol**, Las Setas (the mushrooms) deserve their affectionate moniker, rendered from a curved bloom of criss-crossed wooden panels. There's a city viewpoint at the top and equally fascinating views below at the Antiquarium. The archaeological excavation is of an ancient Roman settlement unearthed during the construction of Las Setas, bringing you two versions of Sevilla in one place.

Palacio de las Dueñas stately home

GLIMPSE SPANISH NOBLE LIFE

The bougainvillea-covered Palacio de las Dueñas is quite the storied stately home. It was the favoured residence of the late Duchess of Alba and her collections of antique furniture, and Semana Santa and football memorabilia (she was a Real Betis fan) deck the rooms surrounding a tropical

Continued on p66

WHERE TO STAY NEAR ALAMEDA DE HÉRCULES

Hostel A2C
No-frills hostel with neat, clean dorms within a few minutes' walk of the Alameda. **€**

Hotel Boutique Doña Lola
Simple hotel with traditional Andalucian courtyard featuring a fountain. Offers choice of rooms and apartments. **€€**

Hotel San Gil
Bright yellow building hiding a decadent, tiled lobby and a pleasantly shaded patio. Elegant rooms. **€€**

CENTRO'S PALACES WALK

Wandering Sevilla's streets, you'll occasionally get a glimpse of a shaded patio, bedecked in foliage, *azulejo* tiles and fountains. Nowadays, some of the city's finest mansions are open to visitors.

Start at the **1 Palacio de la Condesa de Lebrija**, which condenses each of Sevilla's Golden Ages beneath one roof. Like the other palaces, it is largely in the Mudéjar-Renaissance style, with intricate plasterwork arches, *azulejos* and wide stairways fit for a herd of elephants. But it's the Roman mosaics that make this palace special. They were lifted intact from Itálica (see p75) by archaeologist and owner, the Countess of Lebrija, starting in 1901. Upper floor access is by guided tour only (English and Spanish), included in your ticket. There are antiques from all over the world up here.

Wiggle southeast through the Centro streets to the hypnotic **2 Casa de Pilatos**, a Real Alcázar in miniature. This mansion wears its splendour inside and out, where exquisite *artesonado* ceilings, creative tile work and an impressive honey-and-charcoal-coloured courtyard are found. Guided tours of this 15th-century building's upper floor only run when the ducal Medinaceli family aren't in residence.

Open on weekdays, **3 Casa de Salinas** is accessible by guided tour only, with similar elements to the other palaces, including a playful Roman mosaic and the finest Mudéjar *yesería* (stucco and plasterwork) outside of the Real Alcázar.

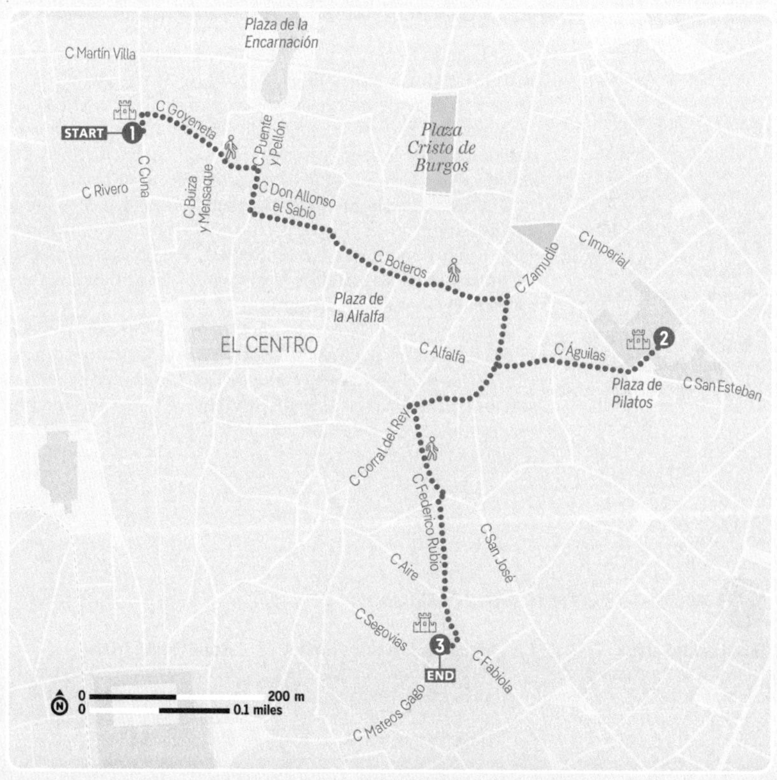

courtyard. Palacio de las Dueñas was also the birthplace of poet Antonio Machado, who took great inspiration from the beautifully sculpted gardens. There's a long list of aristocratic luminaries who stayed here, including Jackie Kennedy and Grace Kelly.

BEST ICE CREAM IN SEVILLA

Sevilla is one of Europe's hottest cities, so ice cream is a particularly welcome treat. Late at night *heladerías* are often as busy as the bars.

Créeme
Family-run ice-cream parlour with decadent flavours, such as El Patio, using orange confit and candied orange pieces. €

Amorino
Innovations abound here; enjoy a gelato shaped like a rose using more than one flavour. €

Bolas
Classics and regional concoctions, such as Sevilla Mora (Moorish Sevilla), comprising walnut, raisin, orange and cinnamon. €

Plaza de España's neo-Mudéjar buildings

FACADE AND BOATING

This plaza is one of Sevilla's highlights. Created for the unluckily timed Ibero-American Expo of 1929, it forms a vast C-shaped curve, cradling a D-shaped moat within, where people row little boats beneath its four bridges. The buildings are primarily neo-Mudéjar, but combine elements of Art Deco, and Renaissance- and baroque- revival architecture in a medley of arcades, *azulejo* tiles, delicate towers and airy vestibules. The bases of the buildings are decorated with tile depictions of maps and historical scenes from each of Spain's 50 provinces. The free **Museo Militar de Sevilla** within showcases regional weaponry and military uniforms.

Fun at Parque de María Luisa

TRACING LOCAL HISTORY, CUSTOMS AND NATURE

The Plaza de España faces the glorious emerald oasis of the Parque de María Luisa. Every part of its 34 hectares is landscaped to provide elegant respite from the cloying heat.

Among the treasures found in the **Museo Arqueológico** are the most valuable relics rescued from Itálica. Expect priceless statues and mosaics, which are only outdated by the Treasure of El Carombolo, a series of crafted gold pieces found just outside Sevilla belonging to the Tartessos civilisation.

For a more modern take on Sevilla, the **Museo de Artes y Costumbres Populares** is dedicated to Andalucian customs, costumes and traditions.

Parque de María Luisa is a great place to take the kids. The four-person pedal-bike rentals are a fun way to navigate the park. The **Museo Casa de la Ciencia** with its Planetarium, and the **Acuario de Sevilla** with its thrilling bull shark tank, are located on the park's edge. Both contain interactive exhibits.

WHERE TO STAY IN TRIANA & CARTUJA

Hotel Zenit Sevilla
Seasonal rooftop pool and quality mattresses, indicative of extra value for money staying in Triana. **€€**

Triana Backpackers Hostel
Tiled lobby and common areas in a traditional Andalucian house close to Triana's best flamenco theatres. **€**

Hotel Monte Triana
Black-and-white marble, and contemporary design in the lobby; space and comfort in the rooms. **€€**

TRABANTOS/SHUTTERSTOCK ©

University of Sevilla

THE SAINTS KEEPING SEVILLA SAFE

You might notice the recurring image of two women in flowing robes standing either side of the Giralda during your time in Sevilla. They are Santa Justa and Santa Rufina, patron saints of the city, and believed to be potters originally from Triana. The annals of history give them credit for protecting the Giralda during 1755's Lisbon earthquake.

Carmen at Antigua Fábrica de Tabacos

CARMEN'S WORKPLACE

This huge former tobacco factory is now the University of Sevilla. Act 1 of Georges Bizet's opera *Carmen* is set here, as the eponymous heroine's workplace. Today you can wander some of the halls; faculty-only areas are clearly marked.

Riverside fortification at Torre del Oro

NAVAL HISTORY AND CATHEDRAL VIEWS

Southwest of the cathedral is a stretch of river with a clutch of key sights. The dodecagonal Torre del Oro is among Sevilla's most renowned sights, with the commanding riverfront position befitting its original military watchtower purpose, when built in the 13th century. Now its walls protect the **Naval Museum**, while its upper ramparts offer good views, particularly at sunset.

MOSAICS APLENTY

The Countess of Lebrija, an early pioneer of modern mosaic extraction and restoration techniques, didn't snaffle all of the mosaics from **Itálica** for her own home. The most precious are protected at the **Museo Arqueológico** (p66), while many more remain preserved at the **Roman ruins** (p75).

B&B Casa Alfareria 59
Run by a delightful couple who have created a quirky, colourful space. Breakfast included. **€€**

Barceló Sevilla Renacimiento
Quirky round buildings with world-class facilities, including pools, three restaurants and a fitness centre. **€€€**

Hotel Kivir Sevilla
Four-star hotel just across the bridge from Triana. Gourmet restaurant and great riverfront views. **€€€**

BEST TAPAS BARS IN SEVILLA

Bar Alfalfa
A snug wedge-shaped bar with tasty tapas, including vegetarian and vegan options, on your plate. €€

Bodega Santa Cruz
Slow-cooked *montadito de pringá* (tender meats and sausage served on crusty bread) is a highlight. €

El Rinconcillo
Purveyors of libations since 1670, in a setting with *azulejos* and varnished wood charm. €€€

PETRA
Inventive takes on popular tapas; good vegetarian and barbecue meat offerings. The tortillas practically melt. €€

Casa Morales
Run by the same family since 1850, a good spot to try the local sherry. €€

ANIBAL TREJO/SHUTTERSTOCK ©

Hospital de la Caridad

Sevillan baroque in Centro & Arenal

GOLDEN-AGE ART, HOLY LOCATION

Some of the finest artworks in Sevilla are found in their intended homes: places of worship. A strong concentration lies where Sevilla's Arenal and Centro merge. Start small at the **Capilla de San José** for a blast of full-on baroque glitz. It is hidden away on a side street between Calles Sierpes and Tetuán. Behind its 18th-century facade is some startlingly lavish decor, culminating in an extraordinary gold altarpiece centred around a sculpture of San José.

Minutes away on Plaza Godínez, 17th-century **Parroquia de Santa María Magdalena** has an unexpectedly vast baroque interior, capped by an octagonal cupola. Its headline act is the colossal gold *retablo* behind the main altar (an 18th-century addition), plus several works by big-name baroque artists Francisco de Zurbarán and Juan de Valdés Leal.

Heading south, keeping to the west side of the cathedral, **Hospital de la Caridad** represents a rare intersection of Sevilla's Golden Age wealthy elites with the impoverished

WHERE TO FIND ROOFTOP COCKTAILS IN SEVILLA

La Terraza del Eme
Spectacular cathedral views and classic cocktails at modern prices at this chic roof-terrace bar.

Terraza Atalaya
Cocktails with a view from 180m up in Torre Sevilla, the city's tallest building.

Corner House Terraza
Wooden decking, handmade tables and grandstand views over the vibrant, treelined Alameda plaza below.

masses. It came about because founder Miguel de Mañara had a vision of his own funeral procession. Quickly extinguishing his hedonistic lifestyle, he ordered Hospital de la Caridad to be built as a hospice for the elderly and impoverished in the 17th century.

Museum at historic Plaza de Toros

SPAIN'S OLDEST BULLRING

Sevilla's white-and-yellow-trimmed bullring has long been a major venue in the bullfighting world. Construction started in 1761, making this the country's first, although it was not completed for another 120 years. Much like a football stadium tour, you can explore Sevilla's bullring and learn about the sport's traditions here without witnessing a fight.

Museo de Bellas Artes fine art

MASTERPIECES IN A MANNERIST CONVENT

You may well see Sevillan baroque painting on many occasions during your time in the city, but none quite like the exhibitions at the Museo de Bellas Artes. The delightful mannerist palace housing the 14 gallery rooms was formerly the Convento de la Merced.

It exhibits 15th- to 20th-century artworks, but it's the Golden Age masterpieces that make this one of Spain's top art museums. Sala V contains the most impressive, and largest, paintings, including Murillo's *Inmaculada concepción*. Don't forget to look up, though, as this room was the former convent's church, and is overhung by a frescoed cupola.

Highlights elsewhere include Zurbarán's *Cristo crucificado* (Sala VI and another in Sala X), El Greco's portrait of his son Jorge Manuel (Sala II), Velázquez's *Cabeza de apóstol* (Sala IV) and Goya's *Don José Duaso* (in Sala XI).

Alameda de Hércules for nightlife

A PLAYGROUND FOR ALL

Sevilla's narrow streets suddenly open up at the Alameda de Hércules, which has two genuine Roman columns at its southern end, topped with statues of Julius Caesar and Hercules. A fashionable promenade in the days of yore, it is still the place to be seen. Cafes and a small playground for younger kids draw families in

BEST RESTAURANTS IN ARENAL

La Brunilda
Tucked down a backstreet, enter through bright blue doors to a modern interior with inventive tapas. €€€

Mamarracha
A trendy modern addition to Sevilla's tapas scene, with similarly eclectic fare on the menu. €€

Bar Postiguillo
It's like wandering into a fancy old barn here, known for its *carrillada* (pork cheek) dish. €€€

A MODERN ROMAN AMPHITHEATRE

Once you've seen the interior of a bullring, it's hard not to conclude that the layout and concept were directly influenced by the Roman amphitheatres that are abundant in Andalucía, such as the one at nearby **Itálica** (p75).

WHERE TO PARTY AROUND ALAMEDA DE HÉRCULES

Cafe Central
A popular place to start/end the night, with tables spilling onto the square. Open until 2am.

Alameda Ritual Club
This stylish LGBTIQ+ friendly bar has a large terrace and stunning old interior.

1987 Bar
Quirky anachronism that's firmly rooted in the '80s, from the music to the framed memorabilia.

the daytime, but clubs and bars make the area the coolest adult's playground in Sevilla at night. As such, the square is the spiritual hub of the city's LGBTIQ+ scene.

Differing Christian fortunes

A TALE OF TWO CHURCHES

On the north side of Centro you'll find two stunning churches with very different fortunes. When the Jesuits were expelled from Spain under the orders of Carlos III in 1767, they left behind a work of genius. **Iglesia de San Luis de los Franceses**, designed by Leonardo de Figueroa and completed only in 1731, has an unusual circular interior with four extravagantly carved altarpieces. The crypt is open to visitors, although even more macabre is the chapel containing saints' bones. It took many years of restoration to bring it back to its former glory.

Walk 400m north along Calle San Luis and you'll come across the city's most venerated religious icon at the **Basílica de La Macarena**. Inside the white-and-honeycomb-coloured neo-baroque church, at the main altarpiece, stands the Virgen de la Esperanza Macarena (Macarena Virgin of Hope), known popularly as La Macarena. Adorned in lavish jewels and a golden crown, the 17th-century statue is a star of the city's fervent Semana Santa (Holy Week) celebrations.

The burnt yellow **Arco de la Macarena** in front of the church is part of the city's 12th-century wall. Here lies the best surviving section, aside from the walls around the Real Alcázar. Built by the Moors, it still wasn't enough to keep Fernando III and his troops out during their reconquest in 1248.

SEVILLA'S SEMANA SANTA

Sevilla puts on one of Spain's most elaborate manifestations of Christian Holy Week. From Palm Sunday to Easter Sunday, hooded *nazarenos* (penitents) carry huge *pasos* (floats carrying revered statues, such as La Macarena) through the streets in ghostly solemnity. Parades lead from their home churches to the cathedral, often in the early evening. The *nazarenos* are members of the city's 50 *hermandades* or *cofradías* (religious brotherhoods, some of which include women), dressed in white robes with pointed conical hoods. Semana Santa's highlight is La Madrugá in the early hours of Good Friday, when several of the city's most venerated statues make their appearances.

Triana & Isla Cartuja's alternative Sevilla

TILES AND MODERN ART

Cross the 19th-century Puente de Triana to the Guadalquivir River's west bank to discover a different Sevilla to the historic neighbourhoods. **Triana** was traditionally a working-class region, where strong contingents of Roma, sailors and ceramics factory workers lived. The area is also a flamenco stronghold, with plenty of places offering classes and workshops, as well as some unique performances.

You will see beautiful *azulejos* from the workshops of Triana throughout Sevilla and Andalucía. **Centro Cerámica Triana** is one of the factories where they were once made. These days it's an insightful museum, with brick-lined kilns on the ground floor and a 1st-floor exhibition detailing the

WHERE TO FIND VEGETARIAN & VEGAN DINING OPTIONS

Veganí
Tiny place serving sandwiches and burgers, some of Sevilla's best croquettes and a tasty pulled jackfruit tapa. €

El Enano Verde
A few minutes from the Alameda. Daily set menu is great value and changes regularly. €

Vegan Rock
Sevilla's best vegan tapas. At the Parque de los Príncipes station along the Metro line. €

RIBEIROANTONIO/SHUTTERSTOCK ©

Puente de Triana

history of ceramics production in Triana, outlining the effect of this industry on the neighbourhood and its residents.

North of Triana is **Isla Cartuja**, dominated by the **Monasterio de Santa María de las Cuevas**, commonly known as **La Cartuja**, which was converted into a porcelain factory by Charles Pickman in 1839. This explains the distinctive bottle-shaped kiln chimneys rising from the midst of a cloister. These buildings serve neither purpose today. Instead, a giant arm and head protrudes from upper-floor windows; not exactly what you'd expect at a former monastery. They belong to *Alicia* by Cristina Lucas, marking the start of the **Centro Andaluz de Arte Contemporáneo**, which combines temporary and permanent modern art exhibits, their incongruity with the historic surroundings adding a further layer of interpretation to the experience.

Family fun in Cartuja

EDUCATION AND EXHILARATION

The **Pabellón de la Navegación** is an interactive, kid-friendly exploration of Sevilla's shipping history, including a look at what life was like aboard the ships bound for the Americas.

Continued on p73

TRIANA'S TILES

Azulejos (ceramic tiles) have been produced in Triana since ancient Roman times, using clay from the riverbanks. Each new set of rulers brought with them new techniques and designs, so that the geometry of the Moors, baroque sensibilities of the 16th and 17th centuries, and the growth of commercialisation in the early 20th century are a history etched in tile. What the last Triana ceramics factory closing its doors in 2012 says about the state of the world today is open to interpretation.

Veganitessen
Popular spot in Mercado de Arenal does a great vegan tortilla. Often closed in summer. **€€**

Habanita
Mostly vegan/vegetarian options, with clear labelling on the menu, at this Cuban restaurant. **€€**

Levies Cafe Bar
Vegetarian-friendly, along with meat options. Creative tapas, such as Camembert in cranberry sauce. **€**

URBAN EXPLORING ON TWO WHEELS

The Sevilla Expo of 1992 commemorated the 500th anniversary of Christopher Columbus setting sail from near Huelva (p91) on a voyage that would see him reach the Americas. In the spirit of the expo's theme 'The Age of Discovery', nothing beats an exploration of this new world gone to seed. Although possible to navigate on foot, Cartuja is connected to central Sevilla by dedicated lanes for bicycles and scooters, making the larger distances more manageable.

Many pavilions were razed and replaced with an array of modern tech start-up offices and government buildings, but the extant highlights are best embodied by the **1 Pabellón del Futuro**, with its towering Ariane 4 space rocket replica, radar dish and winged satellite.

Follow the cycle lane north along the Camino de los Descubrimientos past Isla Mágica on your right until you see two large concrete X-shaped structures. This is the **2 Pabellón de México**, where cacti and a large stone Olmec head reward a little wander around the building.

From here, wiggle through the streets to Calle Leonardo Da Vinci, then head east along the boulevard of large cones belonging to the **3 EEC Pavilion** (representing the European Economic Community, precursor of the European Union). There's something charmingly naive about the hopeful vision projected from an early '90s perspective. Irony is provided by the prominent central cone, with its sun-bleached Union Jack.

Further south, the **4 Esfera Bioclimática**, a giant geometric orb that threatens to come loose and roll down to the river at any moment, dominates a space gradually succumbing to rust and weeds. Nearby **5 Pabellón de Marruecos** looks like the dilapidated palace of a former sheikh.

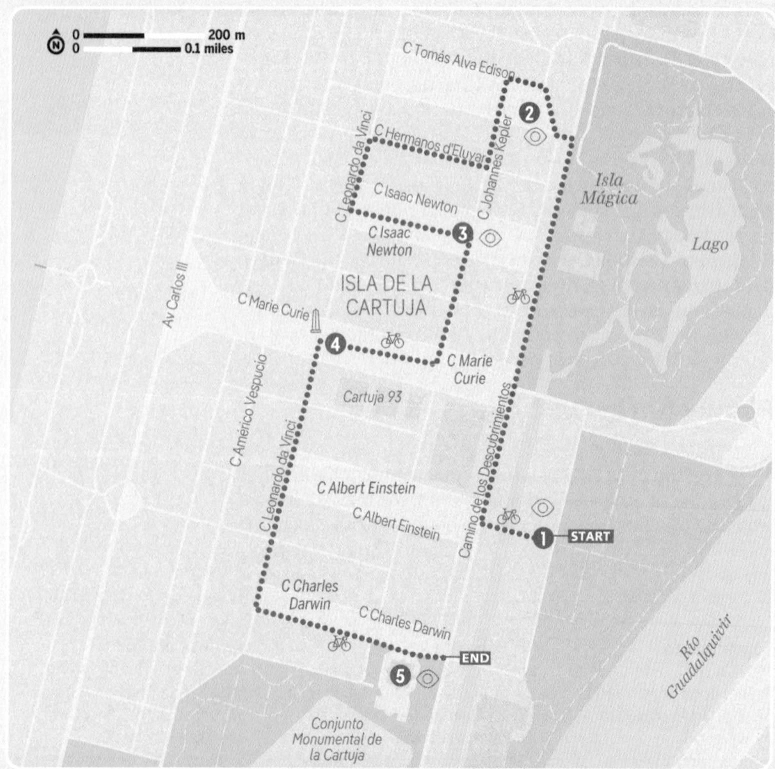

Torre Schindler

Entry to the adjoining **Torre Schindler** is included in the ticket price. The 65m-tall viewing tower gives a different perspective on the city.

Ditch the gears for paddles to get onto the open water. This branch of the Guadalquivir River here is an artificially made inlet, meaning the water is calmer. **Kayak Sevilla** takes great advantage of that with paddling excursions and kayak tours.

At the northern end of this former Expo 1992 zone lies **Isla Mágica**, a theme park catering to all children, although some rides are aimed at specific age groups. It includes a 16th-century ship, roller-coasters and a log flume.

BEST BREAKFAST CAFES IN SEVILLA

Milk Away
Excellent coffee and juices, along with the biggest açaí bowls you've ever seen, crammed with healthy ingredients. Tonnes of veggie and vegan options. €€

Filo
Snug breakfast/ brunch spot, serving *pan con tomate y jamón*, cakes, pastries and fantastic orange juice. €€

La Mala Brunch Rivero
Serves superb eggs Benedict, as well as indulgent Nutella pancakes or healthy fruit smoothies. €€

GETTING AROUND

The streets of old town Sevilla are so narrow that they prohibit most traffic. As such, exploring on foot is a dream. However, that does mean that driving here is tricky and parking, where available, is expensive. E-scooters and mopeds can be found throughout the centre. They are available to hire by the hour and day, often with an attendant app. Servici runs the bikes and has hundreds of docking stations throughout the city. A seven-day pass is the best value if you plan to cycle regularly.

An efficient tram system runs along the Avenida de la Constitución, past the cathedral, and connects to San Bernardo train and bus station to the southeast. This station is also connected to Sevilla's sole Metro line (the L1). Although it passes just south of the centre, it bypasses many of the major sights. The line crosses the Guadalquivir and runs along the southern edge of Triana, and links Sevilla FC's impressive Ramon Sanchez-Pizjuan Stadium to the east.

Sevilla's main train station is Santa Justa, east of Centro. The main bus station, Plaza de Armas, is on the west side of Centro, with both regional and countrywide departures.

Itálica & Monasterio de San Isidoro del Campo
Santiponce
Sevilla

Beyond Sevilla

Sevilla's origins are best understood on its outskirts, via some of Andalucía's finest Roman ruins.

Fertile land to the north of the present-day city was chosen for important settlements by a slew of early civilisations, most notably the Carthaginians, under Hannibal, who were in turn defeated and replaced by the Romans. Much of Rome's first city on the Iberian Peninsula lies buried beneath the current town of Santiponce, although some of the finest remains are neatly preserved at nearby Itálica.

Santiponce is one of Sevilla's many satellite towns. Although most of them have limited immediate appeal to visitors, the monastery at Santiponce could rival most of the religious highlights in Sevilla, with the additional benefit of escaping the city crowds.

TOP TIP

All the sights around Sevilla can easily be visited on a self-guided day trip from the city using public transport.

Santiponce

LUX BLUE/SHUTTERSTOCK ©

JOSERPIZARRO/SHUTTERSTOCK ©

Itálica

THEY CAME, THEY SAW, THEY CONQUERED

The Roman emperors Trajan and Hadrian were both in Itálica. Both rulers would go on to have crucial impacts on the Roman Empire, with Trajan overseeing one of Rome's most successful expansions, while his successor Hadrian was more cautious, building walls in Britain and consolidating Trajan's gains. Quite fitting, given that Itálica was founded by the successful Roman general Scipio, following his defeat of Hannibal (the one with the elephants), during the Second Punic War.

Roman ruins at Itálica

MOSAICS AND AN AMPHITHEATRE

Ancient Itálica is an extensive and arresting set of Roman ruins 30 minutes by bus (M170 A or B) from Sevilla. Much of these remains date to the early 2nd century CE, when son of the city, Hadrian, was the Roman Emperor. This inspired a golden era for Itálica, the results of which can still be explored.

On entry, the path forks to the left. Head this way first, until you reach the broad, paved streets, where houses of the wealthy contain a number of beautiful **patio mosaics**. Those in the **Casa de los Pájaros** (House of the Birds), the **Edificio de Neptuno** (Building of the Neptune Mosaic) and the **Casa del Planetario** (House of the Planetarium), which depicts the gods after whom the seven days of the week were named, are highlights.

Perhaps the quirkiest, though, is a mosaic of little people fighting cranes with spears. It decorated the floor of a *letrina colectiva* (communal latrine) and was potentially designed to draw one's attention away from others as they did their business (the modern cubicle wall may be less creative but is no doubt a more welcome invention).

WHERE'S THE REST?

Many mosaics from Itálica and relics from the pre-Roman peoples who inhabited these lands are on display at the **Museo Arqueológico** in Sevilla (p66).

WHERE TO EAT IN SANTIPONCE & ITÁLICA

Ventorrillo Canario
Close to the Itálica bus stop. Canary Islands dishes served with *patatas arrugadas* and spicy *mojo picón* sauce. €€

Taberna La Romana
Midway between Itálica and Santiponce with classic tapas, such as *croquetas* and *chocos fritos* (fried cuttlefish). €€

Bodeguita Reyes
Simple *platos combinados*, such as *flamenquín* (a fried pork and cheese roll) with chips and salad. €

San Isidoro del Campo

THE STORY OF THE SPANISH BIBLE

Religious deviations didn't sit well with an increasingly radical Spanish Catholic church in the 16th century. Casiodoro de Reina, who lived in Monasterio de San Isidoro del Campo as a Hieronymite monk, fled the Inquisition in 1557, eventually settling in central Europe. His effigy was burned at an auto-da-fé in Sevilla in 1562. While in exile, de Reina became the first person to translate the bible into Castilian Spanish.

Heading back towards the entrance, on your left you'll see thick blocks of stone. These are the outer wall of a stunning 25,000-seat **amphitheatre**, one of the largest Rome ever built. Since the estimated population of Itálica would have been about 15,000 people, it is believed that during the games, the amphitheatre's stands were also used as accommodation by travellers.

But Rome wasn't the initiator of human presence in the area, as the nearby **Dolmen de la Pastora** can bear witness. This prehistoric burial site on the outskirts of **Valencina de la Concepción** is thought to date to the 3rd century BCE.

Monastery of San Isidoro del Campo

GOTHIC CATHOLIC FORTRESS

On the southern outskirts of Santiponce, 20 minutes from Sevilla by bus (M170 A or B), this fortified Gothic monastery was founded by Guzmán el Bueno of Tarifa in 1301. Over the centuries it hosted a succession of religious orders, including the Cistercians and, in the 15th century, the hermetic Hieronymites who embellished the Patio de Evangelistas with striking murals of the saints, and Mudéjar-style floral and geometric patterns. Also outstanding is the church's altarpiece by 17th-century Sevillan sculptor Juan Martínez Montañés.

GETTING AROUND

The hourly bus M170 (A or B) that runs between Sevilla and Itálica archaeological site can be used to travel between Santiponce and the ruins. Otherwise it's a 20-minute walk between the two.

CARMONA

At first glance, you'd be forgiven for thinking that Carmona is Sevilla on a condensed scale. There are Moorish castles, Mudéjar churches, Golden Age palaces and even some well-preserved Roman ruins on the edge of the town. Since the Roman era, Carmona benefitted and grew from Sevilla's prosperity. Even during the Moors' reign, the brother of the Sevillan ruler ran the show in Carmona. Spend any amount of time in town, though, and you'll soon discover there's a completely different atmosphere here; calmer and more sincere.

Carmona's surrounding plains are burnt to a golden crisp in the summer months and surprisingly fertile for the rest of the year. Rising out of them, phoenix-like, the dignified white buildings are an endearing sight. Located on the edge of the region of La Campiña, which encompasses the wedge of land to the east of Sevilla, Carmona is the largest and most significant town from here to Córdoba.

TOP TIP

A handy *ruta turistica* plots a course between the key sights of Carmona. Although there's plenty to keep you looking in front of and above you, a glance occasionally at the ground will pick out the round, marked flagstones and keep you on the right track.

Tombs at Necrópolis Romana

DELVE INTO ROMAN TOMBS

Among Andalucía's most fascinating and important ancient sites is the Roman necropolis in Carmona. A visit is best started in the **museum**, where an informative exhibition details the Roman rituals around death and burial, along with some artefacts excavated from the tombs. There's a good view of Carmona from the viewing platform atop the building.

Beyond the museum building are hundreds of tombs, hewn into the rock between the 1st century BCE and 2nd century CE. Some, such as **La Tumba del Elefante** (The Elephant Tomb) are elaborate family tombs with multiple chambers. Ladders or steps allow you to clamber down into others, often through tight entranceways, where you can see niches for the box-like stone urns (most people were cremated) and hints of faded murals.

Across the road from the entrance are the rocky remains of the **Anfiteatro Romano**, a Roman amphitheatre from

PEDRO'S OTHER PALACE

Pedro I, known as 'The Cruel' by his enemies, is best known for his beautiful palace in Sevilla's **Real Alcázar** (p60), which, unlike the one in Carmona, has survived.

WHERE TO STAY IN CARMONA

Parador de Carmona
Part of the chain of state-owned luxury hotels, the Gothic-Mudéjar touches make this an impressive stay. €€€

Hotel Alcázar de la Reina
Stunning inside and out, from the covered brick patio to the elegant marble-floored bedrooms. €€

El Rincón de las Descalzas
Each room is uniquely designed, while retaining this hotel's original 18th-century townhouse spirit. €€

CARMONA

Prioral de Santa María de la Asunción
Alcázar de la Puerta de Sevilla
Anfiteatro Romano
Necrópolis Romana
Alameda de Alfonso XIII
Plaza de Lasso
Plaza de San Fernando
Plaza del Palenque
C Juan de Ortega
C González Parejo
C Santa Ana
Carretera de Brenes
C B E Cerezo
C Antequera
C Beato Juan Grande
C González Girón
C Barbacana Alta
C Torre del Oro
C Sancho Ibáñez
C Guadalete
Ronda León de San Francisco
C Prim
C Domínguez la Haza
C San Pedro
C La Fuente
C San Felipe
C Anfiteatro
C San Francisco
Paseo del Estatuto
C Enmedio
Av de Jorge Bonsor
C Sevilla
C Real
C Extramuros de San Felipe
Antigua Nacional IV
0 200 m
0 0.1 miles

La Tumba del Elefante (p77)

FOTOEVENTIS/SHUTTERSTOCK ©

Puerta de Sevilla

the 1st century BCE. It hasn't aged well and the sandy arena is circled by rocks now embedded into the yellow-brown ground. It's not open to visitors but you can get a decent view from the road outside.

Alcázar de la Puerta de Sevilla fortifications

AN ENTRANCE WITH A VIEW

Guarding the western edge of the old town is Carmona's fortified main gate, the Puerta de Sevilla. Flowering up all around it is a striking fortress, which displays additions from various eras. Pass through the gate, which looks like a keyhole in the castle's foundation. On your right is the tourist information centre, through which you can access the castle.

The Romans reinforced an earlier structure, which had already been in place for five centuries, and built a temple on top. The Muslim Almohads added an *aljibe* (cistern) to the upper patio.

Keep climbing the steps to the top of the main tower for a hawk-like perch from which to admire the typically Andalucian tableau of white homes and soaring spires.

Santa María de la Asunción church

ELEGANT GOTHIC CHURCH WITH CURIOSITIES

Entering through the **Patio de los Naranjos**, the **Visigothic calendar** carved into a pillar on your right is a great indicator of the many fascinating details of this church. This

HOLY ROOMS

Convento Madre de Dio de Carmona
Nuns still run the chapel, hotel and convent (1520) here, tending gardens and rooms with devotion.

Hotel Monasterio de San Francisco
Palma del Río's huge former monastery has airy, vaulted-ceiling rooms and colourful cloisters.

Hospedería Convento de Santa Clara
Set within Palma del Río's walls, this former convent has patios with orange trees; also an outdoor pool.

Hospedería del Monasterio Osuna
Overlooking Osuna, has a large patio with pool. Views of the city from nearby are excellent.

BEST RESTAURANTS IN CARMONA

Cervecería San Fernando
Waitstaff will happily suggest dishes based on your preferences. The *alcachofas* (artichokes) are excellent. €€

Mesón La Cueva
Alfresco cave-like dining at the foot of the Alcázar de la Puerta. €€

Molino de la Romera
Chargrilled meats in a cosy, 15th-century olive-oil mill, complete with panoramic terrace. *Michelin Guide*–listed. €€€

Mingalario
Traditional tapas bar, complete with hanging hams. Good pork dishes, such as *cochinillo* and *pringá*. €

Pastelería Latidos de Carmona
Head to this bakery for a takeaway snack (the *tartas* are highly recommended). €

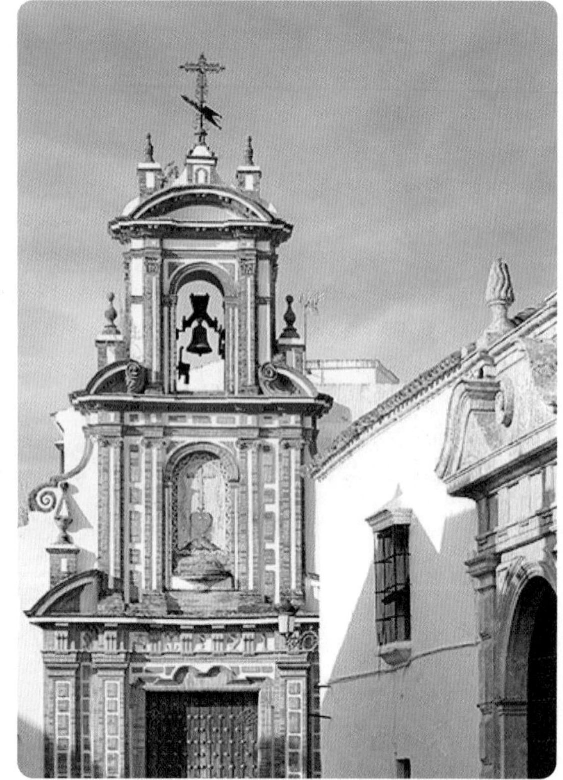

Convento de Santa Clara

12th-century courtyard was originally intended for ablutions before entering a mosque, which was replaced with the current church in the 15th century.

The church interior is crowned by intricate, lofty Gothic vaults above a masterful **altarpiece**, started in 1559, divided into 28 sections framed by gilt-scrolled columns. Each one depicts a biblical scene. A couple of huge scallop shells, symbolising baptism, are placed near the main doors. There's also a small museum upstairs dedicated to ecclesiastical art.

GETTING AROUND

If you are driving from Sevilla, it is easiest to find free parking in the streets near the Roman Necropolis, from where it is a 15-minute walk to the narrow cobbled streets of Carmona's town centre. More central, paid underground parking is found at the Paseo del Estatuto.

RUTA TURISTICA CHURCHES & PALACES

From the Alcázar de la Puerta, you can follow a self-guided walking tour of the town. Start by walking along Calle Prim to **1 Plaza de San Fernando** (aka Plaza Mayor), a popular hang-out for locals. From here, wind through the cobbled streets towards **2 Museo de la Ciudad**, which details Carmona's history from its Copper Age origins (roughly 5000 years ago) to the modern day. The collection includes Roman mosaics and some earthenware vessels, used primarily to store food, dating back to their antecedents, the Tartessians. The museum is housed in the 16th-century Palacio del Marqués de las Torres, which has a Doric-columned doorway that is an attraction in itself.

Next, visit **3 Alcázar de Arriba**, Carmona's other castle. This former Almohad fort was transformed into a palace by Pedro I, but was sadly ruined by earthquakes over the centuries. Most of it remains that way, but for the splendid **4 Parador de Carmona** hotel.

Follow the road south around the castle's outer walls, then drop down towards **5 Puerta de Córdoba**. This Roman gate was built to control access to Carmona from the east. The formidable structure is in excellent condition, with two sturdy hexagonal towers and an 18th-century neoclassical arch.

Wandering back up towards the town centre, **6 Convento de Santa Clara** is a shining example of Sevillan baroque. The two-storey arched cloister gives way to a unique chapel with Gothic ribbed vaulting above a dazzling altarpiece.

Finally, keep walking westward towards Plaza de San Fernando, stopping in at **7 Prioral de Santa María** along the way. The streets around this church have the highest concentration of Golden Age palaces with impressive facades.

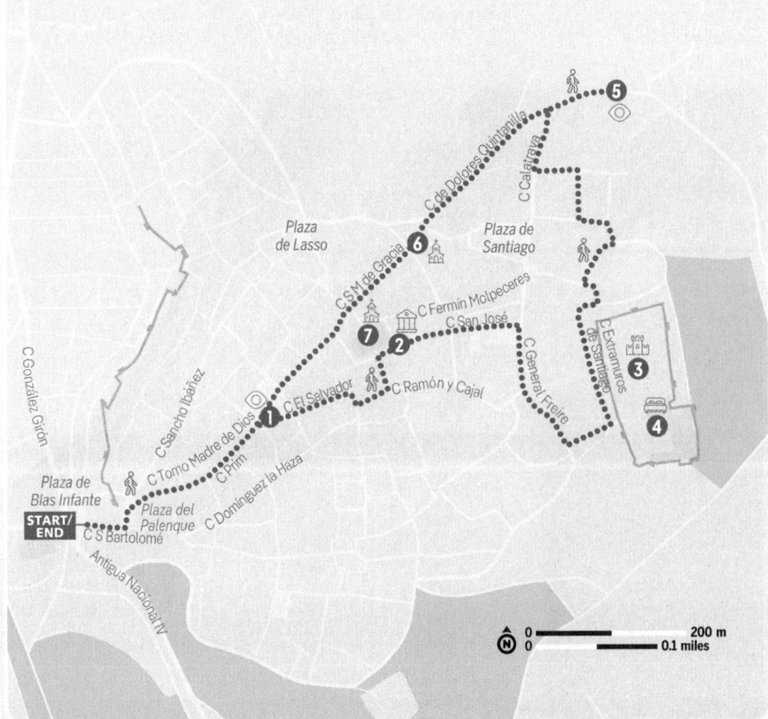

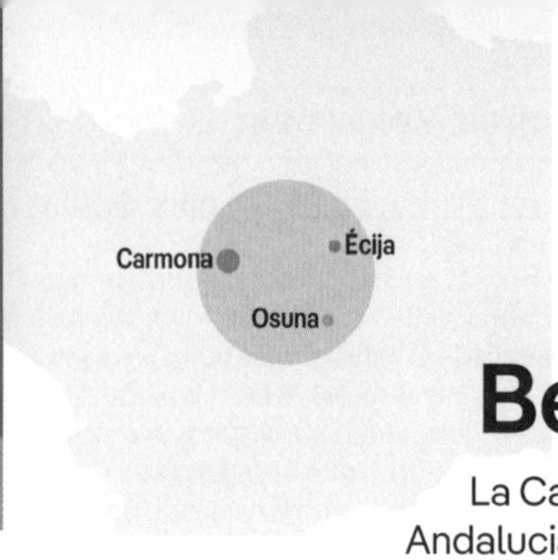

Carmona
Écija
Osuna

Beyond Carmona

La Campiña's towns present varied slices of Andalucian life, culture and history. Choose one that best suits your tastes.

The farmland dominating La Campiña sees some of the hottest annual temperatures on the European mainland, especially approaching Córdoba. But these otherwise desolate expanses make the architectural and cultural treasures found in cities such as Écija and Osuna all the more astounding. Each town has its own distinct flavour. Osuna's narrow grids of undulating streets positively glow in the reflected light of their pristine white exteriors. The town centre, home to some of the finest grand baroque mansions outside of Sevilla, bows under the watchful glare of a mighty Renaissance church on a hilltop. Écija, on the other hand, is a much gentler, friendlier town, with a skyline dominated by a dozen unique, ceramic-tiled church towers.

TOP TIP

Without a car, exploring La Campiña means relying on infrequent local buses. Rideshare app BlaBlaCar is a popular budget alternative.

Palacio de Peñaflor

JOSEP CURTO/SHUTTERSTOCK ©

Museo Histórico Municipal relics

ROMAN RELICS IN A FINE PALACE

It's a two-for-one at Écija's museum. The superbly preserved Roman mosaics, such as the Don del Vino mosaic depicting scenes related to the mythical 'birth' of wine, are housed in the 18th-century Palacio de Benamejí, which sports the most impressive Mudéjar features in La Campiña.

Showy facade of Palacio de Peñaflor

SHOW-STEALING PALACE

Despite being a town known for its churches, Écija's most popular sight is an 18th-century palace. Running the entire length of the street, its flamboyant curved facade, from which it derives its *balcones largos* (long balconies) nickname, is painted with fading frescoes of cherubim and pastoral scenes. The interior is often closed, although occasionally you can pop in and see the vaulted ground-floor stables.

Hilltop Christianity

RELIGIOUS ART AND ARCHITECTURE

Keeping a watchful glare over the town below, the formidable hilltop church, **Colegiata de Santa María de la Asunción**, has a number of baroque paintings by José de Ribera (El Españoleto). Underground is a chapel and pantheon for the Dukes of Osuna, created in 1545. A little further down the hill from the Colegiata is the baroque Monasterio de la Encarnación. The highlight here is the 18th-century Sevillan tile work, depicting various biblical and hunting scenes. Entry to both is by guided tour only (in Spanish).

BEST RESTAURANTS IN ÉCIJA

Agora
You'd expect tapas with this level of presentation and quality to come with a much higher price. Popular place. €

La Reja
Hams hang above the bar at this gourmet-ingredient-focused tapas joint. Seafood dishes are a speciality. €€€

Hispania
A contemporary spin on Spanish dishes, such as wok-fried black rice with *chipirones* (baby squid). Book ahead. €€

PALACE ACCESS

If you want to get behind the doors of a private palace, many in Sevilla open to the public, such as the **Palacio de las Dueñas** (p83).

GETTING AROUND

Osuna is connected to Sevilla via the train line to Málaga. The region's only other train route skirts round the northern edge of La Campiña. Carmona and Écija can be reached by bus via Sevilla and Córdoba respectively. Interconnectivity between the towns on public transport is scant and a car is the best way to travel around. If you are planning to visit Sierra Norte after the towns of La Campiña, having a car is essential. Palma del Río is a useful stopover point midway between Écija and Sierra Norte, or indeed between Sevilla and Córdoba.

ÉCIJA'S CHURCH TOWERS ROUTE

Forty minutes east of Carmona by car is Écija. Its baroque tower-studded skyline has earned it the nickname *la ciudad de las torres* (the city of towers). Although an earthquake in 1755 tragically felled most of them, they were all rebuilt. You can begin at any point on this walk, although if driving, park along Avenida Dr Fleming, near the river. From here head for **1 Iglesia de San Gil's** bell tower, which sits prominently atop Écija's highest neighbourhood. Recent excavations suggest this church was built over the Moorish fort.

Walk northwest from here, towards the billowy red and white belfry of **2 Iglesia de San Juan**. Occasionally, the bell tower opens for visitors to climb. Further north, the brick tower of Gothic-Mudéjar **3 Iglesia de San Pablo y Santo Domingo** is still unfinished.

Following narrow Calle Almonas, you'll come to a leafy plaza enlivened by explosions of magenta bougainvillea. The **4 Parroquia Mayor de Santa Cruz** was once Écija's principal mosque. Echoes of that earthquake are felt in the cracked, roofless atrium; its impressive Gothic arches remain from the original 13th-century church. The cavernous, domed interior features a gold baroque *retablo*.

Finally, head south along the pedestrianised Calle Mas y Prat to **5 Plaza de España**. Just off this, Écija's main square, is **6 Iglesia de Santa María**, the town's finest church. Its Gothic-Mudéjar tower is decked out in white and blue tiles, the interior includes a frescoed dome and a *patio de los naranjos*, suggestive of its origins as a mosque.

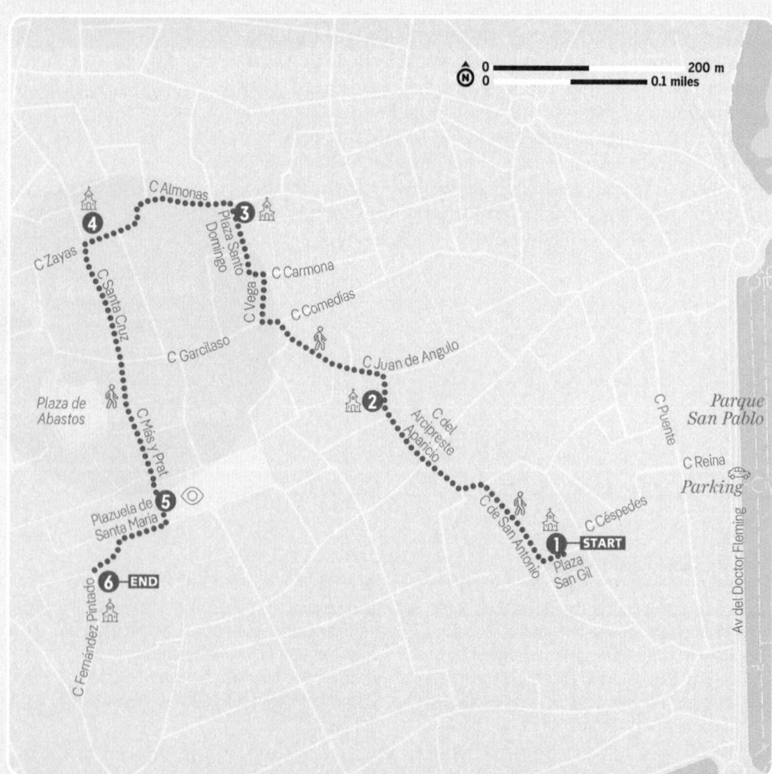

OSUNA'S BAROQUE MANSIONS

An hour's drive southeast of Carmona is the pretty town of Osuna. Park around Calle Alfonso XII. The streets hemmed in between this main artery and calles Sevilla and Carrera are dominated by narrow rows of prim, whitewashed homes. Money found its way from the Americas to this part of Osuna, and Calle San Pedro is the pinnacle of the architectural riches it bought. Generally, most homes are closed to the public, but still hold plenty of interest when viewed from outside.

You can spend a night in **1 Palacio del Marqués de la Gomera**; its pillared main doorway supports a florid balcony above. Ask at the reception to see the 18th-century private chapel, with its gold inlay door panels. A few doors down, **2 Cilla del Cabildo Colegial** (1773), which has been beautifully restored, is a swirling confection of geometric designs and volutes in lemon yellow and ivory. Above the doorway is a sculpted version of Sevilla's famous Giralda bell tower.

South of the Plaza Mayor, on Calle La Huerta, **3 Palacio de los Cepeda** is now Osuna's courthouse. The Churrigueresque, veined marble columns support an entablature, atop which stand two stone halberdiers holding the Cepeda family coat of arms.

One street north is Calle Sevilla. Here, twisted pillars draped with bunches of grapes signal **4 Palacio de Govantes y Herdara**. Facing it is another palace open to visitors, the Palacio de los Hermanos Arjona y Cubas, which houses the tourist information office and **5 Museo de Osuna**. The museum is now part relic exhibition, part reliquary to *Game of Thrones*, which filmed in multiple Osuna locations, including the Plaza de Toros.

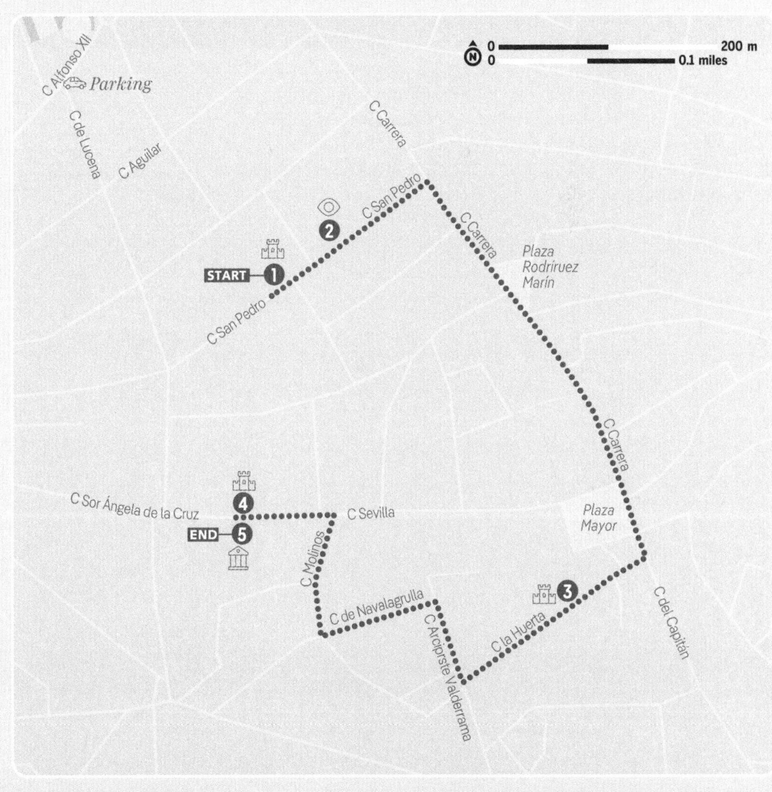

CONSTANTINA & CAZALLA

Constantina and Cazalla de la Sierra are the two major gateways to the Sierra Norte, a natural park that presents the quickest way to escape the heat of Sevilla for a day or two. The narrow medieval streets of Constantina, Sierra Norte's unofficial capital, snake through the forest-clad Huéznar valley, opening up in a town centre lined with handsome 18th-century mansions and traditional cafes. A Moorish castle overlooks the town.

Cazalla de la Sierra is an attractive little *pueblo blanco*, its houses scattered across a hillside in a charming, pell-mell assemblage of streets. Its historic core fans out from Plaza Mayor, which is overlooked by the Iglesia de Nuestra Señora de la Consolación on the south side of town. Both Constantina and Cazalla are ideal bases for hikers. A series of well-signposted *senderos* (hiking paths) have trailheads on the edge of these two urban centres, probing into the surrounding woodland, hills and valleys.

TOP TIP

A train runs at least thrice-daily from Sevilla to Cazalla-Constantina, a station located on the road connecting Constantina and Cazalla de la Sierra. These two main towns occupy the centre of Sierra Norte and are roughly 20km apart by road. A car is the only way to get around easily.

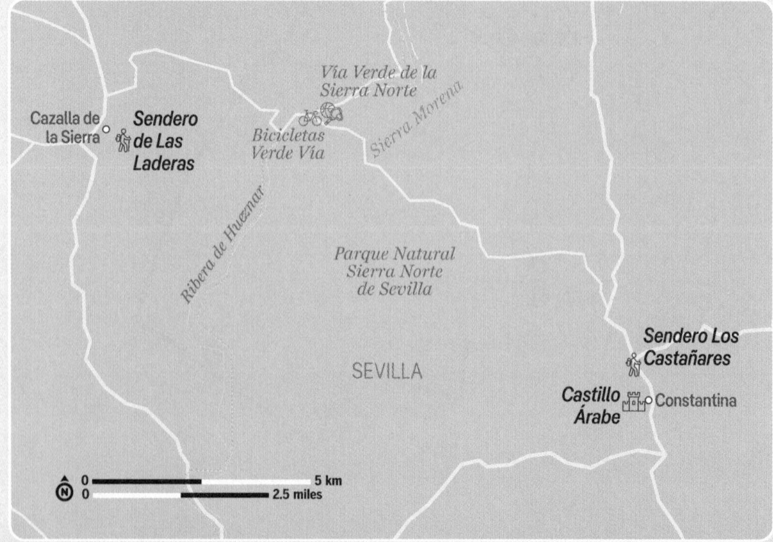

MARIADELAO/GETTY IMAGES ©

Constantina

Valley views from Castillo Árabe

FORTIFIED OVERVIEW OF THE AREA

Constantina's ruined castle is worth the climb for the views alone. Only a shell of the Islamic Almoravid castle's former self remains, but the viewing platform, with a free car park attached, is the perfect spot to get your bearings and a sense of what the surrounding landscape is like. Below, the distinctive Mudéjar bell tower of the Iglesia de Santa María de la Encarnación towers above Barrio de la Morería's huddled clusters of white houses.

Sierra Norte trails from Constantina & Cazalla

HILLTOP LOOPS AND WOODLAND AMBLES

There's likely to be a hiking route to match the timeframe of your visit in this region. Shorter paths, such as the **Sendero los Castañares** (5½km, roughly two hours) loop from the northern edge of Constantina, through thick chestnut woods, to a hilltop viewpoint.

FOR HIKING FANATICS

The Sierra Morena runs southeast from Sierra Norte, towards Portugal. The region around **Aracena** (p97) is particularly good for hiking.

WHERE TO EAT IN CONSTANTINA & CAZALLA

La Toscana
Classic tapas, including smaller bites, and low prices. Menus are usually chalked up. €

Asador los Navarro
Hearty barbecued beef, chicken and pork tapas along the town's *alameda*. The desserts are decadent. €€€

Embrujo Andaluz
Shelves, fridges and floor space crammed with local cakes and produce at this tapas bar-meets-grocery. €€

Agustina
Gourmet cuisine and fine wine in Cazalla. Traditional regional dishes given a culinary makeover. €€€

Cortijo Vistalegre
Converted ranch building with terrace seating. Best known for its *arroz con perdiz* (partridge) dish. €€€

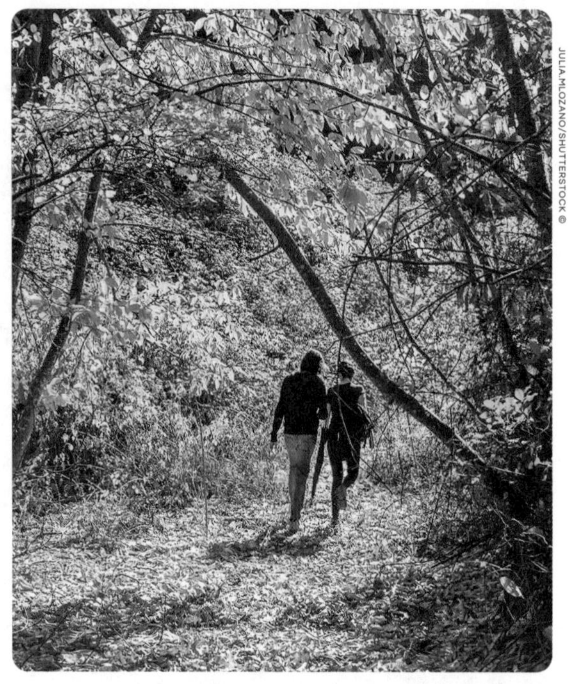

Cazalla de la Sierra

Conversely, the **GR 48** is a 45km route from Cazalla to Almadén de la Plata on the western edge of Sierra Norte and can take anywhere from two to four days on foot. A shorter walk from Cazalla is **Sendero de Las Laderas** (8km, three hours), which leads down to the Huéznar valley, passing through typical Sierra Norte evergreen-oak woodlands, as well as managed farmland with olive groves, chestnut woods and vineyards. There are some steep stretches, so be sure to wear suitable footwear.

Making good use of an old mining railway, the **Vía Verde de la Sierra Norte** is an excellent, 18.7-km cycling (or horse-riding and walking) route that starts from the Cazalla-Constantina train station. It passes north through the Huéznar valley, reaching San Nicolás del Puerto village before bending south again towards the old Cerro del Hierro mines. **Bicicletas Verde Vía** is based just outside the station and rents out mountain bikes.

GETTING AROUND

If you're planning on hiking an A-to-B or loop route without a car, take a train from Sevilla to Cazalla-Constantina station. *Senderos* and a *vía verde* pass close by, although Constantina is difficult to reach on foot from there. Both Cazalla and Constantina are best reached by car.

Beyond Constantina & Cazalla

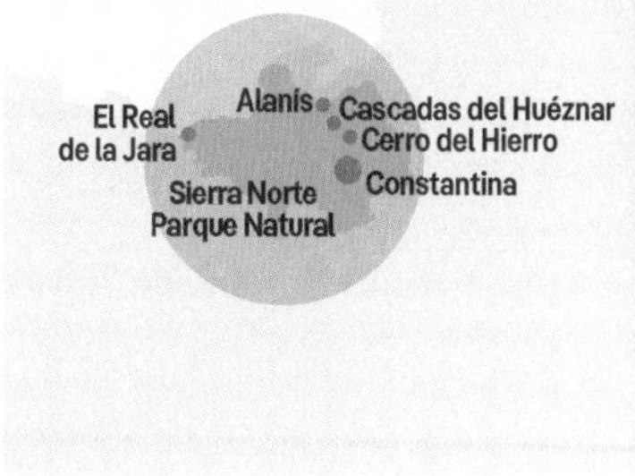

El Real de la Jara
Alanís
Cascadas del Huéznar
Cerro del Hierro
Constantina
Sierra Norte Parque Natural

Leave Constantina & Cazalla to discover charming villages, hilltop castles, remote hikes and natural wonders.

Much of Sierra Norte's potential is locked away in the valleys and hills beyond its quaint towns and villages. Some human impact upon this wide open country is visible in olive groves and old mines, but on many of the trails, you're unlikely to encounter many people for miles. Crisscrossing the landscape, these hiking paths vary from short jaunts to multiday routes.

A great way to explore Sierra Norte in a short space of time is by taking a road trip between the region's natural and human-made highlights. These include castles at Alanís and El Real de la Jara, unique rock formations and old mines at Cerro del Hierro, and waterfalls in the Huéznar valley.

TOP TIP

Sierra Norte enjoys a mild climate. The sunny, flower-filled meadows in spring make April to June the best months to visit.

Cascadas del Huéznar (p90)

SIERRA NORTE DRIVING TOUR

This 50km route, starting at Constantina and ending in Cazalla de la Sierra, offers an all-encompassing road trip of Sierra Norte Parque Natural.

Head first to **1 El Robledo**, a botanic garden and visitor centre on the southern edge of Constantina. You can pick up hiking route maps here. Return back through Constantina, following the A455 north for 3km before taking a right-hand turn onto the SE163, which winds through the hilly countryside. After 8km, there's a signposted turn-off to your right for **2 Cerro del Hierro**. The free car park is surrounded by the dilapidated buildings of a mining industry that once operated here.

Stretch your legs along **3 Sendero Cerro del Hierro** (1.8km, one hour), which leads to a series of viewpoints of the whimsical natural rock formations. Crossing a small bridge near the northwestern viewpoint, you can detour along a path that passes a series of ruins. When it seems to dead-end in scrub, push through into a slot canyon with more ruins.

Back behind the wheel, continue north on the SE163. Just after San Nicolás del Puerto village, take a quick detour left onto the SE7101, which follows an *arroyo* (creek) up the valley to **4 Cascadas del Huéznar** (waterfalls). From San Nicolás del Puerto, take the SE8100 northwest, ploughing on through increasingly remote landscape to **5 Alanís**, topped by a medieval castle.

If time allows, detour northwest, past Guadalcanal, to **6 Sendero Sierra del Viento**. Otherwise, take the A432 south from Alanís to Cazalla. Glimpse hilly vistas and the occasional railway viaduct along this remote route. Cazalla is a natural end point, although you could continue west along the SE179 to Aracena.

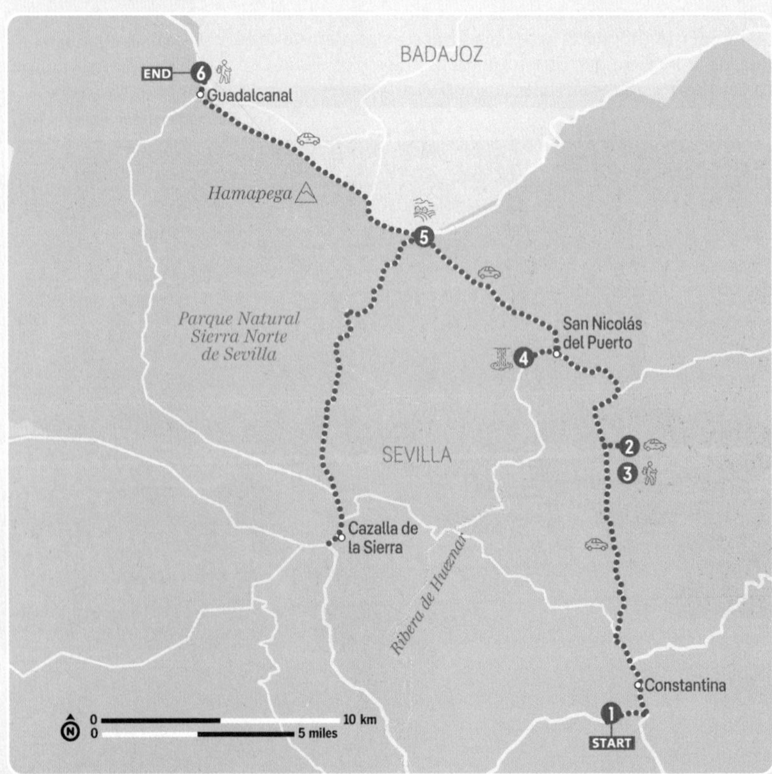

HUELVA

With natural beauty, quieter Costa de la Luz beaches and plenty of historical significance, not just for Spain but globally, it's surprising how off the beaten track Huelva province still feels. Although largely an industrial city, Huelva's centre is lovely, with large, pedestrianised squares that take on a lively evening flair throughout the week. Locals are known as *choqueros*, a nod to the regional penchant for eating *chocos* (cuttlefish).

Noted history here begins with the Phoenicians, 3000 years ago. Much of the Huelva you see is far newer, buoyed mainly by industrialisation under Franco, although Barrio Obrero, built by the Rio Tinto mining company, has a distinctly British feel. Arguably, however, the region's best shipping took place just south of the Tinto estuary. Here, a string of towns produced a generation of great sailors and sea captains, drawing Christopher Columbus to choose it as the staging ground for his voyage across the Atlantic in 1492.

TOP TIP

Where the Tinto and Odiel river estuaries converge in a V-shaped wedge, you'll find the capital of Huelva province. The bus station is on the western edge of the historic centre, the train station is on the southern edge. Plaza de las Monjas is at its core.

BEST CHOCOS

Huelva gained fame for its cuisine as Spain's Gastronomy Capital in 2017, with *chocos* and white shrimp the highlights.

Paco Moreno
Unpretentious spot for all types of lightly battered seafood. €€

Coma Tapas & Punto
Does a good *montadito de chocos fritos* (chocos sandwich) served with alioli. €

Restaurante Portichuelo
A fancier cuttlefish approach at this upscale tapas bar. €€€

Gran Vía Uno
Has a decent wine selection and enticing specials board. €€

MAURO RODRIGUES/SHUTTERSTOCK ©

Museo de Huelva

Museo de Huelva exhibits

ROMAN MOSAICS AND REGIONAL ART

The Romans came here for the mineral wealth, and plenty of relics from that era, including a well-preserved waterwheel and some patio mosaics, have found their way into the permanent collection at this fascinating museum. Seven centuries of Spanish art are also on display upstairs. Salmon-pink **Casa Colón** (Columbus House), a few buildings down from the museum, also stages some temporary art exhibitions.

COLUMBUS'S FESTIVAL

He's still so revered in Huelva that a six-day festival is held every year (late Jul/early Aug) celebrating Columbus's departure for the Americas (3 August 1492). Expect music, dance, drinking and cultural events. For more on Columbus, see p94.

Church of Nuestra Señora de la Cinta

GOTHIC-MUDÉJAR CHAPEL

Azulejo tiles by Daniel Zuloaga within the church depict the story of Columbus promising God that he would pray here during a turbulent traverse of the Atlantic in 1493. Whether or not he came good on his promise is another matter. Take city bus 6, from outside the bus station, 3km north of Huelva.

GETTING AROUND

Huelva's town centre is heavily pedestrianised and everything is easy and quick to navigate on foot. Plenty of local buses run from the stands outside the main bus station, including numbers 2 and 6, which ply the route between the main bus and train stations. If you wish to take a longer walk, a promenade runs for miles along the waterfront past some old relics of the city's mining days.

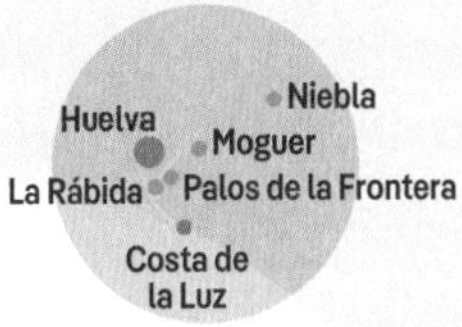

Huelva
Niebla
Moguer
La Rábida
Palos de la Frontera
Costa de la Luz

Beyond Huelva

Costa de la Luz beaches, a day trip to Portugal and the story of Columbus's voyage to the Americas.

Immediately outside Huelva are three fascinating towns, La Rábida, Palos de la Frontera and Moguer, known collectively as the Lugares Colombinos (Columbian sites). Stretching along the eastern bank of the Río Tinto estuary, each one played a crucial role in securing funding and preparing the essentials for Christopher Columbus's fruitful voyage into the unknown. The explorer's legacy still looms large here.

Huelva is also a great gateway to the least-visited stretch of Andalucía's beaches, at least by travellers from abroad. The Costa de la Luz here comprises many kilometres of unbroken sand, often completely devoid of people. On the main road to Sevilla, the historic core of Niebla has Huelva's finest castle.

TOP TIP

Starting early, catch the hourly M403 bus to/from Huelva to visit all three Lugares Colombinos on a long day trip.

Palos de la Frontera (p94)

The Columbus Trail

SHIPS, MUSEUMS AND MONASTERIES

One of Huelva's most intriguing attractions is at **La Rábida**, 20 minutes from Huelva on the M403 bus. In a small artificial lake you will find three wooden caravels. These ships at the **Muelle de las Carabelas** are precise, to-scale replicas of the three vessels – the *Pinta*, the *Niña* and the *Santa María* – that conveyed Christopher Columbus and his 100-strong crew across the Atlantic to make the first documented trip to the Americas. You can clamber all over the three ships, enhancing the appreciation of what life aboard would have been like. An excellent museum with honest, revisionist portrayals of Spain's deleterious effect on indigenous life following Columbus's arrival is a welcome addition.

Before setting sail, Columbus spent plenty of time at the hilltop Franciscan **Monasterio de la Rábida**. Note the statue of the Virgin, to whom Columbus prayed before his voyage, and the exceptional frescoes in its cloister. Another good stop at La Rábida's monument-filled site is **Parque Botánico José Celestino Mutis**, a beautiful botanical garden, which brings together plants and trees from the New and Old worlds.

Columbus actually set sail from **Palos de la Frontera**; its historical prestige is buoyed further for having provided Columbus's two other captains (brothers Martín Alonso Pinzón and Vicente Yáñez Pinzón), half his crew and the two smaller ships. The riches that resulted are particularly evident on the decorated facade of the **Ayuntamiento**. Head north along Calle Colón to see **Parroquia San Jorge Mártir**, a crumbling church strewn with stork nests, where Columbus and his sailors took Communion before embarking. Water for their ships came from **La Fontanilla** well nearby.

The final town on the Columbus Trail is **Moguer**, where Columbus spent a night of prayer at **Monasterio de Santa Clara** upon returning from his first voyage in March 1493. It has a Mudéjar cloister, and a unique 14th-century Nasrid choir stall carved with images of lions and Arabic capitals. A statue of Columbus sits in the plaza in front.

COLUMBUS'S FOUR VOYAGES

Columbus worked hard to gain approval for his scheme to prove the world was round in order to find an alternate route to the spice-rich lands of Asia. The Reyes Católicos (Fernando and Isabel) acquiesced in 1492, leading to four voyages.

The first voyage left on 3 August 1492 from Palos de la Frontera, making first landfall on the Bahamian island of Guanahaní on 12 October. Columbus named it San Salvador (to honour Jesus Christ). The expedition went on to discover Cuba and Hispaniola, returning to Palos in 1493 with only two ships (the *Santa Maria* sank), as well as animals, plants, gold ornaments and six Caribbean indigenous people, all new to Europe, although they were erroneously supposed to be from the 'East Indies' at the time.

Casa Museo Zenobia y Juan Ramón Jiménez

A NOBEL LAUREATE'S HOME

In Moguer, 40 minutes from Huelva by bus M403, you'll find the former home of poet Juan Ramón Jiménez (1881–1958) and his wife – also a poet, writer and translator – Zenobia

WHERE TO STAY ON THE COLUMBUS TRAIL

Hotel La Pinta
Ship-themed lobby with saloon-type bar in Palos de la Frontera. Simple rooms with marble floors. €

Complejo Rural Nazaret de Moguer
Large hotel south of Moguer surrounded by forest and gardens. Has outdoor pool. €€

Hostal Montemayor
Decent, clean budget option on the outskirts of Moguer with free parking. On-site cafe and bar. €

Muelle de las Carabelas

Camprubí. The airy home is an affectionate homage to his life's work. Winning 1956's Nobel Prize in Literature, Ramón Jiménez is best known for a poem called *Platero y yo* (Platero and I), inspired by his beloved donkey. Quotes are rendered in tile throughout the building and audio guides in various languages are available.

HUELVA'S MORE REMOTE BEACHES

Flecha del Rompido
An 8km beach only accessed via hourly FlechaMar ferry from El Rompido (April to October).

Playa de Cuesta Maneli
A blend of nature and quiet sand, via boardwalk from a car park on A494.

Playa de Nueva Umbría
Many kilometres of barely touched sand run along a spit east of La Antilla.

Playa del Parador
Stunning 6km sands at the western edge of Parque Natural de Doñana. Access from Parador de Mazagón.

Costa de la Luz beaches

CROWD-FREE SAND AND SUN

While this part of the Costa de la Luz coastline is well known to domestic tourists, others have yet to cotton onto the fact that some of the region's best beaches can be found here. West of Huelva, the coast south of **Isla Cristina** can be reached in 40 minutes by car or 90 minutes by bus. The pair of long sandy beaches, **Playa de la Gaviota** and **Playa Central**, here are connected by a boardwalk trail. Further east, a nature trail winds through forested marshlands, with good bird watching opportunities.

Also to the west of Huelva are the unpretentious resorts of **Punta Umbría** (20 minutes from Huelva by car) and

COLUMBUS'S TOMB

You can visit the tomb of Christopher Columbus in the **Catedral de Sevilla** (p56), although the remains within weren't confirmed to be his until 2006.

WHERE TO STAY ON COSTA DE LA LUZ

Sol Y Mar
Right on the beach in Isla Cristina. Rooms, although a little dated, have great balconies. **€€**

Barceló Punta Umbría Mar
Huge resort hotel with two swimming pools, good accessible facilities and on-site spa in Punta Umbría. **€€**

Parador de Mazagón
Neo-rustic resort outside Mazagón; empty sand within a short walk. Has two palm-fringed swimming pools. **€€**

GETTING TO PORTUGAL FROM ANDALUCÍA

The Guadiana River forms a natural border between much of Spain's Andalucía and neighbouring Portugal. Where it widens into an estuary, that's where you'll find the main crossings between the two countries. There are no customs or immigration checks when crossing the border, and all cars and buses cross over the International Bridge.

A popular alternative, however, is to take the ferry crossing, a short 15-minute hop, between the pretty towns of **Ayamonte** (Spain) and **Vila Real de Santo António** (Portugal). During the summer, ferries run every half-hour between 9am and 9pm, while the autumn to spring timetable is reduced to between 9am and 6pm around once an hour.

Castillo de los Guzmán

Ayamonte (40 minutes by car). The latter is a pretty little town that has regular ferry crossings to Vila Real de Santo António in Portugal. East of Huelva, the main beach resort is at **Mazagón** (16 minutes by car). From there it is about 30km of unbroken sand and little development until Matalascañas. To escape the crowds, simply pick a spot along the A494.

Niebla's historic old town

WELL-PRESERVED WALLS AND CASTLE

Niebla's old town (25 minutes from Huelva by car or train) exudes history. The focal point is 15th-century **Castillo de los Guzmán**, which has a rather gruesome torture museum in its dungeon and two large interior courtyards. From there, follow the 2km of ochre Moorish wall, which retain 46 towers and five original gates. **Iglesia de Santa María de Granada** was originally a Visigothic cathedral before becoming a 9th-century mosque, and then a Gothic-Mudéjar church in the 15th century.

GETTING AROUND

Damas runs at least five daily buses between Isla Cristina's bus station (Calle Manuel Siurot) and Huelva. They run three to five daily buses to Niebla from Sevilla and three to seven daily buses from Huelva. To get away from it all along the coast, you'll need your own transportation. The M403 from Huelva bus station runs hourly in either direction to the Lugares Colombinos.

ARACENA

In the north of the Province of Huelva, Aracena's gleaming white-and-terracotta buildings sit in a scooped-out valley, presided over by a hilltop castle and chunky medieval church. And while its gastrotourism and market town credentials already make it the regional capital, there's plenty of intrigue beneath the limestone landscape too. Crystalline caverns exhibit natural riches that have been millennia in the making.

This stretch of Sierra Morena uplands, with Aracena at their core, are Huelva's ace in the hole. Temperate, with altitudes around 800m to 900m above sea level, these rolling hills harbour Andalucía's broadest expanses of greenery, clustered in thick stands of holm and cork oaks, juniper and pine. In autumn, the woods are thick with wild mushrooms, while spring wildflowers mean that hiking the region's many exceptional *senderos* is rewarding for much of the year. But perhaps even more enchanting are the outcrops of *pueblos blancos*, clinging like toadstools to the sides of castle- or church-capped hills.

TOP TIP

Most of this region falls within the 1870-sq-km Parque Natural Sierra de Aracena y Picos de Aroche, Andalucía's second-largest protected zone. The main settlements form a diamond pattern at its core, with Aracena in the east and Cortegana in the west, Jabugo in the north and Almonaster la Real to the south.

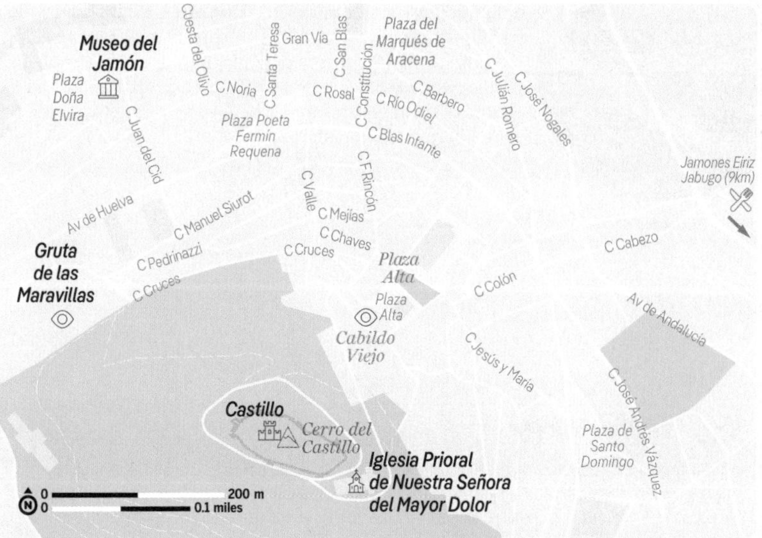

Cerro del Castillo de Aracena

CASTLE, CHURCH, VIEWS

Walking up the road from Plaza Alta, the old town centre with its hulking, 15th-century **Cabildo Viejo**, you reach Aracena's main focal point. The ramshackle **Castillo de Aracena** was built by the kingdoms of Portugal and Castilla in the 12th century, replacing an Islamic predecessor. Jostling for your attention beside it is the Gothic-Mudéjar **Iglesia Prioral de Nuestra Señora del Mayor Dolor**, built by the Knights Templar, with its lofty atrium photogenically framing the surrounding countryside.

THE CATEGORIES OF SPANISH HAM

A colour-coded certification scheme exists to help you know what quality of *jamón* you're getting. It's actually more complicated than you think, with considerations such as diet, the pig's age and weight when slaughtered, and whether or not it's a purebred Iberian pig. *Pata negra* (black label, literally black foot) is the top, running through red, green and white labels in order of quality.

Caves at Gruta de las Maravillas

EERIE UNDERGROUND CAVERNS AND LAKES

Delve deep into the balmy earth on a guided 50-minute subterranean walk. You'll weave through 12 chambers of varying size containing fantastical calcareous formations. The whole site is beautifully illuminated.

Everything hammy at Museo del Jamón

A CARNIVORE'S DREAM

Learn all about how the Sierra de Aracena's landscape and time-tested pig-rearing methods are able to produce Spain's most revered and succulent *jamón*. Audio guides available in five languages. A *jamón* tasting is included in the price.

Meet the pigs

FARM TO TABLE

The town of Jabugo is said to produce the best *jamón* in all of Spain (and thus the world). **Jamones Eíriz Jabugo** is a family-run tour company taking guests to a farm near Aracena to mingle with the pigs in their oak pastures, before the sinister twist of then visiting the salting and curing chambers, where the hams develop their much-vaunted flavour. Tastings included.

Pata negra

GETTING AROUND

Bus infrequency, coupled with the hilly terrain, makes car hire the preferable way to get to Aracena and beyond. It is possible to walk between the caves and castle, although the cobblestone streets make it more challenging for those with restricted mobility.

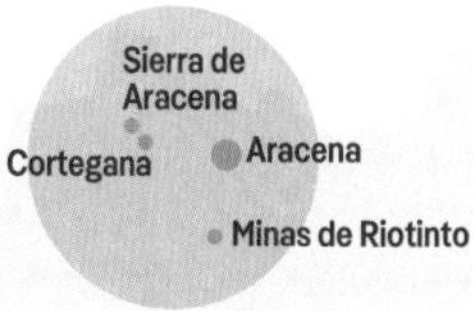

Sierra de Aracena
Cortegana
Aracena
Minas de Riotinto

Beyond Aracena

Castles, mines and countryside beguile and surprise in one of Andalucía's least visited regions.

The Sierra de Aracena stretches north and west from its namesake town, filling a large portion of the province of Huelva, which stretches from Sevilla to the Portuguese border. An undulating profusion of *dehesa* (evergreen oak groves) and verdant hills are crisscrossed by hiking trails and punctuated by picturesque castles, old stone villages and fortified churches.

The clutch of settlements and trails west of Aracena, including Alájar, Linares de la Sierra, Castaño del Robledo, Cortelazor and Almonaster la Real, are among Andalucía's finest. Further south, the land takes on a wilder aspect, striated with ochre, mauve and pewter flecks of mineral-rich soil culminating in gaping pits and a blood-red river at the Minas de Riotinto.

TOP TIP

Download maps from sierradearacena.com and ventanadelvisitante.es. Or pick up guidebook *Sierra de Aracena – A Walk!* and *Sierra de Aracena Tour & Trail Map.*

Linares de la Sierra

WHAT & WHERE TO EAT IN ARACENA

Such natural bounty is provided by the land here. Enjoy wild asparagus in spring; giant, sweet tomatoes in summer; *setas* (mushrooms) in autumn, and succulent, acorn-fed *jamón* all year round.

Rincón de Juan
Try local goat's cheese or ham *montaditos* (small sandwiches) at this rustic tapas establishment. €

Jesús Carrión
Family-run, serving contemporary Aracenan cuisine, such as local boletus mushroom and truffle oil risotto. €€€

José Vicente
Restaurant for fans of melt-in-the-mouth *jamón iberico*. Has all four grades of ham. €€€

JORGE ANASTACIO/SHUTTERSTOCK ©

Castillo de Cortegana

Hilltop Castillo de Cortegana

MEDIEVAL REAL FEEL

Cortegana (35 minutes from Aracena by car) is the quintessential Sierra de Aracena town. Its buildings are sprinkled across a ridge, and lorded over by a castle of questionable provenance. Some accounts say it was started in the 13th century by Pedro Domingo, an out-of-favour knight who had been banished to these hinterlands. Today there are some fantastic panoramic views from its walls and the castle itself has been transformed into a well-preserved museum, complete with suits of armour, tapestries and antique furniture.

WHERE TO STAY IN SIERRA DE ARACENA

Finca Buenvino
Salmon-pink farmhouse off the N433, 10km west of Aracena. Also has writing retreats and cooking courses. €€

Sierra Luz
Simple, large rooms in Cortegana with restaurant and bar attached to hotel. Car parking spaces aplenty. €

Hotel Luz Almonaster
Stylish Almonaster la Real hotel, with a sun terrace and pool out back. Breakfast included. €€

Scarred earth at Minas de Riotinto

RED RIVERS, DEEP MINES AND A MUSEUM

The mineral wealth of the Sierra Morena around Minas de Riotinto (32 minutes from Aracena by car) has long been prized. King Solomon of Jerusalem is said to have mined gold here, the Romans came for the silver and, more recently, the Brits came for the copper when forming the British Rio Tinto company in the 1870s (leading, incidentally, to the foundation of Recreativo de Huelva, Spain's first football club). Sold back to Franco's Spain in 1954, the miners clocked off for the last time in 2001.

A good place to start is the **Museo Minero**, Riotinto's excellent mining museum, where you can buy tickets to as many of the attractions as you want. The museum takes an extensive look at the social history of the mines, including plenty of rock and gemstone exhibits, a 200m walk-through replica of a Roman mine, and a room almost entirely dominated by the *Vagón del Maharajah*, a luxurious train carriage built in 1892 for Britain's Queen Victoria.

You can learn even more about the geology and natural history of these lands, especially the post-mine regeneration, at **Peña de Hierro**, plus gaze into the gullet of an opencast mine. You'll need a car to get here.

Just south of nearby Nerva is the region's highlight: **Ferrocarril Turístico-Minero**, a rickety train ride through the dig-scarred landscape, past rotting infrastructure and old trains that look as though they have been abandoned in a hurry, following the blood-red course of the Río Tinto. Its name ('red river') is due to its unusual red-brown hue from leaching iron and copper. You'll have a chance to disembark at the terminus for ten minutes before the return journey.

BEST RESTAURANTS IN SIERRA DE ARACENA

Arrieros
Unusual pork-based dishes and fantastic *sopa de tomate* (tomato soup). In Linares de la Sierra. €€€

El Padrino Particular
Alájar restaurant serving *tomatá* – a huge, sweet tomato typical of the area – as well as meat dishes. €€

Rincon de Curro
Best known for its *leche frita* dessert, a milk pudding deep-fried in eggy batter. €

THE MAIN MEZQUITA

To see a *mezquita* on a much larger scale, the Unesco-listed **Catedral de Córdoba** (p190) is one of the finest sights in Andalucía.

GETTING AROUND

Damas runs at least one daily bus to and from Sevilla to Cortegana via Alájar or Jabugo. They also run four or five local buses on weekdays between Aracena and Cortegana, often via Linares de la Sierra, Jabugo and Alájar. A daily bus to and from Huelva heads to Aracena via Cortegana. Three daily buses run between Minas de Riotinto and Huelva, but you need a car to see most of the sights there.

SIERRA DE ARACENA DRIVING TOUR

String together the highlights of this area on this one-day road trip from Cortegana to Aracena. Heading east from **1 Cortegana** along the N433, take a right onto the HU8105 after 2km. This road is a lot of fun to drive and leads you directly to **2 Almonaster la Real**.

From the free car park on your right, look out over this delightful little town and see its remarkable Islamic *mezquita*, which dates to the 9th and 10th centuries. Wander through the pleasant central square to find signs pointing out a path leading uphill to this miniature version of Córdoba's great mosque. Just below is Almonaster's 19th-century bullring.

Continue eastwards, round rolling hills covered in cork-oak forest, then turn north onto the N435. Carry on to **3 Jabugo** if you want to pick up some fine *jamón iberico* right from the source; otherwise, take a right onto HU8114 to **4 Castaño del Robledo**, an idyllic little village surrounded by sweet chestnut trees, with not one, but two, huge churches. The most interesting is Iglesia Inacabada (unfinished church).

Pressing further east, turn southwards onto the HU8121 at Fuenteheridos. A viewpoint after 2km, the **5 Mirador de Alájar**, is particularly lovely at sunset, and the nearby Peña de Arias, Montano's small chapel, is an important local pilgrimage site, due to its carving of the Virgin, the region's patron. From here, a series of switchbacks drops you into **6 Alájar**, a contender for the region's prettiest village, with its tight cobbled streets and imposing church.

At this point, you're back on the HU8105. Make one last stop in **7 Linares de la Sierra**. Whoever lays the town's cobblestones has a keen creative streak. Then it's an easy run along the final straight to **8 Aracena**.

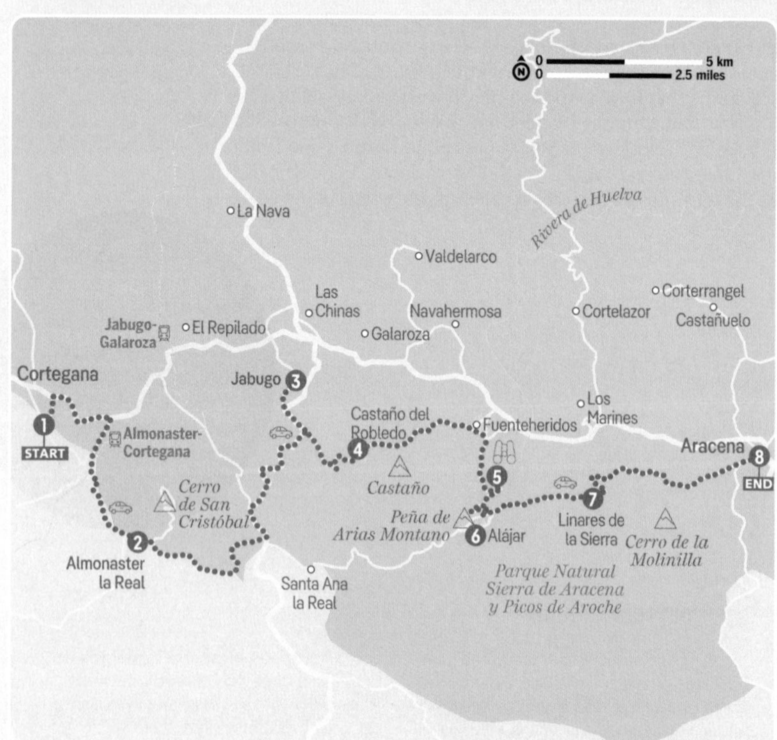

PARQUE NACIONAL DE DOÑANA

Each day, elusive Iberian lynx skulk through the scrub, flocks of flamingos paint the evening skies a pastel pink, and herds of deer bound through the *cotos* (woodland on stabilised sandy soil). Parque Nacional de Doñana has taken a vast expanse of the *marismas* (marshland), once a common feature along Huelva's coastline, and protected it from the sprawling mass of agricultural plastic blighting much of the region. The Unesco-listed wilderness, based around the Guadalquivir delta, is one of Europe's most extensive wetlands.

The 601-sq-km national park, together with bordering Parque Natural de Doñana, which is under less strict protection, provides a refuge for 360 bird, 37 mammal and 21 reptile species. Endangered species, such as the Iberian lynx and Spanish imperial eagle, have bounced back from the brink under close conservation here, despite the encroachment of human infrastructure, farming, hunters and mass tourism.

TOP TIP

Río Guadalquivir makes its merry way south after passing through Sevilla, fanning into a delta. The main course of the river forms the park's eastern border. The park then extends 30km along the Atlantic coast and up to 25km inland. Road entry is via its western flank, using the A483.

Doñana National Park tours

MARSHES, WILDLIFE AND NATURE WALKS

Although visitation to the national park is via accredited agency only, there are various companies running tours into Doñana. The most common type is land-based, with 4WD vehicles the best way to get closer to the exceptional wildlife and birdlife. Other half- and full-day tours with anywhere from four to 30 passengers are available from a flurry of operators.

The larger the vehicle and group, the less likely you'll see the more elusive creatures, such as lynx (although sightings are generally rare). Binoculars are provided on the smaller tours. Bring water and mosquito repellent. If you're lucky, you have a good chance of spotting a lynx and its cubs in the mid–late summer months. Sightings of deer, wild boar and many bird species are more likely. Dawn and dusk are the best times for sightings. Another method of entry into the park is on horseback. Guides are generally talented linguists and have a wealth of experience, information and a keen eye.

There are thought to be around 100 Iberian lynx in Doñana, although numbers tend to fluctuate lower. Sightings are highly coveted, yet they are rare for much of the year. A successful breeding programme noted that 28 pairs added 43 new cubs to Spain's lynx population in 2022 (see lynxexsitu.es for the latest). The **Centro de Visitantes el Acebuche** streams a live video of lynxes in its nearby breeding centre, which makes for pretty exciting viewing even when they're just stretching and grooming, but you can't visit them. Their biggest threat remains cars on the roads around the park.

On the opposite side of the main north–south road that flanks Doñana, close to the entrance to El Rocío, is a **visitors centre** housed inside Palace Acebrón, a former hunting lodge. It contains a museum depicting local life and customs and a rooftop viewpoint. **Sendero Charco de la Boca** is a 3.5km path from the car park through *coto* and along an *arroyo*.

BEST DOÑANA TOURS

Doñana Wings
Nobody runs tours (for exceptional bird watching) quite as well as Doñana Wings, based in Sevilla.

Doñana Nature
El Rocío-based company running private and eight- to 15-person group tours, twice daily.

Discovering Doñana
Offers 4WD private tours.

ANOTHER WAY INTO DOÑANA

While most tours enter the park from the west and south, there are some tours from **Sanlúcar de Barrameda** (p129), in Cádiz province, that cross the mouth of the Río Guadalquivir by boat.

GETTING AROUND

Taking your own vehicle into Parque Nacional de Doñana is forbidden, although you can park at El Rocío, one of the main gateways to the park, and take a guided tour from there.

The most popular option for most visitors is to take a tour from Sevilla, which handles all transportation and access issues in one go.

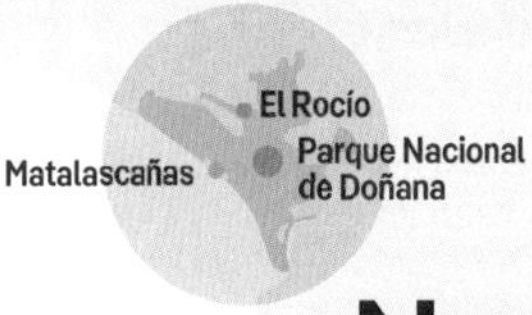

Beyond Parque Nacional de Doñana

Extended beaches, rolling sand dunes and Spain's biggest annual pilgrimage all rub shoulders with Parque Nacional de Doñana.

As the wilderness of Doñana loses its national park protection, the land is chopped up into intensively farmed quadrants. However, a few small towns with entirely different reasons for being do exist, and it is these that offer the most intrigue to visitors. El Rocío and Matalascañas, which both offer good accommodation and restaurants, are Huelva province's main bases for adventures into the Parques Nacional and Natural de Doñana.

Once a year on Whitsunday, El Rocío effervesces with the fervent thrills of the festival Romería del Rocío, as thousands of pilgrims pour into the sandy streets, bringing with them vibrant colour, music and energy. Matalascañas coasts through the summer in a lower gear, for its main function is to serve Spanish beachgoers.

TOP TIP

Staying in El Rocío is a great way to appreciate the energy of this unusual place, while also gaining more options for the varied Doñana tours.

El Rocío (p106)

A DOÑANA YEAR

Winter is vibrant on Doñana's *marismas*, as hundreds of thousands of waterbirds, including an estimated 80% of Western Europe's wild ducks, shelter from the colder north. By spring, the water levels dip, encouraging greater flamingos, herons, storks, spoonbills, avocets, hoopoes, bee-eaters and albatrosses to come and nest around the *lucios* (ponds). By late summer, some of them will move on as the marshes dry out, but the Iberian lynx will be more active in the *cotos*. Genets, wildcats, wild boar, numerous species of birds, and red and fallow deer also roam these areas. Raptors have a good time of it too. Kites and Spanish imperial eagles wheel overhead. By October, the *marismas* start to fill up again and, thanks to the park's protection, the cycle repeats.

Spain's holy wild west

SANDY STREETS AND A HOLY RELIC

The emptiness and the profusion of horses in **El Rocío** lend it a Wild West vibe. But what makes this town feel like no other are the various well-tended buildings belonging to 115 *hermandades* (brotherhoods) and, in the right season, the flamingo-dotted wetlands fringing the town.

Only around 700 people live in El Rocío, so the sand-blown streets are often empty and the wide plaza in front of the brilliant white **Ermita del Rocío** can seem desolate. Within the shrine is a small wooden image of the Virgin, draped in long robes. She is what all the fuss on Whitsunday is about. **Nuestra Señora del Rocío** (Our Lady of El Rocío) also draws visitors and colourful celebrations on weekends.

As the main gateway to Parque Nacional de Doñana, El Rocío is fringed by *marismas*, where herds of deer drink at dawn, horses graze and, at certain times of year, flocks of flamingos gather in massive numbers. **Francisco Bernis Birdwatching Centre**, operated by Spain's national bird conservation group SEO Birdlife, has an excellent hide and observation deck on the southeastern edge of town.

Spain's greatest religious pilgrimage

ROMERÍA DEL ROCÍO

Seven weeks after Easter, on the Pentecost (Whitsunday) weekend, El Rocío's empty, Wild West vibe is transmogrified by up to one million jubilant pilgrims.

It all began when a hunter in the 13th century stopped to rest in the *coto* scrub and the image of the Virgin appeared to him. The rest is fervent history. Pilgrims, led by 115 *hermandades*, come from all over the country to worship a small image of Nuestra Señora del Rocío.

The climax revolves around who gets to carry the Virgin out of the church on a float in the wee hours of Monday morning. The local Almonte *hermandad* naturally have the greatest claim. It's an intense crush and, lamentably, horses have been known to die, despite the presence of voluntary veterinary services. Fortunately, in recent years, Spaniards' rising concern for animal rights is drawing attention to this fact.

WHERE TO STAY IN EL ROCÍO & MATALASCAÑAS

Hotel La Malvasía
Spectacular frontage and some beautiful rooms with floor-to-ceiling windows looking out onto the marsh. **€€**

La Fonda del Rocío
Cheery *hostal* with leafy outdoor patios and simple rooms along a quintessentially dusty El Rocío street. **€€**

Hospedería el Cazadero Real
Horse murals, Romería paintings and a great rooftop view of the Ermita del Rocío and *marismas*. **€**

Storks, Parque Nacional de Doñana

BEST PLACES TO EAT IN EL ROCÍO

ires de Doñana
Andalucian food, exceptional view of the Ermita and marshes. Primarily seafood, but some vegan options. €€€

La Pastelería Pizzas
Pizza, *bocadillos* (sandwiches) and cake make this a good option for tasty food on the go. €

Restaurante Toruño
Traditional Andalucian atmosphere on a shaded square. Specialises in shellfish and meats. €€€

Matalascañas

NATURE AND BEACHES

A resort town primarily serving the domestic market, Matalascañas is hemmed into a 1km chunk of coastline and surrounded by Parque Nacional de Doñana. The small wire fence at the town's eastern edge is all that protects the sand dunes of **Parque Dunar** from the developers here. Wooden boardwalks wind their way up, over and into this extensive dune system.

Horse-riding tours are also provided by a number of companies. Try **Hipica Doñana the Pasodoble**, located at the town's entrance.

Playa de Matalascañas runs for 30km, ending at the Playa de Mazagón. The tall dunes behind this beach, cut through with the occasional boardwalk, make this Huelva's most dramatic coastal area.

ANDALUCÍA'S OTHER NATIONAL PARKS

Despite the vast tracts of natural beauty that make Andalucía so special, only the **Sierra de las Nieves** (p166), west of Málaga, and **Sierra Nevada** (p244), between Granada and Almería, enjoy national park status.

GETTING AROUND

Damas (damas-sa.es) runs buses from Sevilla's Plaza de Armas to El Rocío (two daily, 90 minutes), continuing to Matalascañas (another 25 minutes). There's no direct bus from Huelva to El Rocío (you can take one to Aymonte and change), but it's an easy 50-minute drive to Matalascañas if you've got your own wheels.

Vejer de la Frontera (p136)

CÁDIZ & GIBRALTAR

CULTURAL HEARTLAND WITH BEACHES

The sultry south entices with its sugar-white beaches, original bastions of soulful flamenco, timeless *pueblos blancos* (white towns) and some of Andalucía's best seafood.

If any one region encapsulates Andalucía's cultural complexity and natural beauty, it's Cádiz. The fortunes of Spain's southernmost province have been profoundly shaped by its relationship with the sea. Phoenicians, Romans and Europe's last Neanderthals were all drawn here by the warm climate and bountiful supplies of fish, and the region's bluefin-tuna season now draws foodies from all over the world.

The sea is also the raison d'être for the kitesurf-cool towns of Tarifa and Los Caños de Meca, as well as the naval base and British enclave of Gibraltar, nestling in the shadow of the great limestone monolith and nature reserve of the Rock. It also beckons sun-worshippers to the string of mostly uncrowded white-sand beaches and laid-back small towns along the Costa de la Luz, the province's 200km-long 'spine'.

Inland you'll find other craggy mountains in the hikers' playgrounds of Sierra de Grazalema and Los Alcornocales natural parks, plus beautifully situated *pueblos blancos* (Vejer, Grazalema, Arcos...) that once marked the contested border between Moorish Granada and Christian Spain (hence their 'de la Frontera' suffix).

In the north of the province, Jerez forms part of the Sherry Triangle along with Sanlúcar and Puerto de Santa María. The bastion of Andalucian culture also showcases flamenco in its rawest, purest incarnation, while coastal Cádiz – home to Spain's biggest Carnaval – is the loveliest and most understated of all Andalucian cities.

DULCE RUBIA/SHUTTERSTOCK ©

THE MAIN AREAS

CÁDIZ
Architecture, tapas, flamenco, seafood, beaches. p114

JEREZ DE LA FRONTERA
Andalucian culture, sherry, architecture, flamenco, dining. p125

PARQUE NATURAL SIERRA DE GRAZALEMA
Rugged mountains, hiking, *pueblos blancos*. p130

TARIFA
Water sports, whale-watching, beaches. p138

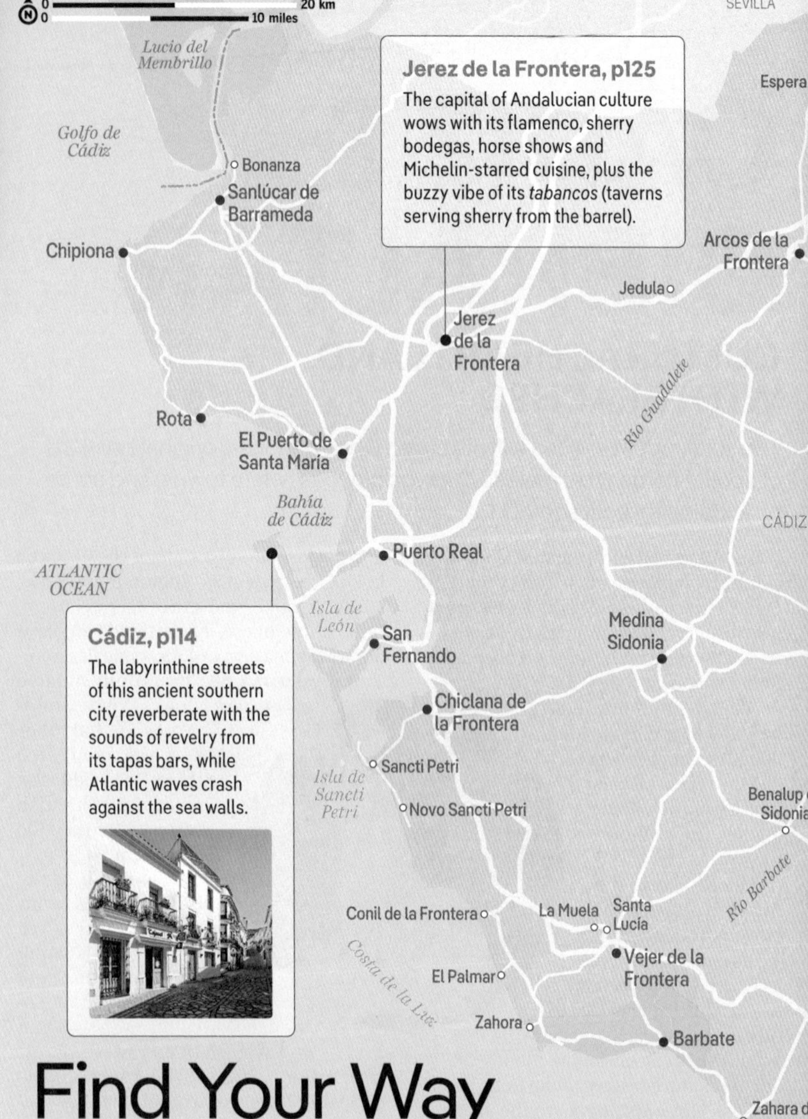

Find Your Way

The Cádiz province is Andalucía's most southerly one, and its attractions are many and rather spread out. We've picked the places that best capture its cultural heritage, culinary legacy and natural landscapes.

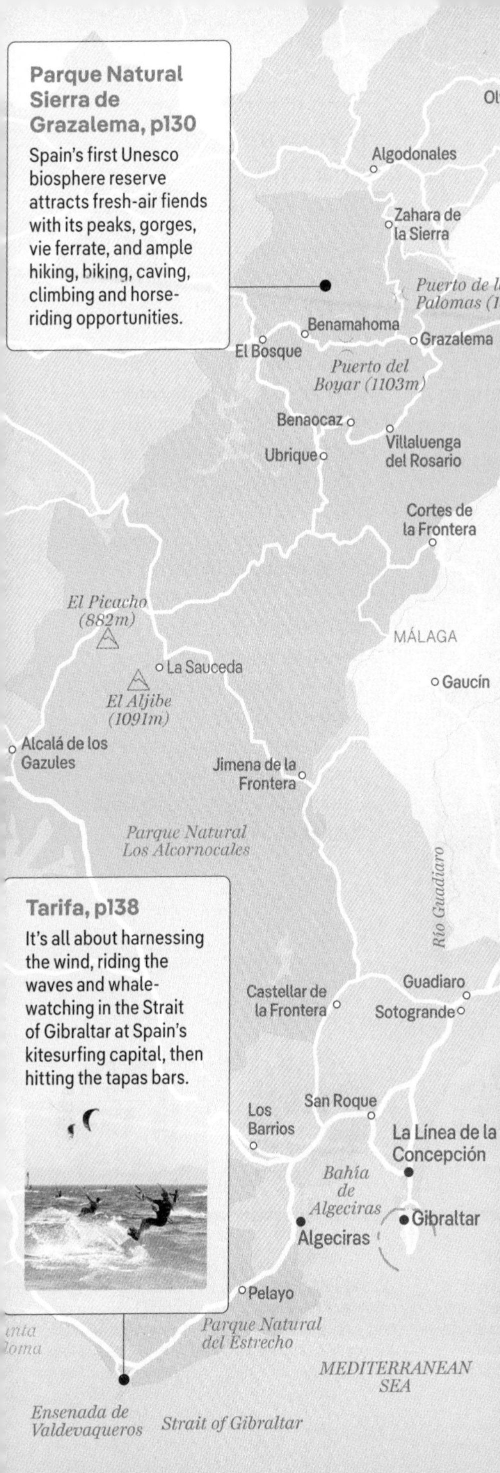

Parque Natural Sierra de Grazalema, p130

Spain's first Unesco biosphere reserve attracts fresh-air fiends with its peaks, gorges, vie ferrate, and ample hiking, biking, caving, climbing and horse-riding opportunities.

Tarifa, p138

It's all about harnessing the wind, riding the waves and whale-watching in the Strait of Gibraltar at Spain's kitesurfing capital, then hitting the tapas bars.

BOAT

The quickest and easiest way to travel between Cádiz and Puerto de Santa María is by boat. CMTBC (cmtbc.es) offers frequent catamaran departures daily.

BUS

Buses serve most destinations and are a cost-effective way of getting around, though visiting remoter *pueblos blancos* requires more planning due to infrequency of services. The main bus companies are Comes (tgcomes.es), Damas (damas-sa.es), Monbus (monbus.es) and CMTBC (cmtbc.es).

CAR

Having your own wheels gives you the most flexibility. There are rental outlets at both Gibraltar and Jerez airports; Jerez tends to have the cheaper rates, but it's a good idea to book in advance.

TRAIN

There are frequent Renfe trains from Cádiz to Puerto de Santa María, Jerez, Jerez airport and Sevilla, with onward services to Madrid.

Plan Your Time

The Cádiz province is a place to meander. Pootle along the coast, stopping to check out unpeopled white-sand beaches, or meander inland to explore *pueblos blancos* and hike rugged mountain trails.

PHOTOOIASSON/GETTY IMAGES ©

Mercado Central de Abastos (p119)

If you only do one thing

- Spend the day wandering Cádiz's historic centre and touring the city's main sights. Grab some breakfast at the **Mercado Central de Abastos** (p119), then stroll the seafront promenade, taking in Alameda Apodaca, Parque del Genovés and Playa de la Caleta before climbing up the cathedral bell tower for all-encompassing views of the city. Grab some lunch at **Sonámbulo** (p115).

- In the afternoon, take in the **Teatro Romano** (p118) and the excellent **Museo de Cádiz** (p119), wander the narrow lanes of Barrio de San Juan, browsing its quirky shops, then hit the tapas bars of Barrio de la Viña, including **Casa Manteca** (p115).

Seasonal highlights

The province hosts festivals year-round. Carnaval is celebrated in a massive way, May–June is of particular import to tuna-lovers, while September brings sherry celebrations.

FEBRUARY

Cádiz hosts its exuberant Carnaval, with costumed revelry, while Jerez celebrates flamenco during the Festival de Jerez.

APRIL

Extravagant Semana Santa celebrations, particularly in Arcos de la Frontera, with floats and processions of the faithful.

MAY

Almadraba season attracts foodies to Costa de la Luz, while sherry aficionados flock to Sanlúcar and Puerto de Santa María.

PABLOAVANZINI/SHUTTERSTOCK ©, ROBERT PAUL VAN BEETS/SHUTTERSTOCK ©, BARMALINI/GETTY IMAGES ©

Travel around for three days

- Drive south for a morning hike along **Sendero del Acantilado** (p124), high above the Costa de la Luz in Parque Natural de la Breña y Marísmas de Barbate. Head to gritty Barbate for a blowout lunch at **El Campero** (p143) if it's *almadraba* (tuna-fishing) season, then spend the afternoon exploring **Vejer de la Frontera** (p136) and dining at **La Judería** (p136).

- On day three, swing by Zahara de los Atunes for a spell on its splendid white-sand beach, or visit the Roman site of **Baelo Claudia** (p121), then take an afternoon whale- and dolphin-watching **tour** (p138) from Tarifa and dine at **El Lola** (p139).

If you have more time

- Ideally, you need a couple of weeks to explore the Cádiz province. Spend a day in **Gibraltar** (p144), venturing to the lofty heights of the Rock on foot. Then head back north, to **Jerez de la Frontera** (p125), for a couple of days' deep dive into traditional Andalucian culture, visiting sherry bodegas, horse shows, *tabancos* and flamenco bars. If you're a sherry aficionado, continue your education elsewhere in the Sherry Triangle.

- If you're a fresh-air fiend, allow several days for hiking and cycling in **Parque Natural Sierra de Grazalema** (p130) and touring *pueblos blancos*, such as Grazalema and Sentenil de las Bodegas.

JUNE

A terrific time for whale-watching off the coast of Tarifa, with orcas and other pelagics drawn by bluefin-tuna shoals.

JULY

Vejer de la Frontera welcomes Spanish and international jazz musicians with an early-July jazz fest and 'gastrojazz' events.

SEPTEMBER

Jerez's two-week Fiestas de la Vendimia involve sherry, *bulerías* (fast flamenco), horse riding and crushing the season's first grapes.

OCTOBER

A month of grape harvests, longer nights, milder temperatures and local food festivals, including cheese tasting and *jamón*-cutting.

CÁDIZ

Sevilla
Cádiz

Founded as Gadir by the Phoenicians in 1100 BCE, sultry, occasionally soporific Cádiz is Europe's oldest continuously inhabited settlement and Spain's most appealing port city. Four millennia of history have left their mark on the ancient centre, surrounded almost entirely by water (and originally an island), rich in historic sights and graceful, centuries-old architecture. Eminently walkable, the city is a pleasure to explore on foot, whether you're perusing its quirky art shops or strolling past the vast rubber figs and spiky dragon trees in the seafront Alameda Apodaca gardens. Less touristy and crowded than its much busier neighbours of Málaga and Sevilla, Cádiz offers a genuinely laid-back Andalucian experience.

There is much to explore here, from the long white-sand beaches further south to the narrow, atmospheric lanes of the centre, with its characterful *barrios* (neighbourhoods), old-school tapas bars packed to the gills with garrulous *gaditanos* (Cádiz residents) and soulful flamenco joints.

TOP TIP

The historic heart of Cádiz sits on a peninsula, fringed by a seafront promenade. Its grids of narrow, centuries-old lanes are split between distinct *barrios* and are best explored on foot. There's underground parking off the Avenida del Puerto, with the ferry terminal and train station just east of the centre.

KNOW YOUR MURGAS

Coros Groups of 30 or so costumed performers, touring on extravagant floats and singing with guitars, mandolins and lutes.

Comparsas Fifteen-strong bands, marching to an accompaniment of guitars and drums.

Chirigotas The jokers of the pack, these groups of 10 wander around Cadiz's bars, singing satirical songs about local events to the tune of *pitos* (reed whistles).

Trios, quartetos, quintetos Small groups performing satirical sketches.

Carnaval!

MAINLAND SPAIN'S MOST EXUBERANT CARNIVAL

If you happen to be in Cádiz between 16 and 26 February, don your best costume and join the *gaditanos* for Spain's biggest, liveliest 10-day singing, dancing and drinking street party (codigocarnaval.com), complete with float parades, street food, fireworks, over 300 *murgas* (bands) and non-stop day and night action.

Carnaval dates back to the 15th century, when the tradition of costumed revelry was imported to Cádiz by homesick Genoese merchants. Banned by military authorities between 1936 and 1948 during the Spanish Civil War and beyond (though it still took place illegally behind closed doors), and tightly controlled during Franco's dictatorship, the fiesta assumed its present exuberant form only in 1977.

A 19th-century customs official, Antonio Rodríguez Martínez (aka El Tío de la Tiza, or 'Chalky'), organised the *murgas* competing in the Carnaval into four main groups: *coros*, *comparsas*, *chirigotas* and the smaller *trios*, *quartetos* and *quintetos*. The performers road-test their witty, bawdy songs, sketches and satirical compositions during the Erizada (sea-urchin party) and Ostionada (oyster party) the two weekends prior to Carnaval before being judged by a panel at the **Gran Teatro Falla**. You can catch the *murgas* in action around the working-class Barrio de la Viña, outside the beautiful yellow-domed **Catedral**, and between the Mercado Central de Abastos (p119) and **Playa de la Caleta**. *Ilegales* – anarchic bands of families and friends who don't compete officially but make a lot of noise! – congregate around Plaza de Topete.

If you haven't booked accommodation months in advance, you won't find a room in Cádiz, but you have the option of staying in Puerto de Santa María or Sevilla instead, and catching ferries or trains packed with costumed revellers to Cádiz during the day.

Cádiz's tapas & tipples

BUZZY BARS AND DELECTABLE BITES

By 8.30pm, a patient queue of locals is already waiting outside **El Faro de Cádiz**. As soon as the doors open, everyone files inside, either to lean on the bar, glass of *manzanilla* in hand, or perch on high chairs in the tile-clad interior. After inhaling some superlative *tortillitas de camarones* (shrimp fritters) or vegetarian-friendly *patatas aliñadas*, move on to the tiny Plaza Tío de la Tiza nearby, elbow your way into **Casa Manteca**, covered in *torero* (bullfighter), flamenco, and Carnaval paraphernalia, and order the *chicharrones* (pork scratchings) or *payoyo* cheese with asparagus marmalade, and the waiters will pass it your way on waxed paper, along with glasses of *oloroso* or *fino* (dry and straw-coloured sherry).

Next, pay a visit to **La Tabernita**, the most popular haunt along Barrio de la Viña's liveliest street. This family-run place excels at creative home-style cooking, so perch on a stool at a street-side table, and chow down on *cazón al coñac* (dogfish in brandy) or cuttlefish-in-ink 'meatballs'.

Move on to rustic-industrial **La Candela** in Barrio de San Juan, which surprises with its floral-stamped windows and rustic-industrial decor. Prop up the bar and watch as strawberry *salmorejo* sauce with tuna tartare and other inspired Andalucian-Asian fusion tapas sails your way from the open kitchen.

If you have any room left, finish off with a visit to Barrio del Mentidero for some kick-ass *arróz meloso con atún* (soupy rice with tuna) or *fideos al ajillo* (garlicky vermicelli) at the funky **Recreo Chico**.

BEST CREATIVE DINING

Sonámbulo
Retro restaurant with rustic furnishings celebrates ingredients from the Cádiz province, with numerous farm-to-table and sea-to-table offerings. €€

Restaurante Contraseña
Dutch chef combines *gaditano* and Andalucian culinary traditions with personal flair, pairing lamb with lavender and prawns with sherry. €€

Código de Barra
Playful seasonal tasting menus capture Cádiz's diverse history in exquisite, beautifully presented platefuls. €€

La Curiosidad de Mauro Barreiro
Local dishes reimagined by one curious local chef, with flavours influenced by his travels. Separate bar and dining-room menus. €€€

WHERE TO SLEEP ON A BUDGET IN CÁDIZ

Casa Caracol
Solar-powered backpacker haunt, with colourful dorms, hammock-y roof terrace, and bike and surfboard rental. €

Planeta Cádiz
Smart bunks with privacy curtains, airy doubles, family rooms with terraces, bike rental and free tours. €

Pension España
Tile-clad historical building with wrought-iron features and snug singles and doubles with shared bathrooms. €

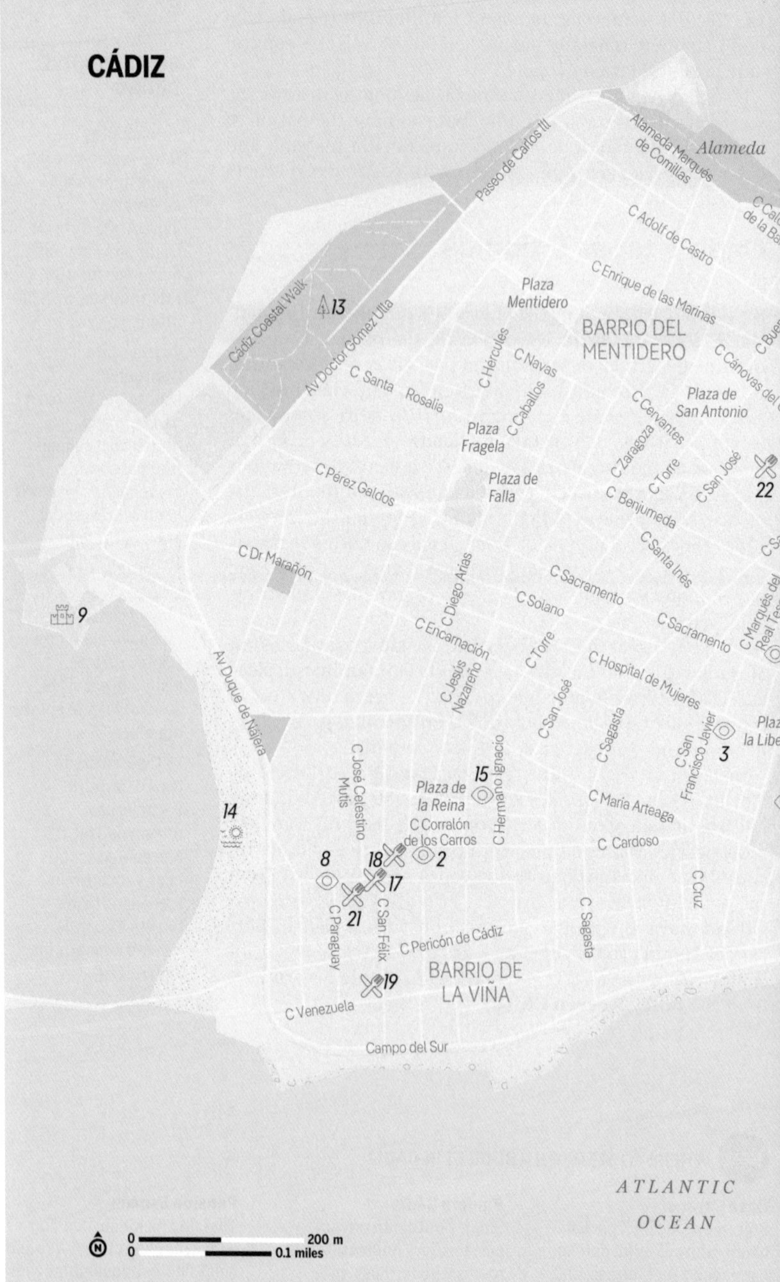
CÁDIZ
Alameda
Alameda Marqués de Comillas
Paseo de Carlos III
C Adolf de Castro
C Enrique de las Marinas
Plaza Mentidero
BARRIO DEL MENTIDERO
Cádiz Coastal Walk
13
Av Doctor Gómez Ulla
C Santa Rosalía
C Hércules
C Navas
C Caballos
Plaza Fragela
Plaza de San Antonio
C Cánovas del Ca
C Cervantes
C Zaragoza
C Torre
C San José
22
Plaza de Falla
C Pérez Galdos
C Benjumeda
C Santa Inés
C Dr Marañón
C Diego Arias
C Sacramento
C Solano
C Encarnación
C Marqués del Real Tesoro
9
C Torre
C Hospital de Mujeres
Av Duque de Nájera
C Jesús Nazareño
C San José
C Sagasta
C San Francisco Javier
3
Plaza la Liber
C José Celestino Mutis
Plaza de la Reina
15
C Hermano Ignacio
C María Arteaga
14
C Corralón de los Carros
C Cardoso
8
18
2
17
21
C Paraguay
C San Félix
C Cruz
C Sagasta
C Pericón de Cádiz
BARRIO DE LA VIÑA
19
C Venezuela
Campo del Sur
ATLANTIC OCEAN
200 m
0.1 miles

SIGHTS

1 Alameda Apodaca
2 Barrio de la Viña
3 Barrio de San Juan
4 Barrio de Santa María
5 Barrio del Mentidero
6 Barrio del Pópulo
7 Calle Ancha
8 Calle Virgen de la Palma
9 Castillo de Santa Catalina
10 Catedral de Cádiz
11 Mercado Central de Abastos
12 Museo de Cádiz
13 Parque del Genovés
14 Playa de la Caleta
15 Plaza Tío de la Tiza
16 Teatro Romano

EATING

17 Calle Virgen de la Palma
18 Casa Manteca
19 El Faro de Cádiz
20 La Candela
21 La Tabernita
22 Recreo Chico

WHY I LOVE CÁDIZ

Anna Kaminski, Lonely Planet writer. *@ACKaminski*

I've been in love with this laid-back southern city ever since I first set foot here as a young backpacker. I instantly took to it – the clamour of the central market, the buzz of the narrow streets around the cathedral, the languor of spending an afternoon beneath the fig trees of Plaza de Mina, the good-natured jostling in the crowded tapas bars. One of my favourite things is an early-morning walk around old Cádiz along the seafront promenade, padding barefoot on the smooth marble tiles in the parks.

JOSERPIZARRO/SHUTTERSTOCK ©

Barrio de la Viña

Exploring Cádiz's barrios

ATMOSPHERIC STREETS, PLAZAS AND SIGHTS

Old Cádiz is split into distinct *barrios*. The oldest part of the city is the cobbled **Barrio del Pópulo**, a formerly run-down maze of lanes and now one of the nightlife spots. It's home to Cádiz's baroque-neoclassical yellow-domed **cathedral**, best appreciated from seafront Campo del Sur at sunset. Inside, don't miss the intricate wood-carved choir (one of Andalucía's finest) and, in the crypt, the tomb of renowned 20th-century *gaditano* composer Manuel de Falla (1876–1946). The entrance fee includes the **bell tower**; ascend the ramp for 360-degree views of the old city, the cathedral's dome and Cádiz's 129 remaining 18th-century watchtowers.

WHERE TO DRINK IN CÁDIZ

Taberna Manzanilla
Drink *manzanilla* from the giant oak barrel at this 1930s sherry tavern plastered with bullfighting posters. €

La Colonial
Stylish bar with sea-view tables on the promenade, a wealth of original cocktails and rare sherries. €€

Rollin' Rock Pub
Sip an IPA to a rock soundtrack beneath posters of Muddy Waters and the Doobie Brothers. €

Tucked away nearby, the **Teatro Romano** was built in the 1st century BCE and would make or break the careers of actors before an audience of 10,000 spectators. Wander amid the restored seating, and peruse the attached museum and the impressive vomitorium beneath the seating area.

Squeezed between Barrio del Pópulo and Cádiz's train station to the east is **Barrio de Santa María**, the old Roma quarter and one of the original homes of flamenco.

Northwest of Barrio del Pópulo, **Barrio de San Juan** centres on the **Mercado Central de Abastos** – Spain's oldest covered market (1838) – with its kaleidoscope of produce stalls and adjoining tapas bars, and the intimate, flower-filled Plaza de Topete. Nearby, the 18th-century **Torre Tavira** is Cádiz's loftiest point; inside, you can spy on people strolling along nearby streets using the camera obscura that projects moving images onto a screen. A couple of blocks north, the historic Calle Ancha is the city's main (pedestrianised) shopping street.

Sitting between Barrio de San Juan and the sea is **Barrio de la Viña**, the old fishing quarter, bisected by the lively Calle Virgen de la Palma, epicentre of Carnaval (p114), and home to some of the city's best tapas bars. Hugging the *barrio*'s western flank, the golden-sand Playa de la Caleta is bookended by the star-shaped, 16th-century **Castillo de Santa Catalina** and a slim stone causeway that juts out into the sea, with walkers lashed by Atlantic spray en route to the polygonal **Castillo de San Sebastián** (1706).

The 18th-century **Barrio del Mentidero** (named after rumours spread on its streets), in the affluent northern part of Cádiz, encompasses the **Gran Teatro Falla**, where Cádiz's annual Carnaval competitions are held; the triangular Plaza Mentidero with its buzzy bars; the beautifully landscaped seafront **parks** – Parque del Genovés and Alameda Apodaca, and the large Plaza de San Antonio. Another highlight is the tree-lined Plaza de Mina, home to the fantastic **Museo de Cádiz**, with its Phoenician marble sarcophagi carved in human likeness, a wealth of Roman statuary and artefacts, and an excellent fine-art collection comprising Spanish art from the 17th to early 20th centuries.

BEST BOUTIQUE HOTELS

Casa de Las Cuatro Torres
Rooms at this 18th-century mansion have stone walls, heavy wood beams, vaulted ceilings and skylights. €€€

Casa Canovas
Luxury fabrics, marble and chandeliers feature at this sensitively updated townhouse hotel. €€€

Hotel Argantonio
Choose Mudéjar-inspired or 'colonial romantic' rooms at this super-central 18th-century home. €€

La Sal by Pillow
Intimate hotel a stone's throw from the cathedral, with fresh, bright rooms. €€

CÁDIZ'S ROMAN HERITAGE

If you've been inspired by your visit to Cádiz's Teatro Romano and want to delve deeper into the Roman history of the province, take to the **Roman trail** (p121).

GETTING AROUND

Cádiz's Old Town is extremely walkable. There are numerous narrow one-way lanes, so if you've driven here, leave your car in an underground car park off Avenida del Puerto. The train station and ferry terminal are both within easy walking distance of the Old Town.

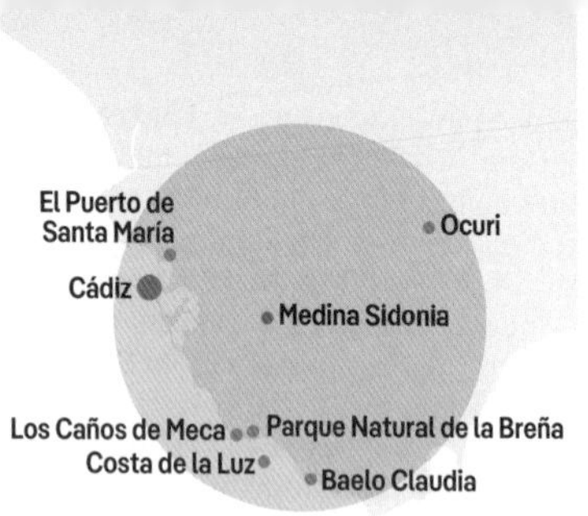

El Puerto de Santa María
Ocuri
Cádiz
Medina Sidonia
Los Caños de Meca
Parque Natural de la Breña
Costa de la Luz
Baelo Claudia

Beyond Cádiz

Cross the bay to the sherry haven of Puerto Santa María, or explore Roman remains, food-centric towns and protected areas.

Cádiz's environs are rich in attractions and Roman remains. Reachable by frequent ferry, its nearest neighbour, Puerto de Santa María, is the southernmost point of the Sherry Triangle and an enjoyable day trip from the city.

A gateway to the northern reaches of Costa de la Luz, Cádiz is an easy drive from the white-sand beaches further south, starting with the city-side strips of sand and ending in the gritty fishing port of Barbate. It's worth taking the slow route through tiny towns along the coast, and hiking high above it in Parque Natural de la Breña, to fully appreciate the natural beauty of the area. During *almadraba* tuna season, eat your heart out along the *ruta de atún*.

TOP TIP

Foodies will want to be sure they're in the area in May–June, during the height of the bluefin-tuna catch.

Baelo Claudia

Cádiz's Roman trail

ROMAN SITES AND HISTORICAL HERITAGE

Before the Moors and the Christian kings, Cádiz province was shaped by six centuries of Roman rule, and vestiges of their civilisation remain in **Gadez** (Cádiz) and beyond.

Detour inland to whitewashed **Medina Sidonia** (Assido-Caesarina) to check out the excavated 1st-century **Cardo Maximus** – the town's main Roman road (look for a child's game etched into a paving stone), plus the archaeology museum with its remarkable underground Roman sewers.

The star of the Costa de la Luz is oceanfront **Baelo Claudia**, overlooking the magnificent Playa de Bolonia and accessed via its namesake village. Thriving on fish-salting and trade with North Africa during the reign of Emperor Claudius (41–54 CE), it was eventually abandoned following a major 3rd-century earthquake. Peruse the museum, then follow the trail through the ruins, past the remnants of the aqueduct and the **Puerta de Carteia** – the town's main gate – before visiting the well-preserved forum, its temples to Jupiter, Minerva, Juno and Isis, the adjoining basilica and the baths. The restored theatre hosts concerts and plays in July–August.

Inland, in the Sierra de Grazalema, you can walk in the Romans' footsteps along an ancient **Roman stone path** that traverses olive groves and cork-oak woodland, connecting the dramatically situated village of Benaocaz with the leather-making town of Ubrique. The Roman town of **Ocuri**, with its surviving tomb, baths, cisterns and dwelling remains, is spectacularly situated 4km from Benaocaz.

BEST ROMAN MUSEUMS

Museo de Cádiz
Reconstructed Roman shipwreck, complete with *garum* amphorae, giant marble Trajan and plenty of statuary.

Conjunto Arqueológico Baelo Claudia
Extensive finds from the nearby site, including mosaics, funerary paraphernalia, coins, oil lamps and adornments.

Yacimiento Arqueológico Romano Carteia
Remnants of a Roman town near Gibraltar, with a temple, salting factory, theatre and villa ruins.

Puerto de Santa María sherry trail

SHERRY TASTINGS, SEAFOOD AND BEACHES

There are three main reasons to take the ferry across the bay from Cádiz or a train from Jerez to this port town: sherry bodegas, outstanding seafood and white-sand beaches. Part of the Sherry Triangle, the town's half-dozen wineries host guided tours that take you through the various stages of sherry production.

An intimate, family-run, 1838-founded sherry winery, **Bodegas Gutiérrez Colosía** is found right beside the catamaran dock. Tours (Monday to Saturday, €15) end with a six-wine tasting. After-dark bodega visits are held from July to September.

ROMAN HERITAGE ON THE SIDE

Delve further into Cádiz's Roman history by visiting the city's **Teatro Romano** (p118), or explore other trails of the **Sierra de Grazalema** (p131) if you're looking for spectacular hiking alongside visiting Roman ruins.

WHERE TO TAPEAR IN PUERTO DE SANTA MARÍA

Bespoke
Snug, rustic-chic sherry and tapas bar, with over 100 wines, and nibbles such as *pescaíto frito* (assorted fried fish). €

Toro Tapas
'Cathedral bodega' with refined tapas, such as Cádiz cheeses with Grazalema honey, and Atlantic prawns. €€

Bar Vicente Los Pepes
Century-old institution, decked out with atmospheric photos. *Atún encebollado* (tuna in onion sauce) is a speciality. €

You'll have seen the giant black-bull billboards all over Spain; now taste the wares of El Puerto's best-known sherry winery. Founded in 1772 by an Englishman, Thomas Osborne Mann, **Bodegas Osborne** offers daily tours (€18) of its ultra-modern production facilities, finishing with a four-wine degustation; book ahead. The superb gift shop stocks the full range, including rare and VORS sherries.

At the far side of town, two-hour tours (Thursday to Saturday, €14) of **Bodegas Caballero** (caballero.es), around since the 1830s, take in both the 'wine cathedral' and the 13th-century Castillo de San Marcos near the waterfront, owned by the same family.

Beyond the bodegas, El Puerto's popular white-sand **beaches** include the 3km-long Playa de Santa Catalina, lined with hopping beach bars, and Playa de Valdelagrana on the eastern side of the Río Guadalete, also with lively *marisquerías* (seafood restaurants).

GARUM: ROME'S KETCHUP

As highly prized as caviar today, and as ubiquitous as ketchup, the Roman Empire's favourite condiment, *garum*, was produced in the Cádiz province in great quantities, if the giant fermentation vats and jars found along the coast are anything to go by.

The quality of *garum* varied dramatically. The upper echelons of Roman society favoured the good stuff, composed of entire fish (mackerel for preference, followed by tuna) fermented with salt and costing as much as US$500 per bottle in today's terms, while the lower classes and slaves had to make do with the cheap equivalent, made of fish guts, blood and salt.

Pungent testimony to the enduring human craving for umami, *garum* factories were kept well away from urban centres, but when the wind blew, well...

Tuna time!

AGE-OLD FISHING SPECTACLE FOR GOURMANDS

Whether you're a killer whale or a Japanese fishing vessel catering to a tuna-loving public, you'll likely find yourself hanging out at the entrance to the Strait of Gibraltar between late April and June, when shoals of *atún rojo* (bluefin tuna) – the largest and most sought-after of the tuna family – migrate from the Atlantic to the Mediterranean to spawn, and which form the bedrock of the Cádiz province's coastal gastronomy.

For millennia, since the Phoenician period (and probably much earlier), fishermen along the Costa de la Luz have taken advantage of this natural bounty. For centuries they've used a fishing technique developed by the Phoenicians and still referred to by the Moorish name *almadraba* ('place for hitting') to lift the tuna out of the sea en masse with nets, drag them ashore and club them to death.

Today, *almadraba* is practised by fishers in Tarifa, Barbate, Zahara de los Atunes and Conil de la Frontera, and involves a circle of fishing boats corralling the fish into a huge net in the middle before the gaffing of the tuna turns the sea red and the *levantá* (lifting of the nets) occurs. Visitors can witness this age-old spectacle via boat trips with **Cádiz Atlántica** (cadizatlantica.com), a sustainable-tourism initiative; allow several days to ensure optimal maritime weather. Alternatively, try *atún rojo* at some of the best local establishments.

WHERE TO EAT IN LOS CAÑOS AND ZAHORA

Las Dunas
Super-relaxed cafe with driftwood sculpture, heaped *platos combinados* and occasional concerts. **€**

Arohaz
Dishes influenced by the chef's global wanderings dominate at this gastrobar; superb *arroces* (rice dishes), too. **€€**

La Bruma
Run by two Patricias, whose creative menu has local classics with a global spin and a killer *tiramisu con whisky*. **€**

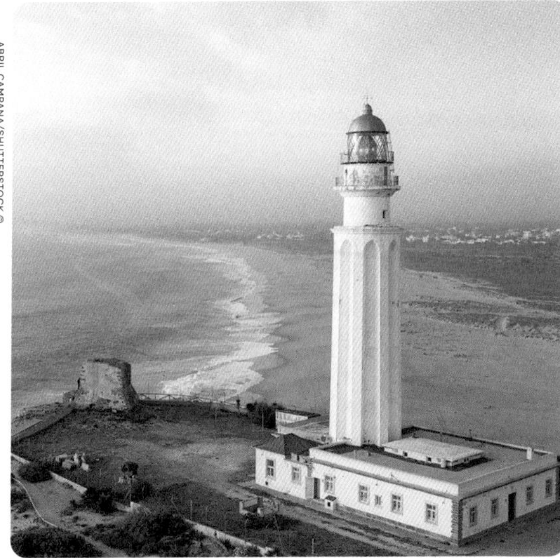

Faro de Trafalgar

Barbate's renowned **El Campero** restaurant serves remarkable 12-course tuna menus (€98) featuring every part of the fish. Reservations essential.

BEST SEAFOOD IN PUERTO DE SANTA MARÍA

Aponiente
Helmed by chef Ángel León, Andalucía's first triple-Michelin-starred restaurant serves uber-imaginative, frequently changing tasting menus (€270). €€€

Restaurante Romerijo
Perch outside this cheap and cheerful place, and order from six types of *langostino* (prawn). €

La Taberna del Chef del Mar
Ángel León's down-to-earth *taberna* (tavern), specialising in sustainably caught seafood. €€

Hiking around Los Caños de Meca & Parque Natural de la Breña

SPLENDID COASTAL TRAILS AND VIEWPOINTS

Surrounded by pine groves, laid-back **Los Caños de Meca**, 16km southwest of Vejer, stretches along a spectacular white-sand beach with freshwater springs *(caños)*. Once a hippie haven, Los Caños still attracts beach lovers of all kinds and nations – especially in summer – with its alternative, hedonistic scene and secluded coves housing nudist beaches, as well as kitesurfing, windsurfing and board-surfing opportunities. It is also a jumping-off point for superb coastal hikes.

From the western end of the seafront, it's a beautiful 20-minute walk along a traffic-free road branching off the main Avenida Trafalgar drag to the landmark 1860 lighthouse, **Faro de Trafalgar**. Battered by Atlantic

MORE SHERRY?

Continue your oenophile education at the celebrated sherry bodegas and *tabancos* in **Jerez** (p125) and sample the unique *manzanilla* sherry in **Sanlúcar de Barrameda**, its sole place of origin (p129).

WHERE TO STAY IN LOS CAÑOS

Casas Karen
Stay in thatched *chozas* (traditional huts), a converted farmhouse or modern, split-level 'studios'. €€

Palomar de la Breña
Inside Parque Natural de la Breña, this 18th-century *cortijo* (farmhouse) turned hotel is a fantastic base for hikers. €€€

Hotel Madreselva
This hacienda-style hotel offers comfy rooms with terraces, a pool, and surfing and kitesurfing courses. €€

BEST PLACES TO BUY ALMADRABA TUNA

During *almadraba* season, follow the *ruta del atún* (rutadelatun.com) to sate your tuna cravings.

Mercado de Abastos, Barbate
Join a tuna auction during *almadraba* season if you want to buy a slab of fresh bluefin.

Calle Alta, Vejer de la Frontera
Buy tuna loin preserved in Iberian pork fat, plus other Herpac tuna products and Andalucian wines.

CAUR, Conil de la Frontera
Gourmet minimarket with full range of Herpac tuna products for sale, as well as locally produced edible specialities.

Torre del Tajo

breakers, it sits on the Cabo de Trafalgar headland, off which Spanish naval power was terminated by a British fleet under Admiral Nelson in 1805. From the lighthouse, you can see a string of splendid beaches; beware of rip currents off the headland's southern tip.

Squeezed between Los Caños and Barbate, 50-sq-km **Parque Natural de la Breña** may be Andalucía's tiniest *parque natural*, but it protects a wealth of habitats, including marshland, umbrella-pine forest, cliffs and mobile dunes from Costa del Sol–type development. Its star attraction is the scenic 7.2km (two-hour) **Sendero del Acantilado** (accessed from car parks along the A2233) that ascends through umbrella-pine groves from behind Hotel la Breña in Los Caños and runs along clifftops that rival Cabo de Gata in their beauty before descending to Barbate's fishing port. The trail's high point is the 16th-century **Torre del Tajo**, with a lookout point soaring above the crashing Atlantic.

GETTING AROUND

Multiple daily ferries run from Cádiz to Puerto de Santa María. Comes (comes.es) buses link Los Caños de Meca with Cádiz via El Palmar, as well as Barbate with Cádiz and Vejer de la Frontera. Parking can be a challenge in summer.

JEREZ DE LA FRONTERA

The venerable home of sherry ('sherry' being the English corruption of the town's Moorish name, Xerex) and the number-one stop in the Sherry Triangle, Jerez is a laid-back, understated city that embodies Andalucian culture just as well as its showier counterparts, Sevilla and Granada. Its biggest draws are its sherry bodegas, dotted around its charming *casco antiguo* (old town) along with baroque and Renaissance palaces and churches. The bodegas' liquid offerings are imbibed in many *tabancos* around town.

With Jerez's sherry dynasties adopting many English upper-class habits, from wearing tweed to horseback riding, it's no surprise the city is also the best place in the region for equestrian art. Making up the flamenco heartland along with Cádiz and Sevilla, Jerez is renowned for the *bulería*, the city's fast-paced, tongue-in-cheek counterpoint to Sevilla's *soleá* laments, best witnessed in the Roma *barrio* of Santiago whence it hails.

TOP TIP

Avoid July and August, when temperatures soar into the mid-40s; visit Jerez in spring or early autumn instead. Don't miss the Fiestas de la Vendimia in September if you're a sherry, flamenco or horse-riding aficionado. Book ahead for flamenco performances, even in *tabancos*, and be aware that accommodation in Jerez is scarce.

Flamenco heartland

EMOTIVE SONG AND PASSIONATE PERFORMANCES

Rooted in the arrival of the Roma people in Spain in the 15th century, and fused with Jewish and Moorish musical elements, flamenco is Jerez's most important musical phenomenon. Jerez, along with Cádiz and Sevilla – three cities that took in refugees – is considered one of the cornerstones of flamenco and is home to a distinctive manifestation of the genre.

Developing over the centuries as the emotive *canto jondo* lament, with *jaleo* (clapping), improvising guitars (*toque*) meeting the needs of the *cantaor* (singer) and staccato dancing, flamenco enjoyed its heyday from the mid-19th century to the late 1920s, then underwent a renaissance in the 1980s as *nuevo* flamenco. When it comes to flamenco *palos* (song types), Jerez is renowned for its fast-paced *bulerías*, in contrast with Cádiz's upbeat *alegrías* and melancholy, expressive *siguiriyas*.

There are three ways to catch a flamenco performance. Rehearsed *tablaos* (choreographed flamenco shows) lack the spontaneity and *duende* (sweet melancholy) of 'pure flamenco' but nevertheless attract top-quality performers, and typically offer dinner and drinks. Traditional *peñas* (private flamenco clubs), run by aficionados, have spontaneous performances. Ask around locally about when non-members may attend; the best time to try is during the two-week flamenco extravaganza of the Festival de Jerez. Finally, many of Jerez's *tabancos* are intertwined with flamenco culture

BEST FLAMENCO VENUES

Tablao la Bailaora, Jerez
Friendly saloon hosting improvised performances at 9.30pm Thu to Sun.

Centro Cultural Flamenco Don Antonio Chacón, Jerez
One of Jerez's best *peñas*, named after the flamenco legend; often graced by top-notch performers.

La Cava, Cádiz
This rustic *taverna* doubles as Cádiz's main *tablao*, with shows on Tue, Thu and Sat at 9.30pm.

La Perla, Cádiz
Spellbinding performances take place at 9.30pm most Fridays.

KNOW YOUR SHERRIES

Manzanilla Delicate, crisp and refreshing dry white, produced only in Sanlúcar de Barrameda. Pair with sushi and seafood.

Fino Fresh, dry, light-coloured wine, ideal as an aperitif. Goes well with olives, tapas, seafood, cold cuts and young cheeses.

Amontillado Fortified, amber-coloured, nutty sherry; dry or with a touch of sweetness. Complements rice dishes, white meat, green asparagus and ripe cheeses.

Oloroso Dark, very dry red; full-bodied and nutty; goes well with red meats, robust stews and mature cheeses.

Palo Cortado Rare, complex 'accidental' sherry halfway between *amontillado* and *oloroso*. Particularly good with spicy foods.

Cream Medium-sweet *oloroso*, a good after-dinner drink. Works with fruit and curries.

Pedro Ximénez Dark, intense, fortified dessert wine. Pair with chocolate or blue cheese.

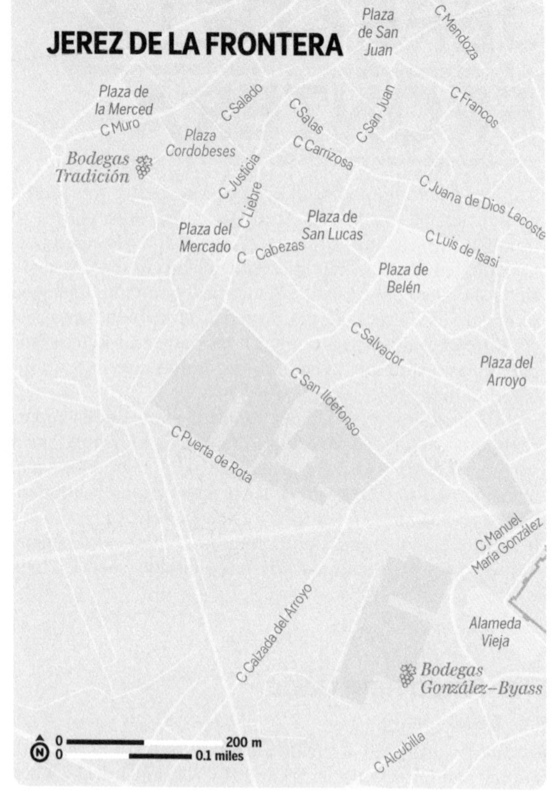

(facebook.com/rutadelostabancosdejerez) – you can often catch a performance over a glass of *fino*.

It's also worth visiting the **Centro Andaluz de Flamenco** (centroandaluzdeflamenco.es), an architecturally-intriguing building that houses a fantastic flamenco resource.

Jerez's sherry trail

WINERY VISITS AND FAMOUS TIPPLES

Britain's love affair with Jerez dates back to the 14th century, when merchants first began trading in *jerez* ('sherry'). Some of Jerez's bodegas were founded by English and Irish Catholic refugees in the 16th century. Today, you can visit many

WHERE TO CATCH FLAMENCO IN JEREZ DE LA FRONTERA

Centro Cultural Flamenco Don Antonio Chacón
One of the best peñas in town (and hence Andalucía); top-notch flamenco performers.

El Guitarrón de San Pedro
Regular performances, occasional art exhibitions, plus extensive sherry tastings and pairings with tapas.

Tabanco El Pasaje
Jerez's oldest tabanco (1925), which once hosted flamenco legend Lola Flores, serves up twice-daily flamenco sessions.

of the city's 20-something bodegas (book ahead) to broaden your oenophile knowledge and sample the sherries.

Sherry, made largely from Palomino grapes, gets its distinctive style from chalky *albariza* soil. Once the grapes have been harvested, they're pressed, then fermented in oak barrels with loose stoppers. A frothy layer of *flor* (yeast) forms on the surface at the end of the fermentation, preventing oxidation and imparting a special flavour to the wine, after which all sherries (except *manzanilla*) are fortified with a grape spirit and enter the *solera* system, where they are mixed with older wines.

Delicate *finos* and *manzanillas* are biologically aged under *flor*, while more robust *olorosos* are matured exclusively by oxidation, as are the sweet sherries made from Pedro Ximénez and muscatel. *Amontillado* and *palo cortado* sherries undergo a combination of biological and oxidative ageing.

The *solera* system consists of American-oak barrels, five-sixths full, lined up in rows up to six barrels high, with 10% to 15% of the wine drawn out and moved from the topmost barrels to the bottom ones three times a year, so the older wine 'educates' the younger, with none of the issues of 'good' or 'bad' years.

Of the bodegas that offer visits, the newish **Bodegas Tradición** (1998) stands out for its top-notch tours (1½ hours; in English, Spanish or German). Its extra-aged sherries (20 to 30 years old) are critically acclaimed, and tastings include four sherries and a visit to its private 14th- to 19th-century Spanish art collection that includes works by Goya, Velázquez, El Greco and Zurbarán.

Home to the famous Tío Pepe brand, 1835-founded **González-Byass** is one of Jerez's biggest sherry houses, just west of the Alcázar, with Jerez's oldest cellars and the superb Lepanto brandy among its products. Basic daily visits (in Spanish, English and German) include the Gustav Eiffel-designed La Concha bodega, and a sampling of two wines; tapas and extra sherries can be added.

Other venues for sampling the tipples include Jerez's famous *tabancos*, dotted around the *casco antiguo*. Mostly dating from the early 20th century, the *tabancos* are charmingly retro, with rustic interiors, typical Andalucian *azulejos* (tiles) and plenty of old-time charm. Jerez has had hundreds of these establishments since the 17th century, but they were reduced to a handful and came close to dying out in the 2000s. A few centuries-old *tabancos* have been given a new lease of life since, as visitors and trendy younger locals join the old-timers, and the number of *neo-tabancos* is on the rise.

GOURMET GASTRONOMY

La Carboná
Cavernous bodega specialising in market-driven dishes, such as boletus rice with razor clams. €€

LÚ, Cocina y Alma
Watch the open kitchen while enjoying an experimental, seasonal tasting menus. €€€

Mantúa
Tasting menus are paired with some of the 200 Jerez wines at this highly innovative restaurant. €€€

Mulai
Gaditano classics like Sanlúcar king prawns and *rabo de toro* (oxtail) are given the globe-trotting treatment. €€

THE REST OF THE SHERRY TRIANGLE

If visits to Jerez's bodegas and *tabancos* aren't enough, head to **Sanlúcar de Barrameda** (p129) to sample the unique *manzanilla* sherry, produced only there, or to **Puerto de Santa María** (p121) for more vintages.

GETTING AROUND

In spite of its size, Jerez is very walkable, particularly the historical centre. Leave your car in one of the car parks outside the maze of narrow one-way lanes. Excellent train and bus connections to all major Andalucian destinations depart from the edge of the *casco historico*.

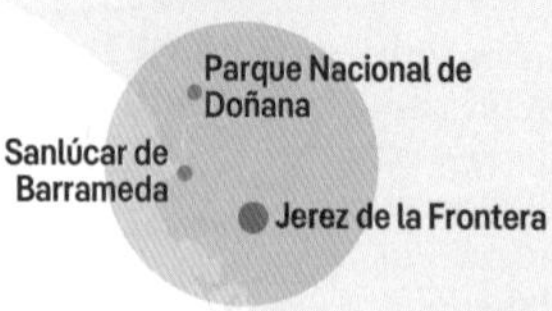

Parque Nacional de Doñana

Sanlúcar de Barrameda

Jerez de la Frontera

Beyond Jerez de la Frontera

Head coastwards to Sanlúcar, another point of the Sherry Triangle, and explore the wilderness of Parque Nacional de Doñana beyond.

Northwest of Jerez, the sherry town of Sanlúcar de Barrameda sits on the edge of the Atlantic, at the mouth of the Guadalquivir River, its microclimate and proximity to the ocean giving its unique *manzanilla* sherry its distinctive salty tang that's prized by connoisseurs. Besides exploring Barrio Alto – the compact, walkable, attractive Old Town with its castle and multiple bodegas – there are multiple beaches to stroll.

Across the river from Sanlúcar, the land dissolves into the vast marshland of Parque Nacional de Doñana – Europe's largest wildlife sanctuary, home to countless bird species, including numerous migrating visitors. The park is accessed only via guided visit, by boat tour or combined boat/jeep excursion; book ahead in summer.

TOP TIP

Visit Sanlúcar de Barrameda during the *manzanilla* festival at the end of May to taste the town's one-of-a-kind type of sherry.

Bodegas Barbadillo

Sanlúcar's bodegas & birdlife

WILDERNESS EXCURSIONS AND UNIQUE SHERRY

Sanlúcar's Atlantic-facing location at the northern tip of the Sherry Triangle, the humid microclimate and the saltiness bestowed by the *poniente* wind enables it to produce one-of-a-kind *manzanilla* sherry (which isn't fortified, unlike sherries in Jerez or El Puerto). Besides visiting sherry bodegas, you may want to wander the narrow lanes and beachside promenade of this appealing, castle-dominated historic town.

Of the bodegas offering guided tours, Barbadillo and Hidalgo stand out. The first sherry dynasty to bottle Sanlúcar's famous *manzanilla*, the 1821-founded **Bodegas Barbadillo** also produces the superb 15-year-old *manzanilla pasada*, as well as Castillo de San Diego, one of Spain's most popular white wines. The on-site Museo de la Manzanilla is well worth a visit. Guided one-hour tours (€15) end with a four-wine tasting. Run by the eighth generation of the founding family, 1792-founded **Bodegas Hidalgo–La Gitana** made its name producing the famed La Gitana *manzanillas*, still produced today along with VORS sherries such as a small-scale *amontillado*. Excellent two-hour introductory tours (€17) finish with tastings in the vine-bedecked courtyard.

Across the Río Guadalquivir, the sand dunes, vast marshlands and pine forests of **Parque Nacional de Doñana** are home to a wealth of wildlife. To visit, hop aboard the *Real Fernando,* departing from the Fábrica de Hielo in Bajo de Guía and operated by **Visitas Doñana** (visitasdonana.com), for three-hour cruises that include two short guided walks, during which you may spot wild horses, flamingos and herons. Alternatively, join one of the land-based excursions in 21- or 29-person 4WDs run by **Viajes Doñana** (viajesdonana.es).

BEST OF SANLÚCAR'S DINING SCENE

Casa Balbino
Perch on the plaza and order superlative *tortillitas de camarones* or deep-fried sea anemone. €

EntreBotas
Bodegas Hidalgo–La Gitana's restaurant blends traditional *sanluqueño* and international flavours, highlighting local produce and sherry. €€

Casa Bigote
Local favourite, specialising in *almadraba* tuna tataki with *salmorejo* sauce and grilled squid with wild-mushroom rice. €€

El Espejo
Plant-filled patio restaurant serving elegant dishes such as *almadraba* tuna tartare or truffled rice with *payoyo* cheese. Wine-pairing menus available. €€

WHERE TO STAY IN IN SANLÚCAR

La Alcoba del Agua
Fourteen stylish rooms fan around a statement courtyard complete with loungers, hammock and lap pool. €€

La Casa
Local breakfasts, room colour schemes inspired by Doñana National Park and touches of contemporary style. €€

Hotel Posada del Palacio
Sensitively updated palace with plant-filled patios and rooms with antique furniture and red-brick arches. €€€

Sevilla
Parque Natural Sierra De Grazalema

PARQUE NATURAL SIERRA DE GRAZALEMA

The crags of the Parque Natural Sierra de Grazalema rise abruptly from the plains northeast of Cádiz, with deep gorges and mountainsides home to an astonishing 1300 plant species, including numerous orchids. The 534-sq-km park, named Spain's first Unesco Biosphere Reserve in 1984, extends into northwestern Málaga province, and is speckled with turquoise lakes, some of Andalucía's most dramatically located *pueblos blancos*, notable for their craftsmanship and local produce, as well as some important Roman remains.

The park is a massive draw for hikers, with 20 excellent trails, some of which throw down the gauntlet even to expert trekkers. Some trails are off-limits from June to mid-October, so it's best to plan accordingly. Cycling, kayaking, paragliding, horseback riding and vie ferrate provide additional outdoor thrills. Pack your waterproof, as this is the wettest part of Spain (Grazalema village logs an average 2200mm annually). Visit during May, June, September and October for the best weather.

TOP TIP

The park's best trails – the Garganta Verde, El Pinsapar, Llanos del Rabel (6.2km) and El Torreón paths – require prebooked permits from the Centro de Visitantes El Bosque (call 956 40 97 33 or email cvelbosque@reservatuvisita.es). Book a month or two ahead. Leftover permits are sometimes available on the day; collect them at the Centro.

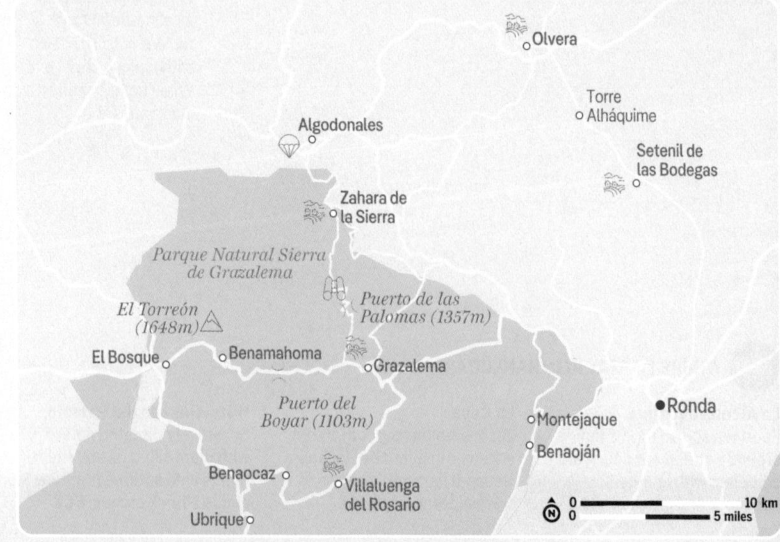

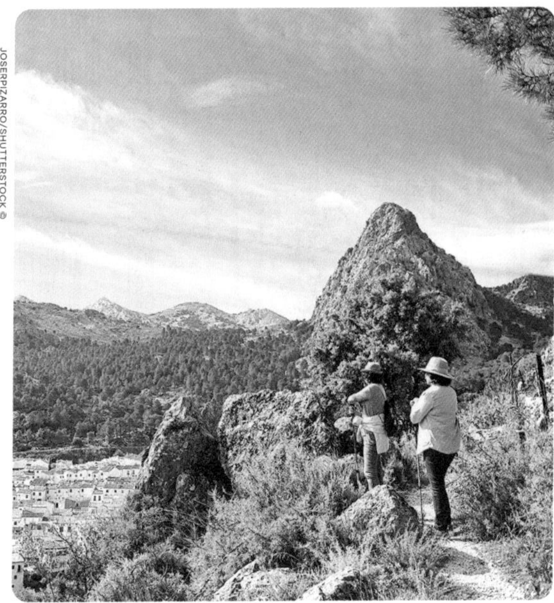

Sierra de Grazalema

Hiking, biking & paddling in the Sierra de Grazalema

GORGE DEEP, MOUNTAIN HIGH

Fantastic hiking awaits in the Sierra de Grazalema, from rambles between scenic *pueblos blancos* along centuries-old paths to the challenging ascent of El Torreón (1648m), the highest peak in Cádiz province.

The moderate 12km-long **El Pinsapar** trail (4½ hours one way) from a car park 2km uphill (northwest) from Grazalema (on the CA91040) to Benamahoma traverses a rare *pinsapo* woodland, with wonderful views of Sevilla and Málaga provinces along the way. These great Mediterranean fir forests of the Tertiary period survive only in southwestern Andalucía and northern Morocco. From 1 June to 15 October you can access part of the trail with Grazalema-based **Horizon** (horizonaventura.com), specialising in nature hikes.

From a trailhead 3.5km south of Zahara de la Sierra (Km 10 on the CA9104 to/from Grazalema), the 2.5km **Garganta**

THE SKY'S THE LIMIT

You can soar high above the sierra's peaks and valleys with the help of long-established paragliding operator **Zero Gravity** (zero-gravity.es), based in tiny Algodonales, the paragliding and hang-gliding centre of Andalucía. Take to the skies as part of a 30-minute tandem flight (€90) or earn your own paragliding credentials through an extensive range of beginner and 'refresher' paragliding courses.

If you wish to scale lofty heights while remaining firmly tethered to the earth, opt for one of PN Grazalema's vie ferrate, with guided trips run by **RSG Aventura** (reservasierra grazalema.com). Located near its namesake village, highlights of the short but tough via ferrata Benaoján include a Tibetan bridge, some thrilling vertical sections and a challenging overhang, with stupendous views from the highest point.

WHERE TO STAY IN THE SIERRA

Tambor del Llano, Grazalema
Rural hideaway in a converted stable, with 10 contemporary rooms, organic home-grown meals and a pool. €€

Al Lago, Zahara de la Sierra
Six rustic-chic rooms at this delightful British-American-run boutique hotel lookout on Zahara's reservoir. €€

No 31 Bed & Breakfast, Olvera
Intimate three-room B&B in a 19th-century townhouse with roof terrace. Canadian owners serve terrific breakfasts. €€

THE CORKS OF PARQUE NATURAL LOS ALCORNOCALES

The southern part of Parque Natural Sierra de Grazalema blends with the northern border of the 1736-sq-km sparsely populated wilderness of Parque Natural Los Alcornocales. Stretching south towards Gibraltar, it encompasses hills densely covered in Spain's most extensive *alcornocales* (cork-oak woodlands), and a handful of remote hiking trails, best accessed from the *pueblo blanco* of Jimena de la Frontera.

Every summer, local *tiradores* (cork-oak strippers) head into the forests to strip bark so it can be turned into wine-bottle corks. However, as the wine industry increasingly moves away from corks in favour of plastic, and the Spanish government comes under pressure to put this important wildlife habitat to other uses, the *tiradores*' and *alcornocales*' future is in flux.

Grazalema

Verde trail descends into the precipitous, lushly green Garganta Verde that's over 100m deep. One of Europe's largest griffon-vulture colonies is here, and sightings of these endangered raptors are common. You'll reach the best viewpoint half an hour into the d-escent. Spelunkers may wish to explore the Cueva de la Ermita at the bottom of the ravine, before the 1½-hour climb back up. Parts are off-limits from 1 June to 15 October (vulture breeding season).

The highly vertical ascent of **El Torreón** is only 3km long but takes around 2½ hours one way. On clear days, you're rewarded with vistas of Gibraltar, Granada's Sierra Nevada and Morocco's Rif mountains. Look for the trailhead 100m east of Km 40 on the Grazalema–Benamahoma A372.

Mountain biking has gained popularity in the park, and there are numerous rewarding routes for everyone, from leisurely beginners' exploration of the park's *pueblos blancos*

WHERE TO FIND CRAFTS AND LOCAL PRODUCE IN THE SIERRA

La Tienda Chica, Ubrique
Local leatherworker Fernando García sells belts, bags, purses, wallets and other accessories at his workshop.

Artesanía Textil, Grazalema
Woven woollen cloaks, blankets, scarves and ponchos are sold at the shop attached to the textile factory.

Quesería la Hazuelas, Grazalema
Watch the production of local *payoyo* cheese, and buy some to take away.

to steep mountain passes and serious off-road biking adventures for the technically skilled. One challenge, should you choose to accept it, is the 12.5km climb to the Puerto de las Palomas (1357m), with wonderful views of Zahara's reservoir and surrounding mountain range. Looking for something flatter? Check out the **Vía Verde de la Sierra** (viasverdes.com) in Olvera, a 36km-long cycling and hiking trail created from a disused 1920s railway line. In Grazalema, **Grazalema Cycling Adventures** (grazalemacycling.com) offers excellent guided rides, has mountain bikes (including e-bikes) for hire, and can provide maps of self-guided routes. You can also hire bicycles along the *vía verde*, and bed down at transformed train stations en route.

For those who prefer being on water to being on solid ground, the picture-perfect turquoise lake at the foot of Zahara de la Sierra is an irresistible lure. You can rent kayaks and SUPs from **Discovery Aventura** (discovery8.com), based by the lake, or even join one of its full-moon-guided kayak tours.

Pueblos blancos of the Sierra de Grazalema

HISTORIC VILLAGES AND SCENIC DRIVES

Inside the Parque Natural Sierra de Grazalema lie a handful of appealing *pueblos blancos*, all with a shared history of forming the Moorish-Christian border for over two centuries, up until the 1492 fall of Moorish Granada. Take a scenic spin along gorgeous mountain roads to visit them.

Sitting at the heart of the Sierra de Grazalema, beneath the rugged peak of San Cristóbal, **Grazalema** is an appealing hiking base, with its narrow, sloping cobbled streets, attractive Plaza de España with a porticoed *ayuntamiento* (town hall) and 18th-century fountain, and whitewashed houses livened up with flowering window boxes and wrought-iron detail. Built on the remains of a Roman settlement, Grazalema has been a wool-production centre since the 17th century.

East then north of Grazalema, the serpentine CA9104 climbs high to the **Puerto de las Palomas** pass (1350m) before swooping down in a spectacular fashion to **Zahara de la Sierra** – a fortified hill village of red-tiled white houses clustered around a vertiginous crag, topped with the free-standing tower of a ruined 12th-century Moorish castle, and surrounded by olive groves. Zahara overlooks the glittering turquoise Embalse de Zahara (Zahara Reservoir), and is a particularly good base for hiking the Garganta Verde.

BEST MOUNTAIN RESTAURANTS IN THE SIERRA DE GRAZALEMA

La Maroma, Grazalema
This gastrobar serves Grazalema's most creative, inspired tapas and *raciones*, making the most of mountain ingredients. €

Al Lago, Zahara de la Sierra
Inventive Andalucian cuisine. Mountain cheese platters and locally caught trout stand out. €€

Casa Palmero, Setenil de las Bodegas
Uncomplicated local fare rooted in family recipes, from goat's-cheese salads to oven-baked sea bass. €

Gastroteka, Ubrique
Family-run restaurant specialising in superlative rice dishes, slow-cooked pork ribs and melt-in-your-mouth oxtail. €€

Setenil de las Bodegas

WHERE TO GET OFF THE BEATEN TRACK

Benaocaz
Reached via a spectacular pass along the A2302; jumping-off spot for the Roman road to Ubrique.

Ubrique
A Republican stronghold during the Spanish Civil War; easy hike to the Roman site of Ocuri.

Benamahoma
Attractive hill village near El Bosque; starting point for the Río Majaceite scenic walk.

THE UNMISSABLE ARCOS DE LA FRONTERA

Marking the imaginary border between the peaks of the Sierra de Grazalema and the vineyards heralding the Sherry Triangle, Arcos de la Frontera is a must-see *pueblo blanco* whose origins predate the Romans. Much about Arcos is beguiling, from its location on a limestone crag high above the Río Guadalete to its soporific *casco antiguo* lined with Moorish and Renaissance buildings, and whitewashed arches soaring above twisting alleyways and Roman-era pillars.

Don't miss the Plaza del Cabildo, with views over the valley below, the centuries-old San Pedro and Santa María churches, or a meal at the bullfighting-themed Taberna Jóvenes Flamencos, with local produce and occasional flamenco performances.

Heading further north and passing through the unassuming farming settlement of **Algodonales** (also a paragliding base), take the A382 for 18km east to **Olvera**, a dramatic scattering of white houses that seems to tumble down a hill topped by a restored Moorish-era castle built into the triangular rock. You can ascend the spiral staircase of the tower for head-spinning views of the village below. A bandit refuge until the mid-19th century, Olvera makes its living from the surrounding olive groves, and is the starting point for the *vía verde* (p133).

Some 14km southeast of Olvera along the scenic CA9120, the streets of **Setenil de las Bodegas** resemble caves due to their position beneath the overhanging ledge of the Río Trejo gorge. The rock forms a natural roof for many of the houses, some of them three storeys high. An abundance of natural light was clearly less of a priority than a good defensive position; it took the Christian army a 15-day siege to dislodge the Moors from here in 1484. You can stay in these cave-houses (formerly used for storing wine), and sample the olive oil, honey and cured meats that Setenil is now renowned for.

A wonderful 13km detour southwest from Grazalema along the A372 brings you to **Villaluenga del Rosario**, the loftiest village in the province (867m), hidden beneath an enormous crag and often obscured by mountain fog. Look out for its ancient Plaza de Toros, hewn out of rock, and buy its award-winning goat's cheese.

GETTING AROUND

It's possible to hike between many of the villages once you're in the Sierra de Grazalema, but to reach many of the trailheads in the park you'll need your own wheels (and to be happy to drive along narrow, winding mountain roads). Comes buses from Ronda serve Zahara de la Sierra; El Bosque, Grazalema, Benaocaz and Ubrique are served by Ronda-bound Damas buses; Damas and Comes buses link Olvera with Ronda, Cádiz, Jerez and Málaga, while Setenil de las Bodegas is connected to Ronda and Málaga by Autocares Sierra de las Nieves.

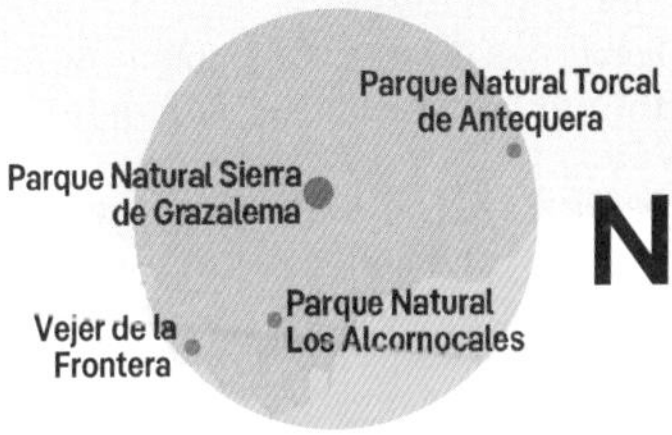

Parque Natural Torcal de Antequera
Parque Natural Sierra de Grazalema
Parque Natural Los Alcornocales
Vejer de la Frontera

Beyond Parque Natural Sierra de Grazalema

Head east into the Málaga province to gorgeous Ronda and Costa del Sol, or west to the remarkable Vejer de la Frontera.

Parque Natural Sierra de Grazalema is surrounded by varied attractions, from nearby mountain ranges and other protected areas, such as the Parque Natural Torcal de Antequera to the northeast and Parque Natural Los Alcornocales to the south, and towns acting as springboards for mountain climbing and hiking, to other striking *pueblos blancos* that once marked the line between the Moorish caliphate and the Christian kingdom.

Heading west, the Sierra de Grazalema gives way to farmland until the Sherry Triangle towns. The beaches of Costa de la Luz are nearby if you head southeast, while inland you can eat your heart out at the foodie Vejer de la Frontera.

TOP TIP

July and August are the hottest months, but Vejer is well worth visiting for its 'gastro-jazz' events in early July.

Vejer de la Frontera

Vejer de la Frontera's food trail

FOODIE TOWN WITH MEDIEVAL STREETS

A strong Moorish influence permeates the sinuous, whitewashed alleyways of this brooding, compact hilltop town, surrounded by 15th-century walls. Vejer has blossomed into a foodie destination over the years; it's a great pleasure to explore the *pueblo blanco* on foot, making serendipitous edible discoveries along the way.

Begin your culinary perambulations on Plaza de España. Stop by **Garimba Sur** for some *arróz negro* (black paella) and a glass of vermouth in the *azulejo*-covered interior before perching beneath the orange trees by **Bar Peneque** and indulging in *atún encebollado* (tuna with braised onions) and *chocos fritos* (fried cuttlefish) tapas while engaging in some people-watching. **Restaurante Trafalgar**, also on the plaza, serves some deceptively simple local delicacies, such as *rabo de toro* (stewed oxtail) and *revuelto de morcilla* (scrambled eggs with black pudding). If you're after Moroccan-inspired flavours, head for **El Jardín del Califa**, one of Vejer's most popular restaurants inside a cavernous, plant-bedecked 16th-century house; reservations are essential. The seasonal Moroccan–Middle Eastern menu includes a traditional meze platter, evening barbecue specials and a superb wine list that combines a fine Moroccan red with noteworthy local tipples from the Cádiz province.

Uphill from the plaza, beneath the church, **Casa Varo** pairs its superb *carpaccio de atún de almadraba*, *albóndigas de chocos* (cuttlefish meatballs) and fine cuts of Iberian pork with one of Vejer's best wine lists. Don't miss **La Judería**, tucked away in a tiny alleyway beneath a stone arch; besides views of Morocco from the terrace, there are stellar rice dishes, superlative *ajoblanco* (cold almond and garlic soup), tuna *bao* buns and a showstopping goat's-cheese cheesecake with honey. Near the Mercado San Francisco, **Corredera 55** features another wonderfully creative menu, with such crowd-pleasers as pork cheeks with cauliflower purée, oxtail *croquetas* and a superb dessert selection.

Exciting new arrivals on the Vejer scene in 2022 include **El Muro Vejer**, a snug restaurant by the city walls where young local chef Paco Doncel turns top-notch local ingredients into the likes of *arróz de Ibéricos* and lightly blowtorched *carpaccio de atún rojo*, and pork *chicharrones* with lemon pearls. Another fantastic newcomer is **La Vinográfica**,

LESSER-KNOWN TAPAS BARS

Sherry educator and local-cuisine expert **Annie B** recommends.

Bar Sumia
Sumia's *tostada de atún rojo con trufa* is fabulous when paired with Calejuella *manzanilla*. My favourite tapa of summer 2022.

El Central de Vejer
The marriage of picked and preserved anchovy is known as a *matrimonio* and this place does it perfectly. Its *tostada de matrimonio* goes particularly well with the local Chardonnay.

Carniceria Guillermo, Mercado San Francisco
They say our *retinto* (free-range cattle), often seen wandering along nearby beaches, is already seasoned with the salty sea spray. Guillermo's melt-in-the-mouth *carpaccio de retinto* comes dusted with grated Parmesan and a squirt of lemon juice.

WHERE TO BUY CRAFTS IN VEJER

Ecléctica Deco
Fun prints from the likes of David Urzua, El Didujo and Sara Luz, plus retro Vejer-related posters.

Cestería Tradicional
The workshop of Juani Marchán sells bags, baskets and accessories crafted from palm leaves and wicker.

Taller de Badillo
Colourful, hand-painted Andalucian ceramics, photographic prints of Vejer's streets and other local goodies.

El Jardín del Califa

serving wines exclusively from select Andalucian producers (luscious white Palominos), an excellent sherry range and superb slow food; its *gambas* (prawns) and *abanico de cerdo Ibérico* (pork) really stand out.

If you're inspired by what you've tasted and want to acquire hands-on skills, you can join **Annie B** (anniebspain.com) for day courses in Andalucian cooking in her beautiful townhouse, or opt for week-long gastrocentric experiences that include food and sherry tours of Vejer, Cádiz and Jerez, and seasonal trips to see the *almadraba* catch. Alternatively, join an engaging sherry and tapas tour with Carlos of **Explorelatierra** (explorelatierra.com).

Vejer de al Frontera is connected to Cádiz, Zahara de los Atunes, Jerez and Sevilla by Comes buses.

BEST BOUTIQUE HOTELS IN VEJER

La Casa del Califa
North Africa-inspired rooms with original stone arches spread across several floors of a 16th-century building. Fabulous breakfasts and *hammam*. €€

La Fonda Antigua
Design-forward hotel with antique doors, mismatched vintage tiles, glass-walled showers and rooftop terrace. €€

Plaza 18
This converted 1896 merchant's house comprises six boldly styled rooms with beamed ceilings, colour-feature walls, international art and Vejer-scented toiletries. €€€

V
Sensitively restored 17th-century mansion with leafy patio. Massages offered in the former *aljibe* (cistern). €€€

WHERE TO DINE NEAR VEJER

La Castillería
In-the-know foodies come here for the succulent wood-fired meats with grilled vegetables, sourced from small farms. €€

Venta El Toro
Family-owned institution specialising in *vejeriego* goodies, including *payoyo* cheese and bread from Conil. €

Bodega Gallardo
Sample locally produced fortified wines, plus the unique Sol de Naranja (think orange-flavoured cream sherry). €

TARIFA

Until the 1990s the compact town of Tarifa that sits on the southernmost tip of Spain, at the confluence of the Atlantic and the Mediterranean, had an unfortunate claim to fame: Spain's highest suicide rate, caused by the unrelenting blowing of the *levante* wind. But the same 'wind of madness', along with its gentler counterpart, the *poniente*, revived Tarifa's fortunes, drawing surfers, kitesurfers and windsurfers from all over, and turning the town into Spain's biggest water-sports centre.

Its present location first settled by Carthaginians and Romans, Tarifa takes its name from Tarif ibn Malik, leader of the first Moorish raid on Spain in 710 CE, the year before the main Islamic arrival on the peninsula. There's a North African vibe to the town, with its labyrinthine whitewashed streets and walled historic core, and Tarifa is the last stop before you hit Morocco, visible some 27km away across the Strait of Gibraltar.

TOP TIP

If you're a kitesturfer, the best time to come to Tarifa is between April and October, when the winds are the most consistent. Tarifa heaves with visitors from late June to late August, so aim for April-May or September-October for less crowded waters; the sea is also warmest in autumn.

CREATURES OF THE DEEP

The Strait of Gibraltar is among the best places in Europe to see pelagic life, particularly between April and October. The highly endangered common dolphin, beautiful striped dolphin and acrobatic bottlenose dolphin are often spotted in these waters year-round. So are families of pilot whales, while the largely solitary sperm whales are occasionally glimpsed in spring. In July and August, orcas tend to congregate at the confluence of the Strait and the Atlantic, on the lookout for migrating bluefin tuna; if you're particularly lucky, you may spot a rare fin whale (the second-largest whale on Earth).

Whales, wind & wave riders

WATER SPORTS AND WILDLIFE WATCHING

Tarifa's legendary winds and optimal conditions along the Atlantic coast have put the town on the map as one of the world's top kitesurfing and windsurfing destinations. There are two winds at work off the coast: the gentler, cooler *poniente* (west wind), ideal for kitesurfing, and the fierce, warm *levante* (east wind) that blows from Africa, particularly during June and July. *Levante* is preferred by windsurfers, and requires considerable skill to harness.

Competitions are held year-round (though winter may be too rough for novices), and during peak season (April to October) Tarifa's hostels, campgrounds, bars and gear-rental shops on Calle Batalla del Salado are packed with bronzed bodies, with many opting for accommodation that doubles as a kitesurfing/windsurfing camp.

One-, two- and three-day courses cost around €100/200/300 per person, based on one instructor per two people; private lessons cost more. Highly recommended, professional kitesurfing and/or windsurfing operators include **Tarifa Max** (tarifamax.com), **Gisela Pulido Pro Center** (giselapulidoprocenter.com), **Freeride Tarifa** (freeridetarifa.com) and **ION Club** (ion-club.net), with multilingual instructors offering courses to suit all abilities.

If you're a first-timer, learning the basics is highly recommended (this writer managed around six seconds on a

kiteboard before flying headfirst into a sand dune), but if you already know the ropes, hit the following beaches in or near Tarifa:

Tarifa Town Beach Kiting prohibited in summer months; strong *levante* offshore. Gusty, unpredictable conditions; best for advanced riders.

Playa de los Lances Broad, white-sand beach stretching for 7km northwest of Tarifa; ideal for beginners but good conditions for pro riders as well.

Playa de Valdevaqueros Three-kilometre-long sandy beach 7km to 10km northwest of Tarifa; crowded in summer with sketchy rocky area. Good cross-shore kiting in low season when the *levante* kicks in.

Los Caños de Meca Wide, partly rocky beach a 45-minute drive north; a good alternative for strong *levante* days in Tarifa.

Palmones Narrow beach a 28km drive in the Algeciras direction; another good alternative for when Tarifa's *levante* is too strong; better conditions in the morning.

TARIFA'S BEST RESTAURANTS & TAPAS BARS

El Lola
Almadraba tuna is the star at this tapas spot, which raises the bar with its creative *raciones*. €€

La Favela
Beautifully presented international fare and Japanese classics, served in a gorgeous stone house overflowing with plants. €€

Bar Anca Curro
Local temple to all things swine-related, with dangling hams, *jamón* platters and *bocadillos* (sandwiches). €

Chilimosa
Low-key, friendly vegetarian and vegan joint, with Middle Eastern dishes using ingredients from the owners' garden. €

Los Caños de Meca

WHERE TO FIND KITING DIGS IN TARIFA

Rebels Tarifa Hostel
Friendly Old Town hostel, offering kitesurfing packages and either spartan bunks or stylish private rooms. €

Beach Hotel Dos Mares
Moroccan-style rooms at Playa los Lances, with an on-site kiting school and outdoor pool for *après*-kiting relaxation. €€

High Flyers Kite House
Snug, stylish singles and doubles, kiting courses for all abilities and stellar lounge-roof terrace. €

DEADLY STRAIT

In 2010 pro kiteboarder Gisela Pulido kitesurfed from Tarifa to Morocco in 35 minutes, racing and beating the Tarifa–Tangier boat. She's not the only one to try to make that journey, albeit in the opposite direction. Each year, hundreds of migrants from sub-Saharan Africa are trafficked to Spain by gangs who pack as many as 30 individuals into rickety, flat-bottomed *pateras* (fishing boats) designed for just six. Boats frequently capsize, and even if the vessel makes it across one of the most treacherous stretches of water on Earth, unscrupulous boatmen occasionally unload the migrants into the water too far from shore, and they drown. Rows of blank crosses in Tarifa's cemetery are a sobering monument to these souls who were only seeking to better their lives.

Another way to get out on the water is to join one of Tarifa's whale-watching outings. Out of numerous operators offering boat outings on the Strait of Gibraltar, the not-for-profit **FIRMM** (firm.org) is among the best. Primarily engaged in studying marine life and dedicated to the protection of marine habitats, it runs ecologically sensitive two-hour tours, sailing up to the maritime border with Morocco and slowing down or stopping the boat altogether when the guide announces sightings off the port, stern or starboard, when there's a controlled stampede of passengers from one side to the other. In July and August, when FIRMM gets notifications of orca sightings, it typically runs longer (three-hour) wildlife-watching trips in the open ocean.

Exploring Tarifa's Old Town

HISTORIC TOWN WITH MOORISH ECHOES

Bookended by the wide, palm-tree-lined Paseo Alameda to the west and the Mediterranean to the south, Tarifa's walled *casco histórico* makes for a wonderful day off from riding the waves.

Built on the ruins of a Roman fort (don't miss the remains of Roman-era walls unearthed in 2010), the 10th-century Moorish castle that became the **Castillo de Guzmán el Bueno** features excellent views of the Mediterranean from its climbable battlements. The castle takes its name from Reconquista hero Guzmán el Bueno, who defended the castle during the Moorish siege of 1294. According to legend, when a Spanish traitor took his nine-year-old son hostage and threatened to kill him unless Guzmán surrendered, Guzmán threw down his own dagger for his son's execution, stating that he preferred to live without a son but with honour.

Across Paseo Alameda from the castle, by the marina, **La Galería del Mar** features evocative original works by a local artist whose use of flotsam and jetsam has won him a loyal following.

More wonderful views of Tarifa's rooftops and across to Morocco's 851m Jebel Musa – one of the 'Pillars of Hercules' (Gibraltar is the other) – are to be had from the **Torre del Miramar**, a lookout tower built into Tarifa's north wall, found near the fortified **Mudéjar Puerta de Jerez**, the main entrance to the Old Town.

Several daily Comes buses connect Tarifa to Cádiz, Jerez, Sevilla, Málaga, La Línea (for Gibraltar) and Algeciras. FRS (frs.es) runs several daily one-hour ferries between Tarifa and Tangier (Morocco).

WHERE TO DRINK IN TARIFA

Surf Bar Tomatito
Rub shoulders with wave-rider types while knocking back a Slippery Nipple shot or signature Tomajito.

Almedina
Cavernous bar built into the city walls, with live flamenco beneath stone arches on Thursday nights.

Taco Way
This place is always hopping, the revelry fuelled by strong mojitos and other tropical-themed cocktails.

Beyond Tarifa

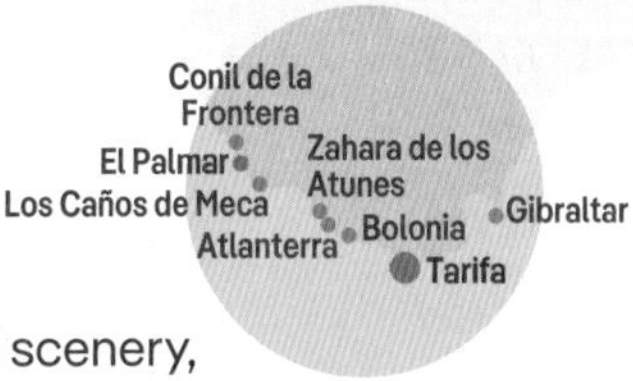

Conil de la Frontera
El Palmar
Zahara de los Atunes
Los Caños de Meca
Atlanterra
Bolonia
Gibraltar
Tarifa

Explore spectacular coastal and inland scenery, from the Costa de la Luz beaches and Gibraltar's Rock to the wilderness of Los Alcornocales.

The only thing south of Tarifa is Morocco, so unless you're Africa-bound and hopping on a ferry to Tangier, the nearby coastline and the rugged interior wilderness beg to be explored.

East of Tarifa, beyond the gritty port of Algeciras (another jumping-off point for Morocco) lies Gibraltar, a weird and wonderful pocket of Britishness overlooked by the monolithic Rock. Northwest of Tarifa, the Costa de la Luz (Coast of Light) is lined with some of Spain's most spectacular (and uncrowded) white-sand beaches, as well as appealing little beach towns, such as Zahara de los Atunes. Inland from Tarifa, the vast, thinly populated wilderness of Parque Natural Los Alcornocales beckons with its mountains, remote villages and cork-oak woodlands.

TOP TIP

Visit Costa de la Luz beaches in June and September, avoiding the July and August crowds but taking advantage of warm weather.

Parque Natural Los Alcornocales

NEANDERTHALS' LAST REFUGE

In 1848, before Neanderthals were recognised by science, the skull of an adult Neanderthal woman was unearthed at Gibraltar's Forbes' Quarry. Other discoveries followed – including flint tools and a Neanderthal child's cranium at the Devil's Tower rock shelter in the 1920s. Eight Neanderthal sites in total have been unearthed around Gibraltar, and it is believed the Rock was home to Europe's last surviving Neanderthals as recently as 24,000 years ago. Excavations of the **Gorham's Cave** complex at the southeastern tip of the Rock are ongoing; it's hoped further finds will provide clues regarding the Neanderthals' extinction or amalgamation with Homo sapiens. While the caves are off-limits to visitors, you can bone up on new discoveries at the nearby **Interpretation Centre** on Europa Advance Rd.

MIGEL/SHUTTERSTOCK ©

Playa de Bolonia

Costa de la Luz's villages & beaches

WHITE SANDS AND CHILLED-OUT VILLAGES

Stretching from the kitesurfer magnet of Tarifa to the marshlands of Huelva's Parque Nacional de Doñana, Cádiz's 200km-long Costa de la Luz is a beguiling string of white-sand beaches and low-key fishing villages. Kitesurfers and sun-worshippers are likely to find their Atlantic-battered haven here.

In tiny **Bolonia**, 15km northwest of Tarifa off the N340, a wooden walkway meanders towards the spectacular white sweep of **Playa de Bolonia**, popular with swimmers and sunbathers, and overlooked by a 30m-high sand dune. Follow the CA8202 for 3km west beyond the Roman site of Baelo Claudia towards the Faro Camarinal, near where a 2km dirt trail leads to **Playa el Cañuelo**, a quiet, golden-coloured naturist beach.

Reachable from Bolonia via a 30km detour around the Cabo de Gracia headland is **Zahara de los Atunes**, a fishing village since ancient times and now a slow-paced resort with low-key hotels, a burgeoning gastronomic scene, and a historical core centred on the ruined 15th-century Castillo de las Almadrabas. Zahara is fronted by the superb 8km-long white-sand **Playa de Zahara**, dotted with *chiringuitos* (snack bars), and catering

WHERE TO STAY IN CONIL AND EL PALMAR

Hipotels Gran Conil
Quintessential four-star resort overlooking Playa Fuente del Gallo, complete with pool and tennis courts. €€€

Almadraba Conil
Elegant wood-beamed rooms surround a courtyard and plunge pool at this updated 18th-century townhouse. €€

Nexo Surfhouse
Chilled-out seasonal B&B with breezy rooms a five-minute walk from El Palmar's beach; surfing lessons offered. €

for families and water-sports enthusiasts with sunbed, surfboard, boogie board and SUP hire.

Four kilometres south of Zahara is **Atlanterra**, a hamlet transformed into a clutch of holiday apartments, where the big draw is the wide, facility-free **Playa Camarinal** that runs up to its namesake lighthouse.

It's a 20km drive north of Zahara, past the fishing port of Barbate, to **Los Caños de Meca**, another laid-back resort. Besides the main **Playa de los Caños**, popular with surfers, and the remote naturist haunt of **Playa la Cortina**, reached via a coastal hike from Los Caños's eastern end, there's the 2km-long, empty **Playa Faro de Trafalgar** that stretches north towards the hamlet of Zahora from the lighthouse – great for sandy strolls but less good for swimming due to powerful currents.

Zahora blends into sleepy **El Palmar**, with a narrow, 2km-long Blue Flag beach. El Palmar comes to life in summer, attracting surfers with its beach breaks, and *chiringuitos* that morph into bars after sundown.

Some 7km north of El Palmar, **Conil de la Frontera** is an increasingly popular beach town that began as a Phoenician fishing settlement. In June it hosts the **Semana del Atún de Almadraba**, with foodies descending on the restaurants participating in the *ruta gastronómica* at the height of the bluefin-tuna catch. The rest of the year its beaches are the big draw, from the family-friendly strand of **Playa la Fontanilla**, lapped at by a mostly gentle Atlantic, to the seven sheltered coves of the **Calas de Poniente** (they'll take some legwork to get to, but you'll likely have them mostly to yourself – and other clothing-optional enthusiasts).

BEST SEAFOOD WITH A VIEW

El Refugio, Zahara
Tuna prepared a multitude of ways and fresh catch of the day dominate at this breezy beachside restaurant. €€

Las Rejas, Bolonia
It's hard to fault the *arroces*, seafood tapas and grilled fish of the day at this local favourite. €€

Casa Reyes, El Palmar
Simple but beautifully executed seafood dishes are the stars at this laid-back beachside haunt. €

Exploring the Rock

MAJESTIC VISTAS MEET MILITARY HISTORY

Soaring to 426m heights, its cliffs plunging steeply to the Mediterranean on its northern and eastern sides, the 5km-long, 2km-wide limestone ridge known as **the Rock** is one of southern Europe's most striking landforms. The top reaches of Gibraltar's biggest attraction fall within the **Upper Rock Nature Reserve**, home to its infamous simian denizens – the Apes of the Rock. According to legend, if these 160 tailless Barbary macaques were to disappear from the Rock, so will the British. (Churchill was sufficiently superstitious to replenish their dwindling numbers during WWII.)

The best way to explore the Rock is on foot. Take the **cable car** (buytickets.gi) from Red Sand Rd to the Top of the Rock,

EL CAMPERO

Legendary **El Campero** (p123), 'the temple of tuna' in Barbate, has a sister restaurant with a great view, Taberna de El Campero, in Zahara.

WHERE TO STAY IN ZAHARA DE LOS ATUNES AND BOLONIA

Hotel Porfirio
Cheerful hotel on the main drag in Zahara de los Atunes; terraced rooms with the sea a five-minute amble away. €€

El Cortijo de Zahara
Moorish rooms, suites with four-poster beds and whirlpool tubs, and a luxe spa overlook Zahara's Playa Atlanterra. €€€

Hostal la Hormiga Voladora
Whitewashed, breezy, wood-beamed doubles and rustic dorms await at this farmhouse overlooking Bolonia's beach. €

and then work your way down via numerous walking trails, scenic viewpoints and historical attractions. Since most sights are located within the reserve, it's cheaper to buy a joint cable-car/nature-reserve ticket (£32/34 one way/return) online in advance (and lets you skip part of the queue to the cable car).

At the top cable-car station you'll encounter some macaques. Keep your distance, especially in summer when they have babies, and never attempt to pet or feed them. Also, carrying food makes you fair game for a mugging.

Heading south from the Top of the Rock, past the macaques' feeding station, brings you to the **Skywalk** – a 340m-high, wedge-shaped, transparent viewing platform overhanging the cliff below. Further along, St Michael's Rd splits in two; head downhill to visit **St Michael's Cave** – a vast cavern (a military hospital in WWII) hung with a wealth of stalactites and stalagmites, with the light show creating the outline of an angel on the cave wall. Alternatively, take the upper turn-off to **O'Hara's Battery**, a 19th-century emplacement of big guns on the Rock's highest point, built to protect the Rock from Spanish incursions.

Nearby, the spectacular (and little-trodden) **Mediterranean Steps** – a narrow, ancient 1.5km path with steep, rough-hewn stone steps – lead down the eastern side of the Rock, with stupendous views en route, before climbing steeply and depositing you at Jews' Gate after a 45-minute hike.

Follow Queen's Rd uphill to the **Windsor Suspension Bridge** and the **Apes' Den** beyond, where macaque sightings are guaranteed. At the northern end of the Rock there's a cluster of WWII sights, including the **Great Siege Tunnels** (gun emplacements hand-hewn by the British during the 1779–83 siege by Spanish and French forces); **City Under Siege** – tableaux of wax figures depicting hardships suffered by locals during the Great Siege; and **WWII Tunnels** (access via 40-minute tour), where the Allied invasion of North Africa was planned. From here, Willis Rd leads you back down into town, past the remains of a 14th-century **Moorish castle**.

A LOCAL'S GUIDE TO EATING IN GIBRALTAR

James Lasry, a lawyer and a Gibraltar resident, recommends places for all moods and occasions.

Gibraltar's multicultural heritage is apparent at **Amar's Kosher Bakery** on Convent Pl between the Convent (where the governors of Gibraltar have lived for hundreds of years) and the Office of the Chief Minister directly across the street. Favourite food? I really like the *japonesa*, an utterly unhealthy but delicious cream-filled local pastry. **Jury's Café** is great for breakfast or dinner. If I'm after fresh fish dishes with sea views, I usually go to **Casa El Pepe** or **El Faro**. If I've got friends visiting who are looking for a lively experience, we head for **Ocean Village**.

Gibraltar: Unique enclave channelling British nostalgia

BRITISH CULTURE MEETS DUTY-FREE SHOPPING

Whether your plane touches down on Gibraltar's spectacularly located runway, or whether you walk across it from Spain's La Línea, you'll find yourself in an over-the-top British corner of the world. As you wander along the narrow **Main Street** in the heart of town, squeezed between the harbour and the

WHERE TO DINE IN GIBRALTAR

Curry & Nigiri
Hole-in-the-wall place run by two brothers, whose superb curries and tandoor dishes rival their sushi.

Jury's Café & Wine Bar
Full English breakfasts by day; imaginative tapas by a Michelin-trained chef and extensive wine list come evening.

Tina's Takeaway
British-Filipino joint serving Gibraltar's best fish and chips, plus superlative *lechon kawali* (deep-fried pork belly).

VADIM_N/SHUTTERSTOCK ©

Rock of Gibraltar (p143)

vast limestone ridge of the Rock, you'll be surrounded by fish-and-chip shops, red phone boxes, Marks & Spencer and Next outlets, and retro 1970s hotels. Also, since Gibraltar isn't part of the European Economic Zone, cigarettes and spirits here are among the cheapest in Europe.

But there's more to Gibraltar than nostalgia and duty-free shopping. Though English is Gibraltar's official language, you'll often hear locals slip into *Ilanito* – an Andalucian dialect peppered with English and other foreign words. And though Britain has scaled back its naval presence, the mother country's maritime history is celebrated at **Nelson's Anchorage** at the southwestern end of town, where a 100-tonne, British-made Victorian supergun commemorates the spot where Admiral Nelson's body was brought ashore from the HMS *Victory* after the 1805 Battle of Trafalgar. The **cemetery**, with its graves of British sailors who perished during the battle, is suitably sombre, while the excellent **Gibraltar Museum** is a stampede through Gibraltar's millennia-long history, from its Phoenician roots to prehistoric finds from the Unesco-listed **Gorham's Cave** to the infamous Great Siege (1779–83).

GLORIOUS GIBRALTAR VIEWS

Cable-car top station
One of the best all-encompassing views of the bay, the marina and the town below.

Europa Point
On clear days at Gibraltar's southernmost tip, North Africa's Rif mountains shimmer on the horizon.

Mediterranean Steps
Tremendous vistas of Gibraltar's eastern side open up as you hike down steep steps.

Skywalk
The cliff falls away beneath your feet at this viewpoint, opened by Mark 'Luke Skywalker' Hamill.

Windsor Bridge
Similar views to the top station, enjoyed from a 71m-long bridge above a 50m-tall gorge.

Gorham's Caves
A viewing platform overlooking the sea gives you views of the Neanderthals' last refuge.

GIBRALTAR MUSEUM

For a closer look at Neanderthal finds from the Gorham's Cave complex, head to the excellent Gibraltar Museum.

WHERE TO FIND THE BEST CHIRINGUITOS

Chiringuito Feduchy Playa
Conil's cliffside haunt with a creative menu starring anemones sautéed with clams and red-prawn croquettes. €€

Chiringuito Sunset Loco Beach
Thatch-roofed bar on Bolonia's beach, serving seafood, along with superb cocktails. €€

El Pez Limón
Pair your sardine *espetos* (skewers), *arroz con atún* and other bites with killer sunsets on Zahara's Playa del Carmen. €€

Ronda (p160)

MÁLAGA

BEYOND THE COSTA DEL SOL

Glorious beaches are just the beginning. Málaga province offers culture, nature and outdoor experiences aplenty.

Fast becoming one of Andalucía's prime tourist destinations, Málaga tempts visitors to explore beyond the region's famous coastline with the variety of experiences it offers.

The heritage cities of Ronda, Antequera and provincial capital Málaga have compelling museums, including Málaga's Museo Picasso, and are a window on the region's history. Charming *pueblos blancos* (white towns) such as Frigiliana, Benalmádena Pueblo and Mijas are postcard pretty and a soothing break from the lively beaches. Rich and varied gastronomy and unique traditional fiestas such as Antequera's Semana Santa (Easter week) celebrations round out the appeal.

Nature-lovers will find interesting species of waterfowl and birds in the lagoon reserve of Fuente de Piedra, and from February to May pink flamingoes come to nest in the lagoon's salt waters. Those with a head for heights will enjoy the Caminito del Rey boardwalk in El Chorro gorge.

Málaga also has more unusual landscapes, such as the evocative limestone formations of El Torcal in Antequera and the Maro-Cerro Gordo cliffs.

The region is a paradise for outdoor enthusiasts. Málaga is synonymous with the Costa del Sol and the popular resorts of Torremolinos and Marbella, but Nerja's river walk and a kayaking tour through the sea-level caves of Maro-Cerro Gordo are a different way to explore the province's natural attractions.

THE MAIN AREAS

Find Your Way

Touring Málaga city, Ronda, Antequera and Frigiliana gives you a great roundup of the region's history, culture and natural landscape, but each in its own right is a great centre well worth uncovering.

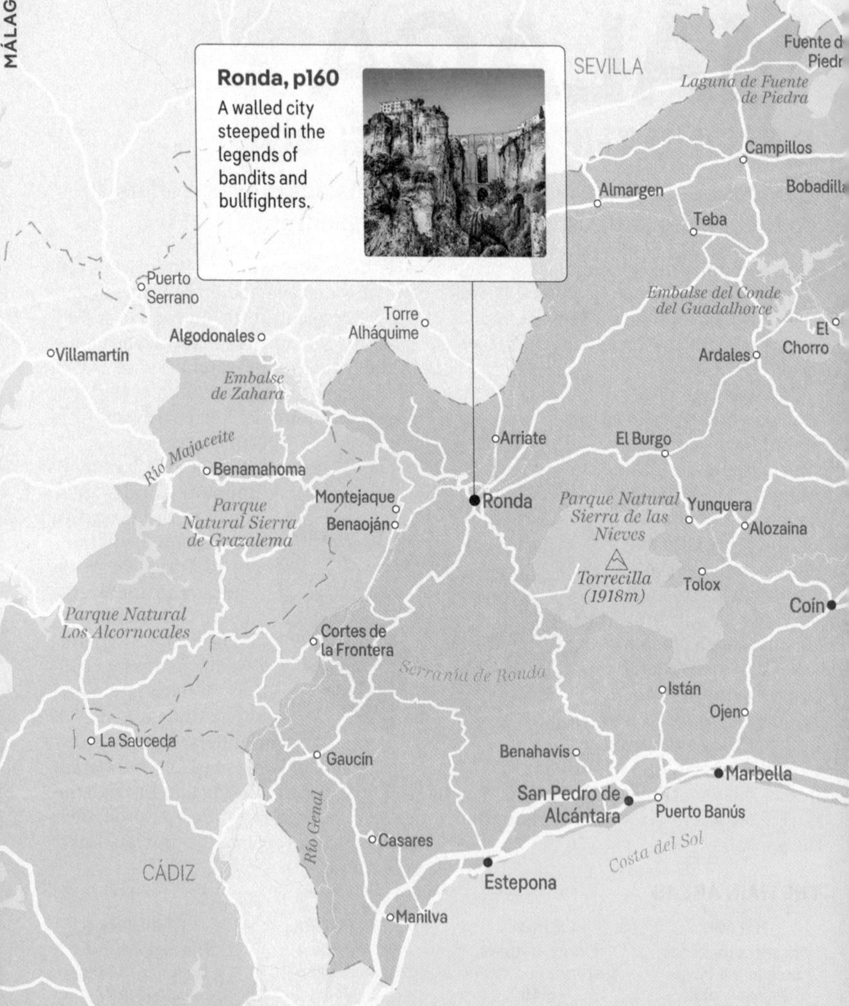

SEAN PAVONE/SHUTTERSTOCK ©, SOPOTNICKI/SHUTTERSTOCK ©

CAR

Hitting the road is the best way to explore the province: you can discover secluded villages and beaches, and tour the wineries scattered across the countryside.

BUS

If you don't have a car, buses are your best bet to reach smaller towns on the outskirts. Buses to and from Málaga city operate from the bus station on Paseo de los Tilos.

TRAIN

Reach the region's main hubs by train from the RENFE station in Málaga and take in the spectacular views along the way. A new high-speed rail route has just opened between Málaga and Granada.

Antequera, p168

The unforgettable El Chorro gorge walk is one of the most popular attractions in the province.

Frigiliana, p177

The beautiful *pueblo blanco* (white town) of Frigiliana is close to glorious coastal spots with panoramic Mediterranean views.

Málaga, p152

A city on the up, full of cafes, museums, a great Moorish fortress – and a fitting tribute to Pablo Picasso.

Plan Your Time

Wander from place to place along the coast enjoying the finest beaches, or venture inland to experience the *pueblos blancos* and historic monuments.

UNAI HUIZI PHOTOGRAPHY/SHUTTERSTOCK ©

Genalguacil (p165)

If you only do one thing

- Spend the morning amid Málaga's hustle and bustle. Visit the **Atarazanas food market** (p154) to take in the sights and sounds and have a bite to eat. Pop over to **Casa Aranda** (p155) for some chocolate and churros.

- Enjoy a glass of local-style sweet wine at **Antigua Casa de Guardia Banderillas** (p156) before visiting the Roman amphitheatre and the Alcazaba.

- Afterwards, head to the bar area of **El Pimpi** (p154), strike up a conversation with your fellow customers and get some tips for the rest of your visit.

- In the evening, unwind and enjoy some *espetós* (skewered sardines) on the beach.

Seasonal highlights

Summer in Málaga can be hot, so stay close to a beach if you visit at this time. Spring and autumn are ideal for wine tasting and hiking.

JANUARY

Málaga's Cabalgata de Reyes (Three Kings Parade) on 5 Jan gives you the chance to see their majesties on elaborate floats.

FEBRUARY

Carnival celebrations across the province; the biggest in Málaga. See the almond blossoms and the pink flamingos arrive for nesting.

APRIL

In Málaga, Antequera and Ronda, each night from Palm Sunday to Good Friday, *cofradías* carry holy images through the city.

Q77PHOTO/SHUTTERSTOCK ©, JESUS COBALEDA/SHUTTERSTOCK ©, KLUBLU/SHUTTERSTOCK ©

Three days to travel around

● After a day in Málaga, head northwest to **Ronda** (p160). See the bridges and take in the stunning views as you learn about the region's multilayered history.

● Spend a day or two driving between the *pueblos blancos*. Be sure to stop at **Genalguacil** (p165) to see the art on display throughout the town. Pick a village where you can do a workshop – possibilities include the family-run cheese factory Quesos Sierra Crestellina in **Casares** (p166) and a bread-making workshop at Hn@s Guerrero bakery in **Benalauría** (p165).

More time up your sleeve

● After getting thoroughly acquainted with Málaga city and Ronda, head northeast to **Antequera** (p168) and enjoy the city's authentic cuisine.

● Beyond, the unique attractions of **El Torcal** (p174) and the **Antequera dolmens** (p172) each merit at least a day of your time. If you're here between February and May, be sure to visit the **Fuente de Piedra nature reserve** (p174) outside Málaga to watch nesting pink flamingos.

● To decompress at the end of it all, head southeast to **Nerja** (p180) and relax on some of the most beautiful beaches in the Costa del Sol.

JULY
Málaga hosts music and dance at the Festival Terral and open-air cinema at many locations – including the beach.

AUGUST
The nine-day Feria de Agosto, launched by a huge fireworks display, is the most ebullient of Andalucía's summer fairs.

OCTOBER
After the nuts are harvested, chestnut trees' leaves change from green to yellow to red. The 'copper autumn' is beautiful.

DECEMBER
Málaga's city centre turns into one big Christmas light – the ones on Calle Larios are nationally famous.

MÁLAGA

Sevilla
Málaga

Málaga has completely reinvented itself in recent years. Once regarded as a playground for young adults, the capital of the Costa del Sol has been revived as a cultural destination with an exciting culinary and arts scene.

Mayor Francisco de la Torre Prados sought to transform Málaga by opening a range of museums, including the jewel in the crown: the Museo Picasso. The cultural efforts paid off when Málaga was in the running to be the 2016 European Capital of Culture.

Loaded with history and brimming with a youthful vigour that proudly acknowledges its multilayered past, Málaga now offers visitors art galleries, a radically rethought port area and a nascent arts district called – perhaps inevitably – Soho.

At the same time, the Alcazaba and Gibralbrafo citadels take the city back to its Moorish past, and the sight of the Roman theatre reinforces just how steeped in history Málaga is.

TOP TIP

You can tackle the centre of Málaga on foot, but you'll need a car to explore the nearby sites. Cycling is possible, but new laws require cyclists to disembark at certain points. Delightful sunset cruises are available from Málaga port for around €20 per adult.

A DRINK WITH A VIEW

The city has many excellent vantage points from which to enjoy light refreshment and gaze down over the city. Our favourites include Terraza Nomadas, Lola at Only YOU hotel, Molina Lario hotel's Piscina, the AC Málaga Palacio hotel, Batik restaurant, Parador de Málaga Gibralfaro, La Terraza de Valeria and Terraza Chinitas.

Museo Picasso Málaga

IMMERSIVE TRIBUTE TO THE MASTER

A fitting tribute to a son of the city, the unmissable Picasso Museum represents a historical milestone: many locals say the museum's opening in 2003 signified the moment Málaga became a go-to destination.

The collection accounts for almost eight decades of Picasso's work and conveys the rigour and creative capacity of a truly gifted artist. The 200-plus works were donated and loaned to the museum by Christine Ruiz-Picasso (wife of Paul, Picasso's eldest son) and Bernard Ruiz-Picasso (Picasso's grandson), and catalogue the artist's sparkling career with a few notable gaps (the 'blue' and 'rose' periods are largely missing).

Conceived as a chronological pathway through Picasso's artistic life, the museum flows from 'Learning to paint' through different halls showcasing important periods, such as 'The portrait as a mirror', 'The adventure of Cubism' and 'Women muses and masks'. Look out for *Vuelta al Mediterráneo* (Return to the Mediterranean), a moving painting that represents a return to Picasso's Mediterranean roots), and *Las Tres Gracias* (The Three Graces), which embodies beauty, love and friendship and shows the influence of Greek mythology on Picasso's work.

Tours help you get the most out of your visit. We Love Malaga and Malaga Discovery are recommended.

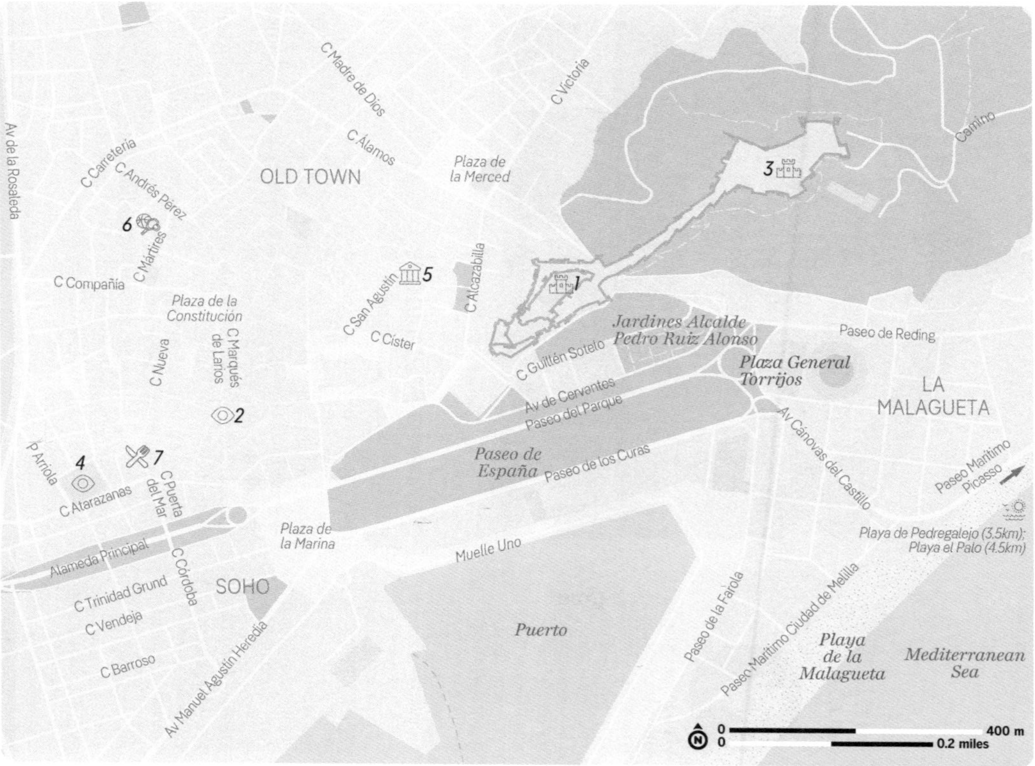

SIGHTS
1 Alcazaba
2 Calle Marqués de Larios
3 Castillo de Gibralfaro
4 Mercado Atarazanas
5 Museo Picasso Málaga

ACTIVITIES, COURSES & TOURS
6 Hammam Al-Andalus

EATING
7 Casa Aranda

OLD TOWN
C Madre de Dios
C Victoria
C Álamos
Plaza de la Merced
Camino
Av de la Rosaleda
C Carretería
C Andrés Pérez
C Mártires
C Compañía
Plaza de la Constitución
C Nueva
C Marqués de Larios
C San Agustín
C Cister
C Alcazabilla
C Guillén Sotelo
Jardines Alcalde Pedro Ruiz Alonso
Paseo de Reding
Plaza General Torrijos
LA MALAGUETA
Av de Cervantes
Paseo del Parque
Paseo de España
Paseo de los Curas
Av Cánovas del Castillo
Paseo Marítimo Picasso
Playa de Pedregalejo (3.5km); Playa el Palo (4.5km)
P Arriola
C Atarazanas
C Puerta del Mar
Plaza de la Marina
Muelle Uno
Alameda Principal
C Córdoba
SOHO
C Trinidad Grund
C Vendeja
C Barroso
Av Manuel Agustín Heredia
Puerto
Paseo de la Farola
Paseo Marítimo Ciudad de Melilla
Playa de la Malagueta
Mediterranean Sea
0 — 400 m
0 — 0.2 miles

Castillo de Gibralfaro (p156)

WHY I LOVE MÁLAGA

Mark Julian Edwards,
Lonely Planet writer
@markjulianedwards

Málaga makes me smile because of the contrasting experiences it offers. In the same day you can chat with local fishermen over *espetós* and also enjoy a luxurious yet affordable *hammam* experience.

The beaches provide perfect conditions for swimming, the Málaga ice cream is delicious and the vibe looking down at the city from the rooftop bars is exquisite. All the food has an unmistakably local flavour. The times spent soaking up the stories at El Pimpi and drinking at the boisterous El Pimpi Florida revealed the city to me for what it was: large and important, yet down to earth and full of charisma.

Mercado Atarazanas

Mercado Atarazanas

HUSTLE, BUSTLE AND FOOD!

Atarazanas food market is a feast for the senses.

First, the entrance: the imposing horseshoe archway in off-white marble (the only remnant of what was once a grand shipyard) will knock your socks off, as will the huge stained-glass window at the far end.

Inside, there's more to admire in the market's three distinct sections: fruit and vegetables, fish, and meat. The immaculate stalls are testament to their owners' careful maintenance – these are family businesses, so the owners take great pride in their stalls' appearance and cleanliness. Try some of the plentiful fresh produce from the local area, from Andalucía and from throughout Spain. You might encounter foods you've never seen, let alone tried.

Be sure to grab a bite to eat inside the market and wash it down with a *caña* (beer) or *vino tinto* (red wine). Try *frito de verduras* (tempura-battered vegetables), *pinchos de gambas, atun o cerdo* (skewered prawns, tuna or seasoned pork) and *boquerones al limón* (deep-fried whitebait with lemon). Don't miss the figs in July and August, mangoes in

WHERE TO EAT

La Recova
Antique shop with a bar inside. Offering gluten-free breakfast plates and tapas, plus handmade homewares. **€**

Mesón Mariano
One of the longest-standing traditional restaurants. Try the *alcachofas fritas* (fried artichokes). **€**

El Pimpi
Iconic restaurant brimming with history and great food. Be sure to check out the celebrity-written barrels. **€€**

October and November, and avocados from the end of November to mid-December. The olive and almond section is fabulous year-round.

One of the best places to enjoy these local treats is **Bar Atarazanas**, which prepares daily seafood and other delicacies. Just outside the market, stop in at **El Colmenero** bakery or have a decadent chocolate-and-churros experience at **Casa Aranda**.

El Palo & Pedregalejo

BEACH HAVENS AND ESPETÓS

The up-and-coming beaches of Playa el Palo and Playa de Pedregalejo are located in the fishing suburbs of the same name. Usually visited only by locals, they offer a more peaceful, less crowded experience than some of the better-known beaches elsewhere in Málaga.

Have a coffee or light brunch at **Hotel la Chancla** or one of the many nearby restaurants and take in the views out over the sand.

In the evenings, enjoy *espetós de sardinas* (skewered sardines) – a Málaga cuisine classic. There are bars and restaurants right on the beach in both El Palo and Pedregalejo where you can eat sardines that have been grilled in an upturned boat by the water's edge.

Each *espetó* typically comes with four or five sardines, with just a touch of lemon for seasoning. The best way to eat them is with your bare hands, as you sit on the beach next to the fisherman who caught and cooked them, chatting about their experiences over a *cerveza*.

Hammam Al-Ándalus

RELAXED SENSORY EXPERIENCE

Blending age-old tradition with some modern twists, the recently renovated Hammam Al-Ándalus captures the essence of the region's ancient Arab baths. The *hammam* has been carefully decorated according to the guidelines of the Moorish tradition, with such highlights as murals and mosaics, and an impressive dome that rests on a series of arches crowning the Central Therm.

The five thermal baths at different temperatures make up the ritual routine of purification and beauty. Along with the steam, resting and massage rooms, the baths form an architectural ensemble characterised by beautiful Nazari decor that induces relaxation of body, mind and soul.

STREET-ART DISTRICTS

Born out of unhappiness among the inhabitants that their neighbourhood had been abandoned by the municipality, **Lagunillas art district** is full of buildings whose exteriors feature the work of local artists. It now draws artists from around the world.

Visiting the district could be the beginning of a street-art tour of Málaga. Start by seeking out the spectacular work of Aintzane Cruceta in the Plaza Esperanza and Calle Lagunillas. To see more international artists' pieces, visit the Soho art district and look for the work of the artists Obey and D'Face on Calle Navalon. You could also see the work of South African artist Faith 41 in Alameda Principal and the work of Belgian artist Roa in Casa de Campos.

WHERE TO STAY

Gran Hotel Miramar
Luxurious hotel occupying a listed building. **€€€**

Hotel la Chancla
Has a terrace facing the Playa de las Acacias. Great place for breakfast. **€€**

Las Acacias Hostal Restaurante
Charming and friendly. Close to Playa de las Acacias-. **€**

Relax as your senses are soothed by atmospheric Andalucian music, the scent of flowers, the taste of traditional tea and the touch of delicate massage.

The standard treatment is the Midra service, consisting of a 15-minute scrub using soapy foam followed by an invigorating 15-minute massage. Afterwards, spend the rest of your time floating around the array of baths. Feel the changing sensations as you enter the baths with different temperatures.

If you want to completely spoil yourself, book a seasonal service. Each of the four services follows a unique set of rituals centred on a particular concept: autumn is detachment, winter is dreaming, spring is rebirth and summer is vitality.

MÁLAGA WINE

The tradition of winemaking in Málaga and the nearby mountains is one of the oldest in Europe. Málaga has long been famous for its sweet fortified wines, made from Pedro Xímenez and Moscatel grape varieties.

In recent years there has been a surge of interest in sweet wines, and Málaga wines are now finding their place on the world stage.

Sample them along with some *banderilla* (skewers) at **Antigua Casa de Guardia Banderillas**. Founded in 1840, this wine bar is brimming with atmosphere and history. Sip from simple little glasses while standing at the long, thin bar and watch as charismatic waiters chalk your bill onto the bar top in the old style.

Views from Alcazaba & Castillo de Gibralfaro

BE TRANSPORTED BACK IN TIME

Like a smaller-scale Alhambra, the 11th-century Alcazaba was the residence of the Arab emirs of Málaga, who created an independent kingdom following the breakup of the western caliphate. At the entrance to the Alcazaba you will see a Roman theatre uncovered in 1951 during building works. The theatre is now used as an auditorium for various outdoor entertainments. Walk among the terraces and patios lined with cypresses, aromatic plants and ornamental pools.

Dominating the city, the Castillo de Gibralfaro sits 132m above sea level on the crest of a long rise. It was built in the 14th century to house troops and protect the Alcazaba.

The Castillo and Alcazaba are located near each other but are not connected. There are separate routes up to each.

Shopping on Calle Marqués de Larios

MARBLE STREETS AND HIGH-END BOUTIQUES

Known simply as Calle Larios, this is the city's main pedestrian and shopping street. It's also Málaga's most expensive street to live on – and the 11th most expensive residential street in all of Spain.

Along this perfectly symmetrical thoroughfare the corners of all the buildings are rounded so the air can flow and help prevent the spread of disease (the street was built in the 19th century). It's the only street in Europe where all the buildings are the same. Uniquely, this and the surrounding streets were built with granite and marble, making the area lighter at night (but somewhat slippery when it rains).

GETTING AROUND

There is an excellent bus network throughout the city. A pleasant cycle path runs from Playa de Pedregalejo into town, but there has recently been a crackdown on people cycling on pavements, so watch out for this. (You may face a steep fine.) There are intercity bus and train stations in town. Both means of transport are comfortable, but be aware that certain destinations only have one bus or train per day.

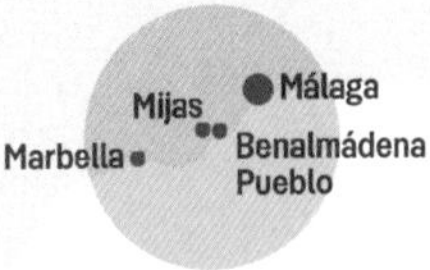

Mijas
Málaga
Marbella
Benalmádena Pueblo

Beyond Málaga

Venture out of the city to discover nearby beach havens, captivating *cascos antiguos* (old towns) and a vibrant market.

The western stretch of the Costa del Sol is less spectacular than the eastern stretch, but some gems are waiting to be discovered.

Benalmádena Pueblo and Mijas are traditional *pueblos blancos* consisting of quiet, scenic streets to walk and small squares where you can sit and watch the day go by. You can even hike between the two towns – an enjoyable option. Known as the Balcón de la Costa del Sol (balcony of the Costa del Sol), these villages offer some of the most spectacular views along the coast.

The old town of Marbella is a gem. Be sure to check out the Avenida del Mar, which serves as a kind of museum of surreal art. It's home to sculptures by Salvador Dalí.

TOP TIP

A car is recommended in this region unless you're heading to one of the main hubs, where there are buses available. Mijas is about a 40-minute drive from Málaga; the bus will take about 1½ hours.

Mijas (p158)

MY PERFECT DAY IN MÁLAGA

Victor Garrido is the owner of tour company We Love Malaga. *@welovemalaga*

I'd start my weekend with a trip to **Mercado del Carmen** – there's outstanding fish and seafood, and it's often cheaper and less crowded than Atarazanas (p154).

I'd have lunch inside at the bar at **El Pimpi**, then head out for a short hike to the **Montes de Malaga** or a more challenging one up **Mt Victoria**. If it's too cold for hiking, I'd visit **Museo Carmen Thyssen**, with its vibrant and uplifting pieces.

In the evening, I'd have a drink at friendly, lively **El Pimpi Florida**, or on the rooftop terrace of the **Lolita Skyview** bar – there's live music at weekends.

Benalmádena Pueblo

CULTURE, BEACHES AND STUNNING VIEWS

Gorgeous Benalmádena Pueblo, southwest of Málaga along the Costa del Sol, is a traditional Andalucian village with narrow streets and squares, and colourful flowers punctuating its whitewashed houses. Take in the **Castillo Monumento Colomares**, a castle-style monument dedicated to the life and adventures of Christopher Columbus, and the **Benalmádena Stupa**, a large Buddhist temple. Stop by the Museo de Arte Precolombino, hosting well-preserved pre-Columbian pieces.

Take bus M-103 to the last stop and walk to the edge of a huge cliff. There, a small trail leads up through the bushes until you come to a breathtaking view of the whole bay below.

Just outside the village, the Butterfly Park is home to more than 1500 butterflies, flying around in a tropical environment.

Venture back to sea level (Benalmádena Costa) for lovely beaches and the **Tivoli World theme park**. The modern Puerto Marina, home to the **Sea Life Benalmádena** aquarium, is said to be one of the most beautiful marinas in the Mediterranean.

Mijas old & new

ART, BEACHES AND CHOCOLATE

Set high away from the coast, **Mijas Pueblo** is the oldest part of Mijas. Wander around this pristinely kept rural Andalucian village before relaxing at one of the beautiful beaches.

For spectacular views, explore the trails that lead from the edge of the village up into the **Sierra de Mijas**. These paths are well signposted and the going is easy enough for most travellers. From this point, you'll be able to see out past Gibraltar to Morocco's Atlas Mountains.

Mijas' Centre for Contemporary Art hosts works by Salvador Dalí, Joan Miró and Pablo Picasso, among others. Look out for the stunning display of Picasso ceramics.

Bioparc Fuengirola will be a hit with the kids. It houses some 200 animal species across four zones: equatorial Africa, the Indo-Pacific, Madagascar and Southeast Asia. In summer the Bioparc is open until 1am.

WHERE TO FIND FUN ACTIVITIES

Potters Lodge
On weekdays, stop in here for a pint and sausage roll. The British owners, longtime residents, are a fount of local knowledge.

Benalmádena cable car
The 15-minute round trip affords incredible views. Allow time at the top to hike to Mt Calamorro.

Mayan Monkey Mijas chocolate factory
Visit the museum and then attend a workshop to create your own chocolate bars.

ANTONIO CIERO REINA/SHUTTERSTOCK ©

Benalmádena Stupa

Marbella culture

PEACEFUL OLD TOWN AND BUSTLING MARKET

Enjoy some respite from the glitzy side of life with a visit to Marbella's beautifully preserved *casco antiguo*, where no cars are allowed. Have lunch in Plaza de los Naranjos, a beautiful square surrounded by orange trees, tropical flowers and cobbled streets.

In **Nueva Andalucía**, located very near Puerto Banús, a Saturday street market (held 8am to 2pm) has stalls selling everything from fashion items and stylish accessories (handbags, sandals, sunglasses) to pictures, antiques and rugs. It's especially busy in summer but popular year-round. You'll usually find something lovely to take home with you and it's always fun to go. Make a beeline for La Red *chiringuito* for an incredible grill.

The **Ralli Museum**, next to the exclusive Puente Romano hotel, has a great collection of works by Dalí and Picasso.

ANTONIO BANDERAS: MÁLAGA'S FAMOUS SON

'Now I know that everything is possible in Málaga,' said actor Antonio Banderas at the 2022 premiere of his second musical, an all-Spanish production of Stephen Sondheim's *Company*. You will hear his name spoken with affection locally. Born in Málaga, Banderas returned to the city in 2019 and is invested in a range of business ventures here.

In 2019 he launched Soho Theatre. He has also created a television production company and a symphony orchestra, and opened four restaurants. A jazz club is soon set to be added to the list.

Banderas regularly takes part in Easter processions as a member of the Cofradías Fusionadas, a coalition of religious brotherhoods.

GETTING AROUND

Each of these areas is easily accessed by bus or car from Málaga.

RONDA

Ronda is a must-see for the spectacular views that surround you as you walk through this magical city. It is split in half by a gaping river gorge that is spanned by an 18th-century arched bridge, the Puente Nuevo. This, together with the famous bullring, serves as the centrepiece of the town.

Along with the Puente Nuevo, two other bridges connect the two parts of the city: the Puente Viejo and the Puente San Miguel.

On the northwestern side of the gorge is the largely modern Mercadillo quarter, while across the bridge is the old, maze-like Moorish town, La Ciudad, and the Barrio de San Francisco quarter. The magnificent bridge apart, Ronda has enough sights and museums to easily fill a few days.

Ronda's bullring was one of the first in the world to stage a *corrida* (bullfight) and has the largest *rueda* (circle of sand used as the bullfighting area) in Spain. It's now a museum, and visitors can stroll out into the arena.

TOP TIP

Ronda is full of hills and windy cobbled streets, so getting around is best done on foot.

Baños Árabes

WINDOW ONTO RELAXATION OF THE PAST

Ronda's Arab baths date from the 10th and 11th centuries, and are made up of three spaces that maintained cold, warm and hot temperatures. Particularly beautiful are the star-shaped ventilation holes in the ceilings.

Visiting these ruined baths transports you back to an older time. Begin your visit by watching a 20-minute video detailing the history of the baths' construction and providing a compelling illustration of what life would have been like within the structure.

With these images in mind, walk through the different rooms, imagining how you might have experienced the place centuries ago.

Learn about the ingenious underground temperature-control system, and most importantly about the baths' second use: they were also a place where locals and visitors would stop to purify and cleanse their bodies before entering the mosque to purify their souls.

Baños Árabes

Plaza de Toros

MUSEUM AND HISTORIC BULLRING

Ronda's bullring is steeped in history. It was one of the first bullrings in Spain to stage a *corrida* and remains one of the largest bullrings in the world, so it has fittingly been

SPANISH GUITAR & FLAMENCO PERFORMANCES

Paco Seco, a local expert in Spanish guitar, delivers an intimate 45-minute performance from 7pm Monday to Saturday at the **Casa Museo Don Bosco**. The garden at the back of the house has a small bar with some of the finest sunset views in Ronda.

On another evening, be sure to catch *Ronda Flamenca* at the **Casino del Socorro**. This traditional flamenco show displays all the discipline, passion and colour of flamenco at its very best. A number of the songs have a strong Ronda influence. Round off the evening with tapas and a glass of wine at any of the restaurant-bars on the Plaza del Socorro.

turned into a museum of bullfighting, open year-round. It's now open only once a year for bullfights, owing to their declining popularity.

Plan time to walk around the bullring and also visit the museum, which contains artefacts such as original posters and clothes worn by the leading matadors, the pen where the bulls are held, the small church where the fighters go to pray before their matches, the indoor dressage ring and the main stables of the Real Maestranza Riding School.

Nowadays most of the Plaza de Toros' income derives from tourism (it attracts 30 million visitors a year), and much of this money supports local cultural and educational initiatives.

WHERE TO EAT IN RONDA

Restaurant Alvacara
Part of Hotel Moneleiro, with outstanding views. €€

Las Maravillas
Down-to-earth place. Try the oxtail. €€

Catalonia Ronda
Hotel restaurant with a fine view of the bullring. €€€

NATURE, WINERIES & MAGICAL SITES

Alfredo Carrasco is a guide at Nature Tours Andalucía. *@nature.tours. andalucia*

One of my favourite places is the **Cueva del Gato** (Cat Cave), with its spectacular entrance. Just in front is a pool where you can swim.

Among the 300 birds you can find in Málaga, I love the raptors. See them in the **Sierra de Las Nieves**. The enchanted forest in **Parauta** is the perfect place to enjoy the copper forest in autumn.

Bodega-Schatz is a pioneer that brought wine to the area. **Chinchilla** wines provide great tours, and **Bodega García Hidalgo** has a really positive local story.

Acinipo archaeological site is one of those magical places that just make you feel better.

RAQUEL PEDROSA/SHUTTERSTOCK ©

Casa del Rey Moro

Casa del Rey Moro

STAIRCASE INTO THE GORGE

The House of the Moorish King is closed, but its gardens are spectacular: split over three levels, they adorn the cliffs of the gorge like giant hanging baskets.

La Mina, the Islamic staircase of 231 sloping steps, enabled Ronda to maintain water supplies when it was under attack. It was also the point where Christian troops forced entry in 1485. The steps get slippery, and are poorly illuminated and narrow in places, so use caution when making your way into the rooms below.

As you descend the stairs you'll pass several halls: the Sala de la Noria (named for the large Ferris wheel used to extract water from the well), the Weapons Room, and the Room of Secrets, where the well is.

The main feature, however, is the view at the bottom. Look out to the river, and look up for an awe-inspiring view of the gorge from below. When you have taken this in, return to the top and relax in the delightful gardens of the mansion.

GETTING AROUND

Ronda is accessible by car, bus or train from Málaga. While the bus journey is direct, you'll have to make one change on the train (at Antequera Santa Ana). It's worth it for the stunning views along the way.

DISCOVERING RONDA WALKING TOUR

Start your walking tour of Ronda's architectural gems at the bullring.

From here, stroll over to the **1 Plaza de España** and prepare for a sight that will take your breath away. Within a few minutes you will find yourself standing on Ronda's terrifying and beautiful **2 Puente Nuevo** (New Bridge), which spans the 120m-deep **3 Tajo de Ronda gorge**. The bridge was completed in 1793 after 40 years of hard work.

Make your way over to the **4 Puente Viejo** (Old Bridge), accessed by pathways that descend into El Tajo gorge in both the 'new' and old parts of town. From the Puente Viejo, take the road that leads off to your right, beyond the old city walls, and after about 10 minutes you'll arrive at the **5 Baños Árabes** (Arab baths). Walking down round the hairpin bend towards the Puente Viejo, you'll come to an archway, the **6 Arco de Felipe V**. Looking back up through the arch you can see the old city walls.

Leaving the Arabic baths, cross the Puente Viejo to reach the other side of El Tajo. It's then a steady uphill walk to reach the elegant **7 Casa del Rey Moro** (House of the Moorish King). Emerging from its lavish gardens, you'll find yourself in the Moorish quarter, known simply as La Ciudad (the Town). Wander about, taking in its charms.

If time allows, pay a visit to the **8 minaret of San Sebastián**. It once belonged to a small mosque possibly dating from the 14th century. After the Christian conquest it became a church called San Sebastián, of which there are no visible remains today, except for the old minaret converted into a bell tower.

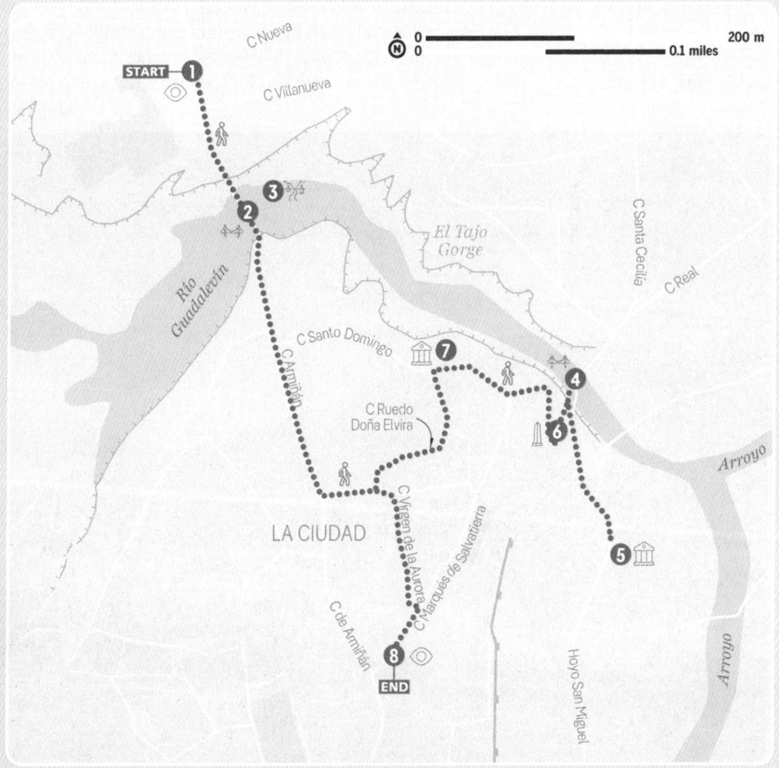

Ronda
Benaoján
El Burgo
Atajate
Parque Natural Sierra de las Nieves
Benalauría
Gaucín
Genalguacil
Casares

Beyond Ronda

Go beyond Ronda and you'll be rewarded with underrated *pueblos blancos* and unspoilt nature.

Compared to those of other provinces, the pueblos blancos near Ronda are relatively untouched by tourists. Spend a day touring several villages, following your intuition as to where you would like to stop, enjoy a drink and stroll around. Be sure to visit La Cueva de la Pileta, which offers a real treat for the senses.

The Parque Natural Sierra de las Nieves has just been declared Andalucía's third national park, offering it the highest levels of protection. This is a source of huge pride to many locals. Best known for its Spanish fir (*Abies pinsapo*), unique to southern Spain and northern Morocco, it is a magnificent place that arguably offers more gentle hiking routes than some of the other parks.

TOP TIP

The easiest way to explore these villages and the park is by car.

Atajate

RUDOLF ERNST/GETTY IMAGES ©

La Cueva de la Pileta

CAVE PAINTINGS, BATS AND DARKNESS

You can only access the unmissable Cueva de la Pileta as part of a group tour – and this adds to the richness of the experience. The expert guide uses her torch to point out the geological and historical riches. Each person also has their own lantern to light their way.

This huge cave is famous for its paintings, many of which were made up to 32,000 years ago. With over 3800 recorded images, it is one of the most important cave-painting sites in Europe. Our guide said the paintings 'changed the notion of what Neanderthals were capable of'. Each chamber presents a visual feast very different from the preceding one. It is extraordinary to observe the precision of the various drawings (horses, fish, goats, turtles, fish).

Highlights include the mineral pools, hearing about the small insects that live within the pools and listening to the echo generated when your guide stamps her feet on the chamber floor. All the while, you'll see bats flying past.

The cave is 23km from Ronda, in the village of Benaoján. Book ahead and be sure to wear enclosed footwear with a good grip.

Pueblos Blancos of the Serrania de Ronda

WANDER FROM VILLAGE TO VILLAGE

With only 180 inhabitants, **Atajate** is the least populated town in the province of Málaga. It has spectacular views from 745m above sea level, and its privileged location and the splendid natural environment surrounding it have made it the starting point of trekking trails. It's also worth visiting for the impressive Iglesia de San Roque.

In **Benalauría** (population 500), be sure to stop by the Bodega 28 metros cuadrados (28-sq-metre bodega) – unsurprisingly, it's the smallest winery in the province.

Pristine white **Genalguacil** (population 400) is not to be missed. Best known as the 'museum town', the village hosts the Art Encounters of the Genal Valley every two years. The winning pieces are installed in squares and streets and have turned the town into an open-air museum. Already, 100 painters, sculptors, photographers and potters have left their mark here. It's great fun to photograph and interact with the bright pieces. Genalguacil has deservedly been named one of the most beautiful towns in Spain.

BREAD & CHEESEMAKING WORKSHOPS

Bread-making workshops take place every day at **Hn@s Guerrero bakery** in Benalauría. Since 1882 the Guerrero family has been making bread every single day in the Plazoleta wood-fired oven using the same artisan recipe.

Nestled in the mountains, and accessed via the Manilva–Gaucín road or by driving up the Casares road, **Quesos Sierra Crestellina** is a family-run cheese factory. There's even the chance to milk the goats in season. The 'museum' also runs guided tours of the factory.

Genalguacil

WHERE TO EAT THROUGHOUT THE VILLAGES

Lla fructuosa, Gaucín
Great value for money; Michelin-starred food with a view. €€

Bar Paco Pepe, Gaucín
Friendly local tapas, on a popular square. €

La Esquinita, Gaucín
Offers vegetarian and gluten-free options. €

Along the route you will pass Algatocín, which is full of cork trees. The bark is harvested every nine years, so the area is divided into nine zones, each to be harvested in turn. Traditionally, mules are used to bring the cork to the road.

Located on the way to Casares, **Gaucín** has thoroughfares full of steep stairs or slopes, white streets and traces of popular Moorish architecture. Its main feature and attraction are the ruins of the Castillo del Águila – located at 150m elevation, so it can be seen from practically anywhere in the municipality.

Beautiful **Casares** (population 3000) is home to the 'sugar cubes' (white houses), piled precariously high and nudging the battlements of a Moorish castle.

WINE IN RONDA

Gema Perez Barea is a wine guide at Milamores Ronda.

Ronda is famous for its different wines thanks to its unique soil and climate, and the love its makers put into the finished product.

We produce wines with Petit Verdot, a grape variety of French origin that arrived in the Serrania de Ronda region in 2002. This is the last grape to be harvested between October and November, and the best Petit Verdot monovarietals in Europe are being made with it.

Among the wineries that produce it are Bodega F. Schatz, Bodega Vetas, Badman Wines, Cortijo Los Aguilares, Bodega Vetas, Bodega Gonzalo Beltrán and Bodega Chinchilla.

Parque Nacional Sierra de las Nieves

EXPERIENCE THE NEW NATIONAL PARK

This newly designated nature reserve is home to over 1500 plant species, 19 of which are found in this area alone. The park also has more than 120 bird species – including various species of eagle – some 1000 ibexes and numerous mountain goats.

The *nieve* (snow) after which the mountains are named usually falls between January and March. **El Burgo**, a remote but attractive village 10km north of Yunquera, makes a good base for visiting the east and northeast of the park (and is a great place for birdwatching).

The park is crisscrossed by trails. The most rewarding walk is an ascent of the highest peak in western Andalucía, **Torrecilla** (1918m). Start at the **Área Recreativa Los Quejigales**, which is 10km east by unpaved road from the A376 Ronda–San Pedro de Alcántara road. The turnoff, 12km from Ronda, is marked by signs. From **Los Quejigales** there's a steep 470m ascent by the **Cañada de los Cuernos** gully to the high pass of **Puerto de los Pilones**. After a level section, you'll be rewarded with incredible views after the final steep 230m to the summit. The easy-to-moderate walk takes five to six hours return.

There's a tourist office (sierranieves.com) in **Yunquera** and other offices in **Tolox** and El Burgo. You should also be able to pick up some park information at the tourist office in Ronda. Autobuses Paco Pepe (grupopacopepe.com) buses to El Burgo depart from Ronda's bus station.

WHERE TO EAT THROUGHOUT THE VILLAGES

Bar Restaurante la Solana, Benalauría
Specialises in steak. Very cosy. **€€**

Restaurante Sarmiento, Casares
Glorious views out over the village. **€€€**

Forge, Casares
Rustic surroundings, and vegetarian and gluten-free options. **€€**

JUMP INTO CHARCO DE LA ESCRIBANA

Halfway between the white towns of Benarrabá and Genalguacil is this unique spot cooled by the Genal River. Jump in and enjoy a swim in this natural lake with its pristine clarity: you'll see fish swimming around you. Gaze up for beautiful views of the mountains. Afterwards, if you're inclined, you can trek all the way to the Venta San Juan inn for a *cerveza* or light lunch.

Waterfall near El Burgo

GETTING AROUND

Exploring the areas outside Ronda is best done by car. Be aware there's only one place in Ronda to hire a vehicle: Auto Ronda Rent A Car. It's closed for siesta from 2pm till 4pm during the week and is open 11am to 1pm on Saturday.

ANTEQUERA

The name Antequera derives from the Iberian name Antikaria, which means 'opposite the enormous line rock'. The town occupies the northernmost part of the province and is rich in landscape and culture. Nearby El Torcal de Antequera is made from limestone that was part of the ocean bottom 150 million years ago.

Known as *el corazón de Andalucía* (the heart of Andalucía) because of its central location, the town sees plenty of travellers pass though – and it's now growing into a destination in its own right.

With more than 30 churches, Antequera has the distinction of having the most churches per inhabitant of all the towns in Spain. The churches are built in a range of architectural styles, from neoclassical to baroque to Renaissance.

TOP TIP

Antequera is still relatively undiscovered by English-speaking tourists, so it's worth doing a little more planning to secure English-speaking tours if required and understand the content of museums before your visit.

MOONLIGHT

From mid-June until mid-September, the village hosts Moonlight, a series of spectacularly backlit concerts and performances at historic locations such as the town's many churches and routes through El Torcal.

Museo de la Ciudad de Antequera

BRINGING ROMAN TIMES BACK

Antequera's town-centre municipal museum displays an impressive collection of Roman artefacts from the surrounding area, including glassware, jewellery, stone carvings, clothing, paintings and fragmentary mosaics. Everything on display has been expertly preserved – even the ornate clothing looks as though it was made recently.

Many pieces are brought to life through illustrations depicting how they would have been used in Roman times.

Efebo, an elegant and athletic 1.4m bronze statue of a boy, was discovered on a local farm in 1952. It's one of the finest examples of Roman sculpture yet found in Spain.

Convento de Belén

BUY TRADITIONAL SWEETS FROM NUNS

Many nuns in the convents of Spain earn their living selling confectionary. Preserved over the ages, their recipes come from the times of the Romans and the Moors. Unfortunately, many convents are closing, so this art may be lost.

The Convento de Belén is run by a cloistered order of Poor Clares. To buy sweets, you'll enter a very small room with a lazy Susan installed on the wall, with a buzzer and price list next to it. When you've decided on your purchase, ring the buzzer. After a while you'll hear the voice of a nun greet you. Tell her what you would like and after a few minutes the

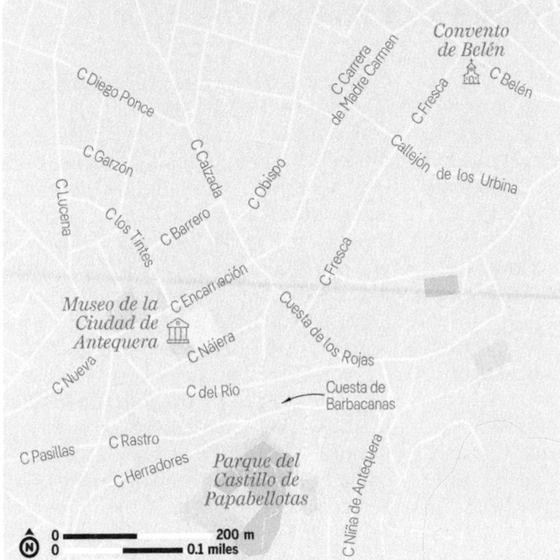

lazy Susan will turn to reveal your order. Take it, then put your money on the lazy Susan and turn it back to the nun.

Alcazaba

WALK THROUGH HISTORY

Favoured by the Granada emirs of Islamic times, Antequera's hilltop Moorish fortress has a fascinating history and covers a massive 62,000 sq metres. The main approach to the hilltop is from Plaza de San Sebastián, up the stepped Cuesta de San Judas and then through an impressive archway, the Arco de los Gigantes, built in 1585 and formerly bearing huge sculptures of Hercules. All that's left today are the Roman inscriptions on the stones.

The admission price includes a multilingual audioguide, which sets the historical scene as you meander along tidy pathways, flanked by hedges and some archaeological remains of a Gothic church and Roman dwellings from the 6th century CE.

Climb the 50 steps of the Torre del Homenaje for great views, especially towards the northeast, and of the Peña de los Enamorados (Rock of the Lovers) – a rock whose profile resembles a human face, long the subject of local legends.

MY PERFECT DAY

Justine Faucon is a tour guide with Visita Antequera. *@visitaantequera*

A day off in Antequera begins early so I can see the sunrise. I have breakfast at Entre Torres or Bar Chicón – I always order *mollete antequerano* (soft Antequeran bread rolls) with extra-virgin olive oil, or ham, cheese and tomato.

Then my dog and I go for a walk. There's always a balcony or a nice patio you've never seen before. Sometimes we walk all the way to the river. When we get back, it's time to meet friends for *cañas* and tapas.

We all enjoy hiking, so we sometimes climb El Torcal (p174). Often we just take in the amazing landscapes surrounding the town.

GETTING AROUND

Málaga airport is only 60km away – approximately 50 minutes by car. There's a good high-speed AVE train service from Málaga Maria Zambrano station. The train stops at Antequera Santa Ana station, 17km from Antequera. You can then take a taxi into the city. From Málaga Central Bus Station, ALSA buses run directly to Antequera.

RUINS, CHURCHES & ALCAZABA WALKING TOUR

Begin your walking tour of the city at the **1 Convento de Belén** (whose construction began in 1628; p168). Notice the stunning, rich decoration of baroque blue plasterwork before heading towards the **2 Iglesia del Carmen**, now a national monument. Observe its rectangular Mudéjar coffered ceiling with butterfly decorations. Head towards the **3 Alcazaba of Antequera** (p169) and take in its history.

Next, take the short walk to the **4 Real Colegiata de Santa María la Mayor** to view the first building constructed in Renaissance style in Andalucía. Inside, settle in for the 20-minute video that tells the fascinating story of the complex. Walk back outside and drink in the beautiful views. If you look out from here you'll see the Roman baths. Discovered in 1988, they date from the 1st century CE and were still in use until the 5th century.

On your way out, walk through the magnificent **5 Arco de los Gigantes**. Constructed in 1585, this building represents an example of late-Renaissance architecture. On top of the gate you will see depictions of a vase of lilies, the castle and a lion: each is part of the city's coat of arms. Looking out to the west, you will see the spectacular **6 Iglesia de San Sebastián**.

If you still have the energy, you could also walk to the **7 Convento de los Remedios**, whose main altarpiece is one of the most beautiful in Antequera. Continue on to the **8 Iglesia de San Juan de Dios**, before returning to visit the incredible Museo de la Ciudad de Antequera (p168) inside the **9 Palacio de Nájera**.

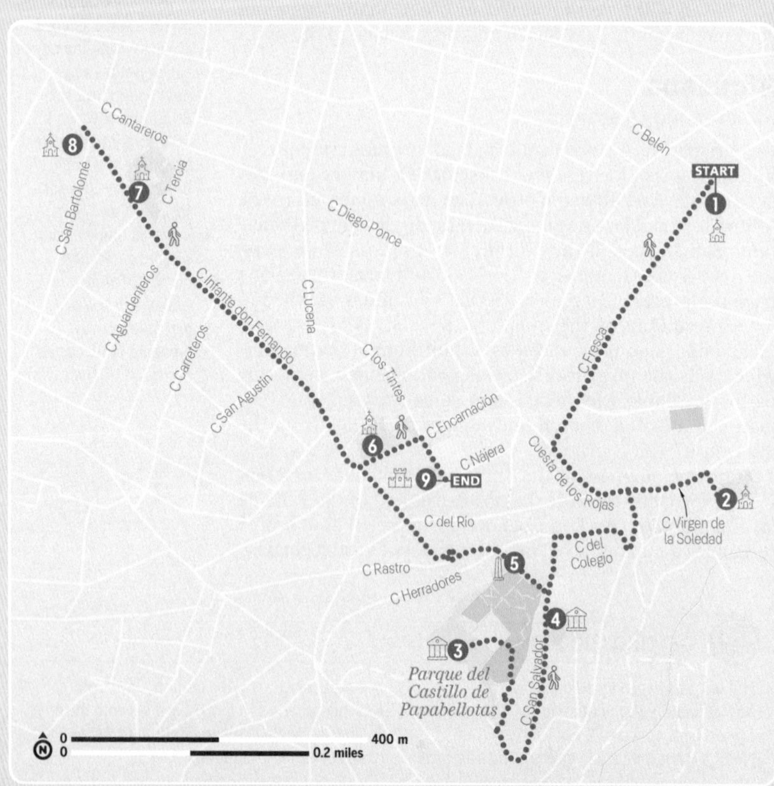

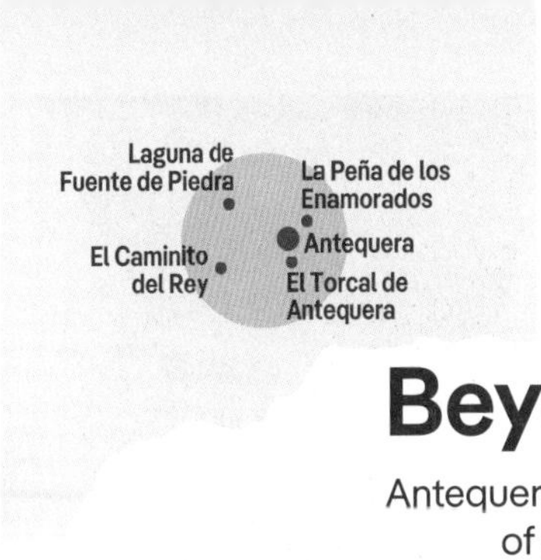

Beyond Antequera

Antequera's surroundings are home to marvels of construction from ancient to modern.

Few places have such a combination of historically important monuments and striking natural environments as the Antequera region.

The Antequera dolmens archaeological site and two of its enclaves, Peña de los Enamorados and El Torcal de Antequera, are Unesco World Heritage sites. El Torcal is one of the most spectacular karst landscapes in Europe. If that weren't enough, the region is also home to the Fuente de Piedra lagoon, which hosts thousands of pink flamingos in nesting season (February to May), and El Caminito del Rey, a walkway pinned along the steep walls of a narrow gorge in El Chorro.

You can visit the sites from Antequera or on day trips from Málaga and other regional cities.

TOP TIP

There's a lot to take in: allow at least three days just to see the highlights.

Viera dolmen (p173)

UNIQUE LOCAL PROCESSIONS & FIESTAS

Antequera's Easter week processions are completely different from those of other Andalucian cities. During the famous Correr la Vega, held on the Thursday and Friday of Easter week, the religious brotherhoods take to the streets and carry their floats to the bottom of a steep hill and, when a bell is rung, start a very exciting race, running with the floats until they reach the top.

During the processions, the streets are almost completely dark, illuminated only by candles and punctuated with the sound of drums.

Some of the most important fiestas celebrate the town's patron saints: in May there is El Señor de la Salud y de las Aguas; in September, the fiestas of the Virgen de los Remedios and Santa Eufemia.

During the last weekend in May there is Agrogant, a farming and livestock fair. August brings the Real Feria (Royal Fair).

Menga dolmen

Antequera dolmens site

GET UP CLOSE TO THE PAST

This extraordinary site consists of three cultural monuments – the dolmens (burial mounds) of Menga (p173) and Viera (p1730), and the *tholos* (tomb) of El Romeral (p173) – and two natural monuments: the mountainous formations of La Peña de los Enamorados (p174; a rock resembling the outline of a woman's face) and El Torcal (p174).

Considered to be some of the finest Neolithic monuments in Europe, the two earth-covered burial mounds were named a Unesco World Heritage site in 2016.

The Menga and Viera dolmens were built by Bronze Age people around 3000 BCE. When they were rediscovered in 1903, they were found to house the remains of several hundred people.

Menga and Viera are just a few metres apart. El Romeral is about 3.5km away.

Before you tour the site, it's well worth watching the short film at the visitor centre to learn more about the dolmens and their connection to La Peña.

WHERE TO EAT

Bar la Socorrilla, Antequera Local and tourist hot spot. Superb location. **€€**

Meson Adarve, Antequera Small family restaurant. Excellent food. **€€**

Recuerdos Tapas Bodega, Antequera High-quality tapas. **€€**

Menga dolmen

BREATHTAKING VIEW OF LA PEÑA

Built sometime before 3500 BCE, this dolmen may be the oldest of the three burial sites at Antequera. It is the largest dolmen in Europe: nearly 30m long, with its largest upright stone weighing 180 tonnes. (The heaviest stone at the UK's Stonehenge weighs 40 tonnes.)

The tomb has three sections: first, an open corridor or atrium porch that would have been partially or completely unroofed; second, a passage or corridor section of four stones; and, third, a passage leading to the large oval-shaped funerary chamber.

As you walk along the tunnel you will see how well preserved the walls are. Once inside, turn around for a surprise: there in front of you is La Peña de los Enamorados! It is unique in continental Europe for a dolmen to align to a natural landmark, so it's not settled whether this was deliberate or a coincidence.

Viera dolmen

A PREHISTORIC FEAT OF ILLUMINATION

Built before 3000 BCE, and so likely to be the second-oldest dolmen at the site, Viera is composed of two sections: an open corridor including a 'door', and a 21m-long passage. At the back is a small sepulchral chamber, accessed through an opening cut into the stone.

The dolmen is positioned so maximal sunlight illuminates the chamber at the spring and autumnal equinoxes – an extraordinary feat of construction. A small number of visitors can witness the equinox at Viera by reservation at the visitor centre next to the dolmens.

El Romeral

ANCIENT OPTICAL ILLUSION

Built around 2500 BCE, the *tholos* of El Romeral is a typical false-cupola tomb. It has a 26m-long corridor with masonry walls and a flat roof, of which 11 large stone slabs remain. At the end of the corridor are two vertical stones followed by two placed closer together, creating the impression of a funnel leading into the 5.2m-wide chamber at the end.

Standing in the chamber, as your eyes grow accustomed to the darkness, look at the wall to the right of the smaller chamber opening. You'll see the 'projection' of the light

DISHES OF ANTEQUERA

Food to try in this region includes *mollete antequerano* (Moorish bread), *porra* (a thick puree consisting of tomato and bread), *guisado de patas* (pork stew), *ajo blanco* (soup of garlic, almonds and bread), *gazpachuelo* (soup of mayonnaise and fish), *pío antequerano* (cod with oranges), rabbit *a la cazadora* (cooked with tomatoes, mushrooms and garlic) and goat *a la pastoril* (cooked with liver, oregano, thyme and paprika). Outstanding desserts include *bienmesabe* (a pudding consisting of ground almonds).

Porra

Sal y Pimienta, Antequera
Simple and friendly, with excellent tapas. €

Arte de Tapas, Antequera
Great tapas and a creative atmosphere. €€

Mesón Adarve, Antequera
A warm welcome and high-quality food. €€€

from the entrance focused by the long corridor. During the afternoon around the winter solstice, the sun shines directly onto this back wall.

La Peña de los Enamorados

SHAPESHIFTING LANDMARK

The 880m-high limestone crag overlooking the town and valley of Antequera is known as La Peña de los Enamorados (Lovers' Rock). It's also called Lovers' Leap.

Whether you see an angular man's face or a young woman's face (different people see different things), try not to rush your time here. Take a moment to simply stop and gaze at this natural phenomenon.

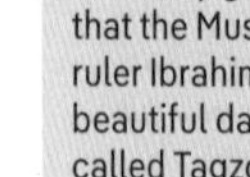

THE TRAGIC TALE OF LOVERS' LEAP

The story goes that the Muslim ruler Ibrahim had a beautiful daughter called Tagzona, who was in love with a handsome young Christian man from the Abencerrajes family of nearby Antequera. The pair ran away together and were chased by Moorish soldiers to the top of the rock. Rather than renounce their love or be captured, they chose to throw themselves over the edge, holding hands – together till the end.

El Torcal de Antequera

STRIKING LIMESTONE FORMATIONS

Since the Sierra del Torcal range emerged from the depths of the sea 150 million years ago, water has penetrated the rocks and chiselled out strange figures and formations. They're nowhere more remarkable than at El Torcal.

Walking through the 17-sq-km park, you'll see views across Málaga, local vegetation (the wild rose trees are stunning) and most likely a griffon vulture – the birds are often seen hovering over the park in search of prey. You may also come across some ammonite fossils.

For an extra-special experience, visit at night. The August moon, which rises far above the peaks, is best seen from Las Ventanillas viewpoint. The harsh edges of the mountain soften in the distance and the rocks take on an almost mystical appearance.

El Torcal is about 30km north of Málaga city, in the direction of Antequera, near Villanueva de la Concepción.

Parque Natural de Fuente de Piedra

VISIT THE FLAMINGOS

The largest lake in Andalucía, the Laguna de Fuente de Piedra becomes a flamingo nesting ground between February and May.

Tour companies provide binoculars and telescopes and go to strategic points where you can observe the flamingos, their breeding colony and other birds. Guides will explain the lake ecosystem and identify the birds you see.

Nearby, visit **Bodegas Málaga Virgen**, one of Málaga's oldest wineries, run by the fifth generation of winemakers

WHERE TO EAT

Restaurante la Garganta, El Chorro
Enjoyable fine-dining experience. €€

Meson Carrion, Alora
Local, friendly feel. €€

Bar Cristóbal, Alora
Good, simple, understated local tapas. €

El Caminito del Rey

BEST WALKING ROUTES AT EL TORCAL

Green route
The shortest and easiest; 1.5 km, about 30 minutes.

Yellow route
Takes you to Las Ventanillas for panoramic views; 2.5km.

Red route
The longest, with a viewing point out to the African coastline; 4.5km.

El Caminito del Rey

WALKWAY ALONG A GORGE

El Caminito del Rey (The King's Path) – so named because Alfonso XIII walked along it when he opened the Guadalhorce hydroelectric dam in 1921 – consists of a 2.9km boardwalk that hangs 100m above the Río Guadalhorce and snakes around the cliffs, affording breathtaking views at every turn.

The caminito had fallen into severe disrepair by the late 1990s, and it became known as the most dangerous pathway in the world; it officially closed in 2000 (though some daredevils still attempted it). Following an extensive €5.5-million restoration, it reopened in 2015; it is now safe and manageable for anyone with a reasonable head for heights.

The boardwalk is constructed with wooden slats; in some sections the old, crumbling path can be spied just below. The walk can only be done in one direction (north–south), and it's highly advisable to book a time slot online; tickets often sell out days or even weeks in advance.

You can walk independently, but guides can point out the best spots for historical context and of course for taking photos.

WHERE TO STAY

Hotel Coso Viejo, Antequera
Converted 17th-century neoclassical palace with rooms overlooking the Plaza. **€**

Hotel Infante Antequera, Antequera
Centrally located and has a rooftop pool. **€€**

La Fuente del Sol Hotel & Spa, Antequera
Exclusive rural hotel on the south slopes of the Sierra del Torcal. **€€€**

THINGS TO DO AROUND EL CAMINITO DEL REY

After your walk along the *caminito*, take a dip in the beautiful clear waters of the **Playa Caminito del Rey**. Relax as you gaze out at the view and watch the odd duck swim by. Enter beside El Kiosko restaurant, one of the kiosks at the bottom of the trail.

Visit the cave-church ruin of **Bobastro** and then go to the end of the road to look out from the viewing point.

Drive to the **Necropolis de las Aguilillas**, a group of seven tombs excavated in the land's rocky substrate between 2100 BCE and 1900 BCE. An easy-to-medium 2km circular path winds past the complex.

Frigiliana

View the shallow layers of earth which rose from the sea some 66 million years ago as the tectonic plates shifted (you will be able to see fossils). With a little luck, you'll also be able to see the Málaga-to-Sevilla train pass through the gorge at different moments!

Good kiosks are at the bottom of the trail, enabling you to quickly get rehydrated, catch your breath and take in the views.

Come in the late afternoon to avoid the crowds – and also the hottest time of the day in summer.

Buses run half-hourly from El Chorro train station to the starting point. From here you must walk 2.7km to the northern access point of the *caminito*, where you'll show your ticket and be given a mandatory helmet to wear. At the end of the *caminito* there's another 2.1km to walk from the southern access point back to El Chorro. Allow three to four hours total for the walk and connecting bus ride, as the views are made for savouring.

The most convenient public transport to the area is the twice-daily train from Málaga to El Chorro station. If you're driving, you can park at either end of the gorge and use the bus to make your connection.

GETTING AROUND

The locations are spread out, so you'll need your own car to visit this region.

FRIGILIANA

With its white houses and narrow streets and passages, the *pueblo blanco* of Frigiliana is regularly voted Andalucía's prettiest village by Spain's tourism authority. Its location in the Parque Natural de las Sierras de Tejeda, Almijara y Alhama makes it a perfect holiday spot for nature-lovers.

El Fuerte, the hill that climbs above the village, was the scene of the final bloody defeat of the Moors of La Axarquía during their 1569 rebellion. The decisive battle of Frigiliana Rock is commemorated on ceramic tiles that can still be seen across the village.

After the expulsion of the Moors, local silk production came to a halt. It was replaced by the sugar-cane industry as the region's main economic activity.

Several daily buses run from Nerja, or you can leave your car at the car park at the bottom of the hill. The A7 motorway links Frigiliana to Málaga and Granada.

TOP TIP

Frigiliana is best explored on foot, but to get your bearings you may enjoy the 30-minute tram journey across the village.

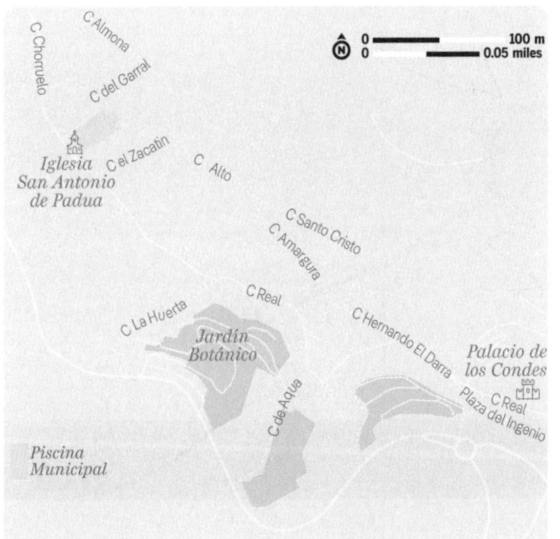

FESTIVAL TIME

In late August, the **Festival de las tres culturas** celebrates Muslim, Jewish and Christian heritage with street performances, fire shows, workshops and concerts, plus the Ruta de la Tapa, which presents the cultures' food specialities in the town's historic centre.

FRIGILIANA WALKING TOUR

Frigiliana is a tangle of narrow cobbled streets lined by whitewashed houses, beautiful flowers and coloured doors standing out against the bright white walls. Small plazas provide shady seating, and the village bars are popular with visitors who come here to taste the local wine.

Walk up the main street, Calle Real, to Plaza de la Iglesia and you'll reach the beautiful baroque-style **1 Iglesia San Antonio de Padua**, Frigiliana's most prominent building. The church was completed in the 17th century. Make a note to come back for dinner at **2 La Taberna del Sacristán** for great food and a close-up view of the church.

Just to the right you will notice the marble **3 Fuente Vieja** (Old Fountain). Adjacent is a clay slab with the symbols of the town's three main cultural influences: the Christian cross, the Jewish Star of David and the Muslim crescent.

Following a walk up the Avenida, at the Plaza de las Tres Culturas, you will find the **4 Fuente de las Tres Culturas** (Fountain of the Three Cultures). Located in the centre of a roundabout, and adorned with the same religious symbols, it represents the union of these three cultures, which coexisted peacefully here for many years.

Wander up to **5 Restaurante El Mirador** for a bite to eat and a stunning view out across the village.

Nearby, visit the **6 Palacio de los Condes** (Condes Palace), popularly known as El Ingenio. Situated at the northernmost point of the old town, this Renaissance mansion operates as the Fábrica de Miel de Cãna, the only traditional factory of this delicious sugarcane 'honey' (aka molasses) in Europe.

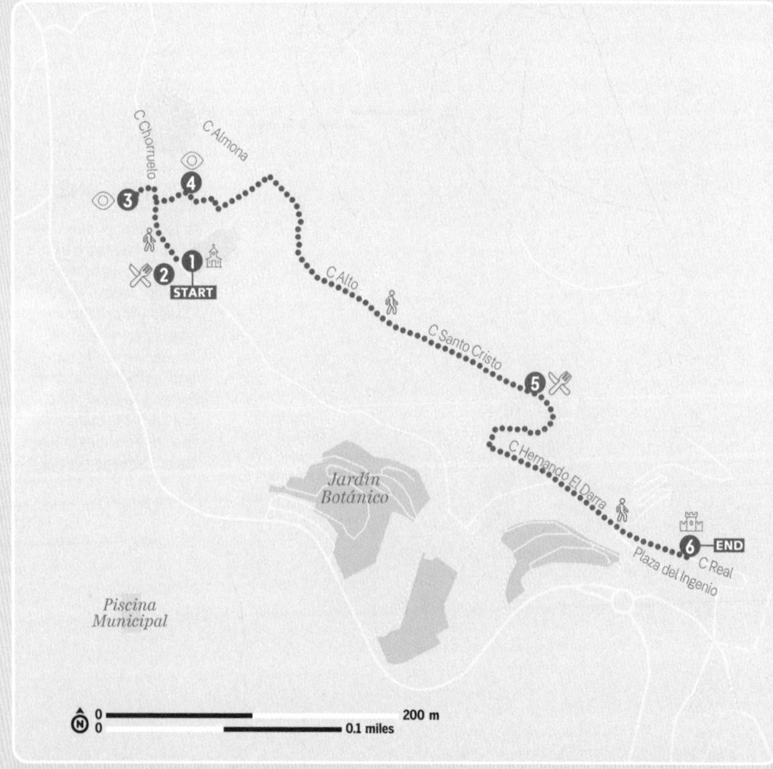

Beyond Frigiliana

Axarquía
El Acebuchal
Frigiliana
Playa de Maro
Nerja
Acantilados de Maro-Cerro Gordo

Frigiliana is the perfect base for exploring the town's natural surroundings.

Situated at the easternmost point of Málaga province, Frigiliana provides easy access to the region's beaches, caves and breathtaking Mediterranean views. Between Nerja and Málaga, the region of Axarquía has a string of towns famous for their avocados and mangoes, wine and olive oil. A stay here can easily be combined with a visit to Granada.

Situated at the easternmost point of Málaga province, Frigiliana provides easy access to the region's beaches and caves, plus breathtaking Mediterranean views.

For beaches, Playa de Maro is a must. If you fancy a different type of water-based experience, try out the ankle-deep Río Chillar river walk. A visit to the bustling tourist resort of Nerja is an option, if only to visit the stunning Balcón de Europa.

If you have a spare afternoon, pop over to El Acebuchal for a history lesson and a meal to savour. Between Nerja and Málaga, the region of Axarquía has a string of towns famous for their avocados and mangoes, wine and olive oil.

A stay here can easily be combined with a visit to Granada.

TOP TIP

With close proximity to some of the best beaches in Andalucía, this region is your ideal chance to unwind and relax.

Playa de Maro (p180)

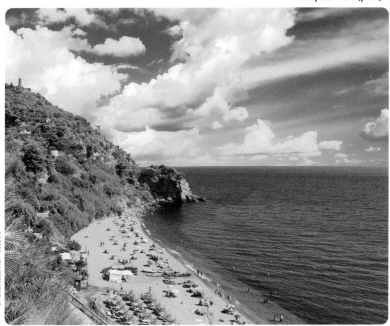

Nerja

THE BALCONY OF EUROPE

Just south of Frigiliana, the coastal town of Nerja draws a high proportion of British tourists, so it can be difficult to discover the Andalucian spirit here. Its incredible views across the Mediterranean and easy access to some of the most beautiful beaches along the Costa del Sol nonetheless make it a worthwhile stop.

The famous Balcony of Europe, once a fortress from which locals scanned the seas for British pirates, is now a stunning viewpoint. It's worth the effort to get up early and watch the sunrise here. Afterwards, grab a coffee and a light breakfast at nearby Anahi cafe.

Around town you'll find simple eateries and places to buy leather bags, plus plenty of shops catering to tourists.

UP CLOSE TO THE CLIFFS OF NERJA & MARO

The Acantilados de Maro-Cerro Gordo nature reserve is home to some of the most magnificent stretches of sand in all of Spain. There are hidden caves, secluded beaches and even a waterfall surrounded by massive craggy rocks.

The best way to experience the stunning cliffs of Nerja and Maro is by sea. Educare Adventures offers tours through the Cerro Gordo, starting at Burriana beach.

Options to explore this magical place include kayak, paddle surf and sailboat. The route takes you through beautiful locations, including Cueva del Lobo, Cascada Doncella, Playa Caleta de Maro and Cascada Grande de Maro.

Some companies enable you to dive in caves that only kayaks can access – an exhilarating experience.

Maro-Cerro Gordo Cliffs

VIEWS TO AFRICA

Standing at one of the scenic lookouts along the Acantilados de Maro-Cerro Gordo on a sunny day, you can enjoy magical views across to the African coast.

You can start a scenic walk at **Balcón de Maro**, in the front yard of Maro's Iglesia de las Maravillas. From here you can see the watchtower of **La Marquesa**, one of four towers erected in the 16th century to keep watch for pirates in the Mediterranean.

Walk along the N-340 toward **Almuñécar** and follow the directions leading to Torre de la Marquesa or Torre de Maro. The cliffs are impressive and the coves magnificent. Next, follow the road to **Cerro Gordo**, a spot that affords the best views of the cliffs and the coast of Málaga.

Access to the coves by car is prohibited.

Beaches

PARADISE ALONG THE COSTA DEL SOL

Consistently voted one of the best beaches in Spain, and surrounded by a protected natural environment, **Playa de Maro** is a haven of hidden waterfalls, underwater caves and some of the best snorkelling around.

The vast sandy expanse of **Playa de Burriana** gets quite full of tourists – but it sure is beautiful. A range of delicious restaurants along its front make it an enjoyable afternoon out. At Ayo, you can enjoy outstanding paella cooked on a

WHERE TO EAT AT THE FISHING HARBOUR OF CALETA DE VÉLEZ

Chinchin Puerto
Family-run restaurant with outstanding service and a great *ensaladilla rusa*! €€

Marisquería Mani
Set a little back from the coast; simple yet high quality with a strong local feel. €€

Bar el Calderón
Warm, friendly feel at this place on a simple terrace. Try the paella. €€

VOYAGERIX/SHUTTERSTOCK ©

Acantilados de Maro-Cerro Gordo

fire pit on the beach or savour fresh fish that's been expertly slow-cooked.

The hidden getaway of **Playa el Cañuelo**, in Nerja, sits on the border between Málaga and Granada provinces. It's not easy to access, but that just adds to its charm. The large Cañuelo cove is dramatically beautiful, with rocks jutting out of the sea at both ends, providing great opportunities to go snorkelling and see brightly coloured fish and corals. A shuttle bus makes the 15-minute trip to and from the beach.

NERJA CAVES

A sight to behold, the Nerja caves consist of two huge 4km-long, 35km-wide caverns with impressive limestone formations, and the world's longest known stalactite – a whopping 32m. Here you can discover art and history while enjoying a walk through the caverns.

The caves are also a venue for musical shows including Nejra's International Festival of Music and Dance, featuring Spanish and international performers.

The Nerja caves are 3km north of Nerja on the outskirts of the *pueblo blanco* of Maro.

El Acebuchal

RESTAURANT WITH A STORY

Exceptionally beautiful El Acebuchal is situated right in the heart of the Parque Natural de las Sierras de Tejeda, Almijara y Alhama.

In the fateful summer of 1948, a whole detachment of Franco's Guardia Civil officers forced everyone to leave their homes. El Acebuchal fell into ruin, becoming known locally as *el pueblo fantasma* (Village of Ghosts).

GRANADA SIDE TRIP

Turn to p225 to plan your side trip to Granada from this easternmost part of Málaga province.

WHERE TO STAY IN NERJA

Hostal Boutique Aurora
Excellent-value-for-money hostel in the centre of town, close to the beach. **€**

Hotel Riu Monica
Perfectly positioned beside the Balcón de Europa, this adults-only hotel is a perfect place to relax. **€€**

Welcome Inn Nerja
Friendly luxury boutique hotel, set outside the city centre, with stunning views. **€€€**

LOCAL FOOD

The Axarquía area's most traditional dishes are *potaje de hinojos* (fennel stew), *emblanco* (chickpeas with tripe) and *el chivo frito* (fried goat) with spices. On cold winter days, you can't miss out on *migas* (a traditional dish of breadcrumbs and accompaniments) – Andalucian *migas* are often fried and eaten with sardines as a tapa. If you still have room for dessert, try *la apropía* and *las marcochas*, two sweet treats made with molasses.

Miel de caña (molasses, commonly called sugar-cane syrup) is produced in Frigiliana and you will enjoy it spread over many dishes (including fried eggplant).

Axarquía

Decades later, Antonio 'El Gumbo', a former resident of El Acebuchal, took the initiative to bring the village back to life. The first house was finished in 1998 and after seven years the project was complete. Most of the village is now restored, although you will still see a few ruined houses.

At Antonio's family restaurant, overlooking lush mountains, you can enjoy a succulent meal made mostly of local and organic produce. The salads are out of this world, as are the homemade breads, desserts, ice creams and family-made olive oils. The house speciality is game, including boar and venison.

Nerja river walk up the Río Chillar

AN ADVENTURE IN NATURE

The Nerja river walk involves slow, steady walking in ankle-deep water as you enjoy striking rock formations, local flora and the unique black dragonfly. If you want to go all the way to Vado de los Patos, it's about 8km there and another 8km to get back (six or seven hours in total). The easier walk to the first pool (Los Cahorros) is about 5km.

WHERE TO STAY IN FRIGILIANA

El Torreón 119
All rooms enjoy sea or mountain views. **€€**

Millers Boutique Casa Rural
A unique family-run *casa rural* situated in Frigiliana's old Moorish quarter. **€€€**

Hotel Villa Frigiliana
Another small family-run hotel, offering stunning views over the mountains. **€€**

At Los Cahorros, the river passes through three cracks in the mountain – a beautiful sight! When you go through the cracks you can touch the walls with your hands. The further you go, the more opportunities there are to dip your whole body into the refreshing river.

Set off early in the morning to avoid the crowds and return before dark. The ideal times to visit are March–May and September–October. Wear comfortable trainers that protect your ankles and are good in wet conditions. Keep in mind that you will be walking on wet and slippery stones.

Park at the public car park on Calle Mirto. You'll need to walk some distance from here to begin the river walk.

If you're here in high season, you could visit the nearby Rio Higueron instead. It's equally enjoyable but less well known.

The farms of Axarquía

TRADITIONALLY MADE FOOD AND WINE

The Axarquía agricultural and winemaking area lies between Nerja and Málaga. It produces 80% of Spain's mangoes.

Guides such as Oletrips and Plan A Málaga can get you behind the scenes at two or three producers, where you can see traditional processes at work. Local winemakers leave their grapes in the sun before they crush them. Raisins are produced by drying grapes in the sunshine for 20 days. Olives are harvested, then processed into oil in a mill.

VISIT AXARQUÍA!

Estefanía Díez is the co-founder of Agualivar Spanish School.
@agualivar

In my home region of Axarquía, **Cómpeta** is the Moscatel town. Go for a tasting at **Bodegas Almijara** (my favourite is the dry white Moscatel).

Árchez, **Canillas de Albaida** and **Canillas de Aceituno** offer mountain views and great hiking. Enjoy the food at **La Sociedad** restaurant. If you want to visit Andalucía's oldest *venta* (inn), head for **La Venta de Alfarnate**.

Take in the sights of the **Lake Viñuela** dam, then enjoy the many restaurants and beautiful hotels nearby. Visit a *chiringuito* such as El Hornillero or La Flaca for a drink or a meal.

GETTING AROUND

A car is best to allow you to enjoy the villages of Axarquía. Drive at least part of the route from Nerja to Malaga along the coastal road, where you will see many *chiringuitos*.

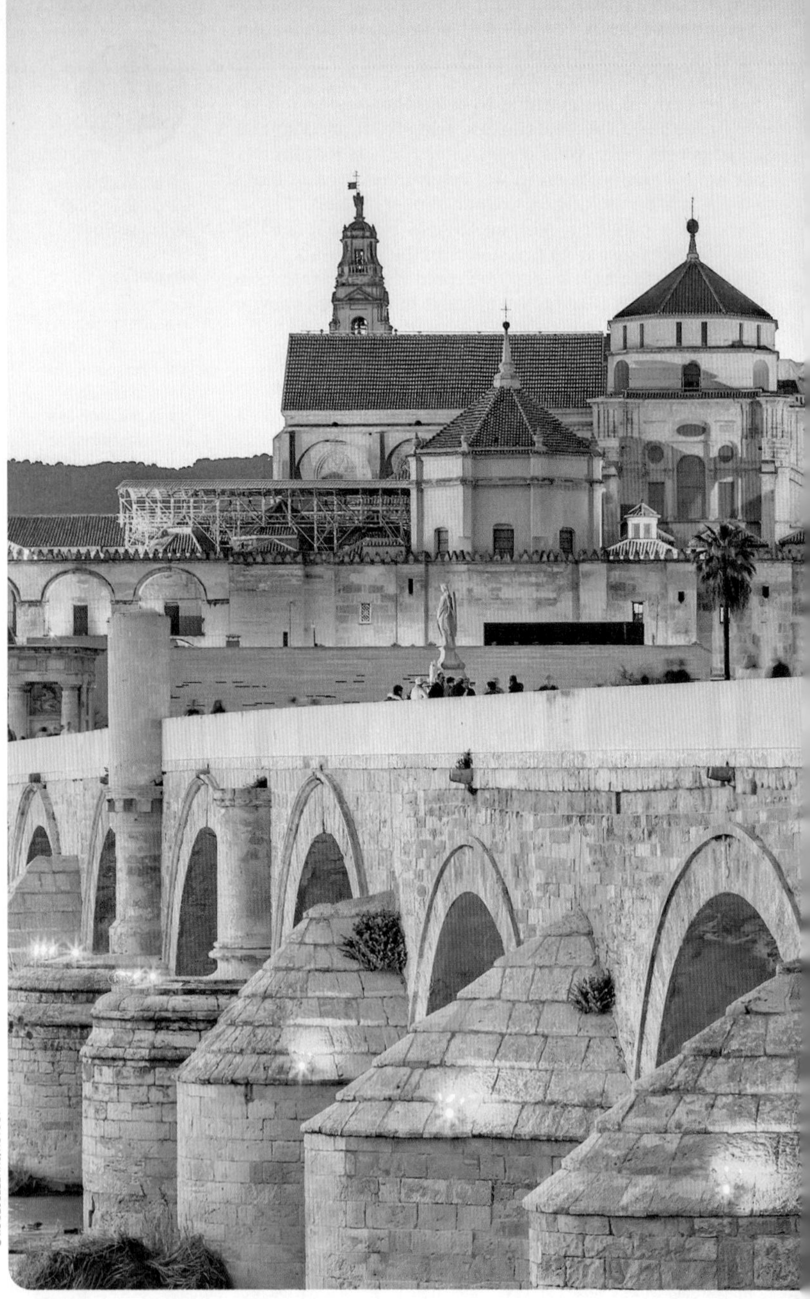

ARCADY/SHUTTERSTOCK ©

Mezquita (p190)

CÓRDOBA & JAÉN

HISTORY, CULTURE AND PROTECTED NATIONAL PARKS

Discover immense natural areas, weather-beaten historical sites and excellent gastronomy in these landlocked provinces in the north of Andalucía

Bordering the searing-hot plains and mountain ranges of the regions of Castilla-La Mancha and Extremadura to the north, Córdoba and Jaén (pronounced as a guttural 'hi- en') lie side by side. This is the most northerly and probably the wildest area of Andalucía. Spain's longest mountain range, Sierra Morena, once the frontier between the Moorish caliphate and the Reyes Católicos (Catholic Monarchs), straddles Jaén and Despeñaperros (the dramatic 'gateway' into Andalucía) across the provinces of Córdoba and Sevilla. It's a wilderness stretching 450km, full of legends of bandits, and home to wolves as well as the rare and hard-to-see Iberian lynx.

This northern area isn't the normal playground for most visitors; many head to Córdoba city, visit the Mezquita (mosque) and leave. There is so very much more. Every town, village, hamlet, turn in the road or brow of a hill beckons. Each province is worthy of standing still in, understanding its people's passion for the land, its locally sourced food and exquisite olive oils.

The provincial city of Córdoba is much better known than its little sister, Jaén. The latter may not have the Mezquita, but its own unique attractions – including the largest Arab baths in Spain and also the best-preserved ones in Europe, not to mention one of the top historical *paradores* in Spain – make it worthy of your time.

THE MAIN AREAS

CÓRDOBA CITY
Architecture, culture, horses and flamenco. p190

SIERRAS SUBBÉTICAS
Rugged landscape and unique white towns. p200

PARQUE NATURAL SIERRAS DE CAZORLA, SEGURA Y LAS VILLAS
Stunning wild scenery and fauna galore. p209

JAÉN, ÚBEDA & BAEZA
Historical sites and great gastronomy. p216

Find Your Way

With mountain ranges, flat plains, rolling olive groves and natural parks, these two land-locked provinces cover a quarter of Andalucía and have a wealth of history, culture, and natural beauty to discover.

Córdoba City, p190
As well as the must-visit Mezquita, you'll experience Córdoba's long history, four UNESCO-protected sites, customs, traditions, and fabulous gastronomy.

Sierras Subbéticas, p200
A large expanse of nature dotted with interesting little towns, often dramatically located, to experience and explore.

CAR

Having your own transport is ideal; stop when you want, change your itinerary on a whim, head for that stunning castle on a hill and choose when and where to stop and eat.

BUS

Between cities or larger towns buses are ideal, but due to the sheer size and often mountainous terrain of this area of Andalucía it's difficult to access smaller towns by bus. The main bus company is alsa.com.

TRAIN

Because of the mountainous landscape, trains are quite limited. Trains can be used between cities, but there are very few to smaller towns. Renfe.com has a map of the stations to help plan a route.

Parque Natural Despeñaperros
Parque Natural Sierra de Andújar
Santa Elena
La Carolina
Santisteban del Puerto
Villarrodrigo
Siles
Orcera
Beas de Segura
Cortijos Nuevos
El Yelmo (1808m)
Hornos
Tranco
Villanueva del Arzobispo
Baños de la Encina
Vilches
Linares
Bailén
Embalse de Giribaile
Villacarrillo
Sierra de Cazorla
Santiago de la Espada
Río Guadalquivir
Torreperogil
Coto Ríos
Parque Natural Sierras de Cazorla, Segura y las Villas
Úbeda
Baeza
Begíjar
Mengíbar
Arroyo Frío
JAÉN
Peal de Becerro
Cazorla
Sierra del Pozo
Parque Natural Sierra de Castril
Jimena
Jódar
Bedmar
Quesada
Mancha Real
Torres
Huéscar
Cabañas (2027m)
Jaén
Parque Natural Sierra Mágina
Sierra de Cazorla
Pozo Alcón
Huelma
Guadahortuna
Alcalá la Real
GRANADA
Guadix

Parque Natural Sierras de Cazorla, Segura y las Villas, p209

Rolling mountaintop pasture land, steep valleys with tumbling rivers and stunning, far-reaching scenery.

Jaén, Úbeda & Baeza, p216

These lesser-visited cities with Renaissance monuments offer free tapas and local fare based on its extra virgin olive oil from the surrounding olive groves.

Plan Your Time

This northernmost part of Andalucía is often overlooked; it shouldn't be. Craft your itineraries around time-warped towns, sleepy mountain villages, ancient traditions, and great gastronomy and free tapas in Jaén province.

MATTEO COLOMBO/GETTY IMAGES ©

Mezquita (p190)

If you only go to one place

● Head to **Parque Natural Sierras de Cazorla, Segura y las Villas** (p209) in Jaén province for the giant, natural wilderness, enticing gastronomy and stunning views. Abundant in history, culture, traditions and wildlife, this is a place that many travellers are unaware of. Peace reigns, so travel slowly and be amazed at the sheer size of the park, 2143 sq km, in a province that has over 66 million olive trees too. It's dotted with charming towns and villages that keep their longstanding traditions, and are topped with ancient castles and watchtowers.

Seasonal highlights

Summers are usually scorching hot, so check out the many wild swimming options before you go. Winters can be cold but sunny, with snow only in the high mountain areas.

JANUARY

Quite cold. Day of the Kings is 6 January, so festivities are still happening. The olive harvest is well underway.

MARCH

Spring looms; fresh, green olive 'juice' is on sale, and it's the ideal season to buy it. Great time for walking holidays.

APRIL

Usually the month of Holy Week. Penitents and processions in almost every city and town.

MIQUELITO/SHUTTERSTOCK ©, ANA DEL CASTILLO/SHUTTERSTOCK ©, MURATTELLIOGLU/SHUTTERSTOCK ©

The cities in three days

● First spend a night in **Córdoba city** (p190) and visit the **Mezquita**, have lunch in a typical tavern, see the **Alcázar de los Reyes Cristianos** (p192), then take in a flamenco show with dinner.

● In the morning wander through the Jewish Quarter to **Plaza de la Corredera** (p193) for breakfast. Pop to the **Palacio de Viana** (p193) to get a taste of the Córdoba patios. Head north to the pasture lands of **Los Pedroches** (p199) and the roaming black pigs before more culture in Unesco-listed **Úbeda** (p218) or **Baeza** (p219) for a night.

● Travel through the olive groves to **Jaén**'s Santa Catalina Hill (p216), take a short stroll to the monumental cross and castle before booking into the hilltop Parador hotel.

Five days of nature & white towns

● With just five days and four nights, head straight to the **Parque Natural Sierras Subbéticas** (p200), resplendent with lovely *pueblos blancos* (white towns), excellent walking and a strategic location to spend a day or two in the larger cities if wanted. **Priego de Córdoba** (p201) and **Zuheros** (p200) within the Natural Park are a must.

● For a fabulous fortress head to Alcalá la Real; for a Roman villa and charming small town – **Almedinilla** (p203); for a gentle stroll take the old olive-oil-train route – **Vía Verde de Aceite** (p207). Fresh air, good food, friendly people and peace abound here.

MAY

Warming up rapidly, but a nice time to explore. A riot of colour everywhere, with Córdoba patios and wildflowers.

AUGUST

August gets very hot in the cities. It is the season for enjoying early mornings, siestas and late nights.

SEPTEMBER

With warm days and cooler evenings, this is a great month for exploring both city and nature.

OCTOBER

For walking and natural areas, October is ideal. The greenery returns and the temperatures are very pleasant.

CÓRDOBA CITY

Phoenicians, Romans, Visigoths and Moors left their mark, and the incredible heritage in Córdoba today. Under Roman Emperor Claudius Marcellus it became Corduba, the largest town in southern Iberia in the days when the Río Guadalquivir was navigable from the Atlantic Ocean up to what is Córdoba city today. The weakening of the Roman Empire and upsurge of the Visigoths saw the city change hands once again. The Moors then took possession in 711 CE and it grew into the Muslim capital on the Iberian Peninsula and the largest city in Western Europe under Abd ar-Rahman I, the independent emir of Al-Andalus.

Being on the plains of the river, it's a flat and easy-to-navigate city. Both old and modern parts merge seamlessly. Be immersed in the evidence of Jews, Moors and Christians living side by side in peace for centuries; it's easy to see why Córdoba has four Unesco listings.

TOP TIP

Head to a Tourist Information Office for a map (Google Maps struggles in the narrow streets) and up-to-date opening hours of the monuments; these change according to the season. Crossing the Roman Bridge and through the Puerta del Puente, also called the Arco del Triunfo, there is a Centro de Recepción de Visitantes office on the right.

COOL CALLES

Neat streets to explore.

Calle de la Hoguera Approach from Calle Céspedes to see the small minaret of the Mezquita de los Andaluces.

Calleja de Pañuelo One of the narrowest alleys in Europe, just elbow-to-elbow wide.

Calleja de los Arquillos Narrow dead-end, ancient street with seven arches.

Calleja de las Flores Prettiest and most photogenic street in Córdoba.

Jewish Quarter & the Mezquita

MESMERISING MEZQUITA AND JEWISH JEWELS

Walk around the outside of the fortress-like walls of the Mezquita to appreciate its sheer size and intricacy. There are several entrances into the ancient courtyard of ablutions, the **Patio de los Naranjos**; the most stunning is the Puerta del Perdón on Calle Cardenal Herrero. Wander in, pass through or stay awhile. This enormous courtyard is divided into three sections, each with its own fountain, and is named after the 90 orange trees there. After the cleansing ritual, enter the Mezquita itself. It is one of the most important Islamic buildings in Spain, and an experience not forgotten easily: a Catholic cathedral inside an ancient mezquita – incongruous, yet true. It's best enjoyed at the beginning or end of the day when few other visitors are around.

While entrance to the Patio de los Naranjos is free, there are separate tickets to go into the Mezquita or up the 54m-high bell tower. The tower has views around town and can help with getting your bearings on this cobbled labyrinth of narrow streets, interior patios and small plazas. Look into doorways for delightful flower-filled patios through metalwork doors. Many patios enter the Patio Competition in May, a lot of which are within the Jewish Quarter.

Wandering down Calle Judíos, pop into the beautifully intricate, square synagogue built in 1315, the only one remaining

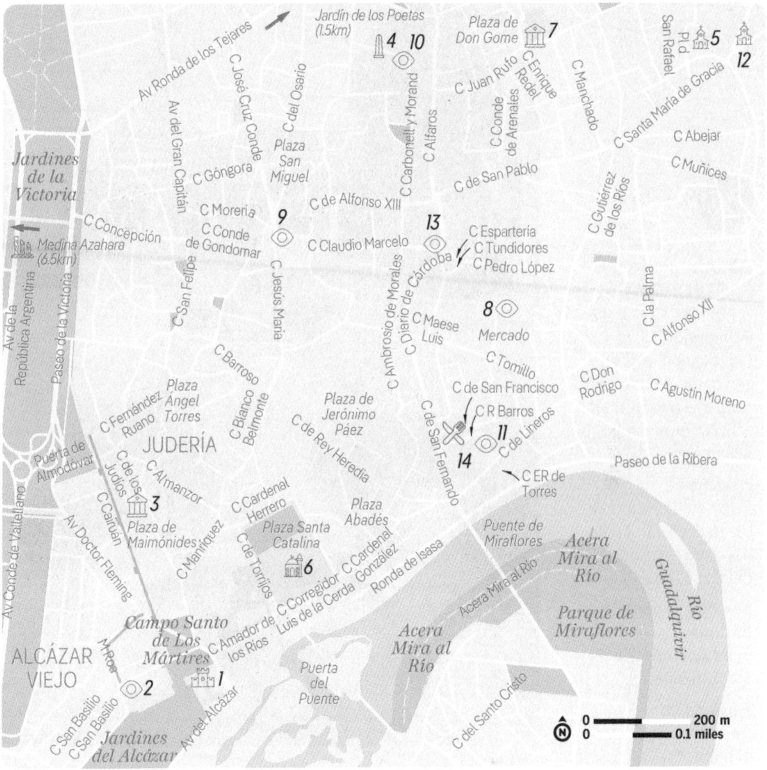

SIGHTS
1 Alcázar de los Reyes Cristianos
2 Caballerizas Reales
3 Casa de Sefarad
4 Cristo de los Faroles
5 Iglesia del Juramento de San Rafael
6 Mezquita
7 Palacio de Viana
8 Plaza de la Corredera
9 Plaza de las Tendillas
10 Plaza de los Capuchinos
11 Plaza del Potro
12 Real Parroquia de San Lorenzo Mártir de Córdoba
13 Templo Romano

EATING
14 Taberna Sociedad de Plateros

in Andalucía. Just up (or down) the street is a fascinating Jewish culture and history museum, **Casa de Sefarad**. On the corner of Calle Judíos is a glorious Mudéjar building with two floors and a beautiful patio that now houses the craft association **Zoco** where shops and traditional crafts can be found.

WHERE TO EAT

Bar Santos
To snack on an enormous tortilla (made with 5kg potatoes and 30 eggs). **€**

Restaurante Regadera
Great local dishes in a modern, light space. **€€**

Bodegas Campos
Lovely old winery; now a charming, old-school restaurant. **€€€**

LOCAL GASTRONOMY

Salmorejo
Chilled tomato, bread and garlic-based thick soup or dip garnished with jamón and hard-boiled egg.

Mazamorra
Thick, chilled almond, bread or cornflour dip (far more delicious than it sounds).

Berenjenas con Miel de Caña
Fried aubergines with black treacle.

Flamenquin
Deep-fried roll of ham/pork loin and cheese with breadcrumbs.

Rabo de Toro
Bull's tail – prepared in a variety of ways.

Palacio de Viana

San Basilio & Alcázar de los Reyes Cristianos

STUNNING ROYAL CASTLE AND GARDENS

The area of **San Basilio** was built as housing for the staff of the **Alcázar de los Reyes Cristianos** and its royal stables – **Caballerizas Reales**. Wander the streets and glance through those open doors or gateways to see where life used to take place: the interior patio or 'Córdoba Patio'. This area also has lots of entries for the Patio Competition in May and several patios are open all year round. The tourist office has a list, but if there's a door open, step in and see. The Alcázar (Royal Fortress) was the first place the Catholic monarchs

WHERE TO SEE GREAT LITTLE MUSEUMS

Museo de la Alquimia
Interesting little alchemy museum on Calle los Judios.

Casa Andalusi
Beautiful Jewish house and courtyard.

La Casa del Agua
Getting water to the city through the ages exhibition.

met with Christopher Columbus while planning their campaign to reconquer the remaining occupied parts of Andalucía. The fortress is home to a castle, rebuilt by Alfonso XI in 1327, and gorgeous gardens remodelled in the 19th century. Ingenious irrigation systems fed the castle and grounds, via aqueducts from the Sierra Morena and Albolafia waterwheel in the nearby **Río Guadalquivir**. Head up onto the battlements for fabulous views. See the displays of 2nd- and 3rd-century intricate Roman mosaics found in the **Plaza de la Corredera** in 1959. The royal stables attached to the fortress are home to the Spanish purebred horse, thanks to Philip II and his desire for a more elegant and agile horse. The beautiful stables, first built in 1570, were partly damaged by fire in the early 18th century, but the original part is a highlight, as is the arena, especially if a horse and flamenco show is on.

San Andres & Palacio de Viana

CAPTIVATING PALACE MUSEUM

The centre of the San Andrés area is the church of the same name built over an old Visigoth church. In front of it is a beautiful octagonal baroque fountain. Behind the church is an oasis, the Jardines de Orive urban garden – just the place to stop awhile when walking from the **Plaza de la Corredera** to the Palacio de Viana.

The **Palacio de Viana**, Spain's best-preserved manor house, is a delightful visit any time of year, but spring is obviously the most colourful time to see the floral creativity in the 12 patios and garden that surround the beautiful palace/museum. When the world-famous **Patio Competition** takes place in May, entrance is free. Each patio is unique, so time is needed to wander slowly through each one. The Renaissance palace is really a five-century mishmash of architectural styles; a grand, private house belonging to the Spanish noble family Viana, and occupied by them from 1425 until the 1980s. The furniture and decor are a frozen portrayal of daily life in times gone by.

Medina Azahara

AMAZING 10TH-CENTURY ARCHAEOLOGICAL SITE

After seeing the wonder of the Mezquita, a visit to the archaeological site of the enormous, fortified city/palace of the Medina Azahara (aka Madinat al-Zahra or 'Bright City'), built in the 10th century, is a must. This major site

OTHER WAYS TO SEE THE CITY

Horse-and-carriage ride
Found near the Alcázar de los Reyes and by the side of the Mezquita.

Tour bus
Open-topped, hop-on/hop-off bus tours throughout the city. Buy tickets online via City Sightseeing (city-sightseeing-spain.com/en/20/cordoba).

Segway/electric scooter/bike
Zip around town on a guided Segway tour or hire a scooter or electric bike with Elektrik (rentabikecordoba.com).

Guided walking tour
Various companies provide free tours: owaytours.com; cordobapie.es; guruwalk.com.

JUDERÍAS

To learn a bit about the history of *juderías* (Jewish quarters) and the Inquisition, see p302.

WHERE TO SEE OTHER FLORAL EXHIBITS

May Crosses Fiesta
Huge crosses made of plants adorn nooks and plazas across the city on 1 May.

Guardians of the Courtyards
Bronze sculptures plus potted plants in Puerta del Rincón, Alcázar Viejo and Plaza del Poeta Juan Bernier.

El Palacio de Viana
With its 12 patios, this museum is a great place for plant lovers, especially in spring.

is at the foot of the Sierra Morena mountain range, yet just a short drive, or bus ride, from the modern city centre. The museum offers intriguing insights into the history, rich indulgence and extravagance of the caliphate. A shuttle bus travels between the museum and car park below and the site above. Visit the museum first to learn about the scale of the former capital city, which covered an area of 1.5km from east to west and 700m from north to south. Excavations are ongoing at this Unesco site, one of the most important archaeological sites in Spain. What is accessible for visitors to see now is an eye-opener into the opulence of its day.

LEATHER ART OF CÓRDOBA

Spain has long been famous for its leather and leatherwork. Even the artistic leatherwork popular in the 16th century of decorated chairs and wall hangings, embossed botanical designs and geometrical patterns found in palaces and stately homes across Europe came from Andalucía. But even before then, a type of leather art called Guadamecí or Omeya was developed in Córdoba during the Muslim caliphate of the 10th century – a highly decorative and skilled art form that was lost for centuries. Guadamecí art has been revived in the city, and José Carlos Villarejo García, taught by his uncle who has taught himself from archives, may be the only person in the world creating these decorative pieces of art. Visit **Casa-Museo del Guadamecí Omeya** to see his exquisite work.

Plethora of plazas

WANDERING STREETS, ANCIENT AND MODERN

The ancient Jewish Quarter merges with modern Córdoba seamlessly: narrow cobbled streets with tiny plazas that change at every junction, from tiny squares to enormous buzzing shopping centres. **Plaza de la Corredera** is a huge Castille-style rectangular plaza, the only one of this type in the south of Spain. Roman mosaics on display in the **Alcázar de los Reyes Cristianos** were excavated from here. Once holding bullfights, public addresses and executions, now it's a great spot for a stop for refreshments and to see the local craft of esparto weaving or the indoor food market.

Miguel Cervantes lived near the **Plaza del Potro** and mentioned it in *Don Quixote*. A large, square traders' marketplace in the 16th and 17th century surrounded by inns, now just the beautiful **Posada del Potro** remains. The statue of the colt (potro) on the 16th-century fountain is a reminder of the trading that took place here before the Hospital de la Caridad was built at the end of 17th century, reducing its size. **Plaza de las Tendillas** is the commercial centre of Córdoba – a large, pedestrian plaza with bars and fountains. Be there on the hour when the clock chimes flamenco-guitar music or join the multitude of people who congregate at New Year's Eve to celebrate the 12 chimes with the eating of 12 grapes – not as easy as it sounds. The marble columns of the **Templo Romano** are just down the road from here. Originally part of the now demolished Convento del Santo Ángel, the **Plaza de los Capuchinos** is more often referred to as its statue – **Cristo de los Faroles**. This ancient statue is surrounded by eight street lights that represent the eight provinces of Andalucía.

WHERE TO STAY

Las Casas de la Judería
Five old houses transformed into one charming hotel. **€€€**

Balcon de Córdoba
Beautiful blend of old and new. **€€€**

Hotel Hacienda Posada de Vallina
Good-value hotel, right next to the Mezquita. **€€**

Plaza de las Tendillas

TYPICAL TABERNAS

Plateros María Auxiliadora
Mezquita-style patio.

Taberna Casa Bravo
Traditional decor, founded in 1919.

El Burlaero
Bullfighting memorabilia.

Casa El Pisto
Nineteenth-century tavern, vintage photos.

La Cazuela de la Esparteria
Looks like a shopfront.

Bodega Guzman
Local wine from the barrel.

San Lorenzo & the patios

PLANTS, PATIOS AND TYPICAL TABERNAS

The area of San Lorenzo dates from the 13th century, when the city was divided into areas after the Christian reconquest (Reconquista). It was a mainly working-class neighbourhood that saw the *Motín del Pan* uprising in 1650 – a fight against famine. Stop by **San Lorenzo church**, which was built over a mosque and replaced a Visigoth church. Visigoth remnants can still be seen, such as the impressive Gothic-Mudéjar rose window. The **Iglesia del Juramento de San Rafael**, with its neoclassical facade, is supposedly where the archangel Raphael appeared to Father Roelas in the 16th century to ask him to guard the city. The **Jardín de los Poetas** is an

FREE FLAMENCO SHOWS

Throughout July and August the town hall puts on free flamenco concerts (until venue is full); cordobaturismo.es. See p304 for more information about the history of flamenco dancing.

Patios de Orfebre
Charming 16th-century house with typical interior patio. €€

Mayflowers
Good natural lighting, friendly and well-located *hostal*. €

Hotel Maestre
Near Patio del Potro, great location, clean and good value. €

WATCHING LOCAL CRAFTSPEOPLE

Head to Calle Puerta de Almodóvar to the shop Cerámica to watch the **potter** at work making flamenco figures.

For guitar fans, Calle San Pablo is the place to go to see **luthier** José Rodríguez at work.

Also on Calle San Pablo watch **cobbler** El Reparador do leather tooling, belt making and shoe repairs.

Fourth-generation **silversmith** Joaquín Espaliú is on Calle Almanzor, near Cerámica.

For esparto **grass weaving** and shop go to the huge Plaza de la Corredera.

JOHN_SILVER/SHUTTERSTOCK ©

San Lorenzo church (p195)

oasis. For a spot of refreshment, the 1868 Taberna Sociedad de Plateros-María Auxiliadora (Tavern of the Society of Silversmiths-María Auxiliadora), with its *mezquita*-style arches and typical patio with orange and lemon trees, serves traditional, local fare. As with the other areas of the city, some of the beautiful interior patios of private houses open to the public during the fortnight of the **Fiesta de los Patios**. The tourist office has special maps showing where each free-to-enter patio is located. All are beautiful and worthy of seeing, but best choose an area where quite a few are grouped together, so there's not so much walking at what is usually a very hot time of the year.

GETTING AROUND

Buses and trains run fairly frequently from surrounding towns. The train station is a 15-minute walk from the historical centre. Arriving by car can be painful if your hotel doesn't have parking or it's a day trip. Take the Avenida Campo de la Verdad road soon after leaving the main E-4; there's free on-street parking to be found.

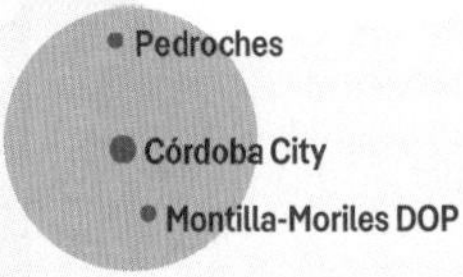

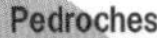

Beyond Córdoba City

Leaving Córdoba city behind, head north to the pasture lands of Pedroches and south to the vineyards of Montilla-Moriles DOP.

Los Pedroches is an area of flatland north of Córdoba city surrounded by mountain ranges, where black Iberian pigs graze calmly on the holm oaks that provide shade in stone-walled fields. Jamón producers and factories abound. Los Pedroches has 17 *pueblos blancos* dotted around the natural landscape, as well as the Cardeña-Montoro Natural Park.

South of the city, the countryside is calmer, with far-reaching views and charming, white, castle-topped towns. These are the plains of the Montilla-Moriles DOP area: vineyards galore with over 50 local wineries. Go at the end of August to see the vineyards being harvested and grapes laid out to dry for several days, and taste those extra-sweet speciality wines of the area.

TOP TIP

If you visit a winery at the finish of harvest, there are often special celebrations, such as jazz concerts, amid the tastings.

Montilla-Moriles (p198)

WHAT ELSE TO SEE IN THE DOP AREA

Villa Romana de Fuente Álamo
Roman villa and architectural site with incredible Roman mosaics in Puente Genil.

Museo de Ceramica
Interesting ceramic museum in La Rambla.

Museo Arqueológico de Ulía
In Montemayor. Don't miss the mirador just around the corner.

Lagar los Raigones
Producers of olive oil and wine.

JOSERPIZARRO/SHUTTERSTOCK ©

Camino Mozárabe de Santiago

Montilla-Moriles DOP wine area

VINEYARDS, WINE AND WINE BARRELS

The Montilla-Moriles DOP is in the plains of the Río Genil and Río Guadajoz; Montilla itself is about 40 minutes south of Córdoba city. A car is by far the easiest method of exploring the area's 17 towns. Montilla-Moriles has been producing wine since Roman times and is the most northerly DOP in Andalucía. You'll notice how the landscape mellows and the earth changes from red to the very pale, almost white, albarizo soil – the same as the sherry triangle in Cadiz – which the Pedro Ximénez grape loves. From this grape a range of wines, from young ones to famous sherries (*fino*, *amontillado*, *oloroso* and *palo cortado*) are produced, as well as dessert wines (muscatel and Pedro Ximénez), which are the most famous. These are wines that are perfect to serve with tapas, for dessert or to accompany cured meats and fish or shellfish.

WHERE TO DO WINERY TOURS & TASTINGS

Bodegas Alvear
In the heart of Montilla, Andalucía´s oldest and Spain's second-oldest winery, founded in 1729.

Bodegas Robles
Third-generation winemakers, now producing organic wines and vermouth too.

Bodegas Toro Albalá
Many-times award-winners; in the same family since 1922.

A visit to a winery or two is a must. Learn about the ancient *solera* method and experience the history and fragrance of the many wineries throughout the area. As wine production and barrel-making go hand in hand, this is the place to see the fascinating craft of barrels being created by hand at various locations, mostly in Montilla itself.

Pasture lands of Los Pedroches

VAST PLAINS, SMALL TOWNS

The name Los Pedroches comes from the Moorish 'land or valley of acorns'. This vast expanse, comprising more than 3000 sq km of rocky terrain and flattish plains of holm oak and cork oak groves, begins around an hour north of Córdoba city. Seventeen unique towns are scattered between the acres of wild meadows, grazed by acorn-feeding black pigs, which makes them difficult to explore by public transport. This is the most northerly part of Córdoba province and where the region of Andalucía borders with the region of Extremadura. Explore by car or do some walking for a slower-paced experience. The **Camino Mozárabe de Santiago** winds through here, a lesser-walked route starting in Almeria.

As in most of Andalucía, *jamón* is served everywhere, but Los Pedroches is home to some of the best. Head to one of the many *jamón* factories to learn about the curing and drying process and for a tasting.

Tiny towns, interesting museums, air-raid shelters and huge stork nests on church towers make for some interesting sightseeing in this hinterland. In the wilds of the **Sierra de Cardeña y Montoro Natural Park** wolves and lynx can be spotted. The Spanish film *Entrelobos*, based on a true story of a boy growing up among wolves, was filmed here in 2010. For stunning views, castle fans should head to the medieval fortress of **Castillo de Sotomayor** in **Belalcázar** and the ruins of **Castillo de Miramontes**, visible from the valley of Los Pedroches in **Santa Eufemia**.

CORPUS CHRISTI FLOWER CARPETS

Scattered around the province, towns of all sizes decorate their streets with *alfombras de flores* (flower carpets) and coloured sawdust to celebrate Corpus Christi, which is the 8th Sunday after Easter. These towns in Córdoba province are where you can see this ancient tradition:

- Ademuz
- Belmez
- Bujalance
- Carcabuey
- Pozoblanco
- Priego de Córdoba
- Valenzuela
- Villanueva del Duque

FOR ROMAN MOSAIC FANS

Roman mosaics can also be seen in the **Alcázar de los Reyes** (p192) in Córdoba city, in the **Roman Villa** (p203) in Almedinilla and in **Cástulo** (p215), Jaén.

GETTING AROUND

Los Pedroches has so much natural beauty and small towns to discover, having your own transport really is a must if you want to appreciate and explore the area to the full.

It's possible to visit the towns in the Montilla-Moriles wine area by bus, although they are not very frequent.

SIERRAS SUBBÉTICAS

The 320,560 sq metre Parque Natural Sierras Subbéticas, not to be confused with the area La Subbética, is almost in the geographical heart of Andalucía. It's an enormous, wild and rugged mountainous area dotted with Moorish watchtowers, limestone peaks and deep ravines. The area was granted Natural Park status in 1988, and since 2006 it's also a Unesco-approved Global Geopark. The beautiful scenery is studded with 17 *pueblos blancos* that are within its borders, each one unique and worthy of exploring.

Hiking and mountain biking, rock climbing and horse riding are the best ways to appreciate the mesmerising scenery. If more gentle walking and cycling is your thing, then the reconditioned train track Vía Verde de Aceite winds – almost level – through the olive groves and sierras of Córdoba's countryside. Birdwatchers and fauna fans, foodies and architecture lovers will all enjoy the Sierras Subbéticas.

TOP TIP

Find out which local fiestas (especially in the smaller towns) are happening during your travel dates and plan your itinerary around them. You may want to join the party or avoid those dates, as everything of interest will be closed.

SOME OF THE FIESTAS IN THE SUBBÉTICAS

Iznájar Fiesta
Third week in June.

Zuheros Fiesta
Second week in August.

Almedinilla Ibero-Roman Fiesta
Second week in August.

Cabra Fiesta
First week in September.

Priego de Córdoba Fiesta
First week in September.

Zuheros Cheese Fair
Around 22 September.

Almedinilla Fiesta
Second week in September.

Zuheros & bat cave

CHARMING TOWN, CAVERNOUS ADVENTURES

Zuheros town is a real chocolate box charmer. It is one of the *Pueblos más bonitos de España* and declared as having Historical and Architectural Interest. Enjoy the first glimpse of its rocky backdrop to the hidden miradors and fairy-tale castle. Birds of prey circle above and the sierras surround the town. Climb the cute 9th-century Moorish fortress that was made larger in the 16th century. Narrow streets and window bars with brightly coloured cascading flowers make it a delight to explore.

Cueva de los Murciélagos (the Bat Cave) is the biggest known cave in Córdoba province. It's a year-round experience, but you'll need warmer clothes if you go in summer; there's a massive difference in temperature between the 30°C+ outside and down the cave. Reservations are necessary and good footwear essential, as the fascinating tour takes about 90 minutes, and you'll drop 65m below ground with 700 steps on uneven terrain. From the vast hall at the start of the tour, it's a 415m loop walk through a series of corridors filled with fantastic rock formations and traces of Neolithic rock paintings showing abstract figures of goats. Be at the cave 15 minutes before the visit starts. The entrance is about 4km above Zuheros town in the Natural Park. The drive up to it is exhilarating; the road twists and

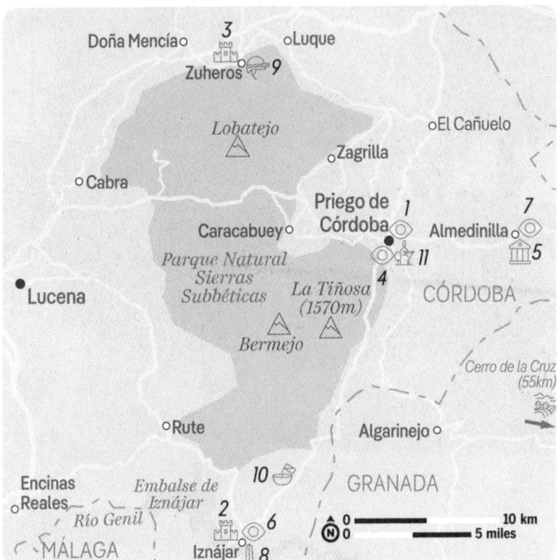

SIGHTS
1 Barrio de la Villa
2 Castillo de Iznájar
3 Castillo de Zuheros
4 Fuente del Rey
5 Museo Histórico de Almedinilla
6 Patio de las Comedias
7 Roman Villa El Ruedo
8 Torre de San Rafael

ACTIVITIES, COURSES & TOURS
9 Cueva de los Murciélagos
10 Finca Las Encinas

DRINKING & NIGHTLIFE
11 Bar Yampe

turns through the looming mountains, with vertiginous views from various lookout points. If you can't fit in a cave tour and/or you don't like bats and the dark, the visitor centre is very interesting.

Zuheros is famous for its Cheese Fair in mid September, which attracts cheeses and cheese lovers from far afield, and many local ones too. It's a great time to visit and try some award-winning dairy produce. It is also an ideal base if you want to walk or cycle on the **Vía Verde de Aceite**, which passes very close to the town. For a gentle warm-up, you can stroll round the village's lower periphery through the **Parque Periurbano**, taking in lookout points and a hanging bridge.

Priego de Córdoba

BEAUTIFUL BAROQUE AND BALCONY VIEWS

If you approach Priego de Córdoba via the A-333, you'll see the *pueblo blanco* perched on rock, with the natural adarve balcony running along the edge, and understand why it's been nicknamed the 'wedding cake' town. Leaving the modern outskirts and heading into the old part of

WHERE TO SEE MORE SUBBÉTICA CAVES

Cueva de los Mármoles
Used as a refuge in the Spanish Civil war, and easy to find near the village of La Concepción.

La Cueva del Macho
In the Sierra Alcaide near Carcabuey you'll find this easy-to-access limestone cave.

Sima de Cabra
First explored in 1841 and mentioned by Miguel de Cervantes in *Don Quixote*, it has a 116m descent.

OTHER TOWNS TO VISIT ON THE CALIPH ROUTE

The Caliph route has some enchanting towns worth adding to your itinerary.

Alguilar de la Frontera
A frontier town with an unusual polygonal square.

Cabra
Has an ammonite as its emblem and a huge number of archaeological sites dating to the Paleolithic times.

Castro del Río
Supposedly of pre-Roman origin, and delightful. Don't miss the Barrio de la Villa.

Espejo
Interesting castle town with famous local pastries that must be tried – *mostachones*.

Lucena
Habited by Jews in the 9th century and with a castle in the town centre, not on a hill.

Montemayor
Fortress town with far-reaching views from the mirador, and an engrossing little architectural museum.

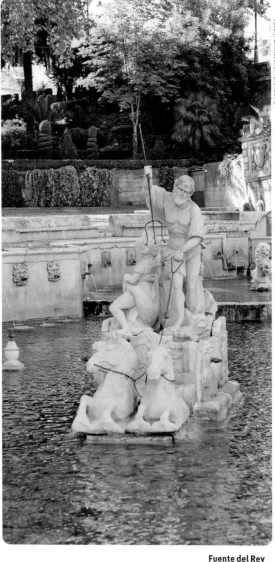

JOSERPIZARRO/SHUTTERSTOCK ©

Fuente del Rey

WHERE TO STAY IN THE SUBBÉTICAS

Casa Olea
Charming, rural escape serving great food near Priego de Córdoba. **€€**

Finca Las Encinas
B&B near Iznájar town and lake. **€€**

Hotel Patria Chica
In central Priego de Córdoba, a hotel/museum with interior patio and private garden. **€€**

town, wonderful architecture woos. Porticos and window bars, stonework and columns from large mansions shout 19th century; it's a delight to wander. Saunter through the narrow streets, be bemused by the balcony's far-reaching views across the sierras.

What draws the crowds to Priego is its plethora of incredibly ornate and extravagant baroque churches, made possible by its silk and textile production in the early 18th century. Some of the churches are more stunning and over-the-top than others, but do visit at least one or two, even if you can't quite face all eight. Ir's worth noting that the opening hours of Priego's churches and other sights have a habit of changing frequently: they are updated weekly on the website of the Oficina de Turismo (turismodepriego.com).

The **Fuente del Rey** (The King's Fountain), a National Monument, is also known as Neptune's Fountain and was built between the 16th and 19th centuries in baroque style. It has 139 waterspouts, three pools and several statues; enticing by day and even better when it's floodlit at night. Bar Yampe is very near to sit and enjoy the trickling fountains while eating or having a drink.

Priego de Córdoba's extra virgin olive oil (*aceite de oliva virgen extra*) is prized across Spain. It has been a source of wealth since ancient Roman times and still today the area's small-scale producers turn out some of the country's finest blends. Oils such as Venta del Barón from the Mueloliva company and Rincón de la Subbética from Almazaras de la Subbética are known internationally and regularly win awards. When buying, go for oils carrying the Denominación de Origen Priego de Córdoba designation, proof that they were produced locally.

BEST PLACES TO EAT IN THE SUBBÉTICAS

Vaquena
En route up to Ermita Virgen de la Sierra. Pasture-fed cattle, extraordinary views.

Casa Frasco
Famous for seafood, but serves other dishes too. In Luque.

Zyrah
Busy gastro bar for good tapas in Priego de Córdoba.

Tres Culturas Restaurante
Dishes inspired by Jewish, Islamic and Christian cultures in Lucena.

Almedinilla

CHARM AND HISTORY

A frontier town, Almedinilla sits between Priego de Córdoba and Alcalá la Real, where the borders of Córdoba, Jaén and Granada provinces meet. It's a small, pretty town with a long and interesting history, but it's the Iberian and Roman legacy that entices visitors. Almedinilla is part of the various routes: the Roman Bética Route, the network of Roman Villas of Hispania, and of the Roman treasures of the South of Córdoba. With its charming rocky backdrop, the town is known locally as the *tierra de sueños* (land of

BEAUTIFUL TOWNS

Spain's Most Beautiful Towns association has 11 towns in Andalucía at the moment; more are added each year. Our featured ones in addition to Zuheros are Baños de la Encina (p222) and Segura de la Sierra (p211).

Casa Rosa
Cosy, welcoming B&B near Almedinilla. €

Casa las Tinajas
Nicely restored town house in the centre of Iznájar. €

Hotel Zuhayra
Great location, good food in Zuheros. €

dreams), because a statue of Hypnos, the god of dreams, was discovered here.

In early August the area comes alive for Festum, a week of Ibero-Romano festivities, with markets, banquets, theatre, and live music. Any other time of year is probably best to visit if you want to see the **Historical-Archaeological Museum**, **Roman Villa El Ruedo** in the town and the Iberian settlement **Cerro de la Cruz** just up the hill.

WHY VISIT IZNÁJAR

Maki Ridout, joint owner of Finca las Encinas, Iznájar shares why she loves the town.

Iznájar is one of the most charming white towns in Andalucía, if not in Spain. It sits on top of a gigantic rocky outcrop and is surrounded by the blue waters of Iznájar Reservoir, the largest man-made lake in Andalucía. The natural beauty and the surrounding countryside are so easy to fall in love with, and its warm and generous people too.

Iznájar has much to offer to visitors of all kinds – adventure, foodie, leisure, eco, wellness, cultural tourism etc. Tourism is still developing, so you really need to explore and discover the hidden jewels in and around Iznájar.

Walking in the Subbéticas

BEAUTIFUL VIEWS AND ENDLESS WALKING ROUTES

Located halfway between Córdoba and Granada, the Sierras Subbéticas are a great destination for walkers, hikers and cyclists. Walks vary from easy and fairly level, like the Vía Verde, to longer and more difficult circular routes – crossing through dramatic scenery with Moorish watchtowers to ancient olive groves, limestone ridges and verdant valleys. There's not a lot of shade here, so even in the autumn, winter and spring take a hat and plenty of water with you. The summer months are not the ideal time to stride out for several hours unless you start very early in the day. With many tracks in the olive groves and old drovers' trails, there is no end to the ground you can travel, but finding signposted routes isn't easy. The owners of Casa Olea in Zamoranos are keen walkers and have many routes uploaded to Wikiloc (wikiloc.com; search 'Casa Olea'). There are also many more routes available at their charming hotel, which is a great base for hikers. Bikes can also be hired here (must be prebooked) and various cycle routes are offered too. All routes are planned from Casa Olea or starting in one of the attractive local villages. Carcabuey is one charming little *pueblo blanco* that has good signposted walking routes.

Iznájar & cooking traditional dishes

DRAMATIC VIEWS AND GREAT GASTRONOMY

Iznájar is a spectacular little castle-topped town with steep streets, charming nooks and gorgeous views. Wander the flower-filled **Patio de las Comedias**, located near the castle and within the city walls, once the stage for theatre shows and comedy sketches. Descend the few steps at the end onto a tiny viewpoint and the **Torre de San Rafael**, one of the towers of the old city wall, and see the spectacular views. The **castle** is also open for visitors and has more of those

WHAT TO VISIT IN PRIEGO DE CÓRDOBA

Parroquia de la Asunción
An astounding mix of Gothic, Mudéjar, baroque and Renaissance work.

Castillo de Priego de Córdoba
Castle with Arab origins, rebuilt in 13th & 14th century. The Keep is a National Monument.

Museo Histórico
Interesting museum, with local finds dating back to Palaeolithic and Neolithic times.

Iznájar

fabulous views. If being by the waterside calls, then the reservoir has a beach area that can be accessed by car, or there's parking on the road further on from Camping ValdeArenas waterside campsite.

Just ten minutes from the reservoir and town is the lovely, rustic **Finca Las Encinas**, which has four charming B&B rooms and offers cooking courses and classes. Welsh chef Clive Ridout and his ex-investment-banker wife Maki Ridout swapped their rat race London life for Devon, then Iznájar in 2004, to open their B&B. Chef Clive teaches about the history of the local food and dishes as you learn techniques to prepare them. If other guests are staying you'll be serving and eating with them and popping back into the kitchen to plate up the next course. You can expect the likes of asparagus with almond sauce, sea bass with tomatoes and black olives, and almond and extra virgin olive oil cake, along with local *fino* wine from Montilla-Moriles DOP and anis from Rute. It's possible to also stay at Finca Las Encinas and enjoy the gastronomic experience without having to cook your own dinner.

THE ROUTE OF THE CALIPHS

The Route of the Caliphs connects Christian castles and Moorish and Christian hilltop fortresses with the most important provincial capitals, Córdoba and Granada, and the frontier territories of Jaén. It´s an interesting, historical route to follow, which can be added to other pleasures, such as winery visits, in some of the towns.

Some of the towns en route, Castro del Río and Baena, both with fortresses and old city walls, are also known for their great local wines.

Alcaudete, another castle on a hill town, visible from miles away, saw many battles and changed rulers many times. Follow signs for the Castillo; there is also parking for motorhomes just below the castle.

GETTING AROUND

Your own wheels is the best way to see the area. Travel by bus is very limited and limiting.

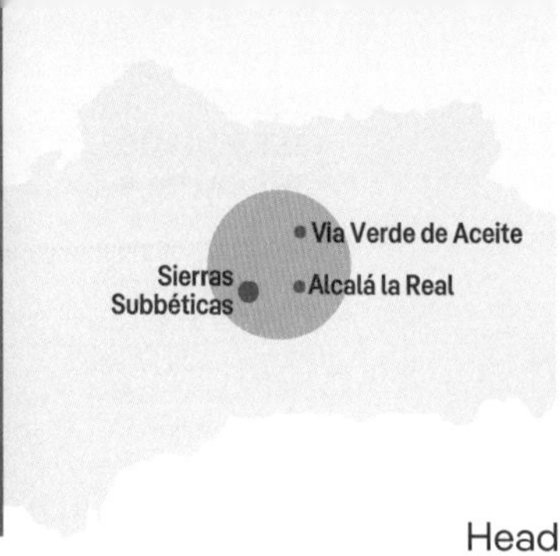

Beyond Sierras Subbéticas

Head to the terrain of olive groves, with fairly level cycling or walking routes, and a fabulous fortress town.

Crossing part of the Subbéticas and linking up with other old train routes, the Vías Verdes or Green Ways are an excellent way to experience the area, travel off road and through the countryside of mainly olive groves. With 26 routes over 600km of Green Ways in Andalucía it shouldn't be difficult to include part of one in your itinerary. Driving 20 minutes slightly north-east from Almedinilla you'll find the fortress town of Alcalá la Real, once within the Granada province. The impressive Fortaleza de la Mota is an enjoyable and interactive history lesson that should not be missed. While you're there, slow down, explore the town, and try the local craft beer.

TOP TIP

Your own wheels are needed here to get off the main routes and explore the picturesque towns and sea of olive groves.

Vía Verde de Aceite

JOSE LUCAS/ALAMY STOCK PHOTO ©

Vía Verde de Aceite for walking or cycling

WALKING THE OLD TRAIN ROUTES

The Vías Verdes or Green Ways are a network of disused train tracks, now reconditioned for walkers or cyclists to travel through stunning countryside with only slight gradients to contend with. The Vía Verde de Aceite is the one of these that passes through the Subbéticas. In its heyday it transported olive oil from Jaén city via Puente Genil towards the coast. This stretch of track can be joined at many points, but to park your car or for a motorhome stopover, the old station at Doña Mencia is the place to head. Hiring of bikes and electric bikes is also possible here. Bikes can also be hired in Martos town, next to the Vía Verde, by the hour, day or half day.

This stretch of Vía Verde is 120km long and has 13 impressive 19th-century metal bridges straddling valleys and rivers en route, a real feat of engineering when the tracks were built. Whether you're walking or cycling, the most attractive part of the route from Doña Mencia is when surrounded by/going through olive groves, very close to the beautiful town of Zuheros (p200). The surface is also suitable for wheelchairs and pushchairs. Get as far as Alcaudete in Jaén province and there's a couple of natural saltwater lagoons that host many visiting waterbirds.

SPRING FLOWER COMPETITIONS IN THE SUBBÉTICAS

Not only in Córdoba city, but also in the Subbéticas, the month of May is all about the flower competitions, with prizes awarded in three categories: Córdoba Patio, Typical Corner, Facade or Balcony. There are usually over 50 entries across the towns of the area, so it's a great time to come and follow the route while seeing more of the charming towns dressed up to the nines.

Alcalá la Real

FABULOUS FORTRESS TOWN

Alcalá la Real is just 1½ hours from Iznájar by car or four hours and several changes by bus. The imposing **Fortaleza de la Mota** announces Alcalá la Real long before you see the town below, with its high church tower and doughty keep rising above the surrounding walls. An enormous three-walled enclosure, one of the largest walled fortresses in Andalucía, sits on a hill that not only protected the townspeople within, but was the last stronghold before Granada. Back in the Middle Ages this fortified hill now looming over the town of Alcalá la Real *was* Alcalá la Real. Alcalá la Real saw many battles over its 150 years as a frontier town, until in 1341 Alfonso XI forced the capitulation of the Moors. Then the townspeople gradually spread outside the walls and the fortress began to decay. Its decline was later hastened when it was occupied by Napoleonic troops and then pilfered for building materials. In 1931 it was made a National Monument

Fortaleza de la Mota

WHAT MUSEUMS TO VISIT IN RUTE

Museo del Anís
Within the Destilerías Duende, distillery since 1908 – great guided tours and tastings.

Museo del Azúcar, la Flor de Rute
Sugar museum, more interesting than it sounds, with statues all in sugar.

Museos del aguardiente anisado de Rute y España
Exhibits and early marketing of over 6000 brands of anisette, popular throughout Spain.

OLD STATION RESTAURANTS & PICNIC AREAS

Some of the former stations of the Vía Verde de Aceite train line have now become favourite stopping points for walkers and cyclists.

Nicol's Restaurante
Old station shop and bar/restaurant in Estación de Luque.

El Pato Restaurante
Old station restaurant, picnic and play area, and motorhome stopover in Doña Mencia.

Alcaudete picnic area
With benches and bike stands at the old Alcaudete station, the last stop before (or after) the saltwater lagoons, Jaén province.

Las Casillas picnic area
Well away from the main road, this old station in Las Casillas is a great family stopping place, Jaén province.

Río Borosa waterfall

and ongoing rebuilding and repairs make it a fascinating insight into medieval life behind walls, complete with a massive, medieval snow-storage house 'fridge' underneath. If you can, take a guided tour of the tunnel complex as well as the fortress. One of the most remarkable features is the inside of the church, where the floor has been removed to lay bare dozens of graves carved out of the rock beneath. In 1967 Alcalá la Real was declared of Historical and Artistic importance. It's an interesting town to visit and a good base for exploring the smaller villages around the area.

In Alcalá you can also visit the **Palacete de Hilandera**, a beautiful 19th-century house that's now a private museum, and the **Centro de Rescate de Anfibios y Reptiles**, a small rescue centre for amphibians and reptiles. Just outside town, head up to **Mirador de San Marcos** to look across at the Fortaleza de la Mota. Sunset is the best time of day.

GETTING AROUND

To get the most out of the Sierras Subbéticas you really need your own wheels. Buses cover town to town but not into the countryside.

PARQUE NATURAL SIERRAS DE CAZORLA, SEGURA Y LAS VILLAS

Captivating, rugged and wild, this is Spain's largest Natural Park, within one of Andalucía's lesser-known provinces – Jaén. As a Unesco Biosphere Reserve, it is an enormous refuge for fauna and, with more than 2000 plant species, for fauna too. The Río Guadalquivir, Andalucía's longest river, and Río Segura begin here, and natural springs, deep valleys, pine-covered peaks and high mountain pasture (which is snow-covered in winter) make it a unique and important natural, protected area. Small historical *pueblos blancos* and hilltop castles, winding mountain roads, endless tracks and vast panoramas mean it's hard not to stop at every viewpoint and get the camera into action. Exploring the park by car, bike or on foot should be leisurely and slow-paced; it's impossible not to relax while breathing in pure mountain air and being this deep in nature, while looking out for wildlife and listening to the soothing soundtrack of birdsong and tumbling waters.

TOP TIP

It's almost a one-road-into-the-park and one-road-out-from-Cazorla town, so it can get busy at weekends, even more so on the Spanish Bank Holidays and last two weeks in August. This means that the smaller tourist offices will be open, but the shorter walking routes will be busy.

NATURAL SWIMMING SPOTS

Mogón
Natural swimming pool on the Río Aguascebas.

Río Borosa
Accessible via most of its length, but this isn't always easy.

Piscina de Almurjo
In Orcera, biggest pool in Spain, fed by the Río Orcera.

Merendero de Peralta (Paraje Natural de Peralta)
Picnic spot adjacent to the Río Guadalentín.

Wild swimming in Río Borosa

RIVER DUNKING IN PURE NATURE

The most popular walk in the Cazorla natural park follows the crystal-clear Río Borosa upstream to its source through scenery that progresses from the pretty to the majestic, via a gorge, two tunnels and a mountain lake. Whether walking this popular route, or going for an icy dunking, the impressive scenery should definitely be on your itinerary when in the Natural Park. Walk the whole route or swim/boulder-clamber up river. Natural crystal-clear pools and miniature cascades amid narrow gorges will make it one of the highlights of your trip. The coolness of the water means it's more of a summer activity, but even in the summer heat it is an experience for hardy souls. The walk alongside the river is at times via a suspended boardwalk, offering a different but always beautiful perspective of the rushing river below. If you don't fancy getting wet or it's too cold, walk the 11km (each way) or at least part of it. The first section of the walk crisscrosses the tumbling, beautiful *río* on a couple of bridges. It does get pretty busy at holiday times and weekends, so go mid-week if you can, and take a wide-brimmed hat and plenty of water; even in winter there are plenty of sunny days. The trackside springs are good and drinkable but the last is at the Central Eléctrica. A torch (headlamp) is comforting, if not absolutely essential, for some tunnels along the walk.

TOP SIGHTS
1 Río Borosa Walk

SIGHTS
2 Bóveda del Río Cerezuelo
3 Castillo de la Iruela
4 Castillo de la Yedra
5 Fuente de las Cadenas
6 Parque Cinegético

EATING
7 Chiringuito Alguacil

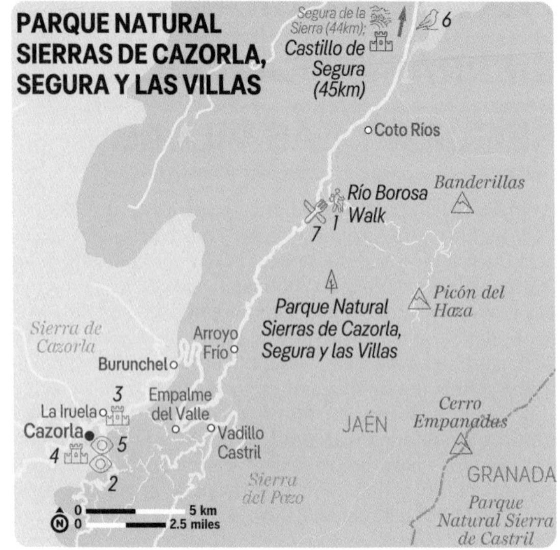

GR247 Bosques del Sur route

MAGNIFICENT CIRCULAR ROUTE WITH STAGES

The GR247, a GR footpath (*Gran Recorrido*) known as Bosques del Sur was created for hikers and mountain bikers in 1986 as the longest walking (or cycling) route in Spain. It's a 309km circular route (478 with the 11 extensions) that weaves on tracks through the rugged limestone crags of the Parque Natural Sierras de Cazorla, Segura y las Villas. The route is broken up into 21 stages, varying between 10km and 20 km each and of differing difficulty. The main route is well-signposted and there are additional extensions to places of interest. If you have time to follow the route it takes you to the source of the Río Guadalquivir, along ancient paths, to historical villages and through gorgeous scenery. Most of the stages of the route start and finish where there are basic services, accommodation, campsites etc. Some of the stages through high mountain plains have only basic refuge huts, which can save lives if weather conditions take a turn for the worse – and this can happen quickly in the higher parts during the winter months. Spring and autumn are the best times to appreciate the scenery.

Jardin Botánico Torre del Vinagre
Botanical gardens with important endemic species.

Centro de Interpretación de la Cultura de la Madera (ciCUM)
Interesting exhibition on timber from the Natural Park.

Museo de Artes y Costumbres Populares del Alto Guadalquivir
In Cazorla's Castillo de la Yedra; also very interesting.

Río Cerezuelo

SHORTER WALKS

Río Cerezuelo
Signposted from Cazorla town. A picturesque, circular route of around 5.5km.

Pico Gilillo
Gilillo peak also starts from Cazorla town but the ascent is steep. A full-day, 20km hike to the Natural Park's highest peak (1848m).

La Cerrada del Utrero
A 2km loop under cliffs to the Cascada de Linarejos waterfall.

Segura de la Sierra, town & castle

IMPRESSIVELY SITUATED CASTLE-TOPPED TOWN

The breathtaking little town of Segura de la Sierra with its recently restored Mudéjar castle deserves its listing as one of *Los Pueblos Más Bonitos de España* – Spain's Most Beautiful Villages. Its location at 1140m above sea level makes it visible from afar. Local cave paintings bear witness to human presence in these lands since the 4th millennium BCE. Wander the narrow streets and it's easy to imagine life in days gone by, as you take in the well-preserved 15th-century Arab baths and admire the views from the town itself. For an even better perspective go up to the castle; there is parking part way but it's still a climb, then of course the outlook gets better still once you've climbed up to the top. This lofty castle dates from Moorish times but was rebuilt after the Christian conquest in the 13th century. Abandoned in the 17th century, it was restored in the 1960s and has now become a 'frontier territory' interpretation centre. If you go while the Air Festival is on in June then there's no better spot to watch the flyers in action than up on the tower.

La Casa de Bicicletas

Ruinas de la Iglesia de Santa María
In Cazorla town, the ruined Renaissance church with some original features still intact.

La Casa de Bicicletas
A quirky guesthouse/museum covered in multicoloured bikes outside and other antiquities inside.

Bóveda del Río Cerezuelo
Subterranean walkway made to create the main plaza above. Book tours at Tourist Office in the Ruinas de Santa Maria.

WHY I LOVE PARQUE NATURAL SIERRAS DE CAZORLA, SEGURA Y LAS VILLAS

Rachel Webb, Lonely Planet writer. *@spaniola*

Every visit to the Park is a different experience. It's a bit of paradise in my home province, yet it's almost a 1½-hour drive to the south of the park and a 2½-hour drive to the north. It's my refuge of peace, an escape into unadulterated nature combined with culture, history, walking and castle towns. Its rugged, natural beauty and peace on an immense scale draws me back again and again – not to mention the indigenous flora and fauna, the fabulous gastronomy and views.

Parque Cinegetico

Cazorla & La Iruela

HISTORICAL TOWNS MEET NATURAL PARK

Cazorla town is the gateway to the natural park and the gorgeous little Iruela, just a couple of kilometres towards the park, is a great introduction to its charm. Stay in one or the other for at least a night. Cazorla sits on a hillside with olive groves stretching out in front and the mountains of the park as its backdrop. Head into the old quarter, especially Plaza de Santa María with its ruined church, and **Castillo de la Yedra** looming above. The dramatic Castle of the Ivy is of Muslim origin, comprehensively rebuilt in the 14th century after the Reconquista, and it offers superb views. Plus don't miss Renaissance-style **Fuente de las Cadenas** for its bars, ambience and views. The plaza may not appear much but was a feat of engineering to create, with the Río Cerezuelo running underneath. It's possible to go down and walk along the underground river from one side of the plaza to the other through the **Bóveda del Río Cerezuelo**. The heart of town is **Plaza de la Corredera**, with a number of

WHERE TO FIND UNMISSABLE MIRADORS

Mirador Merenderos de Cazorla
Picnic spot and viewpoint overlooking Cazorla town.

Mirador del Chorro
Fabulous views and favourite haunt of griffon vultures and bearded vultures.

Mirador de Las Navillas
Not very easy to access, but worth it for the views.

busy bars and the elegant *ayuntamiento* (town hall), in a 400-year-old former monastery building, looking down from the southeast corner.

Castillo de la Iruela is like a ruined, fairy-tale castle perched high above the road with a sheer drop. The 954m-high, 11th-century Moorish, then Templar, fortress is hard to miss if you're going from Cazorla town into the park. If you have time, stop awhile, climb to the top and see the spectacular views, contemplate the complexities of construction and look down that awesome drop, which made it easy to defend. Brooding below is the shell of the 16th-century Iglesia de Santo Domingo, torched by Napoleonic troops two centuries ago. There's parking further up in the village as well as on the road (954m) below.

Wildlife experiences

SPOTTING FAUNA AROUND THE PARK

Whether you walk or cycle, you'll likely see all sorts of eagles, vultures and raptors, along with many types of deer and wild boar, in the park. The Bearded Vulture Breeding Centre, Fundación Gypaetus, created in 1996, is an international project to save bearded vultures, Europe's rarest vulture, from extinction and to reintroduce them to the park and further afield.

The **Parque Cinegético** is a wildlife sanctuary at the southern end of El Tranco reservoir; there are vantage points from where animals can be seen living in the semi-wild. The best time to visit is at dawn or dusk when the animals come out to drink. Taking a 4WD tour with a local guide is highly recommended. They'll take you where there's more chance of seeing wildlife; their local knowledge and history of the park is phenomenal. Seeing wild boar is easy if you head to the bar **Chiringuito Alguacil** before dusk, as boar now come close to feed.

EL YELMO MOUNTAIN

El Yelmo (meaning 'the helmet'), is not only fabulous hiking country but also host to the yearly International Air Festival at the beginning of June. Heading towards the town of Hornos, the mountain is a spectacular sight, with its sheer drop on one side, especially when the air is full of paragliders, hang-gliders flying on their thermals. It's a popular destination for rock climbers too. This 1808m-high mountain is visible from afar. If you like heights, drive up to the summit, but it's not for the faint-hearted. At one point sheer drops fall away either side of the narrow road which leads up to the most incredible, if windy, panoramic views.

GETTING AROUND

Because of the size of this Park, a car is needed to explore the natural areas. Local buses will get you from town to town, but do check out how frequently they run; some of the smaller towns have just one bus a day out to a nearby larger town and one back.

Beyond Parque Natural Sierras de Cazorla, Segura y las Villas

Parque Natural Sierras de Cazorla, Segura y Las Villas
Cástulo

More mountain ranges, castles and watchtowers and, between them, regimented rows of olive groves – the 'Sea of Olives'.

Leaving one mountain range behind, or three in the case of Cazorla, Segura & las Villas, there is always another one on the horizon, many with a castle or watchtower on top. It's because of the terrain that Jaén has so many castles and watchtowers, as it was difficult to protect in the warring days gone by. One way to see some of the legacy left us is to follow the Ruta de Castillos y Batallas or Route of Castles and Battles. Any land that isn't mountainous is covered with olive trees, so visiting an olive oil museum or a mill for tastings is a must too.

TOP TIP

Take your time exploring nature, discovering historical towns and feasting on the local gastronomy in this slow-paced environment.

Cástulo

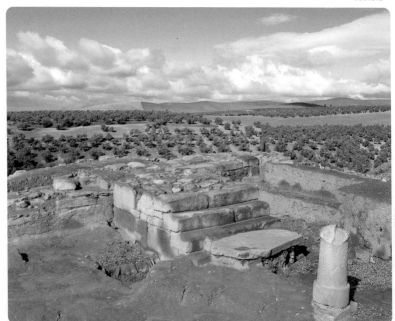

MIGUEL SOTOMAYOR/GETTY IMAGES ©

Route of castles & battles

WATCHTOWERS, BATTLEFIELDS AND AMAZING CASTLES

Leaving the Natural Park behind and heading westwards, within half an hour or so by car you'll reach towns on the Ruta de Castillos y Batallas. The route starts over the regional border in Castilla-La Mancha and makes its way through battlefields and castle towns on its way through Jaén province, finishing at the most imposing fortification of all: the Alhambra in Granada city. Jaén province is said to have more fortifications than any other area in Europe, a testament to its many conflicts of the past, as it is the gateway into Andalucía from the north. It's also where two of Spain's major battles took place: Bailén in 1808, which saw the defeat of the Napoleonic army; and Las Navas de Tolosa in 1212, a turning point for the Reconquista. Follow the whole route of city walls, ruins, battlefields and visitable castles through the west of Jaén province, or pick and choose your own route. It's worth checking when different festivities and re-enactments take place and plan your visit around them.

It is possible to travel between these towns by bus, although services are not very frequent. Good planning is essential to see them all.

BEST PLACES TO STAY IN CAZORLA

Hotel Rural la Calerilla
Rural hotel with gorgeous views, well placed for exploring the natural park. €

Hotel Sierra de Cazorla & Spa
Located in the dramatic town of La Iruela at the gateway of the natural area. €€

Parador de Cazorla
Deep within nature. A great escape for relaxing or walking. €€

Cástulo

ANCIENT HISTORICAL SITES AND MOSAICS

Just under an hour by car from Cazorla town, the Iberian-Roman city of Cástulo has a history dating back to the Greeks and the Phoenicians. It was one of the episcopal headquarters in the Roman Empire period and an important trading centre, due to the mines around the area of Linares and the Sierra Morena mountains. In its heyday it covered 400,000 sq metres, making it the largest pre-Roman city. Cástulo went slowly into decline and, together with the arrival of the Moors, it was finally abandoned in the 14th century when building materials began to be repurposed for the growing cities of Baeza and Linares. What we see today is an impressive collection of artefacts, mosaics and architecture. There are three main sites to visit: the **Yacimiento Arqueológico de Cástulo**, the **Ciudad Ibero-Romana de Cástulo** and the **Museo Arqueológico de Linares**.

WHERE TO TO STAY IN BAÑOS DE LA ENCINA

Hotel Palacio Guzmanes
Very central historical hotel with fabulous views. €

Palacete María Rosa
Ancient 16th-century mansion, now a quirky rustic hotel. €

Hotel Restaurante Baños
Modern, clean hotel with amazing vistas of Baños de la Encina castle. €

JAÉN, ÚBEDA & BAEZA

Introducing the trio of cities with wonderful Renaissance heritage – **Jaén**, **Úbeda** and **Baeza** – and the smaller yet architecturally rich town of **Sabiote**. Jaén, the provincial city, is surrounded by olive groves and dominated by Santa Catalina Hill, with its castle, Parador Hotel and white monumental cross. Úbeda, with the most stunning monuments, and the smaller, more charming Baeza are listed by Unesco as Renaissance Monumental Ensembles. The two cities have much earlier beginnings, but it's their heyday and wealth of the 16th century that give us the many ornate and beautiful sandstone mansions, churches and plazas we see today. They are located just about 8km apart and around 48km from the provincial city of Jaén, with its enormous Renaissance cathedral from which, on a clear day, the silhouette of Baeza sitting on a hill 800m above sea level can be seen.

TOP TIP

As Úbeda and Baeza are so close, it can be tempting to do both in a day; don't. Stay overnight in both if possible to experience the charm of these two very individual cities. Jaén, around 50km away, warrants its own overnight stay for a taste of a much less visited city.

SEA OF OLIVES

The *Mar de Olivos* or Sea of Olive Groves that covers the centre of Andalucía (over 5800 sq miles across the provinces of Córdoba, Jaén, Málaga and Granada), is so important that Spain is campaigning for it to become a protected Unesco landscape. Jaén province alone has over 66 million olive trees and more than 300 olive oil mills within its boundary.

Jaén city

EXPLORING THE CITY AND HEIGHTS

The city of Jaén's old quarter clings to the base of the pine-covered hill of Santa Catalina with its castle, Parador hotel and monumental cross. This hill, a winding 3km ascent above the city, is the place to begin to explore and understand Jaén. Visit the castle, climb those towers and see the mountainous backdrop behind the city sprawl, with the unmissable large cathedral and olive groves fanning out into the distance. The once-Moorish castle was taken by King Fernando III in 1246 and a cross was placed in the ground, at the edge of the hill, after his victory. This is the location of the large cross overlooking the city today, which is reached via a walkway leading from the Parador to the castle. The hotel, a restoration and extension of the castle, is open to non-residents and is worth having a coffee or beer in to see its 20m-high vaulted ceiling.

Down in the city, the 16th–17th-century cathedral should be visited, and the area around it is where the main attractions lie: the Jewish Quarter with typical tapas bars; **Palacio de Villardompardo**, which is home to two museums – the **International Museum of Naïf Art** and the **Museum of Arts and Popular Customs**; and below the palace are the fabulous **Arab Baths**. The baths were converted to a tannery after the Reconquista, then built over completely when the Conde de Villardompardo constructed his handsome palace over them in the 16th century. They were rediscovered in 1913.

TOP SIGHTS
1 Castillo de Santa Catalina
2 Catedral de la Asunción

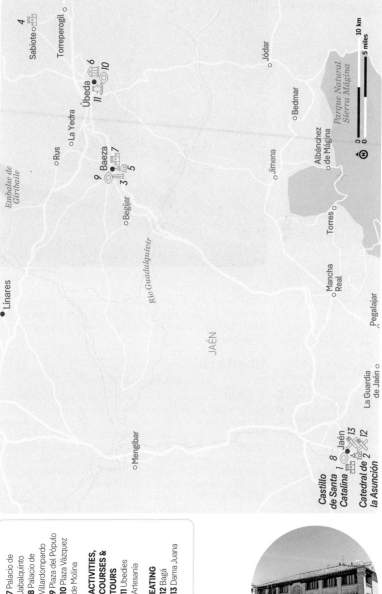

SIGHTS
3 Antigua Carnicería
4 Castillo de Sabiote
5 Catedral de Baeza
6 Museo de Alfarería Paco Tito Memoria de lo Cotidiano
7 Palacio de Jabalquinto
8 Palacio de Villardompardo
9 Plaza del Pópulo
10 Plaza Vázquez de Molina

ACTIVITIES, COURSES & TOURS
11 Ubedíes Artesanía

EATING
12 Bagá
13 Dama Juana

Plaza del Pópulo, Baeza (p219)

HIGHLIGHTS OF JAÉN

David Marmol, a born-and-bred Jaén local, works in tourism PR.

Visit the cobbled villages, such as Baños de la Encina, or the typical white mountain villages that have kept their traditional culture.

With the four natural parks in Jaén province there are idyllic corners to be able to enjoy ecotourism activities – not forgetting the fauna, such as the Iberian lynx, and birds such as the bearded vulture.

Our gastronomy is excellent, based on the EVOO (extra virgin olive oil) of the province, with the highest production and quality in the world. Enjoy our tapas and Michelin-star restaurants.

And last, don't miss our castles, with an agenda of events where you can enjoy them from different perspectives.

Úbeda

The local legend of the lizard is an intriguing tale to investigate, and also take a wander in the San Idelfonso area, which has the city's 1-star Michelin restaurants **Bagá** and **Dama Juana**.

Úbeda city

MONUMENTAL GRANDEUR AND LOCAL CRAFTS

Beautiful Renaissance buildings grace almost every street and plaza in the *casco antiguo* (old quarter) of Úbeda. Charming hotels in several historic mansions, and some top-class restaurants and tapas bars, make a stay here an all-round delight.

A Moorish stronghold until taken by Fernando III in 1234, Úbeda became 'the cradle of Spanish Renaissance' in the 16th century, when the city's aristocratic lions jockeyed successfully for influence at the Habsburg court. Francisco de los Cobos y Molina became state secretary to King Carlos I, and his nephew Juan Vázquez de Molina succeeded him in the job and kept it under Felipe II. High office exposed these men to the Renaissance aesthetic just then reaching Spain from Italy. Much of the wealth that they and a flourishing agriculture generated was invested in some of Spain's purest

WHERE TO STAY

Hostal Estación
As the name suggests, it's right by Jaén's train station. Good, unfussy stay with parking available. €

Hotel Europa
Nicely central in Jaén, nearest the bus station and Plaza de la Constitución. €€

Parador Castillo de Santa Catalina
Up on the hill above Jaén city, this four-star hotel is a 3km walk or an easy taxi ride. €€€

examples of Renaissance architecture. As a result, Úbeda (like its little sister Baeza) is one of the few places in Andalucía boasting stunning architecture that was *not* built by the Moors. Head to the monumental part of Úbeda and it's like stepping back centuries. With dozens of sandstone monuments along with Plaza Vázquez de Molina (the finest examples of Renaissance buildings are here), it's clear why Úbeda became enshrined as a Unesco World Heritage site, jointly with Baeza, in 2003.

As well as beautiful monuments, Úbeda is home to several traditional crafts, pottery and esparto grass. The creation of beautiful green-glazed ceramics is a tradition going back to its Moorish past, with one of the few remaining Moorish kilns still in use at Paco Tito's shop. Check out the pottery at **Museo de Alfarería Paco Tito Memoria de lo Cotidiano** and **Ubedies Artesanía**, with incredible creations made from esparto.

Baeza city

CHARMING NARROW STREETS, MARVELLOUS MONUMENTS

With its beautiful Unesco-listed historic centre, Baeza is easily visited on a day trip from Úbeda – though it has some good restaurants and accommodation of its own that may just tempt you to stick around. Here a handful of wealthy, fractious families, rich from grain-growing and cloth and leather production, are primarily responsible for the marvellous catalogue of perfectly preserved Renaissance churches and civic buildings.

During the Roman Empire, Baeza was known as Vivatia or Biatia, an exchange centre on the Cástulo-Málaga trade route, which transported silver extracted from the mines around Linares. Visigoths then Moors controlled the city until, in 1227, it was one of the first Andalucian towns to fall to the Christians, becoming the civil and religious centre of the area.

It's not a large city, but charming and compact, so walking around, exploring its streets and spotting architectural gems is the way to see it. The Plaza Mayor is the heart of the town, consisting of two plazas, Plaza de España and Plaza de la Constitución, spanning the old town and beautiful Renaissance buildings. The **Cathedral**, **Plaza del Pópulo** and the **Antigua Carnicería** (one of the world's most elegant ex-butcheries) are just some of the not-to-miss monuments. Go up the city walls for the surrounding views and see the **Palacio de Jabalquinto**, a gorgeous grand mansion with a Renaissance courtyard and beautiful baroque staircase.

BEST TYPICAL BARS IN JAÉN

Peña Flamenca de Jaén
Old sherry barrels and original tiles adorn this typical tapas bar.

La Manchega
One of the oldest venues in Jaén, the dining room is downstairs and accessed through the bar.

El Gorrión
Ancient, emblematic bar with a 100-year-old mummified *jamón* on display.

La Espadaña
Sit out or head inside for the authentic wooden-galleried interior patio.

Bar del Pósito
Charming bar on cobbled plaza; atmospheric at night with a glimpse of the illuminated cathedral.

Parador de Úbeda
Historical mansion right on the main monumental plaza. €€

Hotel Palacio de los Salcedo
Striking internal patio in this 16th-century palace in the heart of old town Baeza. €

Hotel Rural Molino del Albaicín
With views of the countryside and Sabiote castle. €

DIEGO GRANDI/SHUTTERSTOCK ©

Baeza (p219)

JAÉN'S RENAISSANCE MASTER BUILDER

Most of the finest architecture that you see in Úbeda, Baeza and Jaén is the work of one man: Andrés de Vandelvira (1509–75). His work spanned all three main phases of Spanish Renaissance architecture – the ornamental early phase known as plateresque, as seen in Úbeda's Sacra Capilla del Salvador; the purer line and classical proportions that emerged in the later Palacio de Vázquez de Molina; and the austere late-Renaissance style (called Herreresque) of his last building, the Hospital de Santiago. Relatively little is known about Vandelvira's life, but his legacy is a jewel of Spanish culture.

Sabiote

FABULOUS CASTLE, ANCIENT STREETS

Lying very close to Úbeda and Baeza, the medieval and Renaissance town of Sabiote is a little charmer, with part of its castle walls and three of its six original access arches into the city intact. Its **castle** is one of the most important military constructions in Jaén province, remodelled by the Cobo family of Úbeda into a Renaissance castle/palace in the 16th century and declared of artistic-historical importance in 1931. It lies in an imposing position, overlooking a vast plain of olive groves, with Sierra Morena and Sierra Mágina in the background. The town has many similarities in the local stonework and style of architecture to Úbeda and Baeza. Have a good meander through its ancient streets, climb the castle tower for those huge views or to spot the enemy coming. If you plan to eat or stay here the 16th-century Renaissance **Palacio las Manillas** is the best in town.

GETTING AROUND

In Jaén the bus station is quite central, just head uphill to the old town. Jaén's train station is quite a steep walk to the old town, but there is a taxi rank outside. You may see tram lines everywhere but they weren't in use at the time of research. Baeza, Úbeda and Sabiote are best reached by car or bus. There is a train station with very few connections outside Úbeda, then it's a car or taxi ride to the city.

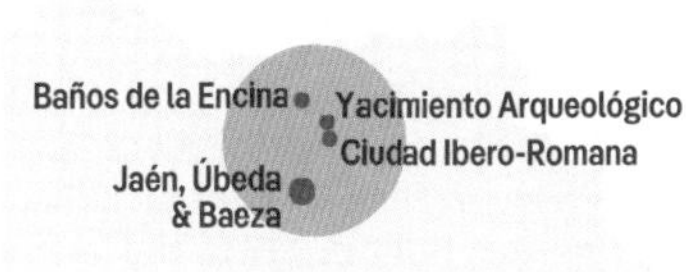

Baños de la Encina
Yacimiento Arqueológico
Ciudad Ibero-Romana
Jaén, Úbeda & Baeza

Beyond Jaén, Úbeda & Baeza

More Renaissance mansions, an enormous castle, some stunning views and Roman mosaics.

Heading northwest from Úbeda and Baeza, the archaeological area of Cástulo and the Ciudad Ibero-Romana and Yacimiento Arqueológico are important sites from Iberian-Roman times. A little further is the fabulous town of Baños de la Encina, with its enormous oval-shaped castle, the oldest one in Spain. On the horizon is the Sierra Morena, a range of rolling, green wooded hills stretching along Andalucía's northern border. And as throughout all of Jaén province, lines of pale-green olive trees – producing one-fourth of all the world's olive oil – carpet much of the landscape.

TOP TIP

A car is a real must-have to explore and to make the most of your time here.

Baños de la Encina (p222)

JAÉN'S LIQUID GOLD

As olive trees reign in Jaén province, so does its liquid gold – the extra virgin olive oil it produces. Every year eight of the region's extra virgin olive oils are chosen from various mills and many towns for a chance to be part of the Jaén Selección chosen oils. Since the event began in 2003, competition has become tougher for the olive mills, as hundreds of products are entered. You can be sure you've bought a good one if it is part of the Jaén Selección.

Baños de la Encina

SANDSTONE MANSIONS, ENORMOUS CASTLE

A 40-minute drive north of Jaén brings you to Baños de la Encina, one of Los Pueblos Más Bonitos de España (Spain's Most Beautiful Towns), which has a fabulous castle on a ridge that can be seen for miles around. Built in 967 on the orders of the Cordoban caliph Al-Hakam II, **Castillo de Burgalimar**, also known as Castillo de Baños de la Encina, is one of the best-preserved and oldesr castles in Europe and is the oldest in Spain. The castle walls are intact, and it's oval in shape with 15 towers, the last of which was added in 1466 by the Castilians, who named it the 'Christian Tower of Homage'. The castle is also known as the 'Fortress of the Seven Kings', as seven kings resided in it in different periods. It was declared a Monumento Nacional in 1931.

The whole town of Baños de la Encina is charming, has some lovely monuments and spectacular views, and it's the only place in Andalucía with a Don-Quixote-style windmill at the opposite end of town to the castle. Wander through the streets with sandstone mansions and through the arch to see the extraordinary oval castle and panoramic views from the huge mirador in front of it.

Olive oil mills & tastings

TASTING JAÉN'S LIQUID GOLD

Olive-oil mills abound across the province, and it's easy to find one to visit en route from one city to another. Alternatively, combine a visit from Jaén city to Oro Bailén mill, which is a 35-minute drive, then carry on to visit Baños de la Encina (another 25 minutes by car). You could also drive 25 minutes from Baeza to the Museo de la Cultura en route to Jaén city half an hour away. Getting to the olive oil mills by bus is not at all easy.

You will see that the *olivo* (olive tree) rules here in Jaén province, and there will be plenty of opportunity to sample several kinds of olives and other local tapas made with local extra virgin olive oil – awarded IGP protected status by the EU in 2019. This is the main olive-growing area in Spain, with over 66 million olive trees and more than 300 olive oil mills, so a trip to an olive-oil factory – or two – is a must.

You can also visit an olive-oil museum to see what an olive-oil mill was like years ago. The **Museo de la Cultura del Olivo** at Hacienda La Laguna, near Baeza, is a great museum

WHERE TO EAT IN ÚBEDA & AROUND

Restaurante la Cantina la Estación
Upmarket food in a dining room with train-carriage-style decor in Úbeda centre. €€

Tapas Bar la Tintoria
Modern and stylish with a great choice of tapas in Úbeda. €

Restaurante El Mesón Despeñaperros
Rustic hotel restaurant serving local game and classic Spanish dishes in Depeñaperros. €€

MIGUELLM/SHUTTERSTOCK ©

Iberian lynx cub, Sierra Morena

showing the original equipment (plus mule), and how the olives were collected, transported, cleaned, crushed and filtered – all rather more cumbersome than today's methods. The museum has a lovely little shop and there are also tours and olive-oil tastings at the modern mill. The award-winning mill **Oro Bailén** near Bailén also does pre-booked daily tours with tastings and explanations of the huge variety and flavours of the different types of oils.

Olives are harvested from October until about February. They are taken straight to oil mills to be mashed into a pulp, which is pressed to extract the oil and then decanted to remove water. Oil that's good enough for consumption without being refined is sold as *aceite de oliva virgen* (virgin olive oil), and the best of that is *virgen extra*. Plain *aceite de oliva* – known in the trade as *lampante* (lamp oil) – is oil that has to be refined before it's fit for consumption. Oils are tested for chemical composition and tasted in International Olive Council laboratories before they can be labelled virgin or extra virgin.

LYNX IN THE SIERRA MORENA

It is believed that only around 100 Iberian lynx existed at the end of the 20th century. Since then, the conservation efforts, including prohibiting the use of poison, building tunnels under busy roads and taking action against poachers, have helped numbers increase to over 1000.

The Mediterranean forest in the Natural Park of Sierra Morena, to the north of Jaén province, has become an important location for their repopulation, and the main area to observe this magnificent mammal in the wild. The primary reason for this success has been the increase in the rabbit population (the main diet of the lynx). Go carefully, quietly and slowly, and you may catch a glimpse of this magnificent mammal at large.

GETTING AROUND

Getting around and covering ground is by far the best with your own transport. Trains only come to Jaén via Córdoba or Madrid. Buses are far more common but probably not as frequent as one would want.

JASON ROTHE/SHUTTERSTOCK ©

Albaicín, Granada (p233)

GRANADA & ALMERÍA

HEARTLANDS, MOORISH ARCHITECTURE & NATURE

Andalucía's highest mountains; remote, pristine beaches; dynamic cities and unique villages; and cave towns and unparalleled Moorish architecture await you here.

Few parts of Andalucía are as diverse as Granada and Almería provinces. One of Spain's great destinations, the city of Granada is home to the country's most magnificent Moorish building, the Alhambra. Moorish-era influences infuse its streets, from the snaking lanes and whitewashed *cármenes* (houses with walled gardens) of the Albaicín historic quarter to the graceful arches of its former Nasrid palaces and centuries-old mansions. Granada's tapas scene is second to none, and Sacromonte, its traditional Roma quarter, still rings with flamenco laments.

The snow-dusted Sierra Nevada mountains provide a scenic backdrop to Granada and double as Andalucía's biggest draw for fresh-air fiends. Challenges include summiting mainland Spain's highest peak, skiing well into April on the breathtakingly high slopes of Europe's southernmost ski resort, and exploring mule trails on horseback.

Northeast of Granada, the barren badlands of the Altiplano are home to unique wineries, Europe's oldest human remains and the beguiling cave town of Guadix. Next door, Spain's sunniest province – Almería – has Europe's only desert. Beyond the appealing port of Almería, its own Moorish fortress and excellent dining scene, the province is home to pristine white-sand beaches, ideal for solitary coastal hikes, spread along the coast of the Parque Natural Cabo de Gata-Nijar. Further west, discover subterranean treasures in the Sorbas and Pulpí caves and hike along the wooded peaks of Los Vélez.

JOSE M. PERAL PHOTOGRAPHY/SHUTTERSTOCK ©

THE MAIN AREAS

GRANADA
Unparalleled architecture & free tapas. p230

PARQUE NACIONAL SIERRA NEVADA
Stupendous hiking & whitewashed villages. p244

ALMERÍA
Moorish fortress & lively dining. p257

PARQUE NATURAL CABO DE GATA-NÍJAR
White-sand beaches & coastal trails. p264

Find Your Way

The Granada and Almería provinces comprise Andalucía's southwest corner, and their attractions are many, varied, and spread out. We've picked the places that best capture the region's unique cultural heritage, culinary legacy and diverse landscapes.

Granada, p230

This beautifully situated, history-rich city entices with the remarkable Alhambra fortress/palace complex, the steep, labyrinthine streets of the Albaicín and Sacromonte and the free tapas served in its bustling bars.

Parque Nacional Sierra Nevada, p244

Beautiful *pueblos blancos* (white towns) clinging to mountain slopes, vertiginous canyons, superb hiking trails and Spain's highest ski resort await.

BUS & CAR

Self-driving offers maximum flexibility. Much is accessible by bus (alsa.com), though services for Sierra Nevada and Cabo de Gata can be limited. Granada city is covered by a handy urban bus network (movilidadgranada.com).

TRAIN & TRAM

High-speed RENFE (renfe.com) trains link Granada to Antequera, connecting with the high-speed Madrid–Córdoba–Málaga AVE line. Slower trains trundle between Granada and Almería. An efficient tram service bisects Granada.

WALKING

The main cities are wonderfully walkable and best explored on foot. Scenic hiking trails connect villages in Las Alpujarras and in Parque Natural Cabo de Gata-Nijar.

rque Natural Sierras de Cazorla, Segura y las Villas
Puebla de Don Fadrique
Almaciles
Huéscar
La Cañada de Cañepla
Castril
Galera
Orce
María
ozo Alcón
Embalse del Negratín
Cúllar
Zújar
Baza
Caniles
Parque Natural Sierra de Baza
Serón
Macael
Río Almanzora
Cóbdar
ALMERÍA
MURCIA
El Pozo del Esparto
Cuevas del Almanzora
Antas
Vera
Villaricos
Garrucha
Mojácar
Cariatiz
Sorbas
Abla
Doña María Ocaña
Gergal
rque Nacional rra Nevada
Tabernas
Lucainena de las Torres
Ohanes
Laujar de Andarax
Canjáyar
Níjar
Carboneras
Rioja
Alhama de Almería
Campohermoso
Agua Amarga
Parque Natural Cabo de Gata-Níjar
Huercal de Almería
Las Negras
Almería
Retamar
Rodalquilar
Santa María del Águila
Aguadulce
Roquetas de Mar
Golfo de Almería
San Miguel de Cabo de Gata
Cabo de Gata
San José
Balerma
Almerimar
MEDITERRANEAN SEA

0 30 km
0 15 miles

Parque Natural Cabo de Gata-Níjar, p264

Stupendous white-sand beaches lapped at by turquoise waters, lofty clifftop viewpoints, superb hiking trails and sleepy villages make up Almeria's best-loved protected area.

Almería, p257

This sultry southern port city with North African vibes and a lively tapas scene is overlooked by the Alcazaba, the Alhambra's sister fortress, and is a springboard for exploring the surrounding 'Wild West'.

Plan Your Time

The Granada and Almería provinces have it all: historic cities, unique culture, uncrowded white-sand beaches, coastal gastronomy, award-winning wines and rugged coastal hiking trails.

SERGEY DZYUBA/SHUTTERSTOCK ©

Alcazaba (p260)

If you only do one thing

- Spend the day exploring Granada and its unmissable sights. Have breakfast at **I Need Coffee** (p236), then set aside a half-day for the highlights of the incredible **Alhambra** (p234), including the unparalleled **Palacios Nazaríes** (p234).

- Stroll back down to the centre via the edgy **Realejo** (p236) neighbourhood to spot the murals by El Niño (Granada's answer to Banksy), then grab some lunch at **El Trillo** (p238).

- Spend the afternoon visiting the **cathedral** (p230) and wandering the hilly, labyrinthine streets of Albaicín. Make it to the **Mirador San Nicolás** (p233) for sunset, then finish off with tapas at **Bar Poë** (p237) or **Más Que Vinos** (p236).

Seasonal highlights

These provinces host numerous festivals year-round. Semana Santa is celebrated in Granada in a big way, while the heat of August brings Almería's biggest city fest.

JANUARY

The Sierra Nevada ski season is well underway, and January 6 (Three Kings' Day) is greeted with processions.

APRIL

Nazarenos (penitents) carry *pasos* (floats) through the streets of Granada during solemn Semana Santa processions.

MAY

Crosses garlanded with flowers adorn Granada's squares for Cruces de Mayo. It's the perfect month for hiking in the Alpujarras.

ADIANY MONTELO/SHUTTERSTOCK ©, AKTURER/SHUTTERSTOCK ©, LUIS OVERLANDER/SHUTTERSTOCK ©

Travel around for a week

- Day-trip from Granada to the unique cave town of **Guadix** (p240) and the surrounding lunar-like geopark, then base yourself in the village of **Trevélez** (p244) in the **Parque Nacional Sierra Nevada** (p244) for a couple of days' intensive hiking.

- Then, make your way down to the coast for a bit of a respite in Almería, spending a day comparing the **Alcazaba** (p260) to its sister fortress in Granada and sampling Almería's tapas bars, including **Jovellanos 16** (p257).

- Finish with two days in **Parque Natural Cabo de Gata-Níjar** (p264), walking the best of Almería's coast from **Las Negras to Agua Amarga** (p268).

If you have more time

- If you can set aside two weeks for Granada and Almería, do it.

- Excellent day trips from Almería include the cheesy but fun Wild West theme parks in the **Desierto de Tabernas** (p262), subterranean explorations of the **Geoda de Pulpí** (p273) or **Cuevas de Sorbas** (p273) and hiking in **Parque Natural Sierra María-Los Vélez** (p263).

- In Granada province, consider roadtripping through the **Alpujarras** (p244) for two days to see the best of the valleys and white villages, detouring to crag-top castle **Montefrío** (p242) and finishing off with a few days of sun, water sports and seafood on the **Costa Tropical** (p255).

JUNE

Noche de San Juan is celebrated with gusto on the beaches, particularly in Mojácar, with dancing, bonfires and barbecues.

JULY

The three-week Festival de Granada showcases contemporary and classical music and dance in the Alhambra and around town.

AUGUST

The Feria de Almería celebrates its patron saint, the Virgen del Mar, with two weeks of music and gastronomic events.

NOVEMBER

The Sierra Nevada ski season kicks off. It's also a low-key time to hike the Cabo de Gata trails.

ALBERTO GARCIA GUILLEN/SHUTTERSTOCK ©, ALFAGUARILLA/SHUTTERSTOCK ©, ALBUM/ALAMY STOCK PHOTO ©, FRAN RODRIGUEZ FOTOGRAFIA/SHUTTERSTOCK ©

Sevilla
Granada

GRANADA

Dramatically situated against the backdrop of the often snow-tipped peaks of the Sierra Nevada, Granada was the Moors' last stronghold in Spain and their legacy is ever-prevalent, found in the horseshoe arches, the *teterías* (teahouses) and tucked-away *cármenes* of the Albaicín (or Albayzín, the historic Muslim quarter). Their most enduring legacy is, of course, the Alhambra: the fortress-palace of the Nasrid rulers whose calligraphy-etched palaces – poetry in stone – are without peer in Europe.

But there is more to Granada than its most remarkable attraction. The city that inspired the work of the great Spanish poet Federico García Lorca gives you the cave dwellings and flamenco *peñas* (clubs) of the Roma quarter of Sacromonte; the hilly, labyrinthine lanes of the Unesco-listed *barrio* (district) of Albaicín; the edgy street art of Realejo and the myriad tapas bars and restaurants in the streets radiating off from the cathedral and central Plaza de la Trinidad.

TOP TIP

To visit the Alhambra – Granada's biggest attraction – you need to book your tickets up to three months in advance from the official website (tickets.alhambra-patronato.es) or by phone. Off-season, a few 'leftover' tickets might possibly be available at the Alhambra ticket office on the day, but this is rare.

LORCA'S GRANADA

Granada's unquiet ghosts include Andalucía's greatest poet, Federico García Lorca (1898–1936), who rose to international fame in 1928 with *El romancero gitano* (*Gypsy Ballads*). He was executed in 1936 at the hands of fascist thugs, for his left-wing political views and his homosexuality. His body has never been found.

Lorca's childhood home, the Museo Lorca in Fuente Vaqueros, 17km northwest of Granada, houses his personal effects. Near the cathedral, the Centro Federico García Lorca stages cultural events. Original furnishings adorn the Huerta de San Vicente, the Lorca family's summer house.

Exploring Granada's Centro

DENSE CLUSTER OF HISTORIC MONUMENTS

Separated from the tangled lanes of the Albaicín by the main Gran Vía thoroughfare, Granada's Centro's more regular grid of streets is densely packed with a wealth of historic buildings.

Contemplate the **Granada Cathedral**'s monumental baroque facade from one of the café tables on the Plaza de las Pasiegas. Built atop Granada's former mosque between 1521 and 1704, this vast Renaissance edifice, designed by architect Diego de Siloé, hides a wonderfully airy interior, with wooden Adam and Eve busts by *granadino* Alonso Cano in the Capilla Mayor. On the facade, look out for the inscription honouring Primo de Rivera, the founder of the fascist Falange, added when Franco had Granada in the grip of terror.

Adjoining the cathedral, the flamboyant Gothic **Capilla Real** (Royal Chapel) is where Spain's Reyes Católicos (Catholic Monarchs), Isabel I de Castilla (1451–1504) and Fernando II de Aragón (1452–1516), who commissioned this final resting place, are seeing out eternity in monumental marble tombs, hidden behind a 1520 gilded wrought-iron screen by Bartolomé de Jaén. (The tombs were desecrated by Napoleon's troops in 1812, so are unlikely to contain royal remains). The monarchs are actually believed to be entombed in simple lead coffins in the plain crypt beneath the chancel, overlooked by a Renaissance monument (the lions beneath their feet identify Isabel and Fernando). Also here are the coffins of their unfortunate daughter, Juana la Loca (Juana the Mad); her husband Felipe

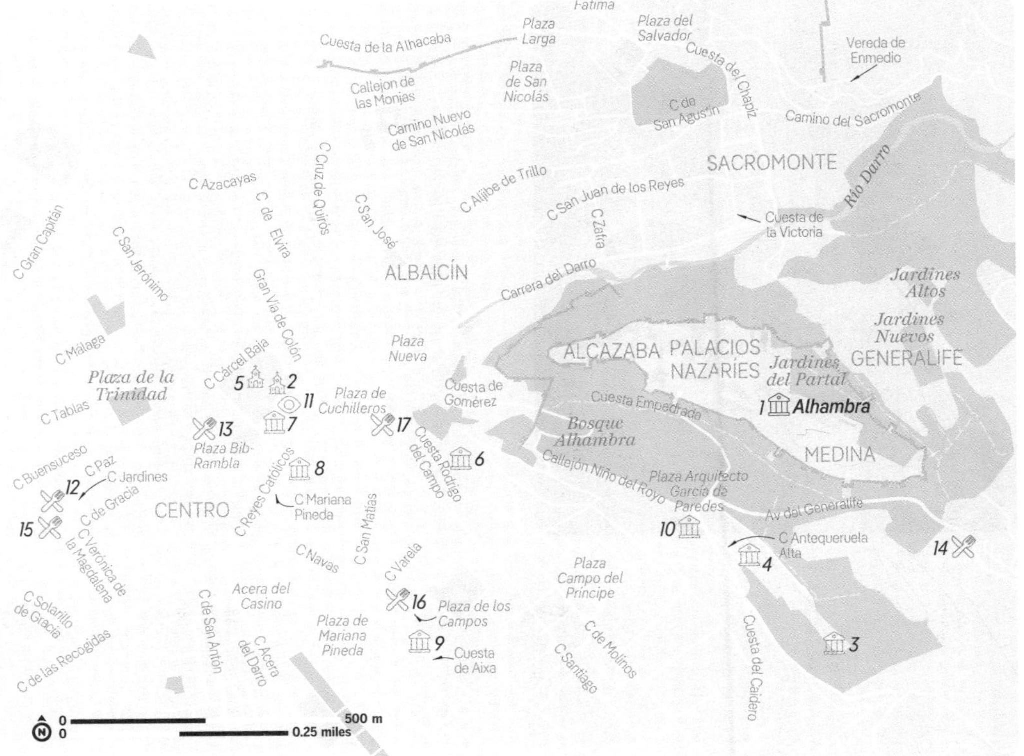

TOP SIGHTS
1 Alhambra

SIGHTS
2 Capilla Real
3 Carmen de los Mártires
4 Casa Museo Manuel Falla
5 Catedral de Granada
6 Centro de la Memoria Sefardí
7 Centro José Guerrero
8 Corral del Carbón
9 El Cuarto Real
10 Hotel Alhambra Palace
11 Madrasa Yusufia

EATING
12 Bar Poë
13 Bar Provincias
14 Casa Torcuato
15 Om Kalsum
16 Taberna la Tana

DRINKING
17 Casa de Vinos la Brujidera

Granada Cathedral

SACROMONTE: GRANADA'S ROMA QUARTER

Northeast of the Albaicín, the city abruptly ends. Urban bustle gives way to scrubland-dotted hills and the Camino de Sacromonte shadows the Río Darro past caves in the hillside – some dating back to the 14th century.

Traditionally a Roma neighbourhood, and the heart of flamenco traditions, Sacromonte is now home to several hundred Roma, immigrants and hippies. There are still flamenco *peñas* (clubs) here, though the performances are hardly impromptu. The main attractions, besides wandering the quiet lanes, are the Museo Cuevas del Sacromonte – a traditional cave home depicting typical life in the *barrio*, and the catacombs and subterranean chapels at the hillside Abadía del Sacromonte.

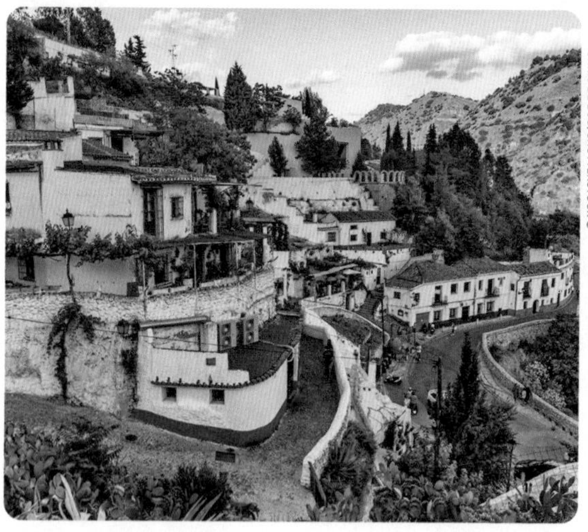

CHRIS DE BUG/SHUTTERSTOCK ©

Sacromonte

el Hermoso (look for 'F' on the coffin); and Miguel, Prince of Asturias, snuffed out by childhood illness.

Opposite the Capilla Real, the **Madrasa Yusufia** (Islamic college) was founded in 1349 by Yusuf I and is still part of Granada University. Inside, highlights include an elaborate *mihrab* (prayer niche), a baroque dome and some coloured stucco.

Just south of the cathedral, **Centro José Guerrero** is a gallery dedicated to *granadino* abstract painter José Guerrero (1914–91), who was influenced by Miró, the Cubism movement and American Expressionism. This museum displays vibrant works from his major periods, as well as temporary modernist exhibitions.

Down an alleyway just east of Calle Reyes Católicos, an elaborate horseshoe arch leads through to the 14th-century **Corral del Carbón**. Originally a caravanserai for Moorish traders (where they slept and stored their wares upstairs), in its various incarnations it's been an inn for coal dealers (hence its name, Coal Yard) and a 16th-century theatre, with spectators watching from galleries above.

Southeast of the Corral del Carbón, **El Cuarto Real** is a sensitively restored 13th-century Nasrid palace. Besides the original fortified tower, look out for the remarkable decorative motifs on the walls and ceiling of the *qubba* (reception room), similar to and predating those in Alhambra's Serallo (p235).

WHERE TO STAY IN A HERITAGE HOTEL

Casa Morisca
Updated 15th-century Albaicín mansion, with timber-beam ceilings and rooms around a turquoise-tiled courtyard. **€€€**

Parador de Granada
Best thing about staying at this former Moorish palace? Waking up in the actual Alhambra. **€€€**

Casa 1800 Granada
Coffered ceilings, stone walls and original panelling meet contemporary decor in a 16th-century building. **€€**

THE DEFINITIVE ALBAICÍN WALKING TOUR

The lanes, alleyways, *cármenes*, Moorish mansions and scenic plazas of the Unesco-listed old Moorish quarter occupy a hill facing the Alhambra. Allow a full day to explore its diverse sights.

Off Carrera del Darro, the **1 Baños Árabes el Bañuelo** is a well-preserved, 11th-century Moorish public bath complex. Light beams into its vaulted brick rooms through octagonal star-shaped shafts, illuminating columns with Roman and Visigothic capitals.

Nearby, occupying the 16th-century Casa de Castril, the **2 Museo Arqueológico** houses fascinating regional artefacts, from Palaeolithic to late Moorish times. Dominating the Plaza del Salvador near the top of the Albaicín, the 16th-century **3 Colegiata del Salvador** was built atop a former mosque. The minaret was converted to a bell tower, but the courtyard still features original *aljibes* (cisterns).

A short wander southwest brings you to the **4 Mirador San Nicolás**, the famous viewpoint for those classic sunset shots of the Alhambra silhouetted against the Sierra Nevada mountains. Further uphill, **5 Palacio de Dar-al-Horra**, a 15th-century Nasrid palace, was the home of sultana Aixa, the mother of Boabdil, Granada's last Moorish ruler. The patios and arches are the only surviving original features, but it's an intimate residence, centred on a central courtyard, with wonderful views across the surrounding neighbourhood.

West and downhill, the **6 Plaza de San Miguel Bajo** is one of Albaicín's most attractive plazas. It's bar-fringed and dominated by the 16th-century Iglesia de San Miguel, by architect Diego de Siloé, superimposed upon the original mosque, of which only the *aljibe* survives. Finish at buzzy **7 Plaza Nueva** via Calle Cruz de Quirós.

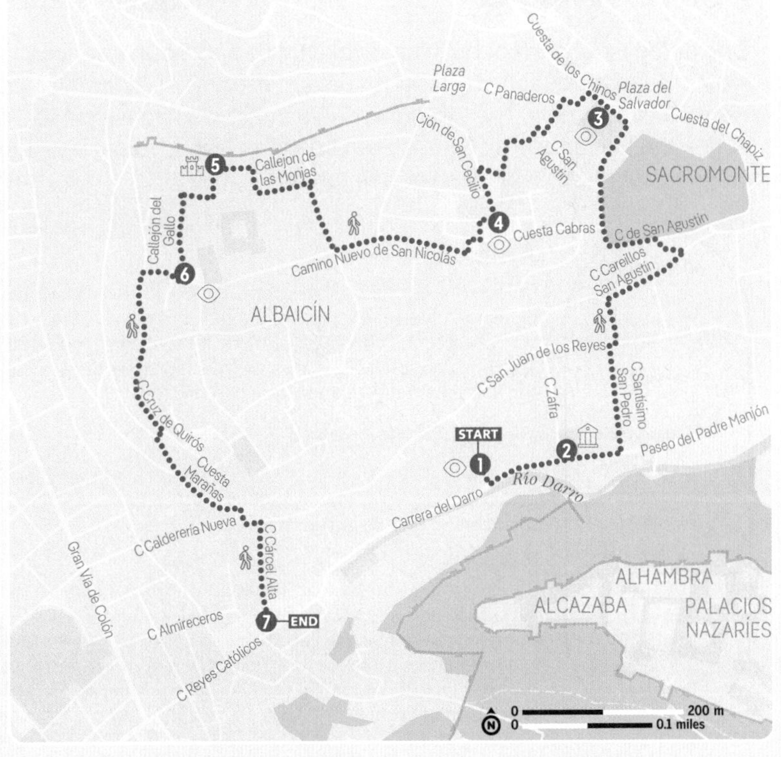

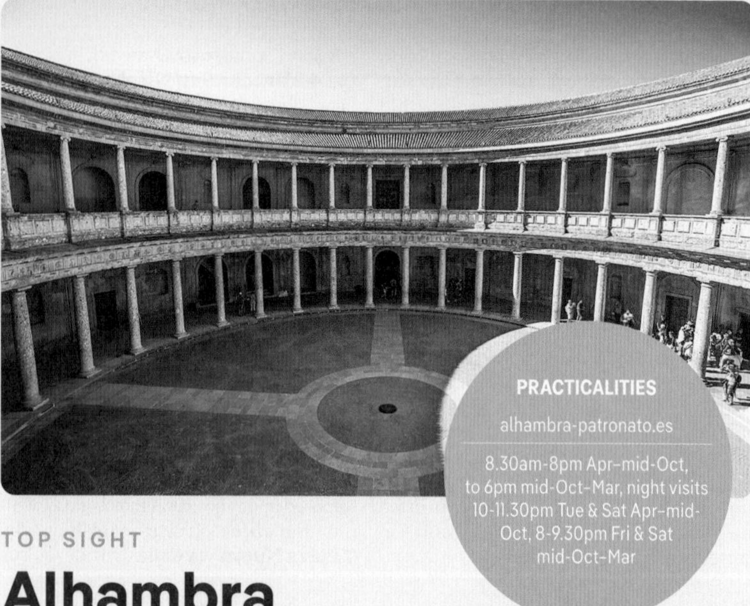

MARQUES/SHUTTERSTOCK ©

PRACTICALITIES

alhambra-patronato.es

8.30am-8pm Apr-mid-Oct, to 6pm mid-Oct-Mar, night visits 10-11.30pm Tue & Sat Apr-mid-Oct, 8-9.30pm Fri & Sat mid-Oct-Mar

TOP SIGHT

Alhambra

One of the most perfect buildings in existence and Spain's second most-visited attraction, the Moorish palace-fortress of Alhambra sits high above Granada. The 9th-century Alhambra was transformed during the 13th and 14th centuries by Granada's Nasrid rulers into the magnificent royal residence you see today.

DON'T MISS

- Palacios Nazaríes
- Patio de los Leones
- Sala de Dos Hermanas
- Patio del Cuarto Dorado
- Patio de los Arrayanes
- Palacio de Carlos V
- Museo de la Alhambra
- Alcazaba
- Generalife

Alcazaba

Occupying Alhambra's western tip, this 13th-century citadel is the oldest part. From the top of Torre de la Vela – the tower where the cross and banners of the Reconquista were raised in January 1492 – are unparalleled views of Albaicín, the Sacromonte hills, and Granada's rooftops.

Palacios Nazaríes

Its walls carved with elegant Arabic inscriptions, this remarkable palace complex was originally divided into three parts: the Mexuar, Serallo and Harem.

Mexuar

Enter through the Mexuar, the 14th-century hall where the sultans would adjudicate citizens' appeals and meet with ministers; beyond is the Patio del Cuarto Dorado, where they gave audiences. Opposite the Cuarto Dorado is the entrance to the Palacio de Comares, with its splendid tile, stucco and carved-wood facade.

Serallo

At the heart of the Serallo, where sultans conducted negotiations with Christian emissaries, is the Patio de los Arrayanes, named after the myrtle hedges around its rectangular pool and surrounded by marble-columned arcades. To the north, the Sala de la Barca, with a copy of its original cedar ceiling, leads into the Salón de los Embajadores – the largest, most striking chamber, with a domed marquetry ceiling symbolising the seven heavens of Islam.

Harem

Continue to the Patio de los Leones, centred on an 11th-century fountain channelling water through the mouths of 12 marble lions. To the south, the Sala de los Abencerrajes features a mesmerising octagonal stalactite ceiling. At the eastern end, the Sala de los Reyes has three leather-lined ceiling alcoves painted by 14th-century Christian artists. To the north, the Sala de Dos Hermanas features a dizzying *muqarnas* (honeycomb-vaulted) dome. Above, the carved wood screens enabled women to peer down from hallways without being seen. Look out over the gardens from the Mirador de Daraxa. The 16th-century Patio de la Lindaraja brings you to the tile-clad Baño Real de Comares, lit by star-shaped skylights. You'll eventually emerge into the terraced gardens of the Jardines del Partal, replete with reflecting pool.

Palacio de Carlos V

In stark contrast to its surroundings, the round Palacio de Carlos V, begun in 1526 by Toledo architect Pedro Machuca, features a Renaissance facade and a two-tiered circular courtyard ringed by 32 columns.

Museo de la Alhambra

This museum features superb tilework, the elaborately carved wooden door from the Sala de Dos Hermanas, and the excavated remains of the Acequia Real (Royal Water Channel). Its tour de force is the 15th-century Jarrón de las Gacelas, a 1.5m-tall red clay vase covered in blue-and-gold enamel and embossed with leaping gazelles.

Museo de Bellas Artes

Standouts include the 17th-century works of *granadino* artist Alonso Cano, sculpture by José de Mora and abstract 20th-century paintings by another *granadino*, José Guerrero.

Generalife

The Nasrid rulers' summer estate takes its name from the Arabic *jinan al-'arif*, meaning 'the overseer's gardens'. The Patio de la Acequia features immaculately tended gardens and distant views of the Palacios Nazaríes; in the Patio de la Sultana, the trunk of a 700-year-old cypress tree marks the spot where Sultana Zoraya allegedly met with her lover Hamet. Nearby, the Escalera del Agua is a marvel, with water channels running down the staircase's stone balustrades.

ALHAMBRA'S HIDDEN SPACES

Each month the Alhambra Board of Trustees give access to select spaces usually closed to the public. The Espacio del Mes is included in general-entry tickets. Past Spaces of the Month include the 19th-century Mirador del Generalife, the 14th-century Sala de Camas de los Baños de Comares and the 13th-century Camino de Ronda.

TOP TIPS

- Access to Palacios Nazaríes is limited to 300 visitors every half-hour; book time-slot tickets as far in advance as possible.
- Alhambra by night is a special experience: book Night Visit Palacios Nazaríes (€8; year-round) and Night Visit Gardens & Generalife (€5; April, May, September & October).
- General (€14) tickets cover all areas, while Gardens, Generalife & Alcazaba (€7) tickets exclude Palacios Nazaríes.
- Bring ID that matches the name on your ticket – authorities are cracking down on scalpers buying up day tickets and reselling them to ticketless visitors hoping for same-day entry by the gate.

MY FAVOURITE TAPAS

Roberto Rodríguez is a guide and local food expert with Granada Tapas Tour.

Tapas hotspots
Some of the best tapas places are in Realejo. Calle Ángel Ganivet has some excellent choices; Calle Navas is too touristy. Some of the smaller lanes near Plaza Nueva also have good places.

Typical Granada dish
Remojón – a typical potato salad with orange and *bacalao* (salted cod).

Best food shop
For superb *jamón iberico bellota* and wines from the Granada province, go to Casa Diego.

Best tapas bar in Centro
Más Que Vinos has a really unusual dish, pork in mustard sauce, and a good selection of local craft beers. And wine, obviously.

Exploring Alhambra Hill & Realejo

ALHAMBRA HILL'S ALTERNATIVE SIGHTS

Found a short walk downhill from Alhambra's Puerta de las Granadas, **Casa Museo Manuel Falla** is the former home of Spain's greatest classical composer, Cádiz-born Manuel de Falla (1876–1946). A friend of Granada's famous poet Federico García Lorca (p230), de Falla spent his key years here until the civil war forced him into exile in Argentina in 1939. The tiny house is just as he left it: cluttered with books and gifts from friends (including Picasso sketches on the walls). Ring the bell to get in; guided visits are given in Spanish, English and French.

Nearby, **Carmen de los Mártires** is a tranquil oasis dotted with cypresses, palms and fountains, with peacocks wandering around and black swans in the artificial lake. The centrepiece is a restored turn-of-the-20th-century mansion. In its past incarnations, the site has hosted a prison, a chapel and a convent.

Swing by the **Hotel Alhambra Palace** on your way downhill. Inside this neo-Moorish edifice, the theatre launched the career of Federico García Lorca during an evening of poetry and song in 1922.

Meandering down Calle Aire Alta, take the tiny lanes into Granada's Judería (former Jewish quarter) and visit the **Centro de la Memoria Sefardí**, dedicated to Granada's Jewish history over many centuries (before their 1492 expulsion). The owners also do Realejo tours by advance request.

Granada & the art of tapear

CITY OF TAPAS

No other Andalucian city does tapas like Granada. Although other *andaluces* consider *granadinos* to be a bit penny-pinching when it comes to the art of *tapear* (tapas bar-hopping), no one can accuse Granada's barkeeps of being less than generous. The old Andalucian custom of offering a free tapa with every drink is alive and well here. These free edible offerings range from a couple of croquettes to small servings of *berenjenas con miel* (aubergine with cane honey), slivers of *jamón serrano* (cured ham), or even mini-portions of rice dishes. In the Albaicín, Moroccan flavours creep in, while fusion tapas are not unheard of in the streets south and west of the cathedral – as well as in the *barrio* Realejo, a particular tapas hotspot.

Drink-wise, you'll encounter everything from *fino* (sherry), popular all over Andalucía, and vermouth (served 'on the rocks'

WHERE TO GO FOR COFFEE

La Finca
Micro-roastery of select beans from around the world from small producers; cosy café; great pastries. €

Sur Coffee Corner
Caffeine-dispensing hole-in-the-wall, with superlative single-origin beans from Barcelona roastery Nomad. €

I Need Coffee
Says it all, really. Excellent coffee, good sandwiches (including bagels) and freshly baked pastries. €

MANUEL ASCANIO/SHUTTERSTOCK ©

Carmen de los Mártires

with a slice of orange) to glasses of robust reds from all over the Granada province and the confusingly named *vino de la costa* (actually an amber-coloured mountain wine from the Alpujarras).

Explore the tapas scene by yourself or opt for expert-led gastronomic tours. Spain Food Sherpas (spainfoodsherpas.com) focus on Granada's speciality dishes and wines from the Alpujarras and elsewhere in Granada, and can organise specialised tastings of local tipples, as well as cooking classes. Well-established Granada Tapas Tours (granadatapastours.com) run a variety of small-group food tours, from craft beer and dedicated Albaicín tapas crawls to 'hidden gems' tours that take you off the beaten tapas trail.

In Centro, **Bar Poë** looks unassuming from the outside, but fills up rapidly with old-timer *granadinos*, students, expats and visitors, drawn by the eclectic cooking of well-travelled owners Ana and Matt. The standout tapas here are spicy chicken livers and potato curry.

Around the corner from Poë, **Om Kalsum** is another Granada stalwart, where B&W photos of flamenco dancers mingle with Moroccan decor and Middle Eastern bites, from mini-tagines to superlative falafel.

EL NIÑO DE LAS PINTURAS

Around the streets of Realejo you'll come across thought-provoking murals that often juxtapose vivid close-ups of human faces with short poetic stanzas. These were created by El Niño de las Pinturas (real name: Raúl Ruiz), a street artist whose works have become renowned throughout the city over the past couple of decades. Though his murals divide *granadino* opinions, most believe that they've infused new life into some of the older corners of Granada. Seek out El Niño's work at vegan restaurant Hicuri and bar Candela opposite; at his old home at Calle de Molinos 44 and on the wall beside the Hotel Molinos.

EL NIÑO'S MASTERPIECE

To see one of El Niño's arguably most famous murals, visit the poet Lorca's childhood home in **Fuente Vaqueros** (p230).

WHERE TO EAT ON ALHAMBRA HILL

Damasqueros
Andalucian-inspired tasting menus with fare such as cod, tripe-and-onion tempura and Iberian-pork carpaccio. €€

Restaurante Vegano Hicuri
Salads and curried seitan sit alongside plant-based renditions of Andalucian favourites and organic wines. €

Faralá
Three tasting menus and expert wine pairings offer a journey into regional culinary traditions. €€€

BEST FUSION DINING IN GRANADA

Picoteca 3 Maneras
South American and Asian flavours infuse boldly reimagined dishes such as pear-and-pancetta gnocchi, and tuna in orange sauce. €€

Ruta del Azafrán
Moroccan starters, hearty Andalucian staples and Asian-inspired tuna dishes get together at this contemporary riverside bistro. €€

Restaurante Masae
Andalucía's marine bounty meets Japanese cooking techniques at this *izakaya* (Japanese tavern). Exquisite prawn sashimi stands out. €€

El Trillo
Ambitiously updated Mediterranean dishes, such as *arróz negro* with ginger aioli, smoked couscous and beetroot *salmorejo* (cold soup) with avocado. €€

WILL PERRETT/ALAMY STOCK PHOTO ©

Casa Torcuato

As old-school as they come, **Bar Provincias** (around since 1945), near the cathedral, is perfect for perching on a stool outside and people-watching as you munch on fried fish and seafood bites.

Near Plaza Nueva, snug, wood-panelled **Casa de Vinos de Brujidera** prides itself on the contents of its wine cellar. Most wines are available by the glass and you can taste everything from Galician *albariño* to organic Granada reds and sherries from Jerez.

In the upper Albaicín, **Casa Torcuato** has been run by multiple generations of the same family since the 1930s. Apart from traditional Andalucian dishes, it's locally renowned for its *arróz* (rice) tapa.

A Realejo favourite, **Taberna la Tana** serves over 500 Spanish wines alongside platters of cold cuts and other superlative bites.

GETTING AROUND

Granada's neighbourhoods are best explored on foot, but public transport gets you to the train/bus stations and between various *barrios*. The following buses (€1.40; €1.50 at night) are handy: C30 Plaza Isabel II–Alhambra (via Realejo); C31 Plaza Nueva–Albayzín; C34 Plaza Nueva–Sacromonte; 4 Gran Vía–Train station; 33 Gran Vía–Bus station.

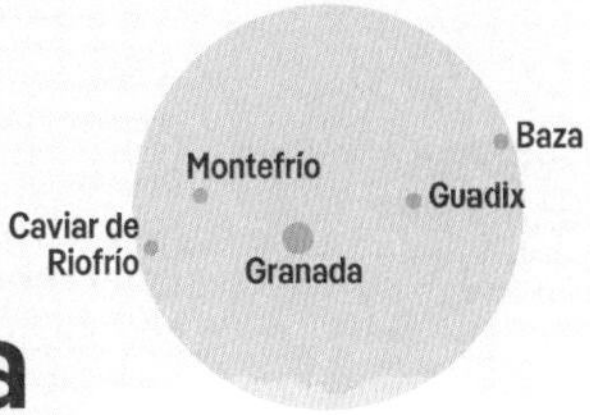

Baza
Montefrío
Guadix
Caviar de Riofrío
Granada

Beyond Granada

Explore vast badlands and cave towns, road-trip to a crag-top castle, and taste unique wines and organic caviar.

Granada is surrounded by fertile land known as La Vega, a patchwork of woods, farmlands and vineyards. Heading west from Granada towards Antequera, you pass by the world's first organic caviar producer, open for visits. Northeast of the city, cultivated land gives way to increasingly hilly and arid terrain until it tops out in a sparsely populated highland plain, El Altiplano, well known for its palaeontological discoveries, as well as its unique wines by small producers. Much of El Altiplano is protected within the 4722-sq-km Unesco Geoparque de Granada; this immense tract of barren semi-desert is hauntingly scenic, and home to the town of Guadix, famed for its cave houses.

TOP TIP

Book ahead to visit the caviar farm. Visit Granada Geopark during European Geopark Week in June for special events.

Guadix

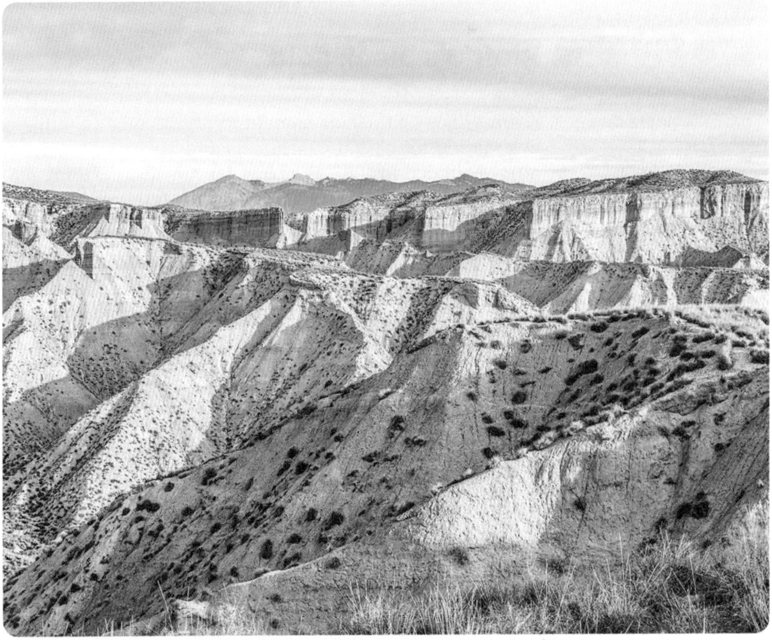

Guadix, city of caves

LUNAR LANDSCAPE & CAVE DWELLINGS

At first glance, dusty Guadix, with its tight medieval core centred on a cathedral, seems indistinguishable from other provincial Andalucian towns. But follow Calle Puerta Ancha through the *casco antiguo* (old town), past the **Alcazaba** (an 11th-century Moorish castle with reddish, crenellated walls and square towers) and along the Calle Cañada de los Perales, and 1.2km south of the centre you'll find yourself in the remarkable **Barrio de las Cuevas**.

Imagine *Star Wars*' planet Tatooine, but with chimneys erupting from undulating russet-brown hillocks with doors, and you get the picture. Sitting against a backdrop of pyramidal brown cliffs, the main cave district consists of around 2000 dwellings – home to around 10,000 people – with the oldest caves thought to have been inhabited since early Moorish times.

Inside a 300-year-old cave-house, the wonderful **Centro de Interpretación Cuevas de Guadix** initiates you into the world of cave dwellers: from how these sustainable dwellings seemingly made for hobbits were originally dug out to the recreated former kitchen, stables and bedrooms. Stop by the whitewashed church opposite (with concealed cave-chapel within) and summit the nearby viewpoint. It's particularly interesting to wander deeper into the district, noticing the contrast between basic cave houses with tiny windows, antennae and whitewashed front and disused and abandoned caves right next door. Note that invitations to visit a cave house often carry a hefty price tag.

I LIVE HERE: GUADIX TIPS

María Paz, a guide at the Centro de Interpretación Cuevas de Guadix, shares her favourites.

Best viewpoint
Mirador Cerro de la Bala is the highest viewpoint in Guadix and the best, though it's above a sketchy part of the Barrio de las Cuevas. From Cuatro Veredas street, it's up an unmarked trail behind the school.

My favourite things
Inside the Iglesia de Santo Domingo is the most beautiful carved wooden Mudéjar ceiling. Nearby are terrific views of the old town from the Mirador de la Magdalena.

Cave restaurants
You can dine in a cave in La Tinaja or the Cuevas Pedro Antonio de Alarcón, near the train station.

Riofrío's black gold

WORLD'S FIRST ORGANIC CAVIAR FARM

A tiny village in the Loja mountains has become an unlikely destination for casual gourmands and Michelin-star chefs alike. Founded in 1963 as a trout farm by fish-farming pioneer Dr Luis Domezain, **Caviar de Riofrío** (caviarderiofrio.com) branched out into breeding critically endangered sturgeon in the 1980s and now produces some of the world's best and most sought-after caviar.

Most caviar today is farmed, since sturgeon are critically endangered in the wild due to overfishing and the destruction of their natural habitat. As sturgeon are river-born fish who spend their lives in the ocean and return to their birthplace

WHERE TO STAY IN A CAVE HOTEL

Cueva de Manuela
Two adorable cave houses in Barrio de las Cuevas, with snug bedrooms, whirlpool baths and roof terraces. €€

Hotel Rural Cuevas de Rolando
Doubles and cave houses at an inviting complex on the outskirts of Guadix. €€

Cuevas Pedro Antonio de Alarcón
Cosy cave bedrooms and living rooms, plus an outdoor pool and restaurant. €€

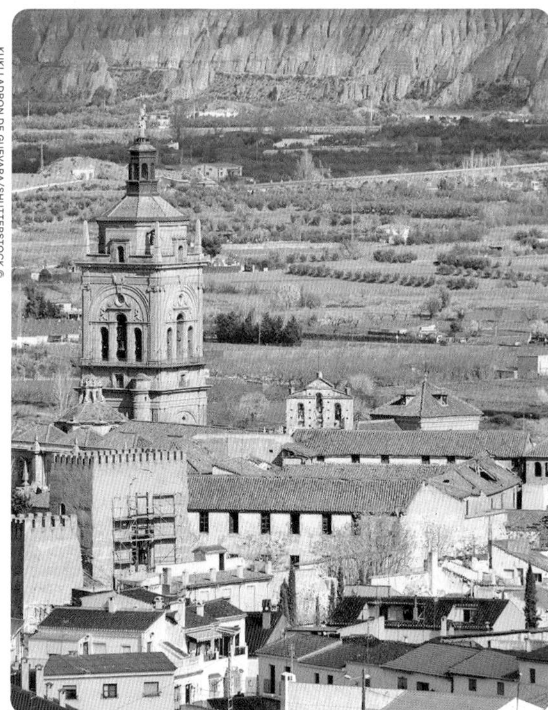

KUKI LADRON DE GUEVARA/SHUTTERSTOCK ©

Alcazaba

to spawn, all farmed caviar is a result of artificial insemination. But Caviar de Riofrío has earned the world's first 'organic caviar' certification, thanks to its proximity to the source of the River Frío (which keeps the sturgeon pools a constant 14–15°C), high standards of animal welfare and use of river plants for waste filtration.

Most of the Riofrío caviar comes from Nacarii and Osetra species, who have to be at least 12 years old before they can start producing caviar, along with some from the Beluga sturgeon, who only reach maturity aged 25. Everything – from spawning to packaging – is done on the premises, ensuring that this caviar is genuinely a 'zero-kilometre' foodstuff.

Caviar and champagne tastings are available for visitors.

CAVIAR 101

Carmen Arriaza,
Caviar de Riofrío.

'We produce three types of caviar: organic, Russian-style and traditional. For organic we add salt and seal it inside glass containers. When you eat it, you feel it pop against the roof of your mouth. Russian-style is caviar that's undergone a two-month maturation process in a special cylinder – a stronger flavour, but it still pops. The taste of traditional-style caviar is achieved by letting it age for four to five months. Its flavour is the most pronounced; it's blacker in colour and it has a buttery texture.

CAVIAR & TAPAS

Taberna la Tana (p238) in Granada is renowned for both its caviar and an exceptional wine cellar full of Spanish tipples. Don't miss it on your tapas bar crawl in Granada.

WHERE TO EAT CAVIAR IN ANDALUCÍA

Restaurante los Patos (Granada)
Tasting menu incorporating caviar, served beneath a flowering trellis. **€€**

Sollo (Benalmádena)
Innovative tasting menus with freshwater fish from Brazilian-born, Michelin-starred 'caviar chef' Diego Gallegos. **€€€**

La Medusa (Málaga)
Oyster specialists with delicious caviar on the menu, as well as matching cava and champagne. **€€**

LAS PEÑAS DE LOS GITANOS

Inhabited by Stone Age people around 3000 BCE, the remarkably well-preserved Neolithic site of Las Peñas de los Gitanos (laspeñasdelosgitanos.es) is well worth a detour. While the cave paintings are currently off-limits, you can view extensive remains of Copper Age stone and clay dwellings, the rock overhangs and caves that provided shelter to the site's earliest occupants and their livestock (cow and goat remains have been found here). Look out for animal carvings on the stone tombs and don't miss Dolmen 23, the best-preserved of the dolmens dotted about the site, with an intact carved entrance. The site is on private land signposted 8km east of Montefrío, off the GR-3410; you'll need advance permission to visit.

Montefrío

Montefrío

LOFTY VILLAGE WITH CASTLE VIEWS

A fantastic day trip from Granada, or a rewarding detour on the drive between Granada and Córdoba or Antequera, Montefrío is spectacularly sited – so much so that *National Geographic* named it one of '10 Villages with the Best Views in the World' in 2015. Surrounded by softly rolling hills, and bookended by two crags, each featuring a church, the village is a cascade of whitewashed, tile-roofed houses overlooked by a clifftop castle.

Take Calle San Sebastián past Montefrío's **town hall** (inside a former 18th-century palace), and a bracing 10-minute climb brings you to the **Castillo de Montefrío** – a palimpsest of ruins that make up this hilltop fortress. The only surviving feature of the original 1382 Moorish construction is its defensive wall. After the Reconquista – Montefrío was

WHERE TO EAT IN MONTEFRÍO

El Pregonero
This atmospheric restaurant specialises in pork: *cochinillo* (suckling pig) and *jamón asado* (roast ham). **€€**

Casa Blanca
Stews, *chuletas* (chops), croquettes and other meaty specials are the order of the day here. **€**

Bar el Cruce
Informal fare, from grilled squid and *huevos rotos* (eggs with ham and chips) to battered fish. **€**

taken by the Reyes Católicos in 1486 – Diego de Siloé was commissioned in 1549 to build the striking Iglesia de la Villa, combining Mudéjar, Renaissance and Gothic styles, within the castle complex. Appropriately, there's now an interactive museum inside, with displays on the reconquest of this part of Andalucía, as well as some gorgeous vaulting.

As for the best views of Montefrío, we'll let you be the judge as to whether they're from the **Mirador National Geographic**, 800m south of town on the A-335, or the **Mirador de las Peñas**, at the end of its namesake street.

Granada's high-altitude wines

UNIQUE TIPPLES

Vines grown above 1000m, an abundance of sunshine, extreme daily temperature contrasts year-round and soil with a high mineral content have all ensured the uniqueness of wines produced in the Granada province. While Granada wines have been produced largely for personal consumption over the centuries, the Denominación de Origen Protegida (DOP; Denomination of Origin; dopvinosdegranada.es) now recognises the importance of the main wine-growing areas of Guadix and El Altiplano – where vines grow at up to 1500m and produce full-bodied garnacha, monastrell, romé, merlot, pinot noir and other fine reds – and the Contraviesa-Alpujarras area between the Mediterranean and the Sierra Nevada, whose high-altitude grapes also yield reds, rosés and whites (the latter from vijiriega, baladí verdejo, torrontés, and niche moscatels, among others). Of the sixty-plus wine producers in Granada, many bodegas now welcome visitors.

Broaden your oenophile education at the eco estate of **Alquería de Morayma** (alqueriamorayma.com), south of Cádiar in the Alpujarras, where you can pair organic reds and whites with food at the excellent restaurant. Also in the Alpujarras, just east of Ugíjar, **Dominio Buenavista** (vinosveleta.com) produces some of the Alpujarras' best wines, such as unique Nolados blends, tempranillo rosés and native vijiriega and chardonnay; tours and tastings available. On the Altiplano, 23km northwest of Guadix, family-owned **Bodega Anchurón** (anchuron.es) is powered by renewable energy and specialises in single-origin reds grown at 1000m.

DETOUR TO BAZA

If you're bodega-hopping on the Altiplano, Baza is worth a detour. Originally an ancient Iberian settlement, it was taken over by the Romans, then became a silk prayer-mat production centre under the Moors; it has a cave-house district (near the bullring) that's less touristed than its counterpart in Guadix.

One highlight is the engaging Museo Arqueológico, housed in a 16th-century wine warehouse. The star exhibit is a copy of the Dama de Baza, a 4th-century BCE painted limestone statue of a richly dressed woman on a throne, found in a nearby necropolis (the original is in Madrid). Also check out the Baños Árabes, one of Spain's most intact 10th-century Moorish baths, with well-defined cold, warm and hot rooms and columned arches illuminated via star-shaped skylights.

GETTING AROUND

Guadix and Baza are served by frequent daily buses from Granada; Baza also connects to Vélez-Rubio, and Guadix to Almería and Málaga. Additionally, there are several daily trains between Guadix, Almería and Granada.

There's a daily bus service from Granada to Montefrío; Ríofrio is on the Granada–Antequera bus route. To explore more remote corners of the Altiplano, you'll need your own wheels.

PARQUE NACIONAL SIERRA NEVADA

Snow-tipped for much of the year, the craggy peaks of the Sierra Nevada provide a dramatic backdrop to Granada's urban landscapes. The 862-sq-km Parque Nacional Sierra Nevada – Spain's largest national park – is home to 2100 of Spain's 7000 plant species, including unique types of crocus, narcissus, thistle, clover and poppy, as well as Andalucía's largest ibex population (around 15,000). It's also where you'll find Mulhacén (3482m), the highest point in mainland Spain, as well as ample day hikes and multi-day trails that beckon serious trekkers and mountaineers. Unpretty mountain town Pradollano provides access to Europe's most southerly ski resort, which leaves you literally breathless at its highest point.

The Sierra Nevada extends about 75km from west to east, with 15 peaks over 3000m. The lower southern reaches – Las Alpujarras – and their dramatic valleys, dotted with age-old *pueblos blancos*, lend themselves beautifully to road-tripping.

TOP TIP

Hiking weather is at its best from July to early September. Outside of this period there's a risk of inclement weather, with snow affecting some of the routes. The Sierra Nevada ski season swings into action in November and typically lasts till April, sometimes extending into May.

BEST MOUNTAIN MEALS

El Corral del Castaño (Capileira)
Creative fare, ranging from meaty classics to a Moroccan-style veg-stuffed *pastela*. €€

Mesón la Fragua (Trevélez)
Traditional Alpujarras recipes with mountain views. €

Alquería de Morayma (Cádiar)
Seasonal farmhouse meals; their own organic wines and olive oil. €€

Las Chimeneas (Mairena)
Excellent Andalucian cooking using organic produce from the British owners' *finca* (rural estate). €€

Alpujarras on two feet

HIKING STUPENDOUS MOUNTAIN TRAILS

There's an almost infinite number of ways to explore the Sierra Nevada from the Alpujarras, from mule paths between villages to multi-week, long-distance trails, with the best months April to mid-June and mid-September to early November. The three villages in the Barranco del Poqueira – **Pampaneira**, **Bubión** and **Capileira**, along with **Trevélez** – are all popular starting points for numerous routes, ranging from 4km-long leg-stretchers to full-day 29km challenges (two to eleven hours); you can summit Mulhacén (p248) from both.

The three long-distance trails traversing the Alpujarras are the 144km-long **GR142**, connecting numerous villages between Lanjarón and Fiñana; the more scenic **GR7** (stretching through five of Andalucía's provinces); and the 300km-long, relatively well signposted **GR240** (aka 'Sulayr'), which passes through the Sierra Nevada at a higher altitude than the GR7.

Moderately challenging hikes from Capileira include the 12km return (5 hours) up the **Río Poqueira valley** to Refugio Poqueira. First, take the reasonably good unpaved road to the abandoned hamlet of La Cebadilla, near the hydroelectric power station. Apart from the initial switchback section up the hill, a beautiful, gently meandering riverside trail leads you through a greenery-filled valley. About halfway along, there's a delightful river-pool for dipping. After you pass the ruins of the Cortijo Las Tomas, it's a steep but straightforward slog up the bare slope to the *refugio*.

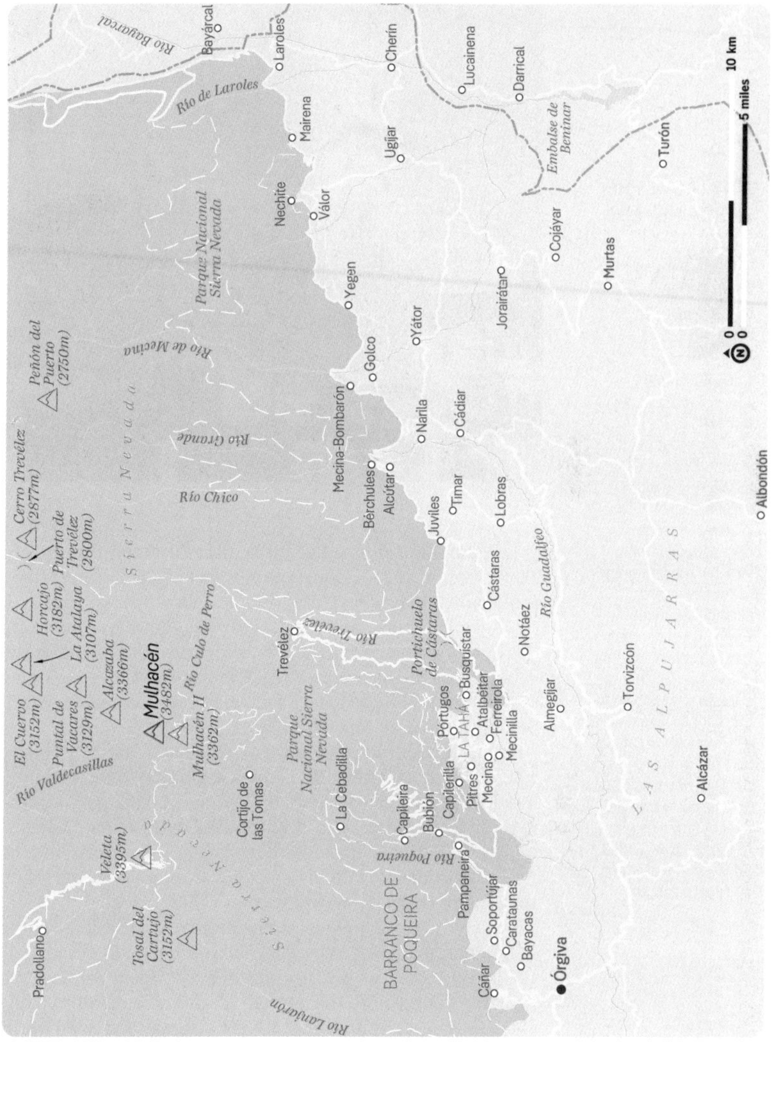

WHERE TO STAY IN TREVÉLEZ & CAPILEIRA

Hotel Real de Poqueira (Capileira)
This welcoming guesthouse features elegant rooms, a pool and a garden restaurant. **€€**

Hotel Fuente (Capileira)
Mountain views and rustic-chic rooms at a Spanish-Belgian hideaway. Perks include massage and guided hikes. **€€**

Hotel la Fragua II (Trevélez)
Alpine-style lodge at the top of Trevélez with spacious, sunny rooms with balconies and heated pool. **€€**

WHY I LOVE THE SIERRA NEVADA

Anna Kaminski, Lonely Planet writer. *@socialhandle*

In winter, I check the Sierra Nevada snow forecast daily. Whenever there's decent snowfall, by 9am the next morning I'm on the slopes, hitting the powder. During warmer months, I try to explore corners of the Alpujarras that are less well-known to me, spend a few days at a mountain retreat, or hike another section of the GR7 or the GR240. I never fail to be awed by the familiar sight of those snow-tipped peaks, some of which I've yet to summit.

SOYAZUR/GETTY IMAGES ©

Pitres

Also starting from La Cebadilla, the 7km **Acequias de Río Toril loop hike** (3½ hours) climbs steeply at the start, past some ruins, before levelling off and following the course of the Acequia Nueva aqueduct, with fine views of Mulhacén. Once you reach the Cortijo de las Mergas at the head of the valley, cross the Barranco de las Carreras, and then scramble up the pathless ridge before following the Acequia Castillejo downhill towards La Cebadilla.

From Trevélez, you can opt for a steep 5km ascent (5 hours return) to the **Mirador de Trevélez**, gaining 900m and linking up with the gentler trail up Mulhacén. You can incorporate the trail into a tough 20km **Siete Lagunas loop hike** by taking Calle Horno up from the village, turning off along the Acequia Gorda and climbing steadily through pine forest and then a bare-sloped, snow-speckled valley, bisected by frigid Acequia Mingo. After you cross it, it's a relatively steep climb to Laguna Hondera, fed by waterfalls of snowmelt. From here, the largely pathless but straightforward ascent up the Culo de Perro takes you to the summit of Alcazaba (3369m), Trevélez's toughest climb. Alternatively, a steady trek westwards connects you to the Mulhacén trail, which you can follow to the mirador before descending steeply to Trevélez.

The best hiking maps of the area are by Editorial Alpina and Discovery Walking Guides. Nevadensis (nevadensis.com) can organise guided hikes, as can many hotels and guesthouses.

WHERE TO STAY IN LA TAHÁ

Casa Ana (Ferreirola)
Beautifully restored 400-year-old house with beamed, rustic rooms. Owner Anne organises walking holidays. **€€**

L'Atelier (Mecina Fondales)
Intimate, French-run, two-room B&B in a 350-year-old house. In-house restaurant serves terrific vegetarian food. **€**

Sierra y Mar (Ferreirola)
A rural hiking base of eight rooms across several houses, with kitchen, library and fireplace. **€**

LA TAHÁ WALKING TOUR

In the beautiful valley immediately east of the Barranco del Poqueira, seven villages make up the former Moorish administrative district of Tahá; this scenic three-hour circuit takes in five of them. Begin in **1 Pitres**, with its Berber-style, flat-roofed houses covered in grey mica, a traditional local architectural style. Taking the narrow path behind Restaurante La Carretera on the main road, veer left as you descend, with the rooftops of **2 Mecina** visible below; fifteen minutes later you'll find yourself near the church at the top of the village. Head down to **3 Mecinilla**, the lower part of the village, following the main road. Once you pass the Bar el Aljibe, turn left at the drinking fountain, take the main street, then take a shortcut downhill through orchards on the edge of a ravine to reach the soporific little maze of lanes that make up **4 Fondales**. Pass through a *tinao*, a traditional, wood-beamed tunnel found in the Alpujarras, to reach El Fuente's wash area in the village's southeast corner. Take the path towards the river, always bearing left. You'll soon find yourself high above the gorge, with the Trevélez bridge ahead. Turn left before the bridge, cross the Río Bermejo and climb up over the rocks towards **5 Ferreirola**. Find the church square and the wash place near it; take the steep path towards **6 Atalbéitar** to find yourself by the church below that village. Check out this untouristed, sleepy hamlet before taking the road back out towards Pitres. Take the right fork to reach a footpath that drops steeply to the river before ascending to an *acequia* (dry irrigation channel) and continuing on past the Refugio los Albergues into Pitres.

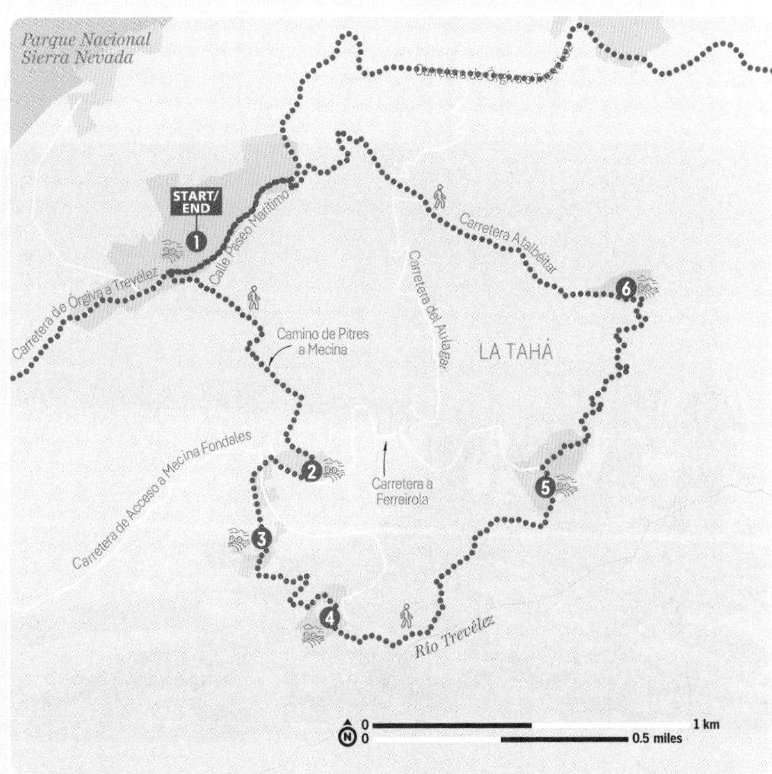

HIKE

The Big One: Mulhacén

Peak-baggers are unable to resist the siren call of Mulhacén, the highest mountain on the Spanish mainland, 3482m above sea level (3718m-high Monte Teide on Tenerife in the Canary Islands claims Spain's number-one spot). Scaling Mulhacén makes for an excellent day hike from the Paraje del Cascajar, reachable by minibus from Capileira between June and November.

1 Paraje del Cascajar

When you start out, Mulhacén doesn't look like much – a rounded hump way up ahead of you. But it's the highest mountain peak around, and you've got a 900m ascent ahead of you.

The Hike: Head up the dirt road. On your left you'll see the shark-fin form of Veleta, the Sierra Nevada's second-highest peak (3396m). Detour to the right after 1.7km, at a 'Trevélez' sign, for the Mirador de Trevélez.

2 Mirador de Trevélez

Spectacular views of the Trevélez valley open up before you, including bird's-eye vistas of its namesake village and the steep descent that is the most direct route to Trevélez.

The Hike: Back on the main track, take the right-hand path at a junction after 450m, heading uphill; then turn left at a fork after 750m.

Mulhacén summit

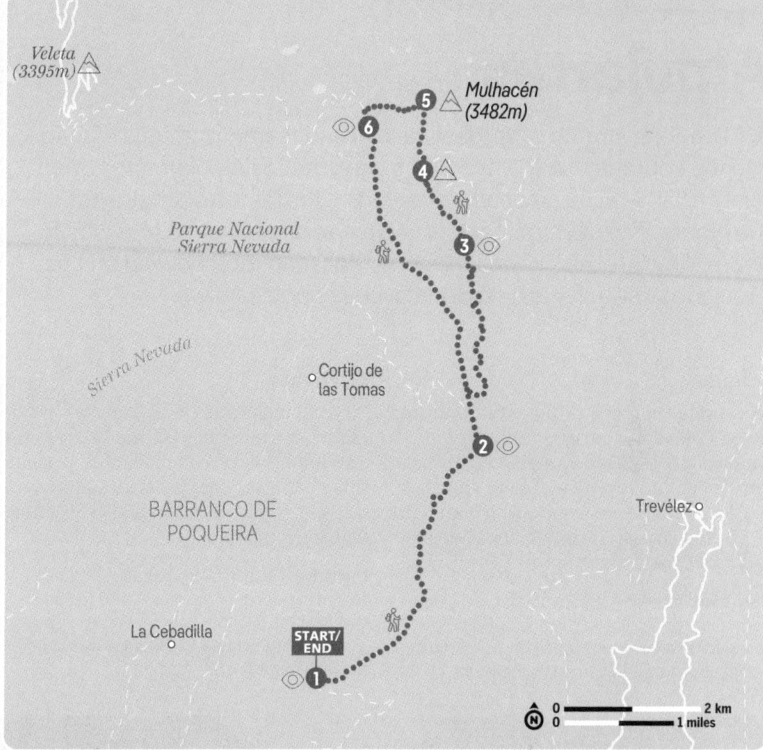

3 Loma de Mulhacén

As you tackle the increasingly steep path up the Loma del Mulhacén (Mulhacén Ridge), you'll find yourself crisscrossing (and occasionally following) an old, abandoned dirt road – a 1960s off-shoot of the old Sierra Nevada road.

The Hike: Passing a Siete Lagunas signpost (leading to another route to Trevélez), continue climbing steadily for 1.75km to reach Mulhacén II.

4 Mulhacén II

Marked by a concrete pillar on the summit ridge at 3362m, the mini-summit of Mulhacén II marks the end of the steepest part of the climb. Vegetation is sparse up here, and you can clearly see the summit.

The Hike: The trail gradient is gentle and it's a straightforward remaining 1km hike across bare rock (with occasional ibex sightings!) to the highest point on the Iberian peninsula.

5 Mulhacén

The summit is crowned with ruined buildings (left over from a 19th-century geodesic survey) and a stone pillar. Beware of the precipice plunging down some 600m to the Hoya de Mulhacén on the north side of the mountain, and enjoy spectacular views of the Laguna de la Caldera and Veleta.

The Hike: A narrow path zigzags steeply down Mulhacén's western slope. Over halfway down, take the left-hand fork to the Sierra Nevada road; the right leads to Laguna de la Caldera.

6 Sierra Nevada Road

This broad dirt track was Europe's highest road in 1935, connecting Granada to Capileira and making the Veleta peak accessible to cars. Closed since 1999 (due to environmental concerns), it's now a straightforward 5km descent to the original junction, and a further 2km to El Cascajar bus stop.

ROAD TRIP

Alpujarras

A 70km-long stretch of verdant valleys and dramatic gorges etched into the southern flank of the Sierra Nevada, Las Alpujarras is famed for its hillside-clinging *pueblos blancos* – the last strongholds of the Moors. The eastern reaches of Granada's Alpujarras give way to arid, rolling land as you near Almería. This road trip, showing off Las Alpujarras' diversity, is best done over a couple of days.

1 Órgiva

The main western Alpujarras market town, Órgiva is a curious mix of *campesinos* (country folk) and hippies, who live in a tent community north of town; Thursday market is good for encountering both. Try Chris Stewart's best-selling book *Driving Over Lemons* for anecdotes of Órgiva life.

The Drive: Take the A-4132 uphill and east before ascending the Barranco de Poqueira. Pass through Pampaneira, turn left at the petrol station, and head up the A-4129 to reach Capileira.

2 Capileira

Pretty Capileira is the Alpujarras' most-visited destination, with the valley's best restaurants and accommodation. Tranquil outside the summer months, it's a terrific base for high-altitude hikes, including Mulhacén (p248).

The Drive: Head back to the petrol station, continuing along the sinuous A-4132 to Pitres – stop for a walking tour through several villages (p247) – then Pórtugos and Busquístar before climbing to Trevélez.

PABLO KAUFMANN/SHUTTERSTOCK ©

 Capileira

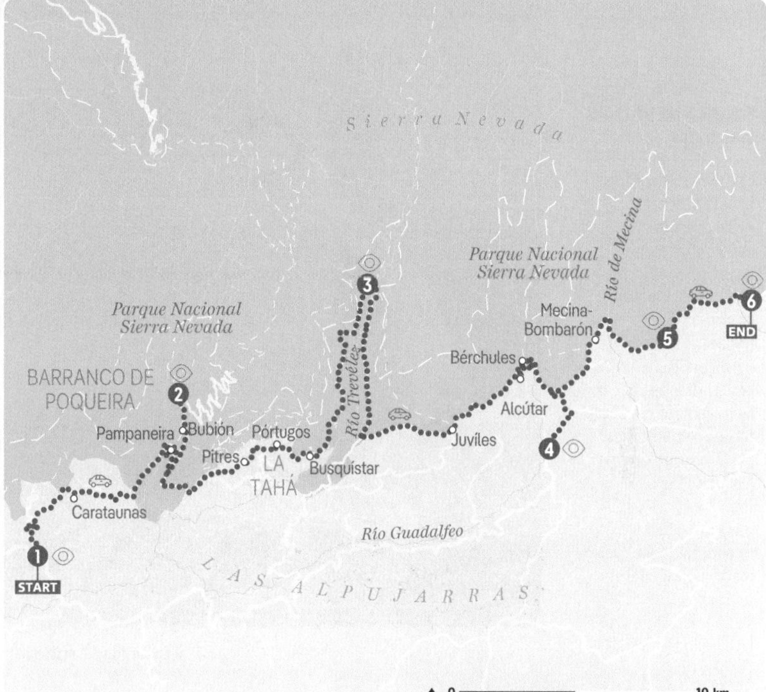

3 Trevélez

Gourmands celebrate Spain's second-highest village (1476m) for its *jamón serrano*. To hikers Trevélez is the gateway to high mountain trails, including one of the main Mulhacén routes. Sitting on the Barranco de Trevélez, the village is divided into three *barrios*: the older, labyrinthine *alto* (high); *medio* (middle); and tourist-centric *bajo* (low).

The Drive: East of Trevélez, the A-4132 becomes A-4130, bisecting Juviles and Alcútar. At the junction, detour to the Río Guadalfeo lowlands along A-4127 and A-348.

4 Cádiar

Worth catching on market days (3rd and 18th of every month), Cádiar celebrates its early October feria by opening the taps on its Fuente del Vino (Wine Fountain). Look for local ceramics and esparto-grass crafts.

The Drive: Head back to the first junction and rejoin the A-4130 as it climbs to Mecina Bombarón, dips down into the Río Mecina valley and ascends towards Yegen.

5 Yegen

Split into *alto* and *bajo* halves, whitewashed Yegen is best known as the home of British writer Gerald Brenan, whose *South from Granada* depicts rural life here in the 1920s. His former house, just off the plaza, is marked with a plaque.

The Drive: It's an easy countryside 6km along the switchbacks of the A-4130 to Válor.

6 Válor

Bookended by deep ravines and clustered around a 16th-century Mudéjar church, Válor was the birthplace of Aben Humeya, a *morisco* (converted Muslim) who led a 1568 rebellion against Felipe II's repressive anti-Muslim policies. Moorish resistance to Christian ascendancy is reenacted during its well-known autumn festival, Moros y Cristianos.

SIERRA NEVADA'S WILDLIFE

The Sierra Nevada's isolated location in Europe's far south, along with its unique geology and microclimates, has created a pocket of incredible biodiversity. In the higher reaches you're likely to spot the sure-footed Spanish ibex, often in large groups (around 15,000 of them live here); you'll have to be lucky to spot badgers, martens, wild cats and foxes. The 60 or so species of native bird include raptors like the golden eagle and Bonelli's eagle, and game birds such as the red-legged partridge; rarely spotted reptiles include the Mediterranean painted frog and snub-nosed viper. The region also has over 2100 plant species, ranging from subtropical fruit trees to the high-altitude Scots pine.

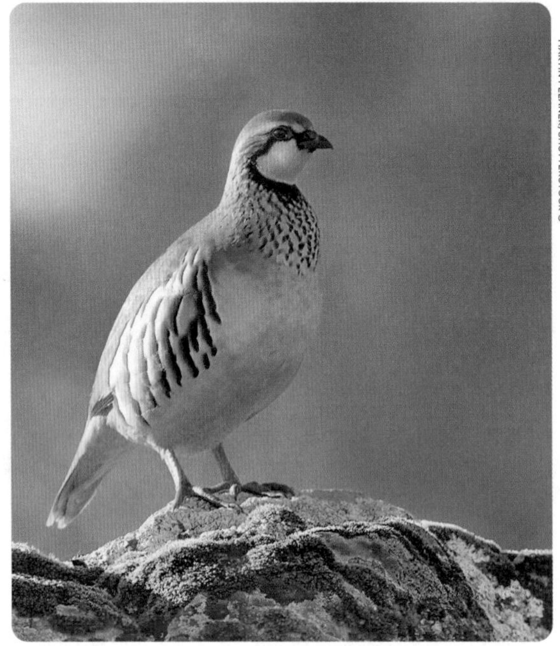

MARTIN PELANEK/SHUTTERSTOCK ©

Red-legged Partridge

Outdoors in the Alpujarras

NON-HIKING OUTDOOR PURSUITS

While many active travellers come to the Sierra Nevada for hiking, there are other outdoor pursuits to tempt you, whether you're looking to hit the powder, explore the mountains on horseback or pursue more adrenaline-infused thrills.

The year's first dusting of snow is usually visible on the mountaintops from late September, but it's not till November that Europe's most southerly ski resort (sierranevada.es), centred on the 2100m-high **Pradollano** village, opens for business. Alpine charm it ain't, but that's okay, since you're here for the snow. A mixture of cable cars, chair lifts and drag lifts link 110km worth of pistes stretching down almost from the top of **Veleta** (3395m), Spain's fourth-highest peak. Of the 131 runs, there are ample green and blue ones

WHERE TO STAY IN THE EASTERN ALPUJARRAS

Alquería de Morayma (Cádiar)
Rustic farmstead amid organic vineyards and woodlands; rooms have wood-beamed ceilings. Superb restaurant. **€€**

Las Chimeneas (Mairena)
Antique-filled, timbered rooms in a British-owned, solar-powered 800-year-old village house; a superb hiking base. **€€**

Hotel los Bérchules (Bérchules)
Family-run hotel featuring rustic rooms with balconies, pool and homestyle restaurant. **€**

for beginners and intermediates, yet enough challenging red and black runs to thrill advanced skiers and snowboarders, along with a Snowpark for freestylers. During ski season, weekends get packed, so come on a weekday if you can. (It's worth staying in Granada and commuting to the slopes rather than overnighting in the overpriced, mediocre ski lodges.) The ski season stretches into April, and after a good snowfall there's nothing finer than hitting the slopes and then driving down to the coast for a *chiringuito* (snack bar) meal on the beach.

Horseback exploration of the Sierra Nevada goes back millennia. You can follow in the hoof-steps of Roman and Moorish cavalry and muleteers taking cargo from the coast to Granada along a spaghetti network of well-worn trails in the Alpujarras on your very own steed. Many of the Moorish-era mule trails are still in use, and local equestrian centres offer everything from gentle trots for beginners through olive groves to half-day ventures and overnight excursions for more experienced riders. One well-established ranch is Caballo Blanco (caballoblancotrekking.com) near Órgiva, in the western Alpujarras; it's also a rescue centre for mistreated horses (tours in English, Spanish and German). Based in **Laroles** in the eastern Alpujarras, sustainable Equi-libre (equi-libre.es) is part farm, part trekking centre, run by the knowledgeable Clara and Antonio, who offer everything from half-day mule or horse treks to three-day mountain expeditions.

Adrenaline-packed activities in the Sierra Nevada include scrambling along via ferrata routes and abseiling down gorges to jump into limpid river pools on canyoning excursions. Nevadensis (nevadensis.com) are an extremely knowledgeable, all-encompassing outdoor adventure outfit based in **Pampaneira**; professional guides offer expert advice and maps, plus organise anything from via ferrata sessions and canyoning to guided hikes and mountaineering courses. In **Bayárcal**, Be Natural (bnaturalsport.com) also offers canyoning, plus Andalucía's longest zip wire, which'll have you flying for 600m over a gorge at high speed.

ALPUJARRAS SPECIALITIES

Besides the yummy *plato alpujarreño* – fried eggs, potatoes, chorizo and *morcilla* (black pudding) – try these local culinary standards:

Patatas a lo pobre Potatoes with green peppers, onions and garlic.

Perdiz en escabeche Partridge in a vinegary onion broth; a Moorish recipe.

Garbanzos y lentejas Chickpeas and lentils, slow-cooked in hearty stews.

Migas Another Moorish crossover dish, made from fried breadcrumbs with bacon, onions and occasionally fruit.

Soplillos Literally 'little breaths' of crumbly almond-based meringues.

Vino de costa Local amber-coloured rosé, sharp and bright, and very refreshing on a hot day.

GETTING AROUND

Outside of the western Alpujarras villages of Lanjarón and Órgiva, which have frequent bus links to Granada, the smaller, remoter villages along the A-4132 and A-4130 are served by a couple of Granada-bound buses per day.

Driving in the Alpujarras is a real pleasure that involves navigating hairpin bends and the sinuous bends of the narrow, scenic A-4132, which connects lowland western Alpujarras with the Poqueira Valley and Trevélez; and the A-4130, which takes you to the eastern Alpujarras. Traffic is typically very light outside Capileria and Trevélez in the summer months.

Beyond Parque Nacional Sierra Nevada

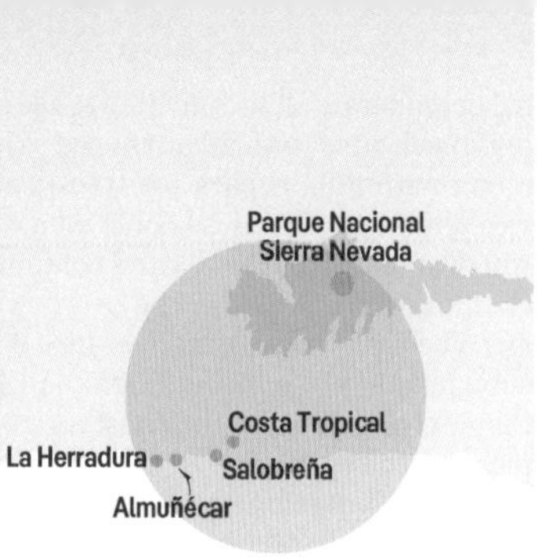

Mix it up with stays in buzzy beach resorts and try your hand at water sports in laidback locales.

You really can go from the ski slopes right to the sea – south of the Parque Nacional Sierra Nevada is the Costa Tropical, named for the subtropical microclimate that has made this coastline a major producer of tropical fruit. Along Granada province's 80km-long coastal stretch of rugged cliffs, punctuated by inviting beaches and hidden coves, Almuñécar is the main resort town, attracting mostly Spanish holidaymakers with its palm-fringed esplanade and two pebble beaches. The quieter pueblo blanco of Salobreña is set back from the sea, its hillside cascade of white houses topped with a castle. Further west, La Herradura's horseshoe-shaped bay is a big draw for windsurfers, divers, kayakers and other water-sports enthusiasts year-round.

TOP TIP

For a quieter stay, avoid the peak (hottest) months of July and August – when all of Spain goes on holiday.

Almuñécar

Highlights of the Costa Tropical

RESORTS, WATER SPORTS & BEACHES

Some 9km east of the unpretty industrial town of Motril, almond and custard-apple trees give way to a striking view of **Salobreña** – 'Salambo' to the Phoenicians, dedicated to the Syrian goddess of love – a millennia-old pueblo blanco surrounded by sugar-cane fields, and a sugar-cane producer since Nasrid times. Like many other Andalucian coastal towns, Salobreña is split in two: the main historical town, set back from the sea, features an attractive hillside centre; white-cube houses; a sensitively restored, formidable Moorish *alcázar* (Muslim-era fortress); and a handsome 16th-century church on the site of a Moorish mosque. Two kilometres away, reachable via #1 bus, is Salobreña's seaside half, centred on two long grey-sand beaches, Playa de la Guardia and Playa de la Charca. Around 8km west of Motril and 15km east of Almuñécar, the town is a fairly quiet, low-key place, but in August it bursts into life for the summer season. During Nasrid times, Salobreña was an important hub and sugar-cane producer.

The N-340 ribbons its way west along the coast for 15km to reach **Almuñécar**. The Costa Tropical's main resort town, Almuñécar heaves in summer as crowds of Spanish holidaymakers and northern European sun-seekers flock to its palm-fringed esplanade and two pebble beaches. In fact, it has been attracting sun worshippers since the first millennium BCE, when it was founded by the Phoenicians as the wonderfully named 'Sexi'. Not very sexy is the waterfront, marred by unappealing high-rise apartment blocks, but Almuñécar grows on you by exploring beyond the Paseo Puerta del Mar promenade. Behind the seafront, you'll uncover a picturesque *casco antiguo* with narrow lanes, whitewashed homes and bar-flanked plazas, topped by the striking 16th-century Castillo de San Miguel. Nestling in its shadow is the Parque Botánico el Majuelo, with well-preserved *garum* (fermented fish sauce) tanks dating to Roman times. Speaking of Romans, it's well worth seeking out the Museo Arqueológico in the Cueva de los Siete Palacios, a former water reservoir: among its local Phoenician, Roman and Moorish finds is a 1700-BCE Egyptian vase featuring the oldest piece of writing ever found in Spain.

Eight kilometres west of Almuñécar along the scenic N-340, **La Herradura** is a fishing village and resort that doubles as a major water-sports centre. Its shimmering

BEST COSTA TROPICAL DINING

La Barraca (Playa Cantarriján)
Beachside *chiringuito* cooking up super-fresh fish and seafood classics. €€

Los Geraneos (Almuñécar)
Charmingly rustic and an excellent-value *menú del día*. €

Mesón de la Villa (Salobreña)
Rustic restaurant specialising in regional fare. €

Araís (Salobreña)
Creative takes on updated Andalucian cuisine. €€

OTHER PRISTINE BEACHES

If Playa Cantarriján and Playa Cañuelo float your boat, head east to check out a string of similarly pristine beaches in **Parque Natural Cabo de Gata-Níjar** (p264), along Almería's coast.

WHERE TO STAY ON THE COSTA TROPICAL

Hotel Miba (Salobreña)
Eight unique rooms with baths, roof terrace with pool and fabulous views across sugarcane fields. €€

Hotel Casablanca (Almuñécar)
Neo-Moorish, family-run hotel with pastel-coloured rooms, close to the beach and Almuñécar's lively centre. €€

La Tartana (Herradura)
Contemporary rooms (some with sea views) in a bougainvillea-draped mansion amidst lush gardens. €€

ACANTILADOS DE MARO BEACHES

The 19-sq-km Paraje Natural Acantilados de Maro-Cerro Gordo comprises precipitous, greenery-clad sea cliffs and three beautiful beaches between La Herradura and Maro (in Málaga province). The best nudist beach in the area is grey-pebble Playa Cantarriján, with wonderfully clear water for snorkelling at the south end and two excellent *chiringuitos*. It's actually two beaches: the main one, with facilities, is family-friendly and clothing-optional; duck through a hole in the cliff to reach the fully naturist beach. (A clifftop footpath high above Cantarriján leads to the Torre de Cerro Gordo, a 16th-century watchtower with tremendous views over the whole coast.) Further south, pristine Playa Cañuelo and its two restaurants can be reached by shuttle bus from mid-June to mid-September.

Maro

horseshoe-shaped bay feels like Almuñécar's more active, less touristed sister. It has a subtle castaway vibe, a lengthy pebble beach, and plenty of holiday apartments and seafront *chiringuitos*. Between Easter and October, busy kiosks along its 2km-long beach rent out kayaks and SUPs. Established watersports operators include Windsurf La Herradura (windsurflaherradura.com), who run sea-kayaking trips for all levels and SUP yoga sessions. Bring your own snorkelling mask (or rent one here) to commune with marine life around the rocks at the base of Cerro Gordo cliffs at the northwest end of the beach. To explore below the waves, sign up for beginner or advanced dives with the well-established Buceo La Herradura (buceolaherradura.com) at the Marina del Este harbour, where you'll find a few other diving operators.

GETTING AROUND

Daily Alsa buses connect Almuñécar, La Herradura and Salobreña from Granada, Almería, Málaga and other cities. From Parque Nacional Sierra Nevada, it's a straightforward drive along the winding, scenic A-44 (past the mountains and the reservoir), and then a coastal stretch along the seaward (also scenic) N-340.

ALMERÍA

Sevilla
Almería

Founded by the Phoenicians and overlooked by an imposing Moorish fortress (the less-embellished twin of Granada's Alhambra), Almería is a busy yet surprisingly charming port city with an illustrious past. During its Moorish heyday, Al-Mariyat ('Mirror of the Sea' to its Nasrid rulers) was a flourishing and modern metropolis, with a sophisticated running-water system and hilltop palace complex surrounded by lush gardens. Falling into decline under the Christian kings from the late 15th century onwards, Almería bounced back in the early 20th century through exporting the province's vast mineral wealth and providing connections to North Africa.

Refreshingly untouristed compared to other large Andalucian cities, Almería is punctuated by palm-fringed plazas and centuries-old churches, and blessed with eclectic sights, interesting museums, an attractive historic core and a sophisticated dining scene – including a plethora of fantastic tapas bars that saw the city crowned 'Spain's Gastronomic Capital' in 2019.

TOP TIP

Avoid Almería in the height of summer, when the city is both extremely hot and very crowded with beach-trippers. Book accommodation well in advance for August's two-week Feria de Almería. The Alcazaba offers particularly wonderful sunset views over the port, and don't miss the up-and-coming *barrio* of La Chanca.

Tapas, tipples & tagine

BEST OF ALMERÍA'S DINING

Taking its food seriously, Almería is justifiably proud of the region's fresh produce and its unique wines, both of which dominate its menus. Whether you're here to partake in extensive *tapear* sessions or indulge in a superlative tagine, there's plenty to tempt you here. The main port in Al-Andalus under the Moors, today's Almería maintains its maritime connections to North Africa, reinforcing its cross-cultural dining scene. With stellar views of the Alcazaba from the roof terrace of its newer branch on Calle Almanzor, local institution **Tetería Almedina** has long been known for its superb lamb tagines, other down-home Moroccan staples and killer mint lemonades. Near the waterfront, unassuming decor at **Restaurante Marrakech** belies the fact that its beef tagine and couscous are second to none.

But Almería is best-known for its tapas scene, defined by the province's raw ingredients: red prawns from Garrucha, plus octopus and other sea bounty. Look out also for *gurullos* with cuttlefish and fried hake cheeks. Several excellent tapas bars are concentrated along Calles Jovellanos. A good place to start is **Taberna Nuestra Tierra**: grab a table outside, order from the menu of Almería wines, nibble on your courtesy tapa and feast on lamb with caramelised peppers, *ajoblanco* (cold almond and garlic soup) and assorted regional cheeses. Around the corner, **Jovellanos 16** is locally popular because

ALMERÍA'S WINES

Of Andalucía's 16 geographical locations granted the 'Vinos de la Tierra' wine classification, five are in Almería province. All these wineries plant their vines at altitudes of 500m to 1200m, so the grapes benefit both from the sun and the highlands' cool nights. Few Almería wines are exported, so the city's bars are among the best places to try them. Look out for high-altitude Valle Almanzora wines; aged reds from Los Velez; Brut Blue from the desert Bodegas Perfer; the smoky, full-bodied Tetas de la Sacristiana from mountainous Laujar; and the intensely fruity, golden-yellow Flor de Indalia from Padules.

ALMERÍA

SIGHTS
1 Alcazaba
2 Aljibes Árabes de Jayrán
3 Catedral de Almería
4 Centro Andaluz de la Fotografía
5 Iglesia de San Juan
6 Refugios de la Guerra Civil

EATING
7 Casa Puga
8 El Quinto Toro
9 Jovellanos 16
10 La Consentida
11 Restaurante Marrakech
12 Taberna Nuestra Tierra
13 Tetería Almedina
14 Tortillería la Mala

this people-watching spot on Almería's 'Tapas Row' serves imaginative bites such as petite red-tuna 'hamburgers' and *secreto con ajo verde* (pork with garlicky sauce), along with a respectable list of local wines.

Further down the street at **Casa Puga**, ancient maps and *azulejos* (tiles) are plastered on the walls, decades-old wine bottles line the shelves and hams dangle from its ceiling. This 1870s institution has a loyal local following, so get here early to have any hope of grabbing a table. Otherwise, elbow your way to the bar and order *bacalao*

WHERE TO STAY IN A BOUTIQUE HOTEL

Murallas de Jayrán
Intimate six-room boutique hotel combines Moorish arches with industrial chic, and circular soaking tubs. **€€€**

AIRE Hotel & Ancient Baths
Airy, contemporary rooms, rooftop pool views of the Alcazaba, and subterranean *hammam* with six pools. **€€€**

Hotel Catedral
Artesonado ceilings meet contemporary decor at this 19th-century hotel overlooking the cathedral. **€€**

LUIS DAFOS/ALAMY STOCK PHOTO ©

Casa Puga

frito (fried cod), *pinchitos* (pork skewers) and tiny *morcilla* (blood sausage) sandwiches, along with local wines from one of Andalucía's best cellars. A couple of blocks south, on Calle Infanta, chargrilled-meat tapas named after celebrities draw the carnivorously inclined to the bright, contemporary **La Consentida**. How about a 'Lola Flores' (beef-cheek meatballs) or a 'Miley Cyrus' (gourmet hot dog)?

A short walk away, on Calle Lucano, **Tortillería la Mala** is another fine ambassador of the contemporary tapas scene, with chilled beats, crimson walls and a youthful ambience. Speciality of the house is the tortillas, omelettes with everything from onions and garlic to prawns and chilli. But if you want to keep it old-school, go for the traditional atmosphere (replete with stuffed bull's head) at **El Quinto Toro** on Calle Reyes Católicos and its classic menu of Andalucian tapas: go for the *albóndigas* (meatballs) and *callos* (tripe).

BEST MICHELIN-RECOMMENDED RESTAURANTS

Tony García Espacio Gastronómico
Contemporary takes on traditional cuisine include prawn carpaccio with swordfish roe and tuna tartare. €€€

Salmantice
Flawless presentation of quality ingredients, from aged Avileña-Black Iberian steak to Asian-style mussels. €€€

Taberna Joseba Añorga
Modern Basque flavours like glazed pig trotters and robalo ceviche tapas, plus a tasting menu. €€€

GETTING AROUND

Several daily Renfe (renfe.com) trains connect Almería with Granada, Sevilla and Madrid, and there are numerous buses daily to all major destinations around Andalucía from Almería's joint bus/train Estación Intermodal just east of the centre. Historic Almería is very walkable, so a car is more a bane than a boon: leave it in one of the underground car parks around the city centre.

ALMERÍA WALKING TOUR

Taking in the labyrinthine Moorish Almedina and medieval Old Town, this walk can be done in around four hours.

Almería's fortress-like **1 Catedral de Almería** (1524) doubled as a refuge from frequent North African pirate raids. Admire the ribbed ceiling of the austere Gothic interior and the chancel with *The Immaculate Conception* by Murillo. Two blocks south, the **2 Centro Andaluz de la Fotografía** puts on top-class photographic exhibitions. Past themes have included 'Hollywood Icons' and 'Nuclear Accident in Palomares'.

Head west through the waterfront park, then north to the 17th-century **3 Iglesia de San Juan**, built over the remains of a 10th-century mosque, with a surviving *mihrab*, fragments of *yesería* (plasterwork) and the *qiblah* wall (indicating the direction of Mecca).

Several blocks northeast, the **4 Alcazaba**, an imposing 10th-century fortress, was once home to 20,000 people. From the battlements are wonderful views over the port and the 11th-century Muralla de Jayrán. Further up are the ruins of the Muslim rulers' palace and the Catholic Monarchs' castle.

Nine blocks northeast is the **5 Refugios de la Guerra Civil**, a 4.5km-long network of underground shelters built during the Spanish Civil War. They accommodated 35,000 people, with shields and ventilation pipes preventing grenade damage. Guided tours (in Spanish) take you through 1km of the tunnels. Book ahead.

Around the corner, the **6 Aljibes Árabes de Jayrán** – well-preserved Moorish 11th-century underground cisterns – once supplied a city of 30,000 people. They morph into a members-only flamenco club by night.

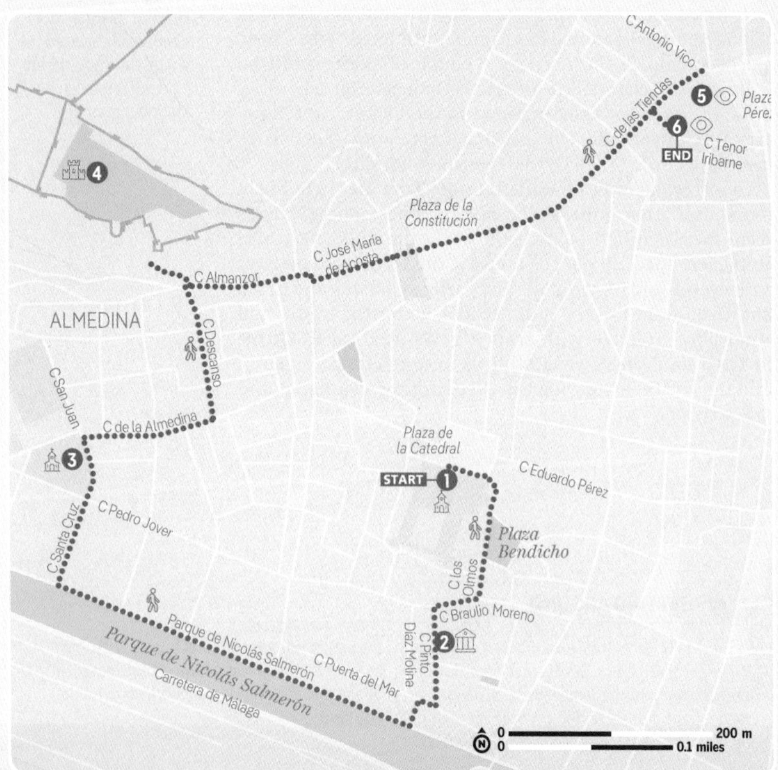

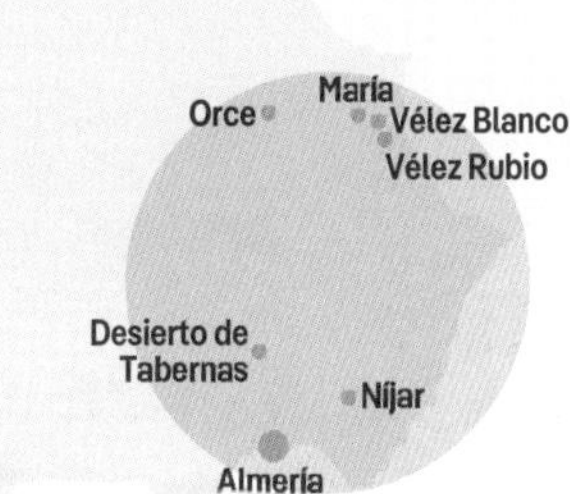

Beyond Almería

Explore the far-flung reaches of Almería province, from the spaghetti-western badlands of Europe's only desert to forest-covered mountains.

The sparsely populated – and occasionally otherworldly – hinterland east and northeast of Almería thrills with its diversity of attractions. Inland of the city-port of Almería lies the almost Mars-like expanse of the Desierto de Tabernas, a cactus-studded desert that's home to 'Wild West' film sets, sitting against the severe backdrop of the arid Sierra de Alhamilla. Blessed with the sunniest climate in all of Spain, the province also throws down a gauntlet to fresh-air fiends in search of new terrain to conquer, with the Parque Natural Sierra María-Los Vélez (further north) providing ample opportunity to stretch your legs.

TOP TIP

Visit outside the scorching months of July and August, and use Los Vélez as a springboard to visit El Altiplano.

Desierto de Tabernas

FILMING LOCATIONS

If you're a movie or TV buff, you'll be thrilled to know that many spots around Almería have made their way onto the big (and little) screen. Famous filming locations include:

Alcazaba (Almería)
Appeared as Sunspear, the palace of Dorne, in *Game of Thrones*. Also featured in the James Bond flick *Never Say Never Again*.

Playa de Mónsul
Sean Connery brought down a German plane here by shooing away a flock of seagulls with his umbrella in *Indiana Jones and the Last Crusade*.

Playa del Algarróbico
A replica of the Jordanian city of Áqaba was built here for *Lawrence of Arabia*.

Desierto de Tabernas
Mikael Blomkvist and Harriet Vanger met in the Australian Outback in *The Girl with the Dragon Tattoo* (2011).

Vélez Blanco

Andalucía's Wild West

DESERT FILM SETS; CRAFTY VILLAGES

Since the mid-1960s partnership between Sergio Leone and Clint Eastwood, the lunar landscape of **Desierto de Tabernas** has been used to shoot spaghetti westerns. Visit the film sets and detour to the *pueblos blancos* of **Níjar**, renowned for its pottery tradition, and **Macael**, known for its marble.

Oasys Mini Hollywood (oasysparquetematico.com) is particularly famous as the set for *A Fistful of Dollars* and *The Good, The Bad and The Ugly* (though *Doctor Who* fans may get a sense of déjà vu there as well). In summer, there are twice-daily shootouts between the sheriff's men and outlaw Jesse James, while dancing girls flash their petticoats dancing the cancan at the saloon. Escape the Wild West overload by visiting the well-curated cactus garden, featuring all things prickly from across five continents.

WHERE TO BUY CRAFTS IN NÍJAR AND MACAEL

La Tienda de los Milagros
Workshop of ceramicist Matthew Weir and artisan Isabel Hernández, producing artistic rugs and stoneware.

La Jarapa
This friendly shop sells colourful *jarapa* rugs, loom-woven from fabric scraps by locals.

Artesanía Muro
This marble workshop in Macael specialises in mortars and pestles, plus goblets and elaborate sculpture.

Fans of *Once Upon a Time in the West* won't want to miss the **Fort Bravo** (fortbravo.org) movie set – still in use – slightly further along the N-340A from Almería than Oasys. Wander through the US cavalry frontier fort and a Mexican border town; among the Native American teepees, set against a dramatic backdrop of gulches and ochre-coloured scrubland; or quench your thirst at the saloon while watching the gunslinging demonstrations and cowboys and outlaws fighting in the main square. Explore the lunar landscape on two-hour horseback rides, or opt for a more genteel horse-drawn buggy ride through 'Texas Hollywood'.

Exploring Parque Natural Sierra María-Los Vélez

ALMERÍA'S FORESTED, MOUNTAINOUS CORNER

The seemingly endless desert landscapes surrounding Almería give way to pine forests and mountainous landscapes of the remote Los Vélez district in the province's northernmost part. Encompassing some 226 sq km of verdant mountain terrain, the Parque Natural Sierra María–Los Vélez is a glorious wilderness, with rocky peaks cloaked in forests of pine and holm oaks beneath golden eagles and peregrine falcons patrolling the skies. Its gateways are three towns – the market town of **Vélez Rubio** (with a superb grill restaurant, Asador Espadín) and the smaller **Vélez Blanco** (with Cueva de los Letreros, a Unesco-protected cave with drawings made before 5500 BC) and **María**. The latter is the highest settlement in the province, from which the unparalleled palaeontology discoveries in tiny Orce are an easy day trip away.

The waymarked trails in the park are at their best outside the summer months, when the weather is cooler. A short leg-stretcher, María's 3km-long **Sendero Umbría de la Virgen** walking trail (about 1¾ hours) follows a circular course around the lower slopes of the Sierra de María, offering an introduction to the local flora; it starts and finishes at María's small botanical garden. A longer challenge is the 13km-long **Sendero Solana de Maimón** (3 hours), a loop trail that runs through the Sierra de Maimón hills southwest of the town. The trailhead is 1.3km along the road signposted 'Cueva de los Letreros' off the A-317, just south of Vélez Blanco.

EUROPE'S OLDEST HUMAN REMAINS

In 1982 Catalan palaeontologist Josep Gibert announced he had unearthed a human skull fragment at Venta Micena, thought to be between 900,000 and 1.6 million years old – potentially the oldest such fragment ever discovered in Europe. Most palaeontologists, however, now believe that it was more likely from a horse or donkey. Gibert died in 2007, but the debate rages on. A second major find was made in 2002 at Barranco León: a 10-year-old child's milk tooth conclusively dated at 1.4 million years old, officially Europe's oldest human remains. You can view the original tooth and the skull fragment replica at Orce's museum, and tour three nearby Palaeolithic settlements during excavations, June to September.

GETTING AROUND

A daily Alsa bus connects Almería with Vélez Rubio, Vélez Blanco and María, with onwards services to Granada from Vélez Rubio. It's an easy drive through stark desert scenery along the A-92N and the scenic A-317. To reach some of the trailheads, as well as Orce (from María) along the desolately beautiful GR-9104, you'll need your own wheels.

PARQUE NATURAL CABO DE GATA-NÍJAR

Sevilla

Parque Natural Cabo de Gata-Níjar

Extending southeast of Almería, the semi-arid, 340-sq-km Parque Natural Cabo de Gata-Níjar is a unique corner of the province. Stretching from Retamar in the west up to Agua Amarga in the east, it encompasses a dramatic coastline punctuated by plunging cliffs and wave-battered lighthouses; some of Andalucía's most pristine, least crowded white-sand beaches, fringed by endemic dwarf palms; sleepy fishing villages and the odd low-key resort town. Inland, you'll encounter abandoned mines, isolated farmsteads, grassy hills and strange rock formations, while the protected area's west side is flanked by the Salinas de Cabo de Gata – a giant salt marsh that's a vital habitat for migrating bird species, including flamingos.

Besides a dozen or so fantastic hiking trails ranging from easy jaunts to full-day coastal tramps, Cabo de Gata is a fantastic place for scuba diving, kayaking, cycling and other outdoor adventures. Outside peak season (July to September), you'll have it largely to yourself.

TOP TIP

Busy coastal hub San José has plenty of accommodation and numerous water-sports operators. Las Negras makes for a quiet experience, with excellent hiking-trail access, while tranquil Agua Amarga is the happy medium, with excellent lodgings, dining and a superb village beach.

DIVE SITES

Cabo's underwater is a diverse playground. Highlights include:

'La Chocolita' A fun, shallow (10m) wreck dive to a sunken steamboat.

Cueva del Francés Take a torch to illuminate the denizens of this small cave.

Playa la Isleta Beginner beach dive, with conger eel, moray, seahorses and shoals of small fish darting around La Punta.

Piedra de los Meros This 26m-deep rock is home to conger eels, morays, haddock and sea bass. Advanced divers only.

Cala los Amarillos Expert dive due to strong currents. Spot cuttlefish, octopus and morays.

Cabo's beaches & water sports

SANDY STRANDS; WATERY ADVENTURES

Cabo de Gata is home to some of Andalucía's best, least-crowded and most beautiful beaches, some reachable by car or public transport, while others will reward a hike.

If you're approaching Cabo from the east along the coastal AL-5106, you'll pass a parking area with a path leading down to the spectacular **Playa de los Muertos** – a long, wide stretch of pristine sand, bookended by cliffs. Further west, the small **Agua Amarga** resort is fronted by a popular white-sand beach, overlooked by restaurants. A short but steep 2km trek (p268) to the southwest leads to **Cala de Enmedio**, a pretty, secluded beach, with slabs for sunbathing. Framed by dramatic headlands and home to hippies, the spectacular white-sand cove of **Playa San Pedro** can similarly only be reached on foot (p268).

If you take the signposted, unpaved coastal road west of San José for 2.5km, you'll reach Cabo's most popular facility-free beach – **Playa de los Genoveses**, a 1km stretch of sand where the Genoese navy landed in 1147 to help the Christian attack on Almería. A further 2.5km along the same road, the wide, pristine **Playa de Mónsul** is dominated by a large free-standing rock that's earned it a place in movie history (p262); due to strong currents, swimming is inadvisable. Tracks behind the large dune at Mónsul's east end lead down to the sheltered nudist **Playa**

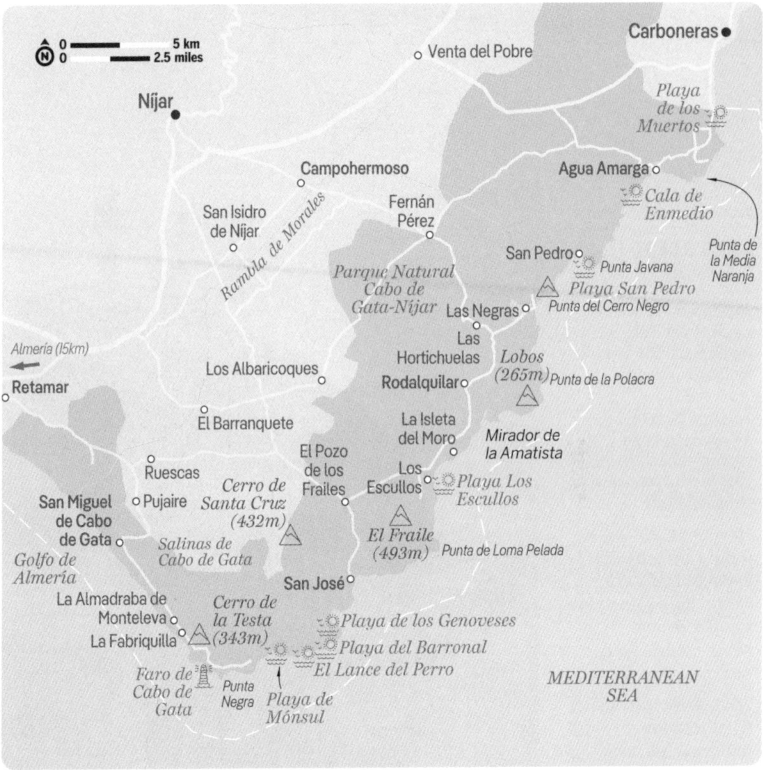

0 5 km
0 2.5 miles
Carboneras
Venta del Pobre
Níjar
Playa de los Muertos
Campohermoso
Agua Amarga
Cala de Enmedio
San Isidro de Níjar
Rambla de Morales
Fernán Pérez
Punta de la Media Naranja
San Pedro
Punta Javana
Parque Natural Cabo de Gata-Níjar
Playa San Pedro
Las Negras
Punta del Cerro Negro
Almería (15km)
Las Hortichuelas
Lobos (265m)
Retamar
Los Albaricoques
Rodalquilar
Punta de la Polacra
El Barranquete
La Isleta del Moro
Mirador de la Amatista
Ruescas
El Pozo de los Frailes
Los Escullos
Playa Los Escullos
San Miguel de Cabo de Gata
Pujaire
Cerro de Santa Cruz (432m)
El Fraile (493m)
Punta de Loma Pelada
Salinas de Cabo de Gata
Golfo de Almería
San José
La Almadraba de Monteleva
Cerro de la Testa (343m)
Playa de los Genoveses
La Fabriquilla
Playa del Barronal
El Lance del Perro
Faro de Cabo de Gata
Punta Negra
Playa de Mónsul
MEDITERRANEAN SEA

Cala de Enmedio

WHERE TO FIND SEAFOOD WITH A VIEW

Costamarga (Agua Amarga)
Seafood paella, fried anchovies and grilled calamari served beneath the trees on a lovely beach. **€**

4 Nudos (San José)
Baby-prawn ceviche, Asian-style tuna, and classic Spanish seafood served inside Club Náutico, at the marina. **€€**

El Manteca (Las Negras)
Toes in sand, order *arróz negro*, grilled catch of the day or fried sardines and anchovies. **€€**

CABO'S BEST VIEWPOINTS

For the most splendid vistas of Cabo del Gata's coastline, head for the following:

Torre de Vela Blanca
All-encompassing views of the south coast from a centuries-old watchtower.

Mirador de la Playa de los Muertos
Splendid bird's-eye view of the arrow-straight, remote beach north of Agua Amarga.

Torre de Mesa Roldán
A 15th-century fortification looking out over the Agua Amarga coastline.

Faro de Cabo de Gata
Stirring views of the jagged, volcanic Arrecife de las Sirenas (Reef of the Mermaids) at Cabo's southernmost point.

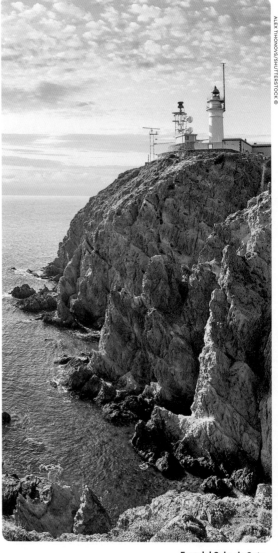

ALEX TIHONOVS/SHUTTERSTOCK ©

Faro del Cabo de Gata

WHERE TO EAT BRUNCH

Café Andrea (San José)
Friendly cafe on the main drag serving *bocadillos* (sandwiches), *tostadas*, coffee and orange juice. €

Taka Tuka (Las Negras)
Crepes, *tostadas* (toast) and freshly brewed coffee on a sunny terrace; also makes excellent ice cream. €

La Ola (La Isleta del Moro)
Superlative *tostadas* with excellent breads, local jams and high-quality toppings, with a side of sea views. €€

del Barronal. Bear left just before Barronal to reach **El Lance del Perro**: this beach, with striking basalt rock formations, is the first of the Calas del Barronal – four gorgeous, isolated coves.

Cabo's cold, clear waters offer some of the best diving (and snorkelling) in southern Spain. The posidonia-seagrass meadows, caves, rocks and canyons shelter eagle rays, sunfish, grouper, angelfish, barracuda, moray and conger eels, and others. Excellent operators include Diving Center Isub (isubsanjose.com), a professional PADI-certified outfit in San José that offers dives for beginners and qualified divers alike, along with snorkelling outings. Another well-regarded operator is Buceo en Cabo de Gata (buceoencabodegata.es) in La Isleta, with a full range of PADI diving courses and beginners' sessions. If you'd rather be atop the waves than beneath them, you can explore Cabo's coast on a guided kayaking trip with Medialun Aventura (medialunaventura.com), a San José outfit that also offers mountain-bike hire, SUP rental and boat trips. The best of both worlds – kayaking *and* snorkelling – is available with Cabo de Gata Activo (cabodegataactivo.com), a friendly outfit located just south of Las Negras.

From mid-June to mid-September, it's paid parking at Playa de los Muertos, Playa de los Genoveses and Playa de Mónsul; traffic is diverted once the car parks are full and beach access is via shuttle or on foot.

Cabo on foot & two wheels

SCENIC CYCLING AND HIKING TRAILS

Dramatic cliffs, deserted white-sand beaches, strange rock formations, abandoned mines and sleepy inland settlements define this unique slice of Almería coast, which is best explored by hiking or cycling.

The hike from the **Faro del Cabo de Gata** lighthouse to **San José** (14km) takes four to five hours. From the lighthouse, a strenuous uphill slog along a 3km-long, hideously potholed road gets you to Torre de Vela Blanca. From here, it's a gentle descent along a wide dirt trail, with vistas of scrub-covered hills descending steeply towards teal-blue waters. You'll pass a couple of secluded coves before reaching the wave-battered Playa de Mónsul. Follow the blue-and-white trail markers uphill to reach the naturist Playa del Barronal. If it's low tide, proceed along the base of the black volcanic cliffs, past the four Calas de Barronal,

Continued on p270

BEST BOUTIQUE HOTELS

La Almendra y el Gitano (Agua Amarga)
Countryside oasis with eight Moroccan-style rooms, hot tub with desert views and a subtly lit pool. €€

Hotel MC (San José)
Clean lines, slate-grey decor with driftwood accents and in-house wine cellar define this boho-chic hotel. €€

MiKasa (Agua Amarga)
Gorgeous villa with individually styled rooms, two pools, a jacuzzi, spa and well-stocked honesty bar. €€€

Hotel Arrecife Calachica (Las Negras)
Private jacuzzis with beach views, tiled rooms with terraces and large outdoor pool. €€

WHERE TO EAT FUSION CUISINE

La Gallineta (San José)
Innovative dishes, including tuna with Cambodian spices and red-prawn carpaccio with citrus and mango. €€

Asador la Chumbera (Agua Amarga)
Hilltop views and excellent wine list paired with superb dishes with a twist. €€

Restaurante Oro y Luz (near Rodaquilar)
Pig trotters with shrimp, squid tartare and other imaginative fusion fare. €€

HIKE

Las Negras to Agua Amarga

Cabo de Gata's most scenic day hike is the 13km stretch (four to five hours) between the villages of Las Negras and Agua Amarga. While this trail, much of which is unreachable by car, is largely shadeless – bring a hat and plenty of water – it's ideal for appreciating Cabo de Gata's stark, desert-like, volcanic landscape, fringed by coastal cliffs and interspersed with largely unpeopled beaches lapped by azure waters.

1 Playa Las Negras

Dotted with fishing boats, this sand-and-pebble beach is refreshingly uncrowded, with sugar-cube-like white houses clustered at the north end. You'll be able to appreciate the views over the picturesque Las Negras bay 20 minutes or so into the walk.

The Hike: Join the wide dirt track that gently ascends the headland. The track narrows to a precipitous coastal path, winding its lofty way towards Playa San Pedro.

2 Playa San Pedro

This white-sand cove lapped at by turquoise waters features a ruined 16th-century castle, which is occupied by an alternative-lifestyle community residing in rehabilitated ruins, new stone dwellings, tents and the odd cave hidden in the greenery. You'll come across gardens, solar panels and even a rustic beach bar flying the Jolly Roger, selling drinks and *bocadillos* (sandwiches) when the mood takes the proprietors.

ROBALITO/SHUTTERSTOCK ©

 Hiking to Playa San Pedro

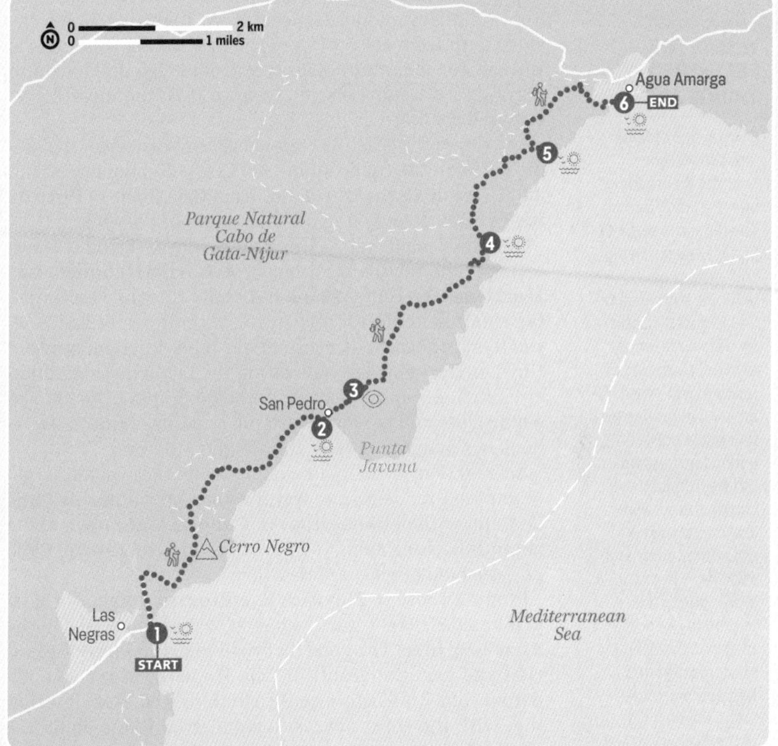

The Hike: Head inland for 50m to another ruined tower. From there, an almost vertical half-hour switchback climb takes you high up the opposite side of the valley.

3 Mirador

At the viewpoint at the top of the climb, turn around to enjoy stupendous vistas of San Pedro beach, the sea and the valley, with more evidence of discreet human habitation in the caves at the valley's far end.

The Hike: The trail levels off and gently undulates its way inland again along scrub-covered hills. After 3km or so, a steady descent brings you to Cala del Plomo.

4 Cala del Plomo

Reachable by car via a dirt road from Agua Amarga, the sandy 250m-long crescent of Cala del Plomo is good for swimming. The beach is occasionally clothing-optional.

The Hike: The dirt road links up with a narrow, sandy footpath that skirts the Cerro de la Higuera hill, bringing you to a junction. The right-hand fork takes you to Cala de Enmedio.

5 Cala de Enmedio

The granite slabs to one side of this smallish, clothing-optional cove sprinkled with driftwood make excellent sunbathing spots. The waves are generally gentle enough to allow swimming.

The Hike: Follow the faint footpath through scrubland to rejoin the main trail visible on the low ridge. Agua Amarga comes into view after a climb over the small Cerro del Cuartel hill. An easy descent brings you to Playa Agua Amarga.

6 Playa Agua Amarga

This beautiful 500m-long sweep of white sand is the prettiest town beach in the whole of Cabo de Gata, with limpid cerulean waters overlooked by several beach bars.

WHERE THE FEATHERED THINGS ARE

Cabo is one of Spain's most important habitats for breeding and migrating birds. The Salinas – some of Spain's last surviving salt-extraction lagoons, southeast of San Miguel de Cabo de Gata – are home to over 80 species of resident waterfowl, drawing migrating pink flamingos between spring and autumn: by late August there can be a thousand. You may also spot other birds such as avocets, egrets and storks during their migration periods; to spy on them, find strategically sited birdwatching hides along the east side of the main road (just north of Almadraba de Monteleva). While hiking along the cliffs, keep an eye out for Bonelli's eagles and eagle owls, as well as the rare Audouin's gull.

before ascending the Morrón de los Genoveses and descending to the Playa de los Genoveses. At high tide, climb the steep path from cove to cove. The first half of this route is suitable for mountain bikes, but from Playa de Mónsul to Playa de los Genoveses you have to take the more direct unpaved road.

Away from the coast, the 3½-hour return ascent of the saddle between the twin summits of Cerro de Limones (411m) and Cerro de Garbanzal (411m) from the village of **Pozo de los Frailes** gives you marvelous views of the coast.

Of the seven official cycling routes, one of the most interesting is the relatively strenuous **Los Albaricoques–Las Hortichuelas** route (22km; 6½ hours return). Starting in the small agricultural settlement 15km north of San José, you'll take the most direct route through the countryside to tiny Las Hortichuelas, navigating the Llano de Doña Francisca ravine – and hideously potholed, unpaved roads – to get up close and personal with the remains of the old farmhouses, Cortijo del Fraile and Cortijo Montano.

An easy, flat, three-hour cycling loop takes you on largely unpaved roads all the way around the Salinas de Cabo de Gata, with optional stops in **Cabo de Gata** town and a potential detour along the paved road to the Faro de Cabo de Gata (add at least another hour).

From San José to **Playa los Escullos** is a gorgeous coastal bike ride (18km return; 4 hours) that can also be done as a day-long hike. The good dirt road takes you past the marina and past the beautiful Cala Higuera (where you can detour for a dip), before gently climbing and then descending, with the coast always in sight. Highlights along the way include remote coves, the Acantilados de los Escullos viewpoint, the remains of the 18th-century Castillo de San Felipe, the golden-sand sweep of the Playa de Piedra Galera and the gorgeous Playa del Arco.

GETTING AROUND

Bus services from Almería are most frequent to San José (two to four daily), with daily or almost-daily services to Las Negras, Rodalquilar and Agua Amarga (more frequent in July and August). Hiking paths connect the villages. Having your own wheels allows maximum flexibility, but you can get by with a mix of buses, taxis and walking.

Beyond Parque Natural Cabo de Gata-Níjar

Explore Almería's coastline and travel to further reaches to sample its subterranean treasures.

Almería's coastline is one of Andalucía's natural wonders, and the stretch east of Parque Natural Cabo de Gata is no exception. Once you pass the fishing port of Carboneras, 11km east of Agua Amarga, you'll pass a string of isolated white-sand coves sitting against a backdrop of scrubland hills. The picturesque Carboneras–Mojácar road then swings inland to a scenic viewpoint before bringing you back down to the buzzy beach resort and some excellent sandy stretches.

Beyond the beaches and the cliffs, scattered around the pottery town of Sorbas and throughout the remote eastern reaches of Almería, cave attractions await – from the world's second-largest geode and prehistoric cave art to a vast cavern complex inviting exploration by spelunkers.

TOP TIP

Visit Mojácar outside the scorching months of July and August for a quieter time. Book all cave tours in advance.

Carboneras

BEST EATS IN MOJÁCAR

Arlequino
Mismatched bohemian decor and panoramic rooftop terrace paired with elegantly presented Middle Eastern fusion cuisine. €€

Tito's
Tuck into fusion-leaning food and tropical cocktails at this wonderfully laid-back beachside bar amid palm trees. €€

Neptuno
Legendary *chiringuito* in Mojácar Playa; specialities include barbecued meats, grilled fish of the day, and rice dishes. €€

Viento Norte
Basque dishes here include grilled octopus and *txistorra* (garlicky sausage); good-value lunchtime *menú del día*. €

ALEX TIHONOVS/SHUTTERSTOCK ©

Mojácar

Mojácar: twixt castle & beach

HISTORIC PUEBLO; BEAUTIFUL BEACHES

A popular beach resort and a charming hill town, Mojácar is divided into two distinct parts. The hilltop **Mojácar Pueblo** – Murgis to the Romans, and Muxacra to the Moors – is the attractive historic centre, a cascade of white-cube houses down a hillside and a jumble of narrow lanes, charming plazas, bars and cafes centred on the fortress-like Iglesia de Santa María. Virtually abandoned in the 1960s, Mojácar was resurrected by a savvy mayor who lured artists to the area with offers of free land, though these bohemian colonies lost ground long ago to second homes and holiday apartments. It's well worth scrambling up to the hilltop **mirador** – originally the site of a castle – for all-encompassing views over the sea and agricultural landscape studded with dwellings and stark volcanic cones just like the one Mojácar occupies.

WHERE TO STAY IN MOJÁCAR

Hostal Arco Plaza
Friendly, excellent-value *hostal* with rooftop terrace and sky-blue rooms; private balconies overlook Plaza Nueva. €

Hostal el Olivar
An olive-themed, boutiquey *hostal* with friendly owners offers three rooms with balconies and a sun terrace. €€

El Mirador del Castillo
Handsome villa at the top of town comprises characterful rooms, a garden and pool. €€

The **Fuente Mora** – a historic marble fountain near the foot of the hilltop *pueblo* – marks the spot where Mojácar's last Moorish mayor, Alavez, met the envoy of the Reyes Católicos in 1488 to negotiate the village's surrender.

Regular buses connect Mojácar Pueblo with **Mojácar Playa**, a modern, low-rise resort 3km away that fronts a 7km-long sandy beach, its seafront promenade lined with restaurants. Further south, **Playa de Bolmayor** is overlooked by the 18th-century Castillo de Macenas, with several clothing-optional coves further along.

Almería's subterranean treasures

UNDERGROUND CAVERNS; GLITTERING CRYSTALS

The labyrinthine underworld in Almería comprises shimmering caverns with giant crystals and places where you can explore underground rivers. Above ground, ancient caves showcase millennia-old paintings. In 2019, geologists from Madrid made a startling discovery in an abandoned silver mine in the Sierra de Aguilón, near the border with Murcia province: the world's second-largest geode, 8m long and 2m tall. Guided tours (geodapulpi.es) take you through tunnels glistening with mineral deposits and show off a cathedral-like cavern with a massive spiral staircase. The tour de force is the descent 50m below the surface, where you climb inside the **Geoda de Pulpí** – a sparkling cave lined with translucent gypsum crystals.

East along the N-340 from Tabernas, **Cuevas de Sorbas** (cuevasdesorbas.com) is a spectacular cave network in the Paraje Natural Karst en Yesos. Some bristle with stalagmites; others feature spiky stalactite ceilings reflected in pools. The two-hour tour includes the galleries of a gypsum cave, while the four-hour combined route involves crawling through tight gaps to reach a second cave with impressive calcium formations.

Near the town of Vélez Blanco, follow a path through the arid landscape for 1.5km until you reach the rockface decorated with *indalos* (matchstick figures with outstretched arms), which are meant to ward off evil, as well as astronomical signs, birds and animals. The red paint looks remarkably fresh considering that the drawings date back to around 4000 BCE!

EXTREME SPELUNKING IN CUEVAS DE SORBAS

If you're a serious caver, then Cueva del Agua (Water Cave), part of the Sorbas cave network, offers extra thrills. Round up three friends (four-person minimum; book a couple of weeks in advance) and join your guide in exploration of this remarkable cave's nooks and crannies, wading through startlingly cold, chest-deep pools of water and watching your torchlight dance on the gypsum crystals. Sorbas' most active challenge (with the biggest crystals) is found inside Cueva de Tesoro (Treasure Cave), where you'll be dangling in a harness above the abyss and rappelling down sheer walls. No prior experience necessary, though you must be reasonably fit; English- and German-speaking guides are available.

GETTING AROUND

Within the Almería province, Alsa buses have good service from the city of Almería to the bigger towns, such as Mojácar, and more sporadic (in some cases nonexistent) service to smaller villages and more out-of-the-way attractions. One or two daily buses run to Vélez Blanco and Sorbas, but to reach the caves, Wild West theme parks in the Desierto de Tabernas, and trailheads in the Parque Natural Sierra María-Los Vélez, you'll really need your own wheels.

TOOLKIT

The chapters in this section cover the most important topics you'll need to know about in Andalucía. They're full of nuts-and-bolts information and valuable insights to help you understand and navigate Andalucía, and get the most out of your trip.

Mijas (p158)

Arriving

Sevilla and Málaga are the primary airports for most travellers arriving in Andalucía; both have numerous on-site facilities and are well connected to their respective cities by public transport. Almería, Córdoba, Granada and Jerez de la Frontera offer a few flights each. Car rental is relatively inexpensive, particularly at Málaga airport.

Visas

EU nationals don't require visas of any kind. Visitors from the UK, Canada, New Zealand, the US and Australia can stay for up to 90 days (in any six months) without a visa.

SIM Cards

Local SIM cards for unlocked phones can be purchased at phone shops to access affordable prepaid data plans. You'll need a photo ID to activate a local SIM card.

Wi-fi

Most hotels, cafes, airports, libraries and other public buildings in Andalucía offer free wi-fi (though the quality varies). Outside big cities, it's best to rely on a local SIM card for data packages.

Money

ATMs are ubiquitous (though withdrawal charges vary wildly), and most businesses accept major credit cards. Some shops, market stalls and restaurants require cash payments.

Public transport from airport to city centre

	Sevilla	Málaga	Granada
TRAIN	n/a	11 mins €2.30	n/a
BUS	40 mins €4	20 mins €3	30 mins €3
TAXI	20 mins €25	15 mins €22	20 mins €30

TO ANDALUCÍA BY BOAT

You can also travel to Andalucía by boat, sailing from the Moroccan ports of Tangier, Nador or Al Hoceima; from Ceuta or Melilla (Spanish enclaves on the Moroccan coast); or from Oran and Ghazaouet (in Algeria). Available routes are Melilla–Almería, Nador–Almería, Oran–Almería, Ghazaouet–Almería, Tangier–Motril, Nador–Motril, Al Hoceima–Motril, Melilla–Málaga, Tangier–Algeciras, Ceuta–Algeciras and Tangier–Tarifa; the most frequent sailings are to/from Algeciras. Routes usually take vehicles as well as passengers, but if you're taking a car, book well ahead for July, August or Easter travel and expect long queues and customs formalities.

Getting Around

Having your own car in Andalucía gives you great freedom, especially if you want to explore remote villages, out-of-the-way attractions, scenic mountain roads and secluded beaches.

TRAVEL COSTS

Rental
From €20/day

Petrol
Approx €1.75/litre

EV charging
€14–15 to a full charge

Train ticket from Sevilla to Málaga
from €25

Hiring a car

Airport car rental is relatively inexpensive, particularly in Málaga; you must be over 21 and have a credit card. Automatic cars are more expensive than manuals. While hiring a small car can make city parking easier, a car with a bigger engine won't struggle with mountain inclines.

Road conditions

Main motorways (*autovía*), toll motorways (*autopista*) and secondary roads are in very good condition; minor roads can have bumpy surfaces and potholes. Some mountain and coastal tracks are unpaved but passable for city cars.

TIP

Take bicycles for free on local *cercanías* (trains); it's €3 for trips over 100km. They must be boxed up on high-speed trains.

DRIVING IN ANDALUCÍA

Except for busy motorway sections passing through cities, motorways and roads in Andalucía tend to be lightly trafficked and generally a pleasure to drive. Overall, Andalucians are good drivers, but tailgating is common and people may cut you off on roundabouts. When driving on winding mountain roads, look out for drivers straying onto your side of the road from the opposite direction. Horseback riders and occasional herds of goats are not uncommon on minor roads in the countryside.

DRIVING ESSENTIALS

Drive on the right.

All vehicle occupants must wear a seatbelt.

Maximum speeds are 120km/h on the *autovía*, 80km/h on secondary highways and 50km/h in built-up areas.

.05

Blood alcohol limit is 0.05%.

Parking

Parking in tiny (often one-way) lanes in medieval town centres and villages is a fool's errand: look for car parks just outside the *casco antiguo* (old town) instead. Some underground garages have very tight spaces. In cities, free spaces have broken white lines; broken blue lines denote resident parking.

Bus

Andalucía is covered by a comprehensive bus service between all major cities and towns, and even remoter villages tend to have one or two daily buses to the nearest city/town. Major bus companies include Alsa (alsa.es), Comes (tgcomes.es) and Autocares Carrera (autocarescarrera.es).

Train

Trains are generally fast, clean and reliable, with very good service between Andalucía's main cities and between Andalucía and Madrid. Booking train tickets in advance via the Renfe (renfe.com) website can save you money on the high-speed AVE routes.

Money

CURRENCY: **EURO (€)**

Credit cards

Major cards are widely accepted throughout Andalucía (in remoter villages, cash is still king). Some motorway toll booths accept both card and cash payment.

Cash or card?

Cash is useful for village restaurants, small purchases, market stalls and public transport. Most hotels and city restaurants accept credit cards (usually only Visa and Mastercard).

Taxes & refunds

Non-EU visitors are entitled to a refund of the 21% IVA on purchases of goods totalling over €90.15 from any shop. Ask for an official DIVA refund form with your purchase, then scan them at a DIVA kiosk at your departure airport.

Tipping

Restaurants & cafes A service charge is usually included in the bill, but most people leave small change if they're satisfied (5% is usually plenty).

Hotels Tip porters around €1.

Taxis Tipping isn't necessary, but rounding up is always appreciated.

HOW MUCH FOR A...

24-hour Málaga Pass discount card
€28

Museum ticket
€3.50–5

Bus ticket from Granada to Almería
€9

Train ticket from Sevilla to Málaga
€25

SAVE a few euros

Bearers of student cards can get reduced admission to museums, as can IYTC card holders. Those aged over 60 or 65 (with ID) usually get free or discounted entry to sights; some discounts are limited to EU passport holders, though. Look for attractions offering combined tickets, which allow you to to save a few euros on individual tickets.

LOCAL TIP

While ATMs are widely available (with the exception of more remote villages), withdrawal fees vary widely. Caixa Rural has some of the lowest fees; Santander Bank's are among the highest.

THE SPANISH ECONOMY TODAY

Spain faces significant economic challenges: low productivity, high structural unemployment, an ageing population, income inequality, plus the fight against climate change – felt particularly sharply in Andalucía, where unprecedented heatwaves and ever more frequent droughts are affecting agriculture. Other external pressures include pandemic-related uncertainty, global supply-chain bottlenecks, and energy price rises. That said, the Spanish government has provided considerable support to its citizens, capping fuel costs and offering free long-distance train travel to commuters, so the Spanish economy is set to reach pre-pandemic levels by late 2023.

Accommodation

Sleep like royalty

Sleep like the monarchs of yore by staying in one of Andalucía's *paradores* – state-run luxury hotels inside sensitively restored castles and palaces, often in stupendously beautiful locations. Alternatives include modern luxury hotels with spas, pools and superb restaurants, and boutique hotels that cleverly combine historical features with dynamic contemporary design, found both in major cities and *pueblos blancos* (white towns).

Budget sleeps

Wallet-friendly alternatives to hotels include family-run budget hotels (*hostales*), with fairly basic single, double and triple rooms; the price almost always includes breakfast. *Hostales* shouldn't be confused with hostels, those backpacker hangouts typically found in main cities, consisting of dorms with shared facilities; common areas good for meeting fellow travellers; and freebies, such as tapas tours, bike hire and pancake breakfasts.

Wilderness stays

National parks (such as the Sierra Nevada) have their share of *refugios* (mountain huts), spaced out along long-distance hiking trails. A fantastic way for fresh-air fiends to access the remoter parts of Andalucía's wilderness, these tend to be rather basic bunk huts with mixed dorms and a dining area serving breakfast and dinner. Booking in advance is wise.

HOW MUCH FOR A NIGHT IN...

a parador
from €150

a bodega
from €120

a B&B
from €50

Go rural

Casas rurales are usually characterful, renovated farmhouses and country houses, run as B&Bs. Some are centuries old, offering immersion into local history; the hosts typically include breakfast with local ingredients – often from their own land – with other meals available on request. Some have restaurants on-site, while other *casas rurales* are independent short-term holiday houses.

Camp out

While wild camping in Andalucía is prohibited in national parks, natural parks and on beaches, there are over 150 campgrounds dotted about the province. Even the most basic campground will have hot showers, electrical hook-ups and a cafe; top-notch places often have minimarkets and swimming pools. Some are naturist (ie clothing-optional). Seafront campgrounds get packed in summer months.

BODEGA HOTELS

Andalucía has several important wine-producing regions and a number of wineries now offer lodgings (some also have excellent restaurants). Staying at a bodega is a unique way of deepening your oenophilic education by sampling unusual, award-winning wines, with the benefit of waking up to vineyard views over rolling countryside. Given how some cutting-edge vintners are bringing back endemic grape varieties and experimenting with live and organic wines, you may be indirectly funding an exciting new tipple – or helping with the upkeep of historic bodegas, at the very least.

Family Travel

Andalucía's sunny climate, well-equipped beaches, and easy-going, child-friendly attitudes make it ideal for families. Numerous sights and attractions keep kids happy, from water sports, castles and amusement parks to child-friendly museums, wildlife-spotting opportunities and exuberant fiestas. Children are welcomed at most restaurants; look for discounted family tickets on public transport.

Sights

Most sights offer children discounts for admission; kids under four years usually get in for free. Some museums offer family-specific tours and workshops for children. Many Málaga museums have entirely free entry on Sundays, and most museums in Andalucía open their doors to visitors, gratis, on Andalucía Day (February 28). Kids are typically charged reduced prices for tours, and many others are free.

Facilities

- Some restaurants and museums have nappy-changing facilities.
- Cobbled streets are difficult for prams and strollers; best to bring a baby carrier.
- Baby supplies are readily available at pharmacies and supermarkets.
- Most hotels have cots and extra beds available (sometimes at extra cost); book ahead.
- Breastfeeding is common everywhere.

Getting around

Under-18s get 40% off high-speed AVE train tickets (kids under four ride free), plus often discounts on ferries; it's full price for bus seats (except small children sitting on parents' laps). Book safety seats in advance if hiring a car.

Eating out

Children are welcomed at most restaurants; some offer high chairs. Many have kids' menus or can serve half-portions; some even have a kids-only *menú del día*. Restaurants don't open for dinner till 8pm, so keep snacks on hand for small stomachs.

KID-FRIENDLY PICKS

Isla Mágica, Sevilla (p73)
Pirate shows, roller-coasters and more.

Oasys Mini Hollywood, Desierto de Tabernas (p262)
Wild West shows, zoo and stagecoaches.

Muelle de las Carabelas, La Rábida (p94)
Scramble around three replica Columbus ships.

Boat trips, Tarifa (p138)
Spot whales and dolphins.

La Geoda de Pulpí, Almería province (p273)
Clamber inside a giant crystal underground.

Castles, Jaén and Baños de la Encina (p216 & p222)
Explore centuries-old battlements.

STAYING AT CASAS RURALES WITH KIDS

The proliferation of *casas rurales* in Andalucía lets you enjoy a wallet-friendly holiday while showing your kids a bit of life in the Andalucian countryside. Some places offer activities such as horse riding or have swimming pools and small playgrounds, or may even provide babysitting services. Others may be happy to show your kids around a working farm, introducing them to animals and having them assist with fruit-picking and egg-collecting. Apart from the tranquillity and plenty of space to run around in, kids can enjoy fresh, farm-to-table food, much of which comes from the land right around them.

Health & Safe Travel

INSURANCE

Spain's public-health system will provide urgent hospital care to everyone, so insurance is not compulsory (though non-EU citizens may get a bill afterwards). Travel insurance is a good idea, since it covers medical care, flight cancellations and lost luggage. EU passport holders can apply for the European Health Insurance Card (EHIC), which covers medical treatment free of charge.

Sunstroke

Andalucía's summer heat is no joke. Always be sure to take plenty of water, a hat and high-SPF sunscreen, especially if hiking; follow locals' lead by staying somewhere dark and cool during the day's hottest hours in July and August. Heat exhaustion and sunstroke are not limited to those two months – don't underestimate the sun's strength, especially at higher altitudes.

Jellyfish

Large numbers of jellyfish are occasionally a problem on the beaches of Costa del Sol during the summer months, following weeks of the easterly levanter wind. The smaller jellyfish are a nuisance and can deliver a nasty sting, but they're otherwise not dangerous; larger ones have a less painful sting. Applying vinegar to the wound helps neutralise the sting.

SOLO TRAVEL

Andalucía is safe for women travelling solo (with the same precautions you'd take anywhere); very occasionally, you may get unwanted male attention.

SWIM SAFELY

Green flag
Safe to swim

Yellow flag
Moderate currents: swim with caution

Red flag
Danger: swimming prohibited

White flag with jellyfish
Dangerous marine life spotted

Black flag
Beach is closed to the public

Cannabis

In Andalucía, it's legal to possess up to 100g of cannabis exclusively for personal and private use. However, it is a crime to purchase cannabis from others, and to consume or possess cannabis in public places. Hotels and other holiday accommodation almost certainly will not allow smoking cannabis on their premises.

THEFT & SCAMS

The main crimes to watch out for in Andalucía are petty theft, pickpockets and the odd scam. Watch your luggage closely in busy public areas, especially parks, plazas and bus/train stations. Beware of pickpockets in tourist-heavy areas. 'Bird poo' scams occasionally occur on the Costa del Sol: culprits spray the victim's back with an unknown liquid, then pickpocket them while 'helping' them.

Food, Drink & Nightlif

When to eat

Desayuno (breakfast): A standard Spanish breakfast: coffee, orange juice, and *tostada* (toasted bread with sweet or savoury toppings), served from 8am to 11am.

Almuerzo (lunch): The biggest meal of the day, with many restaurants offering three-course specials. Sunday lunch can last hours. From 2pm till 4pm.

Cena (dinner): Restaurants open around 8pm but few Andalucians eat out before 9pm. Dinner can last until 11pm or midnight.

Where to eat

Bar: Open early for basic breakfasts, with beer, wine, vermouth and tapas the rest of the day.

Cafetería: Halfway between a cafe and a bar; good for breakfasts and afternoon snacks and drinks.

Asador: Restaurant serving grilled meats.

Taberna: An old-school bar specialising in vermouth or wine. Tapas served.

Restaurante: Anything from basic restaurant to fine-dining establishment.

Chiringuito: Beachside kiosk serving fried fish and seafood.

Marisquería: Upmarket seafood restaurant.

Bar de copas: Specifically a cocktail bar, open late and not serving food.

MENU DECODER

Menú del día: A fixed-price, three-course meal, typically served at lunchtime and occasionally excellent value.

Menú degustación: A tasting menu consisting of at least five courses.

Tapa: The smallest size of a dish that you can order.

Ración: Large helping of a dish, typically meant for sharing.

Media ración: Half of a large dish, usually enough for one person.

Entrantes: Starters to share – sometimes under the heading *para picar* ('to pick at').

Primeros: First courses of a *menú del día* (eg soup, vegetable dish, paella).

Segundos: Second courses of same (eg meat or fish with potatoes).

Carnes: Red meat dishes

Ensaladas: Salads

Pescados: Fish dishes

Mariscos: Seafood dishes

Postres: Desserts

Una caña: A small beer

Vino de la casa: House wine

HOW TO...

TAPEAR

Stories regarding the origin of the 'tapa' (meaning 'lid') vary. According to one, in the 13th century King Alfonso X stopped at a beachside bar in Cádiz province and a strong gust of wind blew in his direction; a quick-witted waiter rushed to place a slice of *jamón* (cured ham) atop his glass of sherry to keep out the sand. It may also come from the old Andalucian custom of doing the same with a slice of bread to deter flies.

Tapas are now synonymous with Andalucía's dining scene. While the custom of a free tapa with every drink is no longer widespread, it lives on in select bars in Sevilla and the majority in Granada. To *tapear* (eat tapas), you can either hop between tapas bars and order a drink in each one, or settle on one place and make a meal of it.

HOW MUCH FOR A...

Espresso
€1.20

Tostada
€3–4

Helado (ice cream)
€2.50

Tapa
€2–4

Media ración
€5–8

Glass of wine
€2–4.50

Lunch at a chiringuito
€20

Dinner at a Michelin-starred restaurant
€100–150

HOW TO...

ORDER COFFEE

While Andalucians are not Europe's biggest coffee drinkers, they have the same passion for it as other Mediterraneans, with an element of social ritual to its consumption. For breakfast, many opt for milky coffee, quite often consumed in a bar, occasionally accompanied by a pastry or tostada; it's followed by a stronger brew in the afternoon. When meeting friends or work colleagues, Andalucians tend to gather for coffee at cafes instead of someone's home.

Most Andalucian coffee is espresso-based, served in small glasses or cups and less watered down than in northern Europe. While the proliferation of speciality coffee shops has added some extra vocabulary to the list, Andalucians generally have their coffee the following ways:

Spanish coffee

Much of Spanish coffee is *torrefacto* – with sugar added to the beans before roasting, a tradition dating to the Civil War. The sugar burns during roasting, giving the beans a stronger, more bitter taste.

Espresso: A tiny cup of very strong black coffee.

Café solo: A synonym for espresso.

Café largo: A large, strong black coffee.

Americano: A café solo with hot water added to dilute it.

Cappuccino: Practically unheard of (outside of a Starbucks).

Cortado: A small cup of espresso with a dash of milk.

Café con leche: Hot milk and coffee served in equal amounts. Only consumed in the morning.

Carajillo: Coffee with a splash of alcohol, such as brandy or Baileys.

Café con hielo: Summer version of any coffee drink, with a few ice cubes thrown in.

Bombón: Half-and-half: condensed milk at the bottom, espresso on top.

GOING OUT

A night out in Andalucía often starts with meeting friends after work, sipping a beer or an aperitif in a bar or on the *terraza* (terrace) of some plaza. Andalucía is particularly well-geared towards al fresco libations: even in winter, there's plenty of sunshine and most bars offer outdoor seating. Around 8pm, the kitchens open, and sometimes people order a few *raciones* – croquettes, or platters of cold cuts – instead of dinner, or else head to an actual restaurant for a sit-down meal.

Alternatively, grab some dinner at home before heading out again, since the evening action doesn't really start picking up until late. In Sevilla, Granada, Málaga and other big cities, revellers fill the streets, particularly on hot summer nights, moving between the tapas bars of Barrio Santa Cruz in Sevilla, Granada's Realejo or Málaga's historical centre, getting a drink here, a tapa there. Around 11pm, bars really start to fill up, so you may have to stand outside with your drink, then elbow your way back in to place your order at the bar.

If you want to hit some nightclubs, don't go before 1am – they're pretty empty before then, and DJs often play until 6am or so. Many clubs are pretty casual and don't have a strict dress code, but it's a good idea to look at the club's social-media feed beforehand to figure out what to wear. Some clubs offer free entry to women.

Responsible Travel

Climate change & travel

It's impossible to ignore the impact we have when travelling, and the importance of making changes where we can. Lonely Planet urges all travellers to engage with their travel carbon footprint. There are many carbon calculators online that allow travellers to estimate the carbon emissions generated by their journey; try resurgence.org/resources/carbon-calculator.html. Many airlines and booking sites offer travellers the option of offsetting the impact of greenhouse gas emissions by contributing to climate-friendly initiatives around the world. We continue to offset the carbon footprint of all Lonely Planet staff travel, while recognising this is a mitigation more than a solution.

Stargazing

Be wowed by the night sky at the Astronomical Observatory (astrotorcal.es) in El Torcal de Antequera. The high-altitude Sierra Nevada Astrophysical Observatory (osn.iaa.csic.es/en) offers facility tours during the day in July and August.

Cork forests

Stripping cork-oak to turn the bark into wine-bottle corks is an age-old profession; supporting it economically helps preserve the cork-oak woodlands of Parque Natural Los Alcornocales, so buy bottles with corks rather than cheaper plastic stoppers.

Eating local

Another excellent way to support the local economy in a province with high unemployment is to patronise local restaurants in villages. You'll also get top-notch fresh produce, most of which is grown locally.

Traditional crafts

Many of Andalucía's villages still practise age-old traditional crafts, from weaving and pottery to marble- and leatherwork. Purchasing these crafts helps to keep traditional culture alive while simultaneously supporting local artisans.

Sustainable wood

You'll encounter numerous wooden souvenirs during your travels around Andalucía – those made of wood harvested from sustainable forests are marked with the FSC or PERF label.

Stop for a meal at Puerto de Santa María's **La Taberna del Chef del Mar** (p123), where sustainably caught seafood is the order of the day.

Eat green with Sevilla's best vegan tapas at **Vegan Rock** (p70), or enjoy the home-grown vegies at **Chilimosa** (p139) in Tarifa.

Select winemakers in Ronda (wineronda.com) are dedicated to producing award-winning wines, combining an unusual mix of grape varietals and using only sustainable, organic and biodynamic techniques.

Andalucía is Spain's most arid province – some parts are actual desert – so it's important to conserve water as much as possible. Carry reusable water containers (the tap water is drinkable) and shower efficiently.

Marine conservation

Many come to Tarifa for whale- and dolphin-watching in the Straits of Gibraltar. The excellent FIRMM (firmm.org) does marine mammal research and conservation, and also offers tours (in English) that treat the animals with respect.

Volunteering

European Solidarity Corps (youthforeurope.eu) have numerous opportunities for young travellers prepared to stay longer in Andalucía. Volunteering projects are an excellent way of improving your language skills while directly contributing to local communities.

Explore Spain's hundreds of **Vías Verdes** (Green Ways), disused train tracks converted into cycling and walking routes (p44).

Málaga is incorporating new electric buses into its fleet to achieve zero emissions by 2030.

The Global Sustainability Index ranks Spain in 12th place worldwide. The country has produced a roadmap for achieving carbon neutrality by 2050, aiming to get 74% of its electricity from renewables by 2030.

Electric cars

If hiring a car, get a hybrid or electric, which are more fuel-efficient. There's also free parking for electric cars in designated places, and numerous charging points, in villages as well as larger towns and cities.

Ditch the car

Explore the mountains and the countryside on foot and by bike along the Vías Verdes (viasverdes.com), a network of recovered rail-trails. Also try the hiking and biking trails between villages in Sierra Nevada and beyond.

RESOURCES

worldpackers.com
Volunteering with various social enterprises, including animal rescue.

andalucia.org
Info on Andalucía's protected areas.

iucn.org
Climate-change-related environmental issues in Spain and beyond.

Contribute to Andalucía's reforestation projects by booking a tour with responsible-travel company Andalucia360Travel (andalucia360travel.com).

LGBTIQ+ Travellers

Spain is one of the world's most progressive countries for LGBTIQ+ issues. Openly gay people have served in the Spanish military since 1979; antidiscrimination laws were introduced in the 1990s; in 2005 same-sex marriage was legalised. There are well-established queer communities in Torremolinos, Málaga, Sevilla and Granada, but even elsewhere, LGBTIQ+ visitors are unlikely to face discrimination.

Festivals & parades

Sevilla hosts Andalucía's largest pride festival, Orgullo de Andalucía (orgullolgtbiandalucia.es), in late June; a week-long slate of concerts, exhibitions and parties culminates in a parade to the Alameda de Hércules on the final Saturday. Granada, Córdoba, Málaga, Almería, Huelva and El Puerto de Santa María all host their own Pride events the last week in June, with lively drag events in Málaga and Huelva in particular. Almería highlights issues faced by trans people with their 'diverse identity exhibition', while Granada and Huelva try to outdo each other with LGBTIQ+-themed window displays.

RESOURCES

The websites travelgay.com and patroc.com have helpful listings of gay-owned and gay-friendly accommodation, bars, clubs, beaches, cruising areas, health clubs and associations. Both have special sections for Sevilla and Torremolinos. Other useful websites include gayseville4u.com and gaytorremolinos4u.com.

GAY DISTRICTS

Andalucía's liveliest gay scene is in Torremolinos, closely followed by the scenes in Málaga, Sevilla and Granada, but there are gay- and lesbian-friendly bars and clubs in all major cities. Some cities produce special leaflets, guides and maps advertising gay-specific sights, such as Sevilla's Municipios Orgullosos de la Provincia de Sevilla (turismosevilla.org).

Tourism & safe networks

Out of Office (outofoffice.com) organises gay-centric tours, and is a good general resource. MisterBandB (misterbandb.com) is an extensive guide to LGBTIQ+-friendly accommodation, while Further Afield (furtherafield.com) also lists inclusive accommodation on their site. Málaga-based Federación Andaluza Arco Iris (federacionarcoiris.blogspot.com) is an organisation that campaigns for equal opportunities for LGBTIQ+ people.

All things drag

Fans of the art of drag can see local performers shine in the spotlight of Torremolinos' Gala Drag Queen del Carnival Gay – Andalucía's drag event of the year. Benalmádena follows suit with their Drag Queen Gala.

OLDER MINDSETS

Generally speaking, Andalucía is welcoming to everyone, including LGBTIQ+ travellers. However, older generations, particularly in rural areas, might have different ideals and make the occasional rude remark. Andalucian cities can also feel more progressive than smaller rural towns and the countryside, though attitudes everywhere are slowly moving towards greater acceptance.

Accessible Travel

Andalucía does have accessibility issues, but efforts are being made to promote tourist accessibility for travellers with different needs.

Accessible beaches

Andalucía has numerous beaches with access ramps for wheelchairs, adapted facilities, opportunities to participate in water sports, devices for visitors with sensory disabilities and more.

Airports

Andalucía's airports offer assistance for passengers with reduced mobility and visual and hearing impairments; ask your airline at least 48 hours before departure. Málaga, Sevilla and other airports offer disabled parking, adapted toilets and lifts with Braille buttons.

Accommodation

Newer midrange and top-end hotels in Andalucía have wheelchair access and adapted bathrooms, whereas many B&Bs and guesthouses don't have lifts. Book accommodation through Access At Last (accessatlast.com) to ensure your needs are met.

FREE APPS

TUR4all is a handy app providing info about levels of accessibility in over 1300 tourist establishments across Spain.

GoogleMaps has a useful 'Accessible Places' feature that shows accessible parking, seating, entrances and restrooms.

Cobbled streets

Even in cities where public transport is wheelchair-friendly, cobbled, narrow, and sometimes steep streets, lack of ramps up on the pavement and other obstacles present ample challenges for disabled travellers.

Public transport

New city buses and trams in Málaga, Sevilla and Granada can accommodate wheelchairs. Train stations in Sevilla and Córdoba are fully accessible, while those in Málaga, Cádiz and other major cities are partially accessible.

FESTIVALS

In July, events take place across Andalucía as part of Disability Pride Month, designed to bring attention to challenges that people with functional diversity face, as well as focusing on present-day opportunities.

RESOURCES

Accessible Spain Travel (accessiblespain travel.com) Organises accessible tours, transport and accommodation in Córdoba, Granada, Malaga and Sevilla for travellers with limited mobility.

Disabled Accessible Travel (disabledaccessible travel.com) Another useful resource for booking disabled-friendly accommodation, transfers and tours in main Andalucian cities.

Mobility International USA (miusa.org) Advises travellers with disabilities on mobility issues and runs an educational exchange programme.

Málaga's commitment to 'museums without barriers' means that the Picasso Museum (p152) hosts interactive tours and workshops aimed at visitors with diverse needs. Málaga Museum (museosdeandalucia.es) and the Automobile and Fashion Museum (museoautomovilmalaga.com) both have touchable exhibits with signs in Braille.

MARCELINA1982/GETTY IMAGES ©

GR7, Parque Natural Sierra de Grazalema (p130)

HOW TO...

Hike Andalucía's Trails

With over three dozen protected areas, Andalucía is a hiking destination par excellence, with some of Spain's most exciting and varied terrain. Besides countless day hikes there are two long-distance trails – the GR7 and the GR240.

Pick your trail

The GR7 ('GR' stands for *gran recorrido* – 'long-distance trail') is part of a Europe-wide network. Its Andalucía section is around 1250km long, starting from Tarifa, bisecting the Alcornocales and Grazalema protected areas and then splitting at Villanueva de Cauche. The northern branch heads for the Sierras Subbéticas and Parque Natural Sierras de Cazorla, Segura y las Villas; the southern branch passes through the *pueblos blancos* of Sierra de Almijara and the Alpujarras villages of Sierra Nevada. The 270km-long GR240 (Sulayr, or 'mountains of the sun' to the Moors) does a high-altitude loop around Sierra Nevada's rugged terrain and takes 15 to 19 days to complete.

Decide when to go

April to July and September to October are best for the GR240: the trail's northern half can be treacherous or even impassible in places due to winter snowfall, and the August heat can reach you even in the high Sierra Nevada. The GR7 can be hiked during the winter months, but is best avoided altogether in summer, when temperatures are unbearably hot and fire risk may close some trail sections.

Plan your accommodation

You can plan both treks around staying in villages en route, since both trails are helpfully divided into day-hike chunks. Accommodation is limited in some of the smaller Alpujarras villages and gets booked up weeks ahead in popular spots like Capileira. The GR240 is divided into 19 stages, but you can combine shorter stages to make use of eight *refugios*.

Gear up

Layers are a must year-round, as is waterproof gear. Sturdy hiking boots, first-aid kit and torch are essential. Sleeping bag and emergency bivvy bag are good considerations for the GR240; if hiking it during colder months, consider packing crampons. While both trails are reasonably well-marked, it's well worth investing in Editorial Alpina maps and downloading the Gaia GPS app.

WHAT'S A REFUGIO?

Andalucía's hiking-trail accommodation (*refugios*) varies greatly. Some are free, first-come-first-served, ultra-basic shelters that are nothing more than stone huts with perhaps a table, fireplace and a few bare bunks where you can lay your sleeping bag if you get caught in the open as daylight is fading. Others are full-service *albergues* (mountain hostels) offering mixed-sex dorm rooms with bedding, cooking facilities, a bar, breakfast and dinner provided on request, and perhaps even gear for sale. Refugio Postero Alto (refugioposteroalto.es) on the GR240 requires advance bookings, particularly during busier warmer months.

Nuts & Bolts

OPENING HOURS

Opening times vary seasonally and are typically more reduced during winter and/or peak summer (depending on location).

Banks 8.30am–2pm Monday to Friday

Cafes & bars 8am–11pm

Restaurants 1–4pm and 8pm–midnight

Bars & clubs 10pm–6am

Central post offices 8.30am–8.30pm Monday to Friday, to 2pm Saturday

Shops 10am–2pm and 5–8pm Monday to Saturday; big supermarkets 10am–10pm Monday to Saturday

Smoking

Smoking, including e-cigarettes, is banned inside all bars and restaurants in Andalucía, though many still smoke in outdoor seating areas. Most hotels don't allow smoking in any of their rooms.

GOOD TO KNOW

Time Zone
GMT/UTC +1 in winter, GMT/UTC+2 during the daylight-savings period

Country Code
34

Emergency number
112

Population
47.4 million

Toilets

Public toilets are rare. Pop into a shopping centre, or grab coffee in a bar to use the toilet.

Internet access

Most businesses offer free wi-fi, as do many cities and towns for public spaces.

Electricity 230V/50Hz

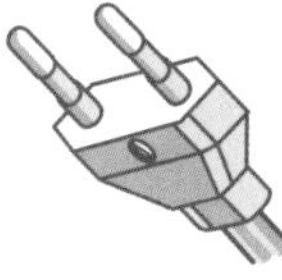

Type C
220V/50Hz

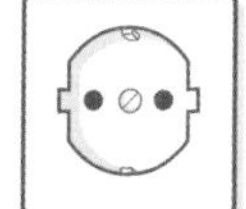

Type F
230V/50Hz

PUBLIC HOLIDAYS

On public holidays, businesses and non-essential services usually close. Towns also celebrate their patron saint's holiday. Spain has nine national holidays:

New Year's Day
1 January

Good Friday
March/April

Labour Day
1 May

Feast of the Assumption
15 August

Fiesta Nacional de España (National Day)
12 October

All Saints' Day
1 November

Constitution Day
6 December

Feast of the Immaculate Conception
8 December

Christmas
25 December

Andalucía also observes:

Día de los Reyes Magos
6 January

Andalucía Day
28 February

Maundy Thursday
March/April

Language

English is quite widely spoken, especially in larger cities and popular tourist areas, but less so in rural villages and among older Spaniards. Learning a little Spanish before you come will, in any case, greatly increase your appreciation of the country.

Basics

Hello. Hola. *o·la*
Goodbye. Adiós. *adiós*
Yes. Sí. *see*
No. No. *no*
Please. Por favor. *por fa·vor*
Thank you. Gracias. *gra·thyas*
Excuse me. Perdón. *per·don*
Sorry. Lo siento. *lo syen·to*
What's your name? ¿Cómo se llama Usted?. *ko·mo se lya·ma oo·ste*
My name is ... Me llamo ... *me lya·mo ...*
Do you speak English? ¿Habla inglés? *a·bla een·gles*
I don't understand. No entiendo. *no en·tyen·do*

Signs

Abierto Open
Cerrado Closed
Entrada Entrance
Mujeres Women
Hombres Men
Prohibido Prohibited
Salida Exit
Servicios/Aseos Toilets

Time

What time is it? ¿Qué hora es? *ke o·ra es*
It's (10) o'clock. Son (las diez). *son (las dyeth)*
It's half past (one). Es (la una) y media. *es (la oo·na) ee me·dya*
yesterday ayer. *a·yer*
today hoy. *oy*
tomorrow mañana. *ma·nya·na*

Emergencies

Help! ¡Socorro! *so·ko·ro*
Go away! ¡Vete! *ve·te*
Call the police! ¡Llame a la policía! *lya·me a la po·lee·thee·a*
Call a doctor! ¡Llame a un médico! *lya·me a oon me·dee·ko*

Eating & drinking

What would you recommend? ¿Qué recomienda? *ke re·ko·myen·da*
Cheers! ¡Salud! *sa·loo*
That was delicious. ¡Estaba buenísimo! *es·ta·ba bwe·nee·see·mo*

Talk like a local

What's up? ¿Qué pasa? ke pa·sa
Great! ¡Genial! *khe·nyal*
How cool! ¡Qué guay! *ke gwai*
That's fantastic! ¡Estupendo! *es·too·pen·do*
Really? ¿En serio? *en se·ryo*
You don't say! ¡No me digas! *no me dee·gas*
Sure. Claro. *kla·ro*
OK. Vale. *va·le*
Of course! ¡Por supuesto! *por soo·pwes·to*
Whatever. Lo que sea. *lo ke se·a*
Hey! ¡Eh, tú! *e too*
Listen (to this)! ¡Escucha (esto)! *es·koo·cha (es·to)*
Look! ¡Mira! *mee·ra*
No way! ¡De ningún modo! *de neen·goon mo·do*
Just joking. Era broma. *e·ra bro·ma*

NUMBERS

1
uno *oo·no*

2
dos *dos*

3
tres *tres*

4
cuatro *kwa·tro*

5
cinco *theen·ko*

6
seis *seys*

7
siete *sye·te*

8
ocho *o·cho*

9
nueve *nwe·ve*

10
diez *dyeth*

DONATIONS TO ENGLISH

Numerous – you may recognise armada, aficionado, embargo, fiesta, machismo, plaza, salsa ...

DISTINCTIVE SOUNDS

Note that *kh* is a throaty sound (like the 'ch' in the Scottish loch), *r* is strongly rolled, *ly* is pronounced as the 'lli' in 'million' and *ny* as the 'ni' in 'onion'.

Quick grammar tip

Spanish has a formal and informal word for 'you' (Usted and tú respectively). The verbs also have a different ending for each person, like the English 'I do' vs 'he/she do**es**'.

False friends

Warning: some Spanish words look like English words but have a different meaning altogether! For example, *suburbio* is 'slum district' (not 'suburb', which is *barrio*).

Four phrases to learn before you go

1 What time does it open/close?

¿A qué hora abren/cierran? a ke *o*·ra *ab*·ren/*thye*·ran

The Spanish tend to observe the siesta (afternoon rest), so opening times may surprise you.

2 When is admission free?

¿Cuándo es la entrada gratuita? *kwan*·do es la en·*tra*·da gra·*twee*·ta

Many museums and galleries in Spain have admission-free times, so check before buying tickets.

3 Where can we go (salsa) dancing?

¿Dónde podemos ir a bailar (salsa)? *don*·de po·*de*·mos eer a bai·*lar* (*sal*·sa)

Flamenco may be the authentic viewing experience in Spain, but to actively enjoy the music you'll want to do some dancing.

4 How do you say this in (Catalan/Galician/Basque)?

¿Cómo se dice ésto en (catalán/gallego/euskera)? *ko*·mo se *dee*·the *es*·to en (ka·ta·*lan*/ga·*lye*·go/e·oos·*ke*·ra)

Spain has four official languages, and people in these regions will appreciate it if you try to use their local language.

SPANISH IN THE WORLD

Over the last 500 years, Spanish in Latin America has evolved differently to the Spanish of Europe. Among other differences, you'll easily recognise Latin Americans by the lack of lisp in their speech – ie *cerveza* (beer) is ther·*ve*·tha in Europe but ser·*ve*·sa across the Atlantic. Within Spain, Spanish, or Castilian **(*castellano*) is** primarily the language of Castille (covering the largest territory in Spain). However, Catalan, Galician and Basque are also official languages, and locals in these regions are very proud of their own language.

THE ANDALUCÍA

STORYBOOK

Our writers delve deep into different aspects of Andalucian life

Puente Nuevo, Ronda (p163)

A HISTORY OF ANDALUCÍA IN 15 PLACES

Andalucía's warm climate, seafarer-friendly shores and strategic location on the Mediterranean have made it one of the oldest inhabited parts of Europe and attracted a succession of prominent civilisations, each keen to claim the land for their own. These are Andalucía's diverse stories, from prehistory to the present day.

THE EARLIEST PART of Europe to be inhabited by human beings, and the last stand of Neanderthals, Andalucía has played a unique role in the development of humanity. As Spain's southernmost region, located at a meeting point of continents and oceans, it's come into contact with sophisticated civilisations from the eastern Mediterranean and North Africa – all of which have helped to shape it.

It's difficult to reconcile the agrarian image from the 15th to the early 20th centuries with the innovative role that Andalucía played millennia ago. Cultural cross-pollination from Egypt and Mesopotamia around 6000 BCE brought the revolution of agriculture – the plough, crops, livestock – and with it pottery, textiles and villages, followed by Spain's first metalworking culture. The Phoenicians and the Romans built cities, roads and aqueducts, while the long Moorish interlude made Andalucía the centre of Islamic culture in Europe. Andalucía's tenure as the gateway to the Spanish American empire was followed by centuries of decline under the Christian kings and the 20th-century dictatorship. And yet, while present-day Andalucía faces numerous challenges, its unique, beguiling character sets it apart from the rest of Spain.

1. Alhambra

MAJESTIC MOORISH MONUMENT

Arguably Spain's most architecturally perfect building, the Moorish palace-fortress of Alhambra became the seat of Nasrid rulers in Granada just as the Christian Reconquista was gathering momentum elsewhere in Andalucía. In fact, this last Moorish stronghold survived for as long as it did because its astute rulers joined forces with Fernando III to help him sack Moorish Sevilla. The elegant Palacios Nazaríes saw numerous deadly intrigues, including a civil war between supporters of two wives of the same sultan, while in the immaculately tended gardens of the Generalife a sultan's wife brought about the fall of a dynasty by dallying with her consort.

For a tour of the Alhambra, see p234

2. Orce

EUROPE'S OLDEST TEETH

In 1982 the nondescript town of Orce in the badlands of Granada's Altiplano made international headlines when a local palaeontological find was thought to redefine what we know about human history in Europe. Catalan palaeontologist Josep Gibert found a human skull fragment, claiming that it was that of a Palaeolithic-era child of indeterminate gender who had been devoured by a great hyena. More importantly, he claimed the skull was between 0.9 and 1.6 million years old, which would have made it the oldest find of its kind. Major controversy followed, though a more recent find has cemented Orce's place in history.

For an in-depth glimpse of Europe's prehistory, visit the museum in Orce (p263)

3. Mezquita

CATHEDRAL WITHIN A MOSQUE

Córdoba's 8th-century Mezquita is one of the greatest works of Islamic architecture in the world – one that makes you glad that the Christian monarchs saw it fit to accommodate the Christian cathedral inside it rather than demolish the Moorish edifice altogether. Within, the forests of marble columns, topped by red-and-white arches, and the rather austere Gothic chapel, sporting carved mahogany choir stalls and a baroque ceiling, reflect Córdoba's transition from a great city of learning at the heart of the western Islamic empire to one in decline, following its conquest by Fernando III of Castile.

For more on the Mezquita, see p190

4. Catedral de Sevilla

CATHEDRAL LIKE NO OTHER

After Sevilla had been captured from the Almohad rulers in 1248 by Fernando III, and its mosque-church was damaged by the 1401 earthquake, legend has it the powers that be decided to build a cathedral, the likes of which Spain had never seen: 'Let's construct a church so large future generations will think we were mad.' And so they did, with architects incorporating the mosque's original minaret into the Giralda (bell tower) and constructing an astonishing gold altarpiece in the Capilla Mayor. Columbus, who set sail from Sevilla to the New World, is seeing out eternity in a marble sarcophagus within.

For more on the Catedral, see p56

V_E/SHUTTERSTOCK ©

5. Baelo Claudia

ROMAN CITY BY THE SEA

Arguably Andalucía's most important Roman site, the oceanfront Baelo Claudia on the Costa de la Luz rose to particular prominence during the reign of Emperor Claudius (41–54 CE) on the production of *garum* – the Roman Empire's favourite pungent condiment, made of fish fermented with salt – and on trade with North Africa. It's unclear why the once-prosperous city fell into decline, though a major 3rd-century earthquake is thought to have played a major part, but many vestiges of a long-gone civilisation remain, from the aqueduct and the town's main gate, to the forum, the temples where its residents made offerings, the basilica, the baths and the theatre.

For an in-depth visit to Baelo Claudia see p121

6. Real Maestranza

THE BIRTHPLACE OF BULLFIGHTING

Immortalised in novels, songs, poetry and films – most notably in Bizet's *Carmen* – Sevilla's white-and-yellow-trimmed bullring that seats up to 14,000 spectators is Spain's oldest (construction began in 1761) and, to aficionados, the most beautiful. Many legends, clad in their *trajes de luces* (suits of light), have faced off against their bovine adversaries on the sand of this very arena, from Manolete and Curro Romero to Juan Belmonte. If you're a matador, appearing here is the ultimate honour. It's possible to visit the arena and the attached museum without partaking in death in the afternoon.

Opt for a guided tour of the Maestranza and the Museo de Toros to learn more about bullfighting (p69)

7. Puente Nuevo

GORGE-SPANNING BRIDGE

Devotees of Hemingway's *For Whom the Bell Tolls* will recognise the descriptions of Ronda's famous bridge that straddles the dramatic Río Guadalevín gorge, connecting La Ciudad with the Mercadillo quarter. Built between 1759 and 1793 to replace the older, hastily built 1734 version that collapsed into El Tajo gorge in 1741, taking 50 souls with it, it's Ronda's most striking sight, best appreciated from the trail descending into the gorge. Both Nationalists and Republicans are believed to have thrown prisoners to their deaths from the chamber beneath the central arch, used as a prison during the civil war.

To explore Ronda further, go to p160

8. Refugios de la Guerra Civil

ECHOES OF CIVIL WAR

On 31 May 1937, Almería residents awoke to the sound of explosions. In retaliation for the Republican attack on the German cruiser *Deutschland*, the German cruiser *Admiral Scheer* and four destroyers shelled the city, killing 20 civilians. Others were luckier: they hurried down into the network of concrete tunnels beneath the city and lived to see another day. The Republicans' last holdout in Andalucía, Almería came under repeat attack from Franco's forces during the course of the war, with surgeons working flat out in the operating theatre beneath the ground to save the wounded.

For a tour of Almería's shelters, see p260

9. Úbeda's Jews

HIDDEN JEWISH HISTORY

Prior to the 1492 expulsion, Úbeda's Jews played an important role in the town's civil life as tanners, silversmiths, tax collectors and shoemakers, and most of the time they coexisted peacefully with Moors and Christians. Post-expulsion, only *conversos* (Jewish converts to Christianity) remained, some of them practising the Jewish faith in secret. Historic buildings such as Casa Andalusí, with its Star of David etched into a 14th-century Gothic-Mudéjar column and a cellar that may have been used as a clandestine place of worship, provide a glimpse into a lost world, as does the sensitively restored 13th-century Sinagoga del Agua.

Discover more about Úbeda on p218

10. Rock of Gibraltar

APE-GUARDED MILITARY FORTIFICATIONS

Attended in perpetuity by its simian guardians (tailless Barbary macaques, aka the Apes of the Rock, replenished during WWII by Churchill for fear that if they were to disappear, so would the British) and soaring to great heights, the giant limestone Rock of Gibraltar made a natural naval base for the British. Its upper reaches are dotted with military fortifications that reflect the turbulent story of this centuries-old British outpost: the 19th-century O'Hara Battery guns, discouraging Spanish incursions; the Great Siege Tunnels (hewn by hand to repel Spanish and French forces); and WWII tunnels (where the Allied invasion of North Africa was planned).

For more Gibraltar sights, see p144

11. Museo Picasso

THE MASTER'S WORK OVER THE DECADES

In 1881 one of Málaga's most famous sons was born. He would go on to transform 20th-century art as we know it by inventing Cubism. The Picasso family home on Plaza de Merced aside, the unmissable Museo Picasso offers an in-depth insight into the artist's work, with a focus on all his major artistic periods, barring the 'blue' and 'rose' periods – notable by their absence. Besides a painting of his sister Lola that the artist painted when he was only 13, look out for such highlights as sculptures made from clay, plaster and sheet metal; numerous early sketches; a quick stampede through Cubism; and some absorbing late works when Picasso developed an obsession with musketeers.

For more on Picasso's work, see p152

12. Dolmens de Antequera

MYSTERIOUS NEOLITHIC TOMBS

Narrow entryways welcome you into the subterranean gloom of two of Europe's finest Neolithic burial chambers, the stone walls of the tunnels and the supporting rock slabs still faintly inscribed with rune-like carvings. Constructed around 2500 BCE by Bronze Age inhabitants of present-day Antequera, the Dolmen de Menga and Dolmen de Viera mounds were named a Unesco World Heritage Site in 2016. They are extraordinary feats of engineering that saw their builders shift slabs weighing as much as 180 tonnes and construct the Menga chamber mouth so that it's illuminated by the sun rising behind the Peña de los Enamorados rock formation in midsummer.

More on this captivating site on p172

13. Castillo Santa Catalina

BESEIGED HILLTOP CASTLE

High above Jaén, Cerro de Santa Catalina is topped with what has been a near-impregnable fortress. Near-impregnable, because even a hilltop castle with all-encompassing views of the surrounding hills can be hobbled by treason and the cutting off of vital supplies. From early Iberian civilisations that built their settlement on these lofty slopes to the fortress in its various incarnations, this land has changed hands on several occasions. The Almohad and Almoravid dynasties held their own against the Christian Reconquista, but after four failed sieges (two by Alfonso VII, two by Fernando III), Fernando finally managed to overrun the Moorish forces in 1246.

Plan your approach to this fortification on p216

14. Muelle de las Carabelas

LAUNCHPAD FOR THE NEW WORLD

On 3 August 1492, Genoan explorer Christopher Columbus set sail across the Atlantic from the waterfront below the Monasterio de la Rábida for what turned out to be the Americas. He had a mandate from the Catholic Monarchs, Fernando and Isabel, to seek out a new maritime route to India, China, Japan and the Spice Islands, and his modest fleet comprised three ships: the *Niña*, the *Pinta* and the *Santa María*. When visiting this recreation in Sevilla of the 15th-century wharf, and clambering aboard the three life-size replicas of Columbus' ships, what strikes you is how small they were, and how perilous the journey must have been.

For an in-depth visit to the museum, see p94

15. Espacio Brenan

REMOTE LITERARY BOLTHOLE

In the 1920s, disillusioned with middle-class life in England, Bloomsbury Group writer Gerald Brenan relocated to the remote village of Yegen in the Alpujarras, bringing with him a library of 2000 books. He rented the Fonda de Manuel Juliana – now turned into a fascinating museum – and spent years writing his autobiography, *South from Granada*, basing it on the village characters, traditions, fiestas and superstitions he'd observed in Yegen during his time there. Eventually he had to relocate to Churriana after becoming embroiled in scandal and getting a young girl pregnant, but not before his depictions of Alpujarras life made it into print.

For more on Yegen, see p251

MEET THE ANDALUCIANS

Your first encounter with an Andalucian might be overwhelming. Expect a hug, a handshake and a kiss on either cheek, sometimes all at once. ESPERANZA FUENTES introduces her people.

THANKS TO THE many cultures that have influenced this land, there is not one Andalucian character, but many. And yet Andalucians are united in their pride at being from here, in their intellectual heritage and in the region's many other benefits. Any Andalucian will tell you their gastronomy is the best in the world.

If you visit different cities in Andalucía you will see that not everyone speaks alike. This region, the second-largest in Spain, has several distinct accents and ways of pronouncing words. These differences are notable overall between the western and eastern provinces.

But despite these contrasts in speech, most Andalucians have the same way of communicating. Generally, Andalucians are quite expressive when speaking; they speak faster than people do in other areas of Spain, and with rhythmic intonation. They have no problem raising the volume of their voice or gesturing if it will make you understand them better. It may seem rude to strangers, but all of these mannerisms are designed to make visitors feel at home.

When you walk through the streets in the evening, you'll quickly see that Andalucians know how to enjoy and take advantage of everyday pleasures. It's not mere frivolity; it's an appreciation of life's simpler things. For that reason, even though knowing how to dance flamenco is not a requirement, most people here will have fun with it, even if some can't get the beat no matter how hard they try.

Having said that, you might be surprised to learn that not every Andalucian is keen on Semana Santa. Although most Andalucians consider themselves Catholic, only 23% say they are the practising type. And while Holy Week is well recognised for its cultural and touristic value, the event is devoid of religiosity for many.

Despite this, roughly 1.2 million Andalucians have 'María' somewhere in their name, such as 'José María' or 'María del Carmen'. This tradition continues to prove quite durable, remaining popular ahead of newer naming trends, which often start in Andalucía before catching on elsewhere in Spain. In 2016, for example, the region registered Spain's first girl named Khaleesi.

When you come to say goodbye to an Andalucian it won't be a sad farewell, but it will be long. So if you don't have much time, plan to leave earlier than you need to. Farewells are usually eternal, with a handshake, hugs and two intense kisses not unlikely.

The most populous region

Andalucía is the most populous region in Spain, with almost 8.5 million inhabitants. Of these, only 7.77% are foreigners. Perhaps unsurprisingly, Málaga and Almería, on the southern coastline, contain the highest proportion of non-natives. On the other hand, 2 million Andalucians live outside the region.

AN ANDALUCIAN PROUD OF HER ROOTS

I was born and raised in Sevilla, the capital of Andalucía. I'm 40 years old, almost the average age of the Andalucian population, which is 42.7 years. That's below the Spanish average, which stands at 44 years.

Like many Andalucian families, mine settled in this land because of the Spanish Civil War. My grandfather was from Cádiz and had to escape to another province. He ended up in Sevilla, and here he met my grandmother, the daughter of a woman from Madrid who found shelter in the city of orange trees to survive in the post-war period.

I am proud to be from here, among other reasons because Andalucians have fought to advance and improve, making Andalucía one of the most attractive areas in southern Europe. Every year some 30 million national and international tourists visit this region, which is a benchmark for the country's tourism.

Catedral de Sevilla (p56)

HIGH FLIERS/SHUTTERSTOCK ©

UGLY QUESTIONS: THE INQUISITION & RELIGIOUS EXTREMISM

The liberation of Spain turned the country into a prison for non-Catholics from the 15th century to the 19th century.

CÓRDOBA, SEVILLA, JAÉN, Granada and Lucena all have *juderías* (Jewish quarters). But aside from a few architectural traces, far less of Spain's Jewish legacy survives than it should. The language, the food, the music and the way of life are all conspicuously absent. The *barechu* (call to prayer) in the synagogues was silenced and the buildings were converted to Christian churches. For over 500 years, the legacy of the Spanish Inquisition has cast a shadow over the country. Finally, the stories of Spain's Jewish population are starting to be told and the long-term damage of the Inquisition addressed.

Back in 1469, it was a good time to be a Spaniard. The Reyes Católicos, Fernando II de Aragón and Isabel I de Castilla, were wed, uniting Spain's two largest kingdoms. There was hope in the air that centuries of occupation and war were finally coming to an end.

It soon became clear that the celebratory mood would only extend to the country's Christian population. The Reyes Católicos gradually decided that only Catholic orthodoxy would do for their newly restored hegemony. This decision sounded a death knell for the Moors, who clung on in Spain at Granada, and only then by paying tribute to Castile. It would prove to be even more disastrous for Spain's Jewish population. Events in the 12th and 13th centuries, where holy Crusades in Europe mirrored the similarly polarised religious conflict in Spain, had set a fundamentalist tone, as war is wont to do.

Threats to Spain were now largely perceived as being non-Christian in nature. It was a dangerous state of mind. The next logical step was to remove those threats, while simultaneously expanding Spain's influence overseas. Thus, the Inquisition was initiated by papal bull in 1478 and instituted in 1480. Christopher Columbus' first voyage in search of a new trade route to Asia was funded in 1492. Between them, these two acts created shockwaves at home and abroad for centuries.

The first decade of the Inquisition saw non-Christians presented with three awful alternatives: convert to Catholicism, be expelled from Spain, or die. Under the guise of rooting out religious heresy, the Inquisition's main purpose early on was to divest Spain's Jews of their possessions and any socio-political power they had. Of particular concern to the Reyes Católicos

were a group known as the *conversos*, former Jews whose families had converted to Christianity decades earlier to avoid the anti-Semitism that was already pervasive following the Black Death of the 1390s. (Jews were made the scapegoats, and this led to pogroms.)

In something akin to a modern-day conspiracy theory – often perpetuated by powerful Christian families who stood to gain the most from dispossessing them – the *conversos* were blamed for a variety of societal problems, including subsequent plagues. Many were also charged with continuing to practise Judaism in secret. This may have been true in some cases – certainly given the reasons behind that initial wave of conversions – but it only acted as kindling to fuel the stubborn old fires of suspicion.

Fernando and Isabel, along with the Grand Inquisitor, *fray* Tomás de Torquemada, proved themselves ruthlessly effective in their bigotry. They placated many powerful Christian families by removing powerful Jewish families from the country or forcing them into ghettos. The first auto-da-fé (literally 'act of faith') took place in 1481 in Sevilla. Any convicted heretic who did not confess at this public event was burned at the stake. The Catholic Church was not messing around.

But the biggest blow to Jewish life in Spain came in 1492. The Reyes Católicos released an edict that intensified the persecution of religious minorities. The properties and businesses of non-converted Jews were confiscated. It is the main reason those *juderías* in Andalucía feel so empty today.

Accurate data is scarce, but in all, between 160,000 and 350,000 Jews and *conversos* are thought to have fled the country. Some were executed. By the end of the year, a papal bull also sealed the fate of the Native Americans. It gave the Spanish a deadly legitimacy, as though handed down from God, to ensure the conversion or eradication of anybody of any other faith. Spain's darkest period of fundamentalist terrorism was in full swing.

Plunder and pillage brought great riches from the Americas to Spain. Meanwhile, various Native American groups lost devastating percentages of their populations to European armaments and diseases such as smallpox, to which the New World had no immunity. There was bad news for non-Catholics at home, too. *Moriscos* (former Muslims) were targeted next, and by

Museo del Castillo de San Jorge

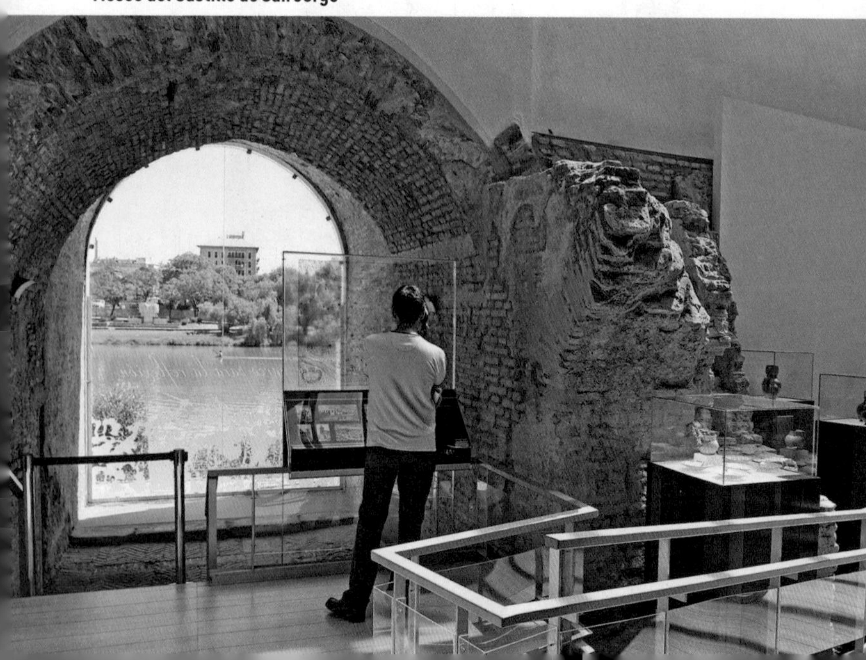

1614 hundreds of thousands of them, including those who'd previously agreed to a baptism, were expelled.

Perhaps predictably, there was a backlash to Catholicism from within the church. Protestantism and other sects of Christianity thrived elsewhere in Europe. Their followers were not immune to the Inquisition, forcing many Spanish Christians to flee the country as well. As the fundamentalism of the Catholic Church mushroomed, excommunications drew Spain into conflict with other nations. The Spanish Armada of 1588 was a particularly ill-judged naval blunder that harmed Spain's navy and buoyed that of Britain for decades to come.

But despite the escalating conflict at home and abroad, the riches of the New World and the fear and fervour of Catholicism at home meant that, despite Spain's ailing empire, the Inquisition endured until 1834. As with the numbers of expulsions, figures for those put to death during the Inquisition are broadly unreliable, although the most conservative estimates still suggest 32,000 executions took place in Spain. Many more people were tortured.

FOR OVER 500 YEARS, THE LEGACY OF THE SPANISH INQUISITION HAS CAST A SHADOW OVER THE COUNTRY.

As outlandish as the Inquisition may sound today, the conspiracy theorists never went away, and the damage continues to reverberate in some of Spain's naves. In August 2022, it was alleged by Israel's liberal *Ha'aretz* newspaper that many Catholic churches in Spain still hold anti-Semitic 'blood libel' memorials. 'Blood libel' was a conspiracy theory stating that Jews performed religious rituals using the blood of abducted Catholic children. It is perhaps no coincidence that the first 'blood libel' theories popped up just after the Inquisition began in 1480. The Cathedral-Basilica of Zaragoza still has a chapel dedicated to one of these alleged abductees, holding a service there each October.

In light of this pressure, Spain's Catholic Church announced an investigation. It's too soon to tell whether this is mere lip service or a meaningful attempt to right the ongoing wrongs of the Inquisition. However, other less conservative arenas of society are beginning to address the issue with more rigour. The Spanish period drama *Heirs to the Land*, released on Netflix in 2022 and based on the book by Ildefonso Falcones, is set largely in a Jewish community around the time of the Inquisition. Although it's a dramatisation with plenty of artistic licence, it may be the closest you'll get to seeing life in Spain's *juderías* as it may once have been lived.

You can learn more about Jewish history in Spain at Granada's Palacio de los Olvidados (Palace of the Forgotten) in the Albaicín neighbourhood (p233). It includes exhibitions on Andalucía's Jewish heritage and history, plus the legacy of the Inquisition.

In Sevilla's Triana neighbourhood you'll find the Castillo de San Jorge, which is steeped in notoriety for being the headquarters of the Inquisition from 1481 to 1785. At the time of research, it was undergoing extensive refurbishment with plans to open a museum about the Inquisition, albeit with no confirmed completion date listed.

Palacio de los Olvidados

Flamenco, Sevilla
JON CHICA/SHUTTERSTOCK ©

ROMANI KINGS & QUEENS: THE ORIGINS OF FLAMENCO

Flamenco is so much more than a genre or style. It's a feeling, a shared moment between the stage and the aisles that speaks with the voice of countless generations, cultures and peoples as one.

IN THE LATE 1980s a band called the Gipsy Kings found their way onto music charts around the world with their self-titled album. Although they were from France and the official genre, Catalan rumba, emerged from Barcelona's Romani community, the roots of their music were undoubtedly in Andalucian flamenco.

While those songs deservedly found an audience, aficionados of pure flamenco knew that something would always be lost between the recorded studio performance and the listener's ear. Flamenco's power hinges on its live spectacle – on the ebb and flow of energy in the room, the raw passion, the emotional honesty and, often, the spontaneity of the act itself. To fully appreciate it requires being there as it unfolds.

Flamenco has four core parts. The *toque* (guitar) and the *jaleo* (crucial to the rhythm) form the musical foundation, on which the *cante* (song) and the *baile* (dance) are built. When one or more of those elements isn't interacting with and informing the others, something is lost. The *baile* and much of the *jaleo* cannot make it onto a recording.

The *jaleo* is the most ephemeral and interactive element, consisting of various aspects such as *pitos* (finger clicking) and polyrhythmic clapping (known as *palmas*) to accentuate the distinctive rhythms and styles (*compás* and *palos*) of the flamenco song. The *palmas* is accompanied by shouts of encouragement (also part of the *jaleo*) such as '*olé!*', which sometimes come from the audience's own energy, as well as that of the musicians as they play. That conversation between the parts is like different eras of the past communicating with one another through a sonorous wormhole in time.

Scant published testimony or description of flamenco exists from before the mid-19th century, making any definitive assertion about its specific origins

difficult. But by breaking down the art form into its four constituent parts, you can start to understand the inspiration behind each section.

The story of flamenco's *toque* style dates back to Moorish rule. The oud, a soulful stringed instrument, was brought across the Mediterranean to enliven the courts of Moorish rulers. The great musician Ziryab even founded music schools in Andalucía in the 9th century. Although guitars did not form part of flamenco until much later, virtuosity with stringed instruments was instilled in Andalucía early on.

Around that same time, thousands of miles away, the itinerant Roma flowed freely into Europe by way of Turkey, Persia and the Indian subcontinent. Great similarities exist between the *baile* style of flamenco and that of *kathak*, which means 'story' in Sanskrit. The Kathak people were also nomadic, travelling throughout Rajasthan and the Indo-Gangetic Plain telling stories of Krishna through dance and song. The similarities range from the expressive movements of the hands to the types of flowing dresses worn by female dancers.

The Roma imbued their music and *baile* with an intrinsic sense of fluidity and embellishment. During their peregrinations, they picked up elements of folk traditions from everywhere they passed through, so that by the time the Roma started to arrive in Andalucía in the 1400s, new folk influences were seamlessly blended into their own cultural idioms. Improvisation is still a fundamental part of all good flamenco.

In Andalucía, the Roma encountered the haunting rhythms of Andalucian string music. After the oud but before the guitar there was the vihuela, a 15th-century instrument with six strings tuned like a lute. It's possible that this is where flamenco really started to take the form known today, and it then gradually transformed even closer during the guitar's rise to popularity in the late 18th and 19th centuries. Nowadays, some of the biggest names and most prolific proponents of the flamenco aesthetic, such as Paco de Lucia (1947–2014), are guitarists.

But central to it all, and perhaps the most purely Roma aspect of flamenco, is the *cante*. If you take the classical repertoire of *cante jondo* (deep songs), you can hear the Romani oral tradition at work. *Cante jondo* is the purest form of flamenco. Its poetic lyrics deal with themes of sorrow, loss and heartache. Songs existed to entertain and simultaneously to perpetuate stories and shared history among those peoples, many of whom were illiterate. They served as a form of collective memory.

You don't need to understand the lyrics to feel the *dolor* (grief) of every impassioned *grito* (lament) and the longing in every quavering, smoky vocal movement. Overcoming great despair is an integral theme of many flamenco songs. Singers usually sit at the centre of the stage, underlining the importance of this core Romani influence as a song's guide or director, from which the guitar, percussion and dancers take their lead.

Flamenco singers have the unenviable task of inspiring *duende*. Much like an actor's big-screen close-up, there's no room for artifice here. The best singers bare every inch of their souls, leaving them floating in the room like conjured spirits. This intense raw emotion, when done right, is enough to make a stone gargoyle well up. And yet *duende* is difficult to categorise in words. In an essay on the concept, poet Federico García Lorca characterised it as 'a force not a labour, a struggle not a thought'.

To see a great flamenco performance is to instinctively understand the word *duende*. From the singer, *duende* flows into the performances of everybody else on stage and back again, heightening the emotion yet further. 'The great artists of Southern Spain, Gypsy or flamenco, singers, dancers, musicians, know that emotion is impossible without the arrival of the duende', wrote Lorca.

Perhaps the simplest way to describe *duende* is as an expression of life's darkest recesses. Nobody knew these hardships more keenly than those who dealt with the persecution and oppression of the Inquisition. The Roma were forced onto society's fringes, maintaining urban footholds in

Sevilla's Triana neighbourhood or in the sierras. Here, flamenco rubbed shoulders with the folk styles of other oppressed groups in those neighbourhoods, such as the Jews and *moriscos* (Muslims forcibly converted to Christianity). This could certainly have added ingredients to the art form.

Whenever *duende* makes an appearance, the *jaleo* of '*olé, olé*' is an automatic response, both from those on stage and from the audience. The word does not have any meaning beyond its emphatic use as an exclamation of approval. These emphatic utterances could have originated with the *moriscos*. Still today, Islamic cultures have the *takbir*, often uttered as an expression in Arabic of 'Allah! Allah!' or '*Allāhu akbar*', which serves many purposes, including as a joyful exclamation.

It is unlikely a coincidence that the end of the Inquisition in 1834 was soon followed by the first written records of flamenco, after otherness in Spanish society was no longer persecuted. By the 1850s it was enjoying an explosion in popularity, with flamenco's golden age taking root in Sevilla (where *cafés cantantes* came into vogue). The Roma, freer to travel once more, took their art with them all around the Iberian Peninsula.

A new wave of Christian conservatism descended on Spain when Francisco Franco's dictatorship began in 1939. But by then flamenco was being promoted, along with bullfighting, as a national tradition and an ideal form of Spanish identity. You could argue that the Andalucian art form had made it to the big time. Ironically, this was at odds with Franco's simultaneous suppression of the very people whose traditions informed flamenco in the first place.

During this time, flamenco made more sense than ever to those who performed it, especially the songs of nostalgia and hardship. But any art form under the guidance of a political entity loses its ability to function properly. Flamenco was ripped away from those who sang it and was co-opted, imbued with manufactured values and frozen in an idealised and inert state. Suppression is the enemy of creative expression. Cue the underground, once more.

ANDRZEJ LISOWSKI TRAVEL/SHUTTERSTOCK ©

THE BEST SINGERS BARE EVERY INCH OF THEIR SOULS, LEAVING THEM FLOATING IN THE ROOM LIKE CONJURED SPIRITS.

A certain form of flamenco survived in smaller, more secretive holdouts called *peñas*, run by aficionados. When Franco died in 1975, flamenco flourished – just as it had after the end of the Inquisition. Practitioners, like much of Spanish society, quickly demonstrated a desire to embrace innovative ideas and discover fresh forms of creative expression. As if making up for lost time, the art form dabbled with other styles of world music and in turn became better known to the world. The Gipsy Kings formed a few years later.

These days you will find all sorts of flamenco on show. It would be unfair to label the popular *tablaos* of Sevilla and Málaga as tourist traps – the performers in them are usually exceptional. And while the twice-nightly shows might not lend themselves to the spontaneity purists may require of flamenco, you will likely feel as though you're part of something moving, entrenched in the moment and yet utterly timeless.

Above: Performance, Sacromonte (p232)

CONSERVATION: THREE PROTECTED SPECIES

Creatures once on the brink of extinction in Spain are, with a little help, regaining a foothold in the Andalucian wilderness.

IT'S EARLY MORNING and mist hangs over the open water, clumping around rose-tinted congregations of flamingos as they sift the *lagunas* for food. Nearby, wild horses graze the scrub and deer venture from their shield of forest in thirsty trepidation.

In the denser forest beyond, an Iberian lynx skulks through the undergrowth, surveying the long, straw-dry grass for rabbits. Above, a vast dark shape scuds over the land, an imperial eagle watching intently for the slightest movement.

Doñana National Park's protected land is the only reason this timeless scene still exists. If you look at the land from above, you'll notice swaths of territory gleaming white and grey, particularly around Almería and Huelva. It takes a tremendous amount of effort to protect what little green remains. Humans have relegated the region's once abundant wildlife to a few isolated pockets, with no safe natural corridor between them, and these only exist thanks to willing governmental protection at the behest of persistent and insistent conservationists.

But thanks to the energy and willingness of NGOs, conservationists and prescient political leaders in the Andalucian government, it's not all gloomy skies ahead for local wildlife. Since the 1980s, dozens

Clockwise from top left: Iberian lynx, Spanish imperial eagle, flamingos, bearded vulture

of critically endangered species have been plucked from the brink of extinction. Here are three examples.

Iberian lynx

The story of this striking wild cat *(Lynx pardinus)* perfectly illustrates the challenges and potential for conservation efforts in Andalucía. These fascinating creatures, with their characterful ear tufts and mutton-chop sideburns, are unmistakable.

Despite their customary prey being rabbits, their predatory nature augured ill when encountering humans. When they weren't hunted, new dams flooded their hunting grounds. When myxomatosis and other diseases decimated the rabbit populations from the 1950s onwards, the lynx rapidly went from being a free-roaming species throughout the Iberian Peninsula to near-extinction.

A 2001 census discovered that fewer than 150 individuals remained. They held on in isolated pockets at Doñana and Jaén's Sierra de Andújar. With no way to connect the two populations, this meant diminished gene pools that, left unaltered, would have had further negative impacts on the beleaguered creatures, leaving them more susceptible to degenerative ailments and disease.

The solution was the Acebuche Centre, a few miles north of Matalascañas, where individuals from each isolated group were interbred in captivity in 2004. The first year produced three new kits, and those offspring were first released into the wild in 2009 and 2010. In 2022, 28 captive lynx couples added 43 kits to the population. This, coupled with habitat preservation and attempts to bolster rabbit populations in lynx breeding grounds such as Doñana, has proven a tremendous success.

Protection of this delicate feline has been an international effort. The borders of Andalucía – and indeed those of Spain or Europe – don't mean anything beyond a human control context. That's why European Commission oversight and funding has aided several more programmes through the years, leading to the reintroduction of lynxes to parts of Spain and Portugal where they have been lost for decades.

Real numbers in the wild are hard to confirm, although it is estimated that the population passed 1000 in 2021. Around 700 now roam Spain's wild scrublands and forests.

Spanish imperial eagle

Rabbit scarcity didn't just harm the lynx. It was indicative of a blight on all tertiary consumers, in the sky and on the land. Raptors felt the impact most, with Montagu's harrier and barn owl numbers still currently in decline in Andalucía. But the Spanish imperial eagle *(Aquila adalberti)* was once critically endangered globally, due to two major factors: food shortages and power lines.

The latter were particularly deadly around Doñana until anti-electrocution insulation was fitted onto transmission towers. These eagles are much more elegant than their primary cause of death would suggest. Their wingspans can reach 220cm, making them smaller than golden eagles but still an intimidating presence in the sky. Their tawny crowns and white shoulders contrast with black-brown wings and body.

Removing the main human-made threats and improving land conditions so that primary and secondary mammal populations started to thrive again bolstered the Spanish imperial eagle's survival prospects. Its numbers have increased from only a handful a few decades ago to 129 breeding pairs in Andalucía alone.

Bearded vulture

By 1986 the bearded vulture *(Gypaetus barbatus)*, also known as the lammergeier, was extinct in Andalucía. The Andalucian government formed a task force in 1996 to try to reverse that sad fact by releasing individuals back into the mountains.

One of Europe's most fascinating birds, the bearded vulture's name in Spanish, *quebrantahuesos*, translates to 'bone breaker', which refers to their habit of dropping bones onto rocks from great heights to access the marrow within. They have wingspans of up to 280cm and, unlike most vultures, have feathered necks.

In 2015 the first bearded vultures to breed in the wild in Andalucía since the species' local extinction four decades earlier marked a huge step forward in their conservation. By 2021 there were five breeding pairs in their high mountain habitats north of Jaén. If the region's other conservation stories are anything to go by, that number will continue to climb, continuing the Andalucian government's growing legacy of successful environmental protection and diversification.

Lorca in 1919

PHOTO12/UNIVERSAL IMAGES GROUP VIA GETTY IMAGES ©

FEDERICO GARCÍA LORCA: EVOKING ANDALUCÍA

In a career spanning only 18 years, Federico García Lorca cemented his reputation as Spain's greatest poet and playwright. His depictions of Andalucía are more vibrant than any photograph.

Parched land
quiet land
of immense nights.
(Wind in the olive grove,
wind on the sierra.)

NOBODY HAS WRITTEN of Andalucía quite so evocatively as Federico García Lorca (1898–1936). Life and death are elegantly wrought through the distinctly colourful lyricism and vivid manner of his poetry and plays.

Born in Granada to wealthy landowner parents, Lorca spent his youth exploring the rural climes of Fuente Vaqueros, 17km northwest of Granada. This area, known as the Vega, encompasses fertile farmland and encroaching mountains. His family later moved to Huerta de San Vicente, once a village and now consumed by the swelling suburbs of Granada. It was here he began to understand Granada's rich multiculturalism, where Jewish, Roma and Spanish influences combined with the stubbornest remnant of Arabic and Berber cultures in Spain, a final Moorish outpost in a Catholic sea.

Despite the privilege of his upbringing, Lorca was discriminated against for being homosexual. Perhaps it was this commonality of societal rejection with Spain's other outcasts that allowed him to identify with their struggles as they manifested through music, such as flamenco. Later he was similarly drawn to the African American spirituals of Harlem while staying in New York.

The lines of poetry above come from his *Poema del cante jondo* (Poem of the Deep Song), which he wrote in the early 1920s and named after the *cante jondo* style of flamenco that, from his youth, deeply influenced him. Lorca's early work perfectly sums up that blend of Arabic tonal inflections and Roma traditions that underpins flamenco, while focusing thematically on the harsh realities of life in Spain's poorest region. His poetry always demonstrated a keen emotional intelligence. Each stanza drips with desire, frustration and suffering. An example is this passage from '*Romance sonámbulo*' (Dreamwalker Ballad):

Green how I want you green.
Beneath the gypsy moon
things are watching her
and she can't watch them.

Andalucía exists in living colour on Lorca's pages: 'the mountain, like a thieving cat, arches its back of sour agaves', or 'Cypresses have flourished, like green-haired, hollow-socket, giant heads, pensive and in pain', or 'O white wall of Spain! Black bull of sorrow!' Those lines come from his early, middle and late poetry, respectively. Throughout his oeuvre, Lorca imbues the region with character and personality. To read Lorca's poetry is to know Andalucía.

The same goes for its people. 'Romance *sonámbulo*' formed part of Lorca's breakout work *Romancero gitano* (Gypsy Ballads), which explores the life and customs of the Roma through the prism of his boyhood interactions with them in Fuente Vaqueros. It is a work filled with nostalgia, magical realism and grief.

Some people level the claim that Lorca exoticised the victimhood of the Roma and other groups in his work, but that would overlook the fact that the poems admire rather than exploit Roma history and culture. At the time, Spain was ruled by the military dictatorship of Primo de Rivera. Around Europe, fascism was taking stubborn root, and would spawn a period of history so ghastly that Rivera's rule would come to seem comparatively utopic.

The Roma were among those who had suffered the most when ultra-conservative rulers were allowed too much power. In '*La monja gitana*' (The Gypsy Nun), it's as though Lorca's pushing back against injustice and ignorance, against the repressive Inquisition mentality towards a people who only wanted to live in freedom:

The church growls in the distance
like a stricken bear.
How well she embroiders,
such finesse!
On the straw-yellow cloth
she'd like to embroider
flowers of her imagining.

Lorca was a core member of the Generation of '27, which brought movements primarily associated with art at the time, such as surrealism and futurism, into Spanish poetry. The group's first meeting in Sevilla in 1927 preceded the release of *Romancero gitano* by one year. It was a rich time for Andalucian writing that acted both as a support network and a catalyst for lyrical invention.

At this point at the turn of the decade, death gradually saturates Lorca's work. One of his greatest poems is '*Llanto por* Ignacio Sánchez Majías', about his brother-in-law, a bullfighter and fellow poet, who was gored to death by a bull in 1934.

He looked for dawn
and dawn was finished.
He seeks his firm profile,
sleep sets it adrift.
He sought his beautiful body
and found his opened blood.

Lorca's final years from 1933 and 1936 saw him increasingly address the rise of fascism in Spain, which he opposed by asserting his socialist ideals on the stage. Three of his tragedies: *Bodas de sangre* (Blood Wedding), *Yerma* (Barren) and *La casa de Bernarda Alba* (The House of Bernarda Alba), which deal with themes of entrapment and liberation, today rank among his best-known works.

Accurately capturing the *duende* of a place does not give a work its longevity, though. Lorca's words are still praised because they communicated beyond Andalucía, beyond Spain, and even beyond Europe, speaking to humanity's shared sense of life's meaning. These were sentiments that the horrors of war could only reinforce.

Lorca's own life ended in the same kind of fathomless tragedy that his words so ably explored when detailing the grief of others. In 1936, as the Spanish Civil War raged through an odious and vitriolic early phase, he was seized by Franco's right-wing Royalists, pushed through a kangaroo court, unceremoniously shot and thrown into an unmarked grave outside Granada. He was just 38. Curiously prophetic, Lorca had already written his own eulogy in 1929:

I understood they had murdered me.
They searched the cafés and the graveyards and churches,
they opened the wine casks and wardrobes,
they destroyed three skeletons to pull out their gold teeth.
Still they couldn't find me.

To this day, his remains lie undiscovered beneath that parched land. Beneath those immense nights.

INDEX

A

F

Map Pages **000**

Map Pages **000**

'Four millennia of history have left their mark on Cádiz (p114), surrounded almost entirely by water, rich in historic sights and graceful, centuries-old architecture.'

Anna Kaminski

'Sevilla (p56), the Andalucian capital and jewel in the region's cultural crown, is a luminous introduction to this region of Spain, with a rich blend of historical phases.'

Paul Stafford

THIS BOOK

Design Development Marc Backwell

Content Development Mark Jones, Sandie Kestell, Anne Mason, Joana Taborda

Cartography Development Katerina Pavkova

Production Development Sandie Kestell, Fergal Condon

Series Development Leadership Darren O'Connell, Piers Pickard, Chris Zeiher

Commissioning Editor Amy Lynch

Product Editor Hannah Cartmel

Book Designer Catalina Aragón

Cartographer Rachel Imeson

Assisting Editors Janet Austin, Amy Lysen, Maja Vatrić

Cover Researcher Fergal Condon

Thanks Sofie Foldager Andersen, Gwen Cotter, Esteban Fernandez, Clare Healy, Gabrielle Stefanos

LEFT: UNAI HUIZI PHOTOGRAPHY/SHUTTERSTOCK © RIGHT: LILIANA MARMELO/SHUTTERSTOCK ©

Paper in this book is certified against the Forest Stewardship Council™ standards. FSC™ promotes environmentally responsible, socially beneficial and economically viable management of the world's forests.

Published by Lonely Planet Global Limited
CRN 554153
11th edition – June 2023
ISBN 978 1 83869 163 9

10 9 8 7 6 5 4 3 2 1
Printed in China